ZATCH BELL!™

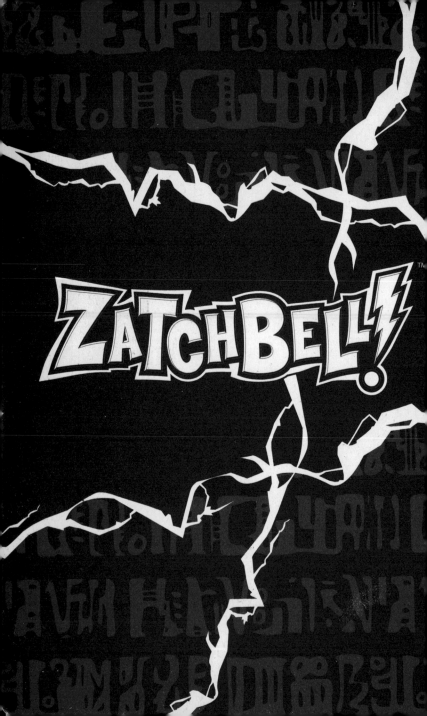

ZATCH BELL!
Vol. 14

STORY AND ART BY
MAKOTO RAIKU

Translation/David Ury
Touch-up Art & Lettering/Gabe Crate
Design/Izumi Hirayama
Special Thanks/Jessica Villat, Miki Macaluso,
Mitsuko Kitajima, and Akane Matsuo
Editor/Kit Fox

Editor in Chief, Books/Alvin Lu
Editor in Chief, Magazines/Marc Weidenbaum
VP of Publishing Licensing/Rika Inouye
VP of Sales/Gonzalo Ferreyra
Sr. VP of Marketing/Liza Coppola
Publisher/Hyoe Narita

Printed in the U.S.A.

Published by VIZ Media, LLC
P.O. Box 77010
San Francisco, CA 94107

10 9 8 7 6 5 4 3 2 1
First printing, August 2007

www.viz.com
store.viz.com

ZATCH BELL!™

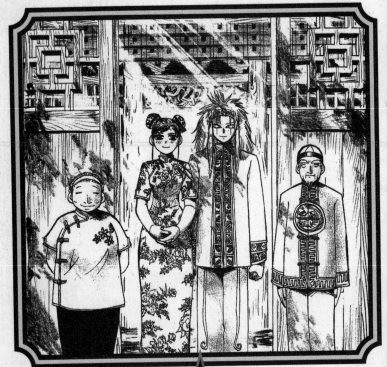

STORY AND ART BY

MAKOTO RAIKU

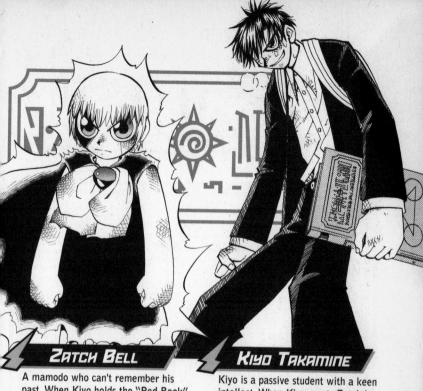

 ## ZATCH BELL

A mamodo who can't remember his past. When Kiyo holds the "Red Book" and reads a spell, lightning bolts shoot from Zatch's mouth. He is fighting to be a "kind king."

 ## KIYO TAKAMINE

Kiyo is a passive student with a keen intellect. When Kiyo meets Zatch he assumes ownership of the "Red Book" and starts to grow up.

✪ THE STORY THUS FAR ✪

The battle to determine who will be the next king of the mamodo world takes place every 1,000 years in the human world. Each mamodo owns a "book" which increases its unique powers, and they must team up with a human in order to fight for their own survival. Zatch is one of 100 mamodo chosen to fight in this battle, and his partner is Kiyo, a junior high school student. The bond between Zatch and Kiyo deepens as they continue to survive through many harsh battles. Zatch swears, "I will fight to become a kind king."

As the battle rages on, the number of remaining mamodo has dwindled to less than 40. Meanwhile, Zofis, who plans on becoming king, has brought the mamodo from 1,000 years ago back to life. Zatch and Kiyo are furious when they find out what Zofis has done and decide to attack his home base!

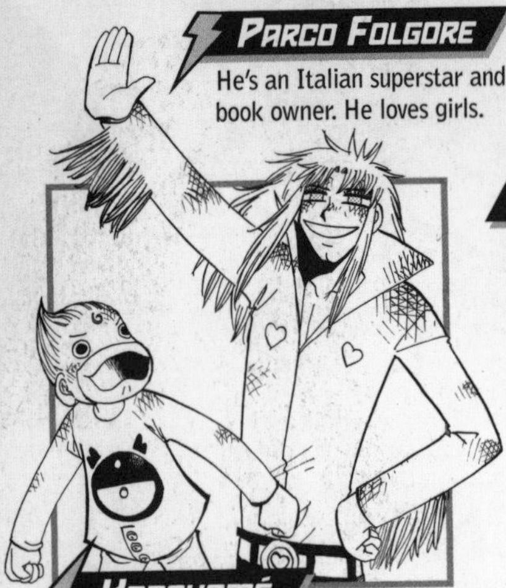

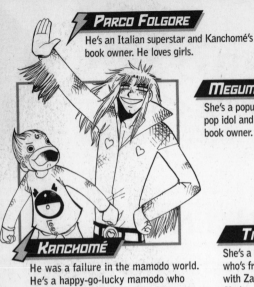

Parco Folgore

He's an Italian superstar and Kanchomé's book owner. He loves girls.

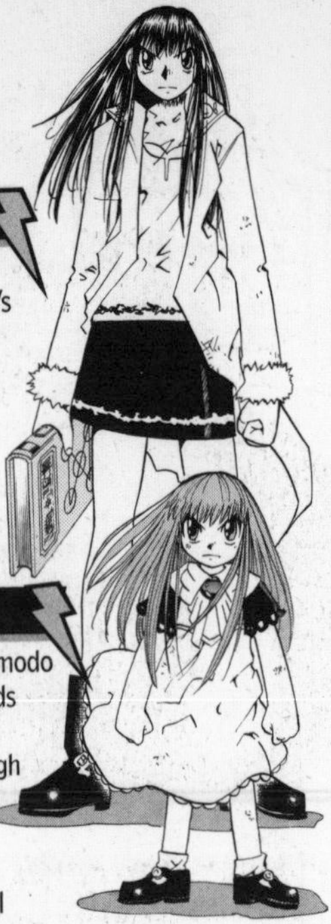

Megumi

She's a popular pop idol and Tia's book owner.

Kanchomé

He was a failure in the mamodo world. He's a happy-go-lucky mamodo who makes mistakes all the time, but...

Tia

She's a mamodo who's friends with Zatch. She's a tough cookie.

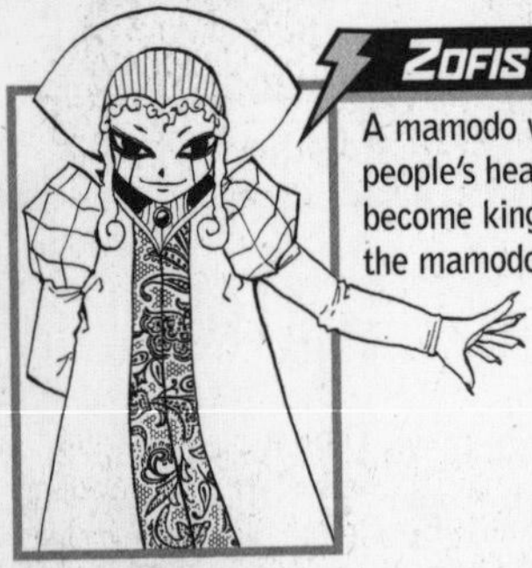

Zofis

A mamodo with the power to control people's hearts, his mission is to become king by using the strength of the mamodo from 1,000 years ago.

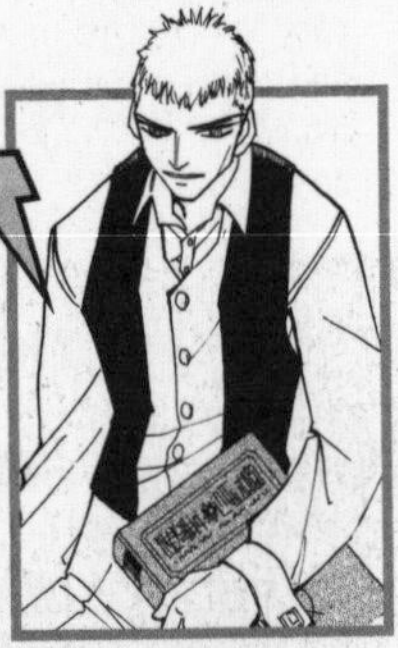

Kafk Sunbeam

Ponygon's book owner who somehow completely understands Ponygon's emotions...! He works as an engineer in Japan.

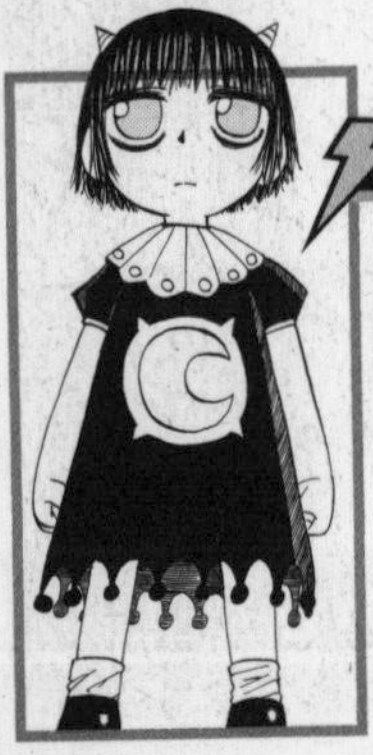

Laila

A 1,000-year-old mamodo who betrays Zofis and helps Kiyo and Zatch.

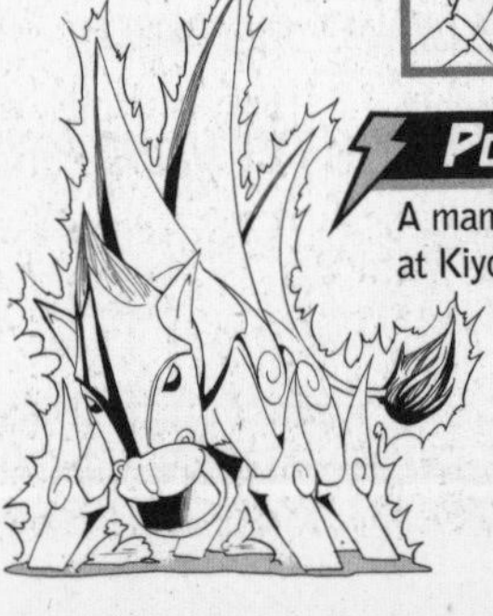

Ponygon

A mamodo who stays at Kiyo's house. He finally found a book owner!

ZATCH BELL! 14

CONTENTS

LEVEL 124: Conversations of the Heart

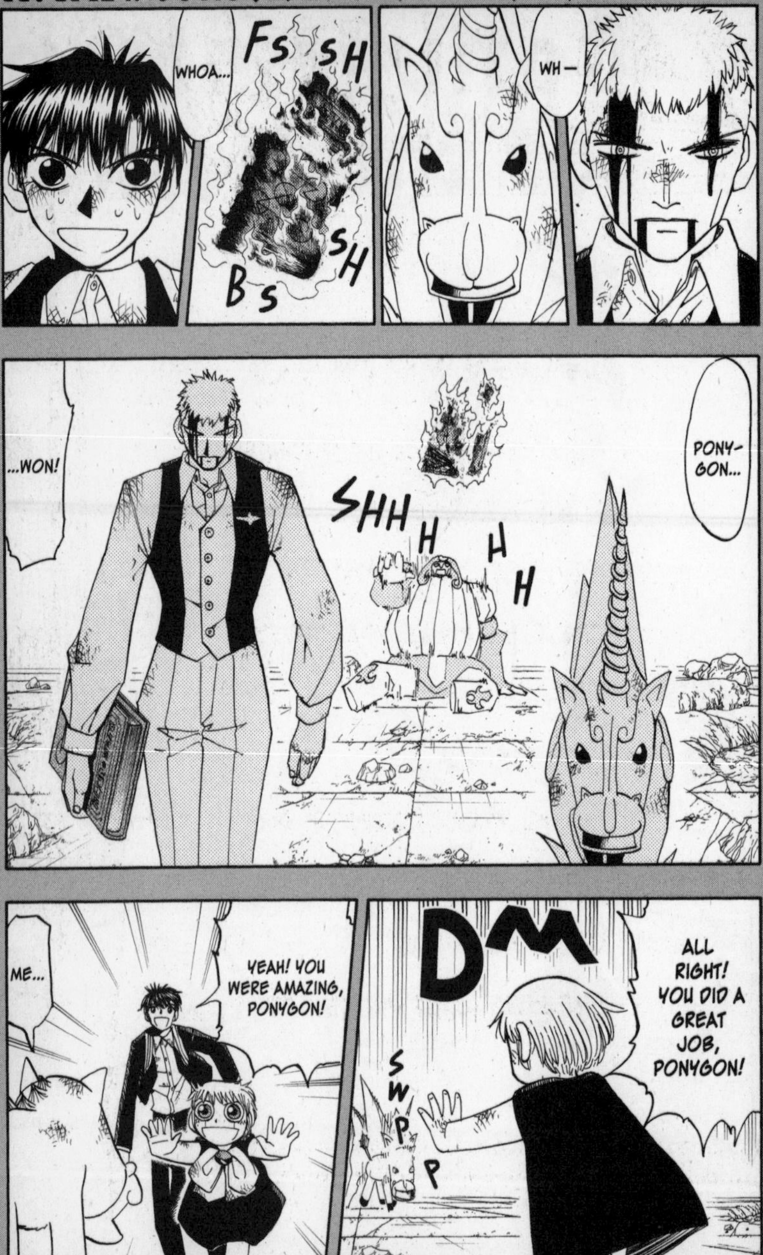
WH—
WHOA...
FsSH
BsSH
PONY-GON...
SHHHHH
...WON!
DM
ALL RIGHT! YOU DID A GREAT JOB, PONYGON!
SWPP
YEAH! YOU WERE AMAZING, PONYGON!
ME...

LEVEL 124: Conversations of the Heart

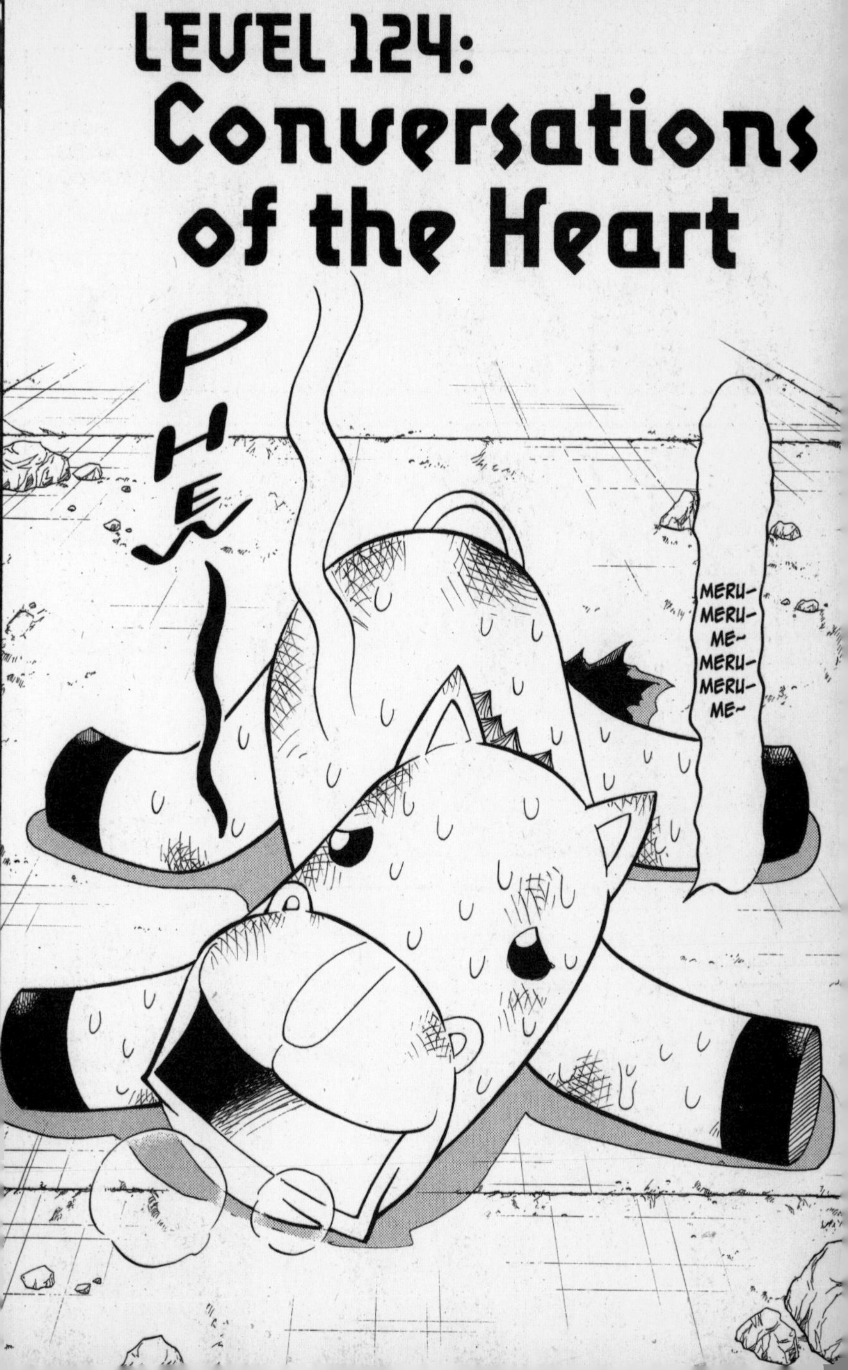
MERU-MERU-ME- MERU-MERU-ME-
PHEW~

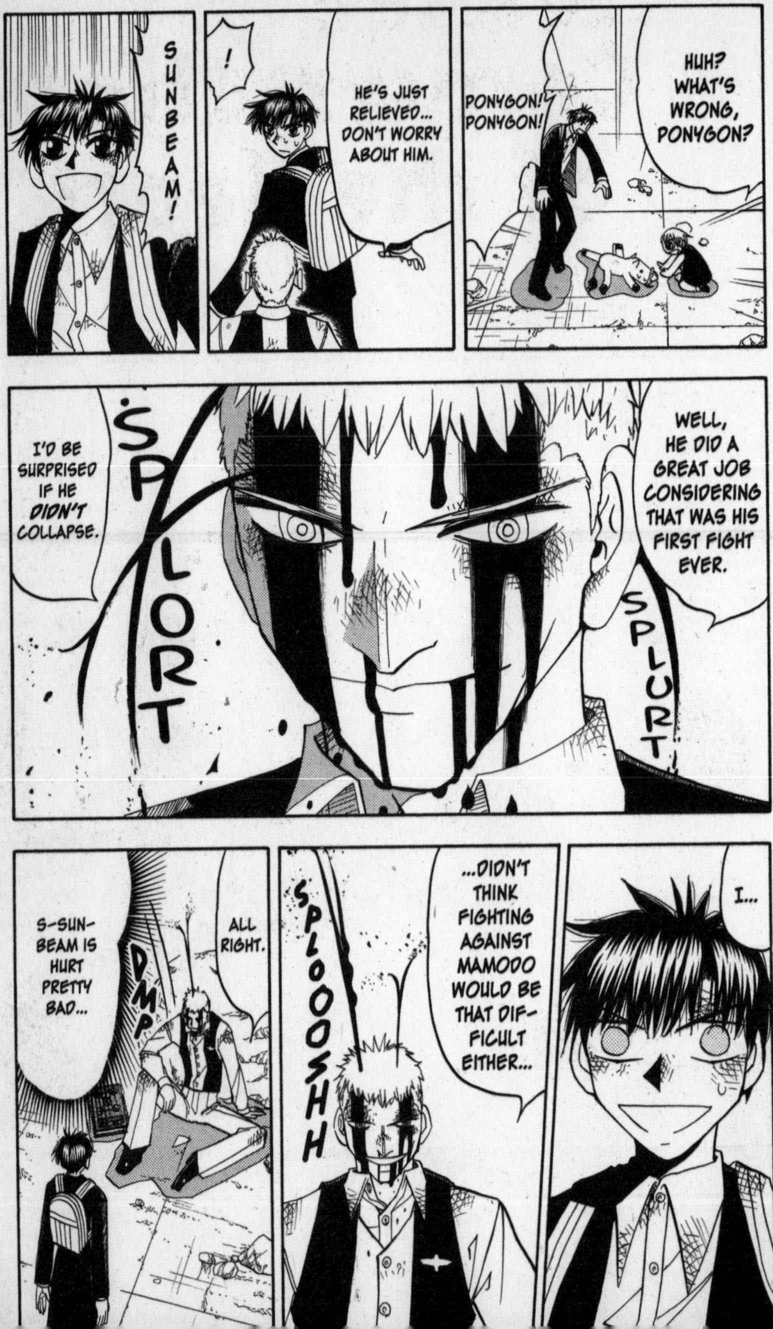
HUH? WHAT'S WRONG, PONYGON?
PONYGON! PONYGON!
!
HE'S JUST RELIEVED... DON'T WORRY ABOUT HIM.
SUNBEAM!
WELL, HE DID A GREAT JOB CONSIDERING THAT WAS HIS FIRST FIGHT EVER.
SPLURT
SPLORT
I'D BE SURPRISED IF HE *DIDN'T* COLLAPSE.
I...
...DIDN'T THINK FIGHTING AGAINST MAMODO WOULD BE THAT DIF-FICULT EITHER...
SPLOOOSHH
ALL RIGHT.
DMP
S-SUN-BEAM IS HURT PRETTY BAD...

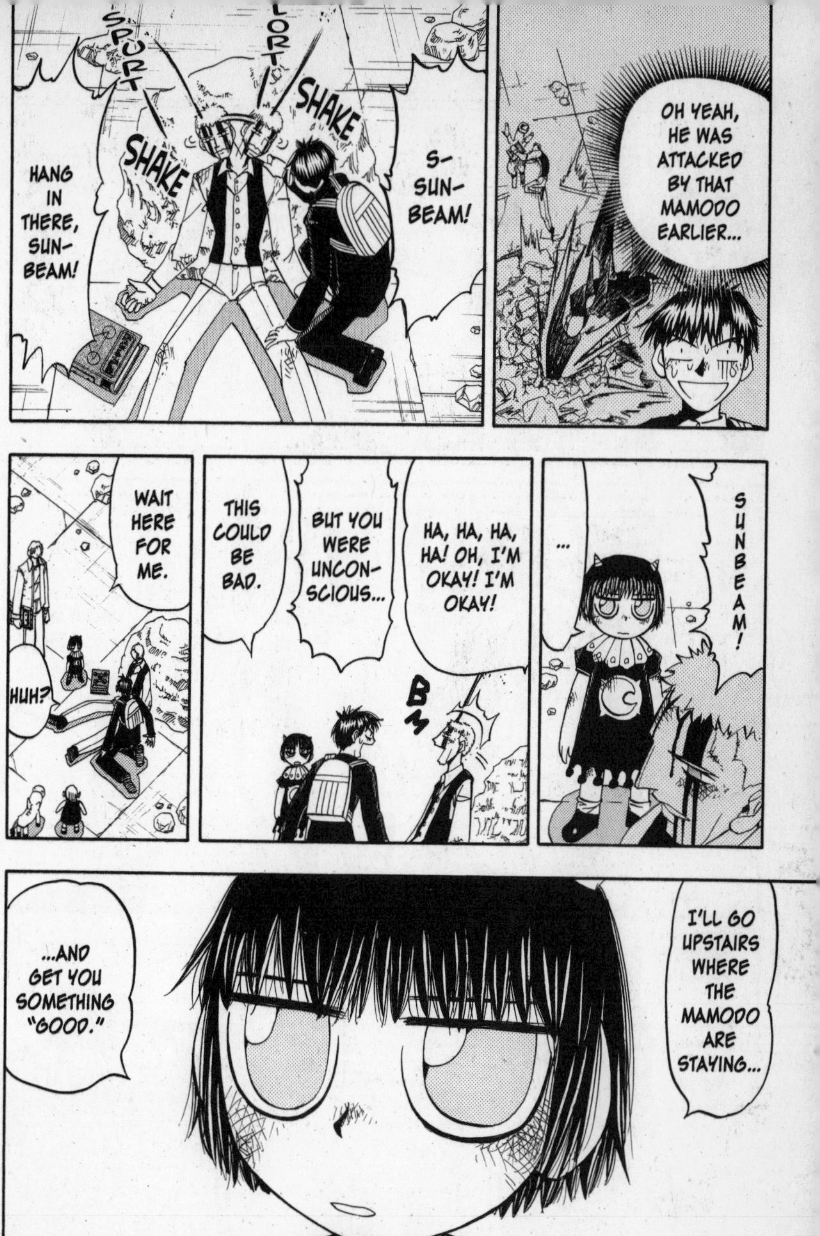
OH YEAH, HE WAS ATTACKED BY THAT MAMODO EARLIER...
LORT
SHAKE
S-SUNBEAM!
SPURT
SHAKE
HANG IN THERE, SUN-BEAM!
SUNBEAM!
...
HA, HA, HA, HA! OH, I'M OKAY! I'M OKAY!
BM
BUT YOU WERE UNCON-SCIOUS...
THIS COULD BE BAD.
WAIT HERE FOR ME.
HUH?
I'LL GO UPSTAIRS WHERE THE MAMODO ARE STAYING...
...AND GET YOU SOMETHING "GOOD."

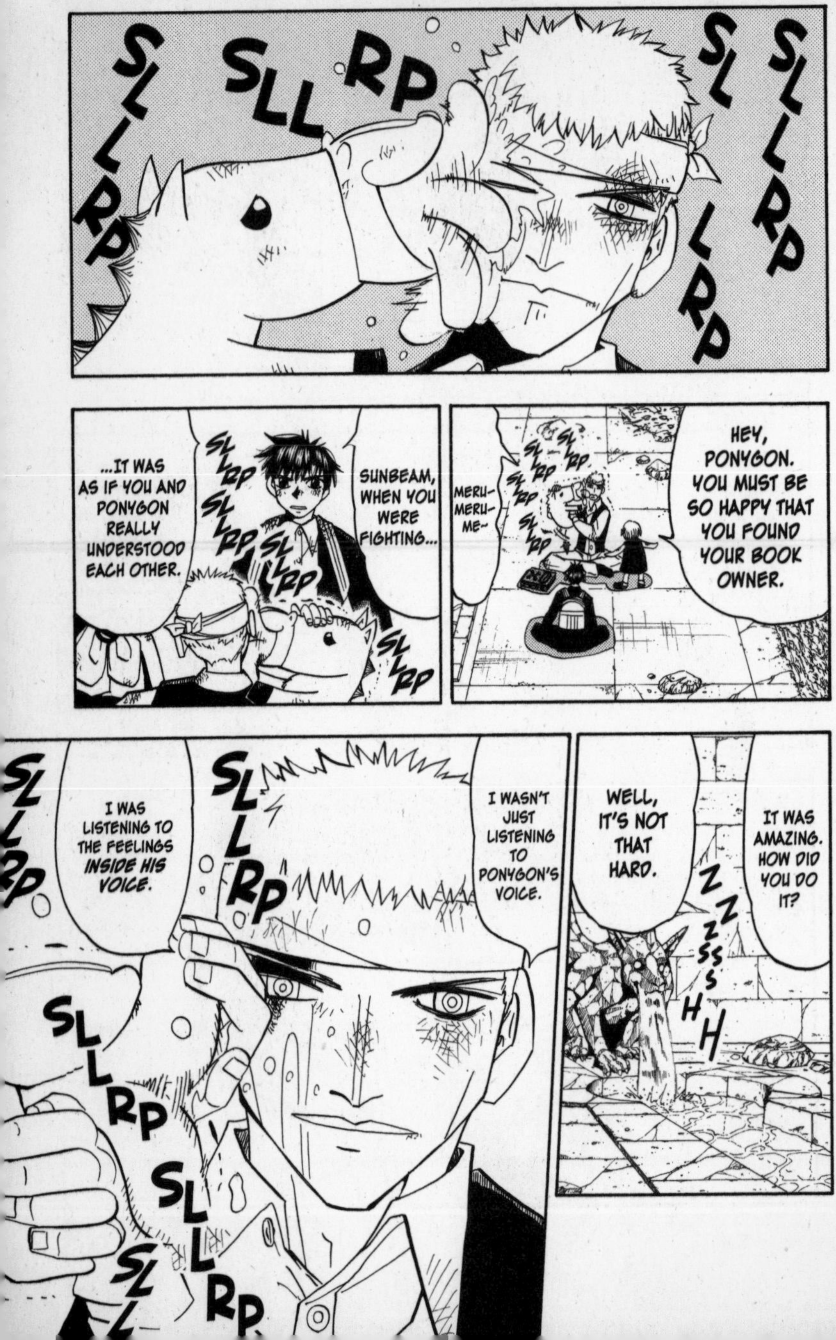
SLLRP
SLLRP
SLLRP
SLLRP
HEY, PONYGON. YOU MUST BE SO HAPPY THAT YOU FOUND YOUR BOOK OWNER.
MERU-MERU-ME~
SLLRP
SUNBEAM, WHEN YOU WERE FIGHTING...
...IT WAS AS IF YOU AND PONYGON REALLY UNDERSTOOD EACH OTHER.
SLLRP
IT WAS AMAZING. HOW DID YOU DO IT?
WELL, IT'S NOT THAT HARD.
ZZZSSSHH
I WASN'T JUST LISTENING TO PONYGON'S VOICE.
I WAS LISTENING TO THE FEELINGS INSIDE HIS VOICE.
SLLRP
SLLRP
SLLRP

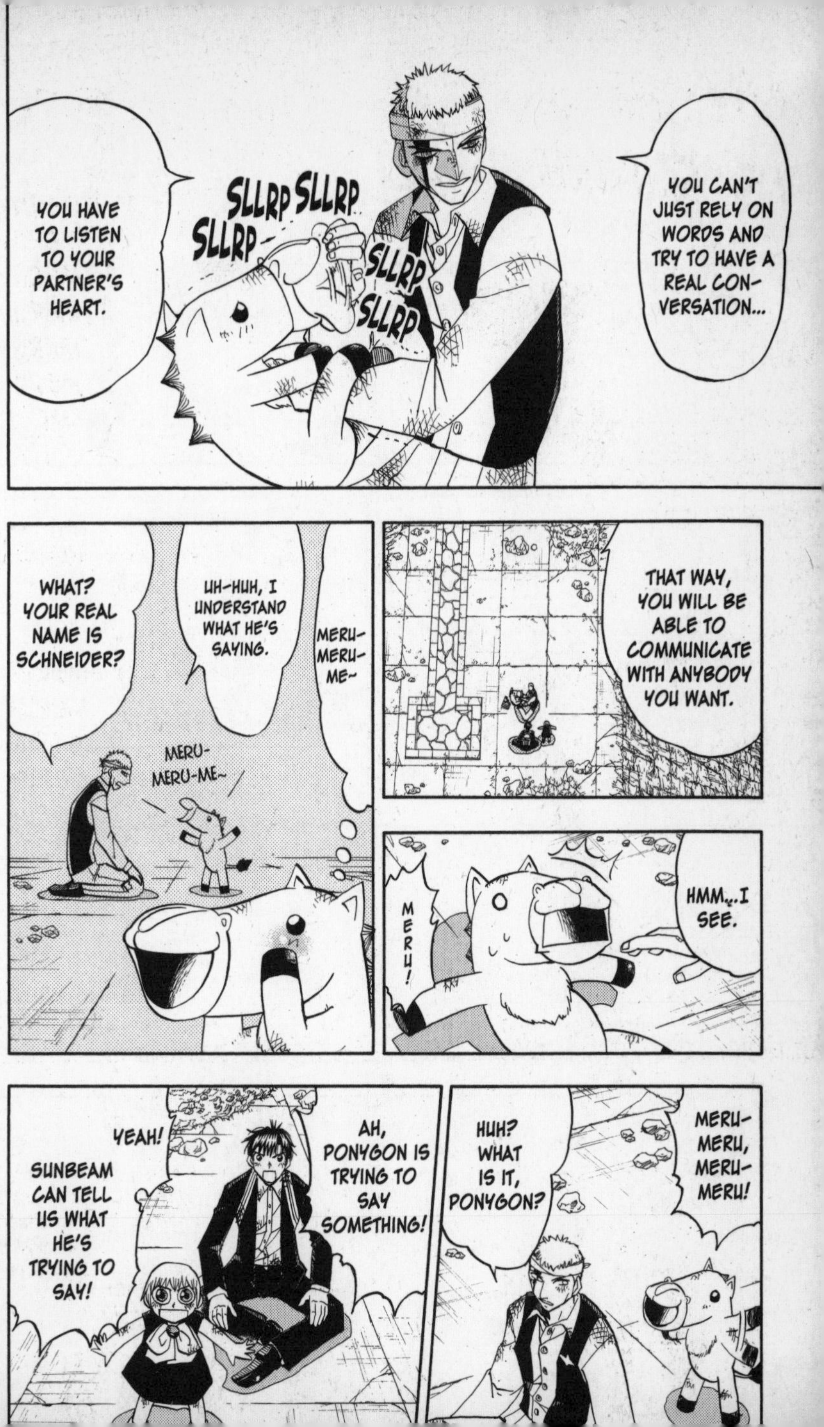
YOU CAN'T JUST RELY ON WORDS AND TRY TO HAVE A REAL CON-VERSATION...
SLLRP SLLRP
SLLRP
SLLRP
SLLRP
YOU HAVE TO LISTEN TO YOUR PARTNER'S HEART.
THAT WAY, YOU WILL BE ABLE TO COMMUNICATE WITH ANYBODY YOU WANT.
HMM...I SEE.
MERU!
MERU-MERU-ME~
UH-HUH, I UNDERSTAND WHAT HE'S SAYING.
WHAT? YOUR REAL NAME IS SCHNEIDER?
MERU-MERU-ME~
MERU-MERU, MERU-MERU!
HUH? WHAT IS IT, PONYGON?
AH, PONYGON IS TRYING TO SAY SOMETHING!
YEAH!
SUNBEAM CAN TELL US WHAT HE'S TRYING TO SAY!

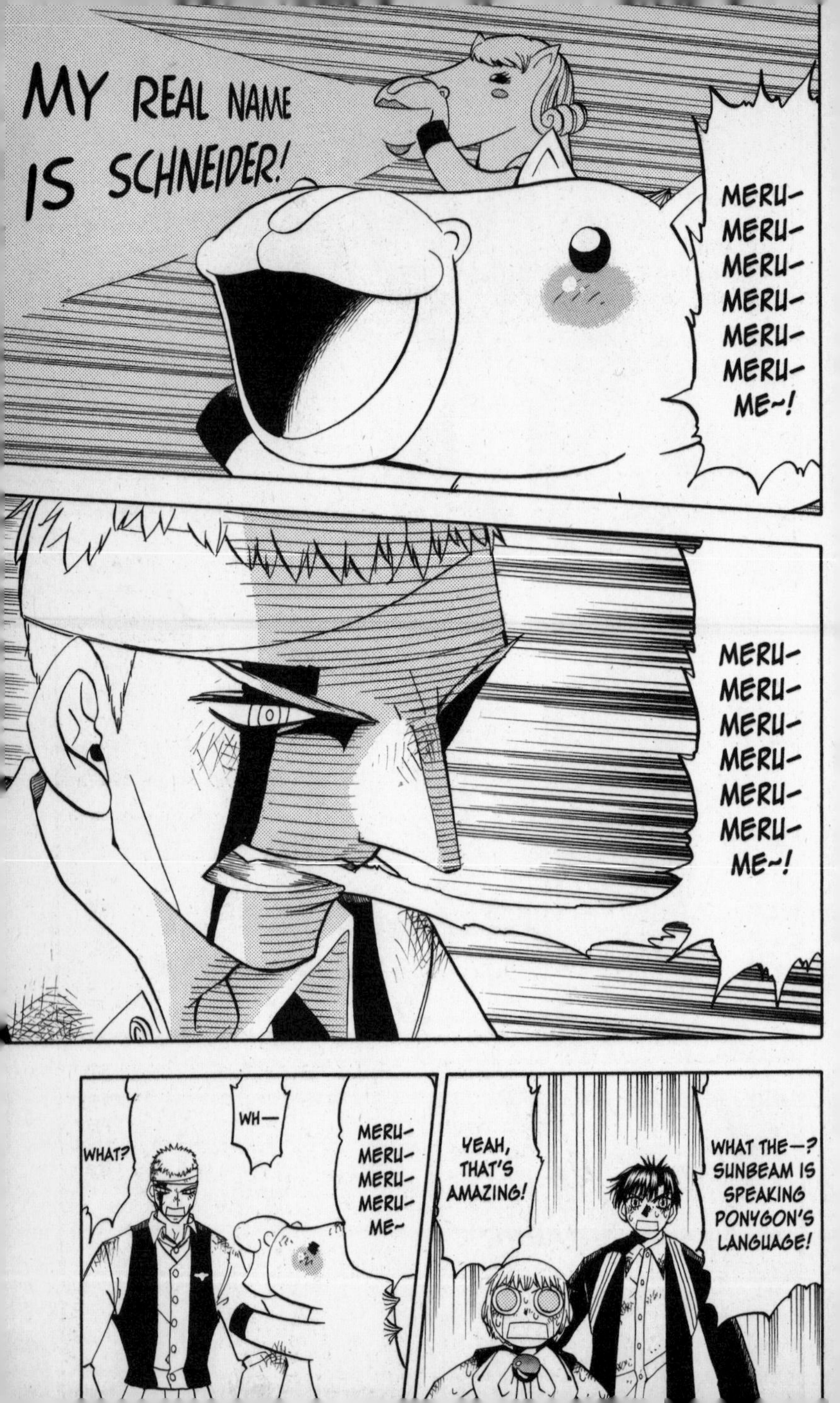

MERU-MERU-MERU-MERU-MERU-MERU-ME~!
MY REAL NAME IS SCHNEIDER!
MERU-MERU-MERU-MERU-MERU-MERU-ME~!
WHAT THE—? SUNBEAM IS SPEAKING PONYGON'S LANGUAGE!
YEAH, THAT'S AMAZING!
MERU-MERU-MERU-MERU-ME~
WH—
WHAT?

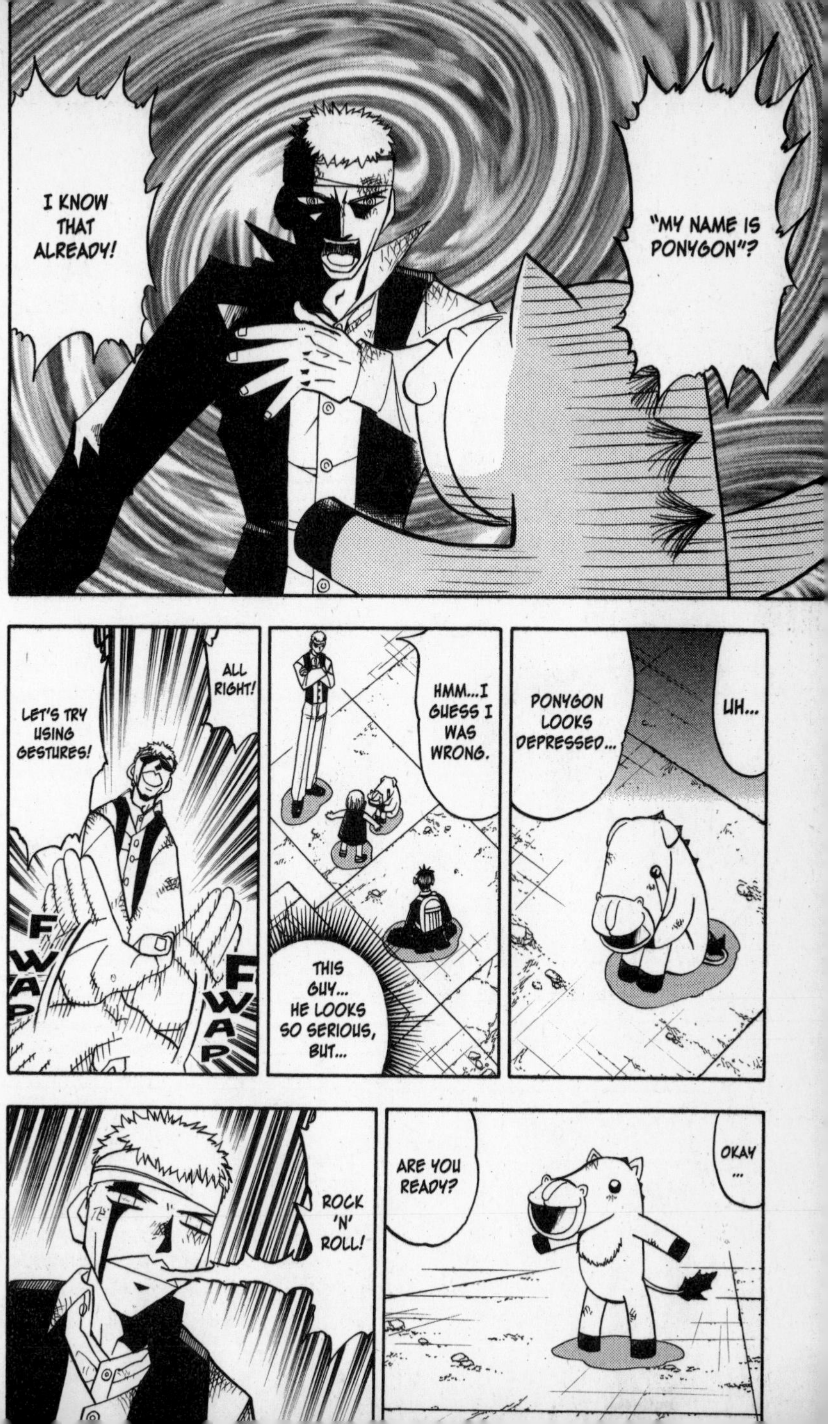
"MY NAME IS PONYGON"?
I KNOW THAT ALREADY!
UH...
PONYGON LOOKS DEPRESSED...
HMM...I GUESS I WAS WRONG.
THIS GUY... HE LOOKS SO SERIOUS, BUT...
ALL RIGHT!
LET'S TRY USING GESTURES!
FWAP
FWAP
OKAY ...
ARE YOU READY?
ROCK 'N' ROLL!

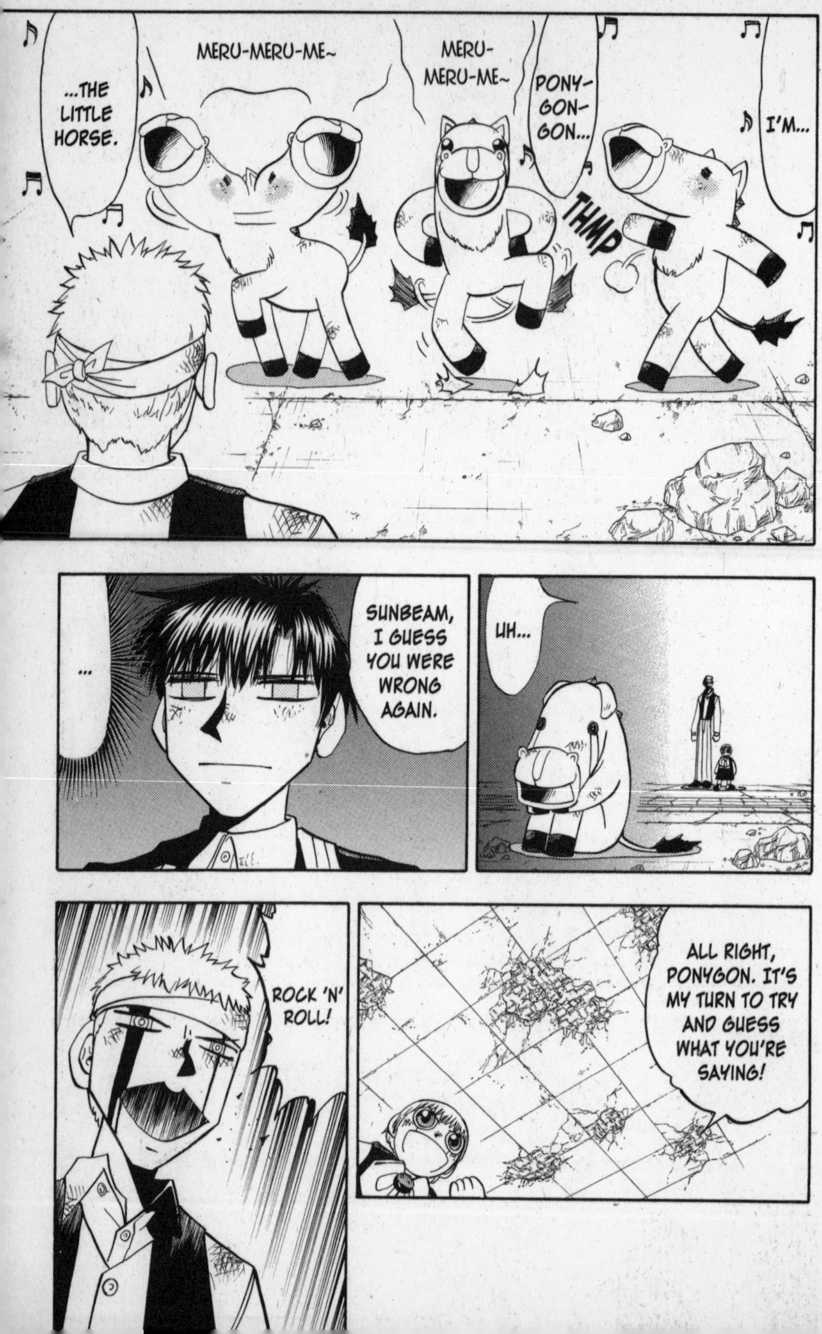
I'M...
PONY-GON-GON...
THMP
MERU-MERU-ME~
MERU-MERU-ME~
...THE LITTLE HORSE.
UH...
SUNBEAM, I GUESS YOU WERE WRONG AGAIN.
...
ALL RIGHT, PONYGON. IT'S MY TURN TO TRY AND GUESS WHAT YOU'RE SAYING!
ROCK 'N' ROLL!

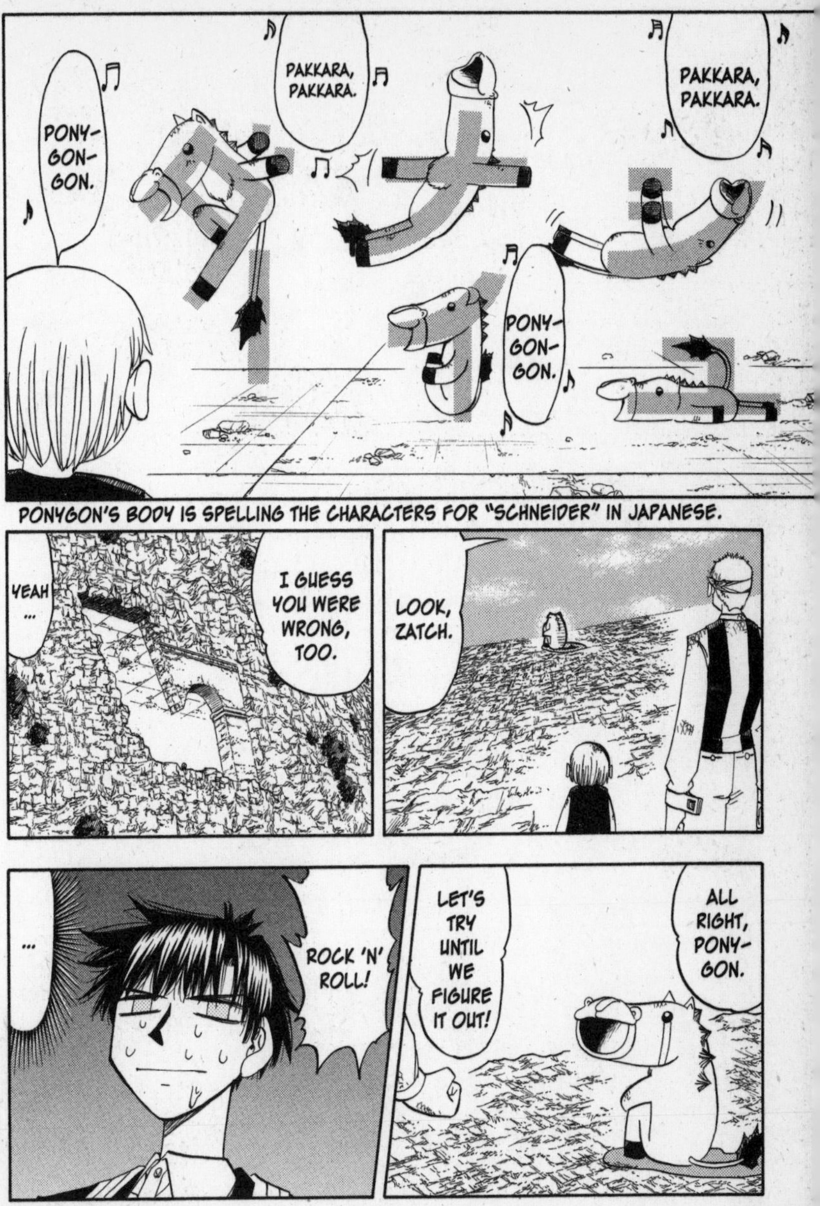
PAKKARA, PAKKARA.
PAKKARA, PAKKARA.
PONY-GON-GON.
PONY-GON-GON.
PONYGON'S BODY IS SPELLING THE CHARACTERS FOR "SCHNEIDER" IN JAPANESE.
LOOK, ZATCH.
I GUESS YOU WERE WRONG, TOO.
YEAH ...
ALL RIGHT, PONY-GON.
LET'S TRY UNTIL WE FIGURE IT OUT!
ROCK 'N' ROLL!
...

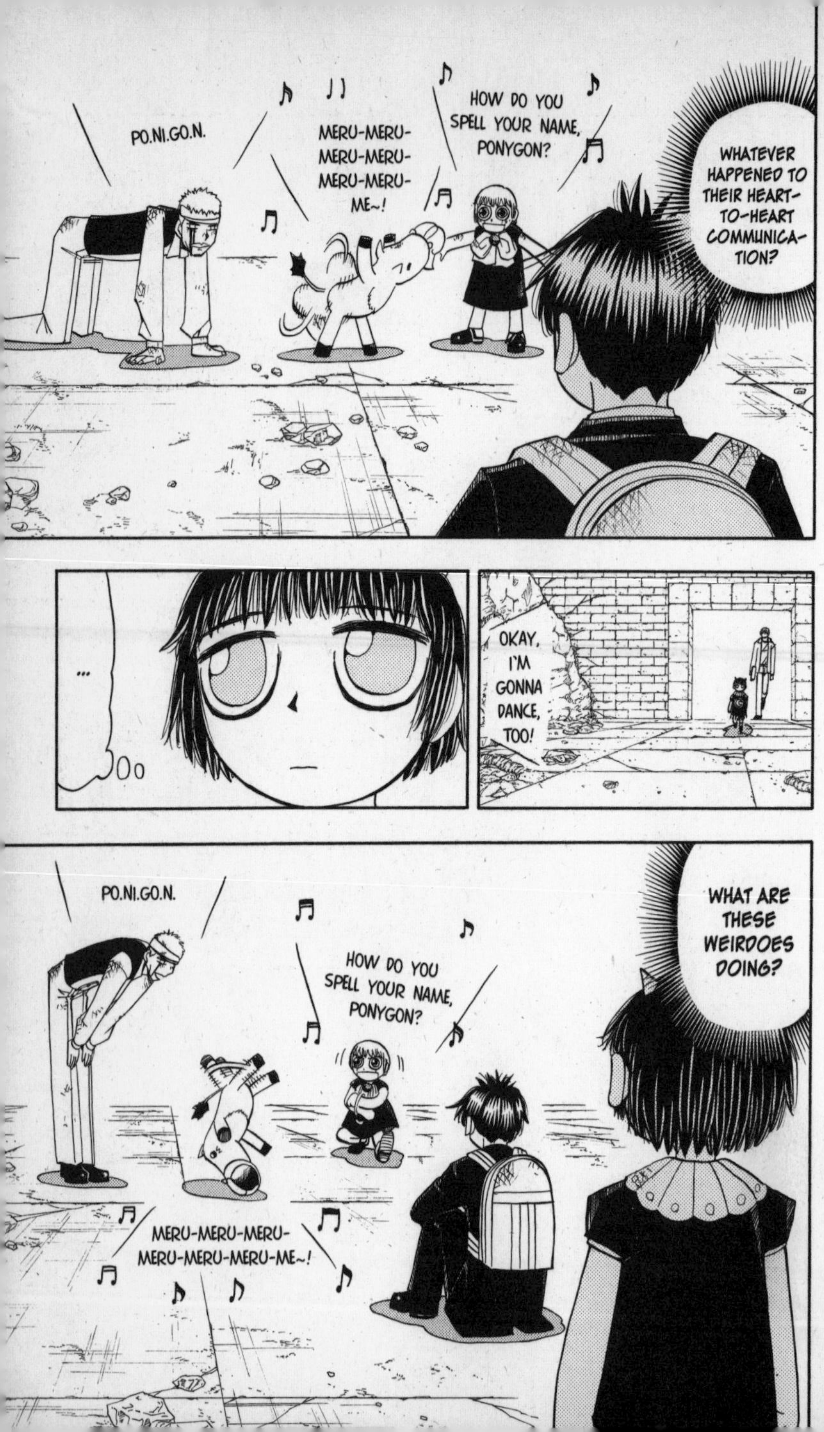

WHATEVER HAPPENED TO THEIR HEART-TO-HEART COMMUNICATION?
HOW DO YOU SPELL YOUR NAME, PONYGON?
MERU-MERU-MERU-MERU-MERU-MERU-ME~!
PO.NI.GO.N.
OKAY, I'M GONNA DANCE, TOO!
...
WHAT ARE THESE WEIRDOES DOING?
HOW DO YOU SPELL YOUR NAME, PONYGON?
PO.NI.GO.N.
MERU-MERU-MERU-MERU-MERU-MERU-ME~!

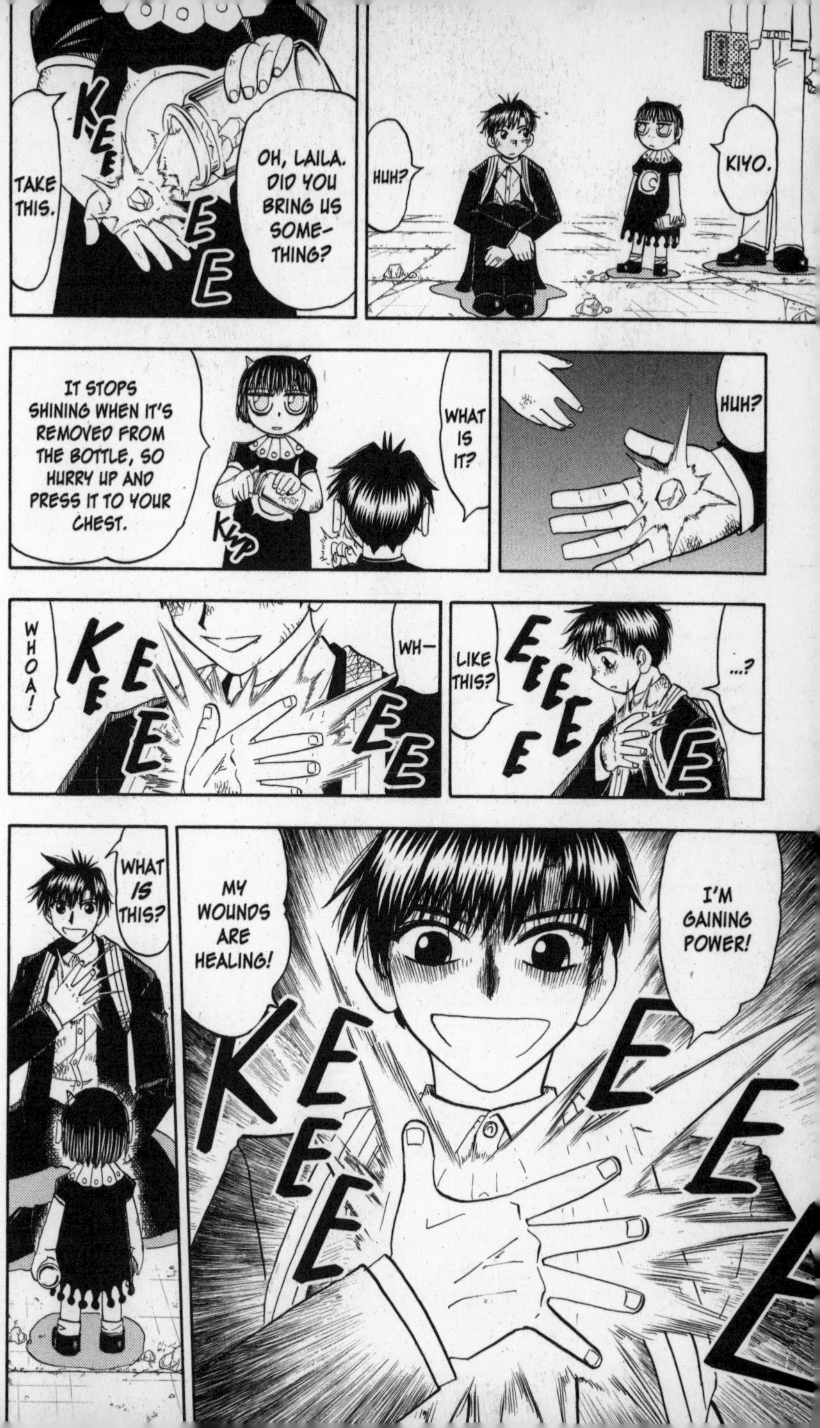
KIYO.
HUH?
OH, LAILA. DID YOU BRING US SOME-THING?
TAKE THIS.
KEEEEE
HUH?
WHAT IS IT?
IT STOPS SHINING WHEN IT'S REMOVED FROM THE BOTTLE, SO HURRY UP AND PRESS IT TO YOUR CHEST.
KWP
...?
LIKE THIS?
WH—
WHOA!
I'M GAINING POWER!
MY WOUNDS ARE HEALING!
WHAT IS THIS?

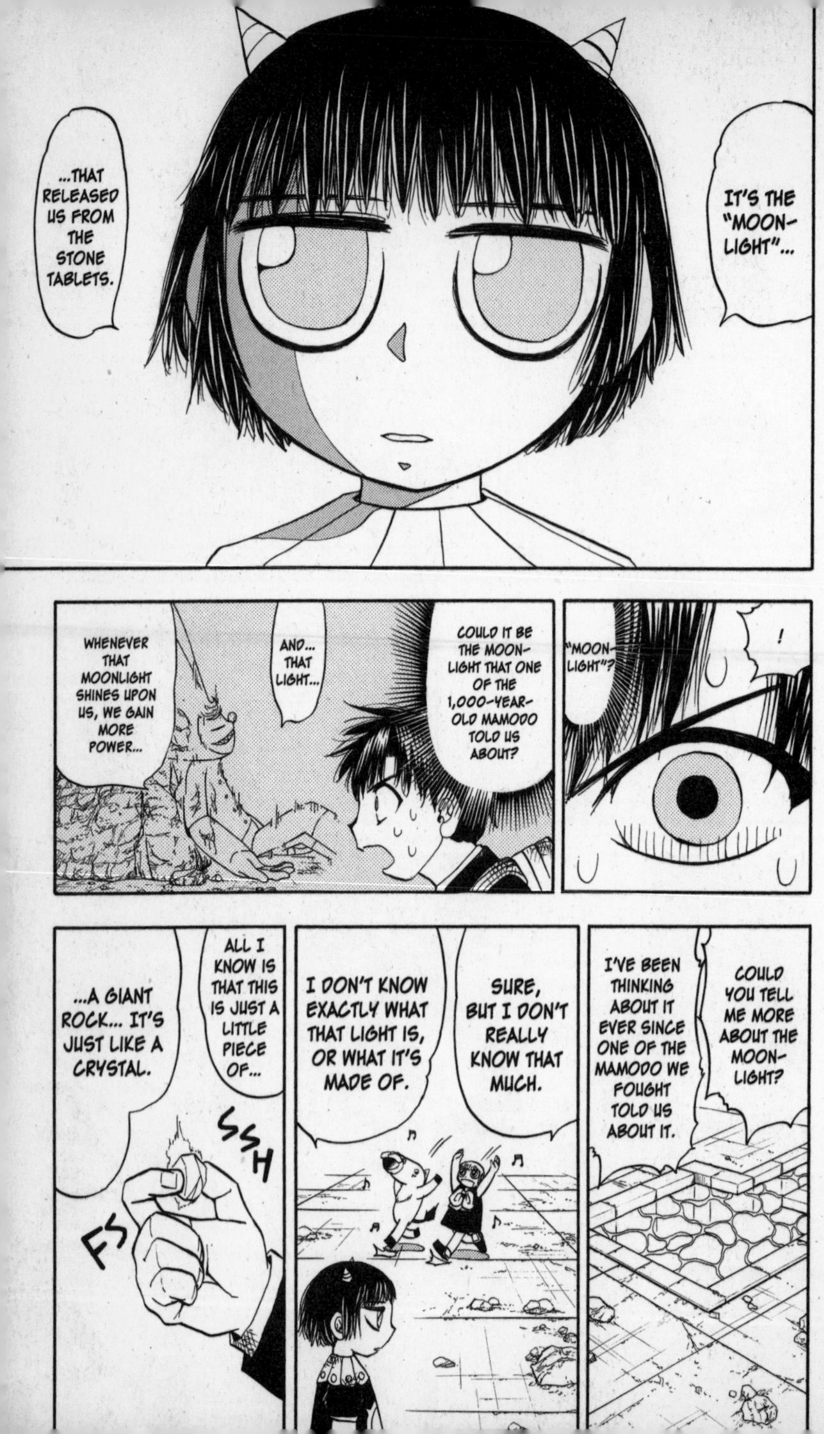
IT'S THE "MOON-LIGHT"...
...THAT RELEASED US FROM THE STONE TABLETS.
!
"MOON-LIGHT"?
COULD IT BE THE MOON-LIGHT THAT ONE OF THE 1,000-YEAR-OLD MAMODO TOLD US ABOUT?
AND... THAT LIGHT...
WHENEVER THAT MOONLIGHT SHINES UPON US, WE GAIN MORE POWER...
COULD YOU TELL ME MORE ABOUT THE MOON-LIGHT?
I'VE BEEN THINKING ABOUT IT EVER SINCE ONE OF THE MAMODO WE FOUGHT TOLD US ABOUT IT.
SURE, BUT I DON'T REALLY KNOW THAT MUCH.
I DON'T KNOW EXACTLY WHAT THAT LIGHT IS, OR WHAT IT'S MADE OF.
ALL I KNOW IS THAT THIS IS JUST A LITTLE PIECE OF...
...A GIANT ROCK... IT'S JUST LIKE A CRYSTAL.
SSH
FS

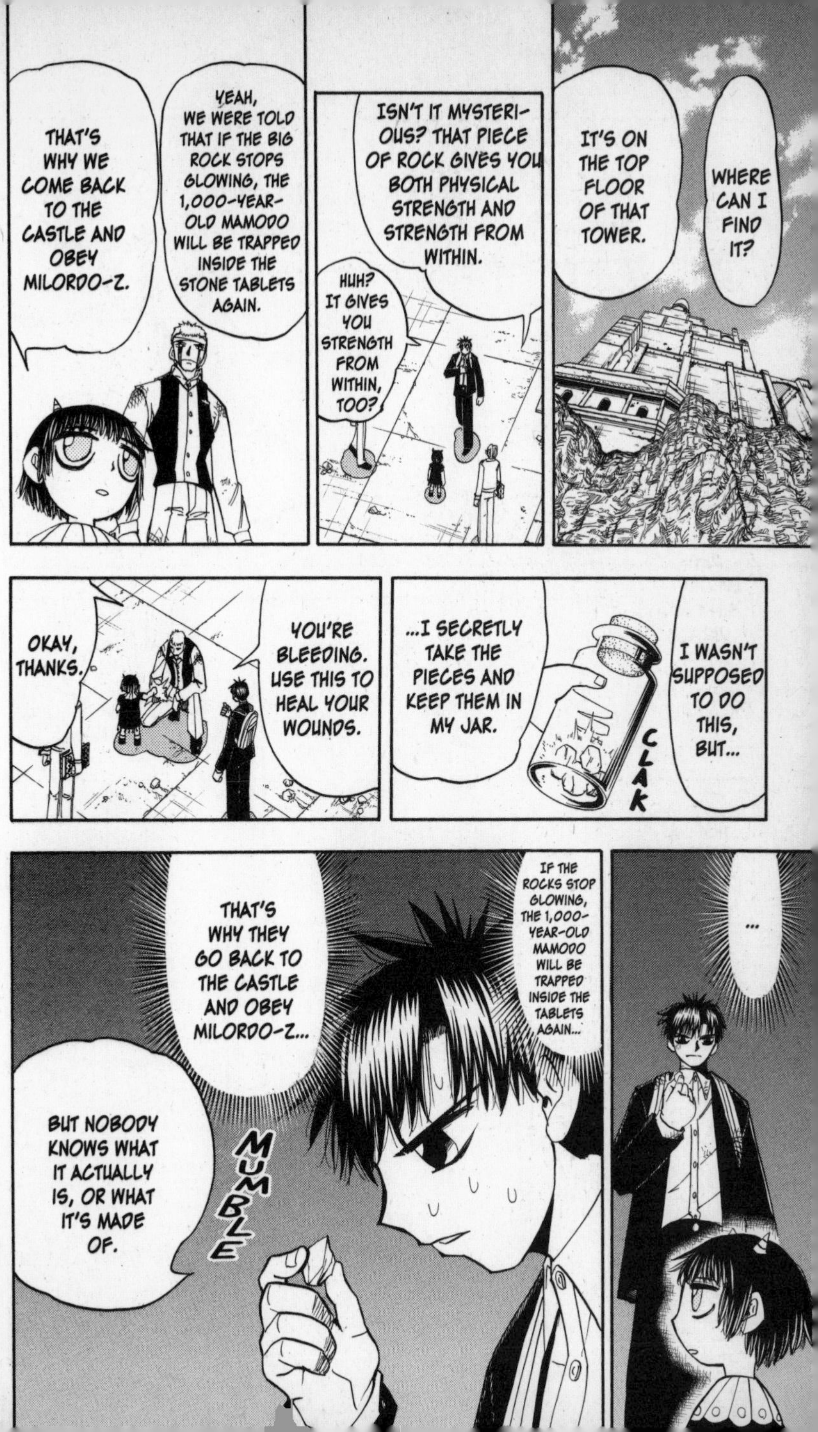
WHERE CAN I FIND IT?
IT'S ON THE TOP FLOOR OF THAT TOWER.
ISN'T IT MYSTERIOUS? THAT PIECE OF ROCK GIVES YOU BOTH PHYSICAL STRENGTH AND STRENGTH FROM WITHIN.
HUH? IT GIVES YOU STRENGTH FROM WITHIN, TOO?
YEAH, WE WERE TOLD THAT IF THE BIG ROCK STOPS GLOWING, THE 1,000-YEAR-OLD MAMODO WILL BE TRAPPED INSIDE THE STONE TABLETS AGAIN.
THAT'S WHY WE COME BACK TO THE CASTLE AND OBEY MILORDO-Z.
I WASN'T SUPPOSED TO DO THIS, BUT...
CLAK
...I SECRETLY TAKE THE PIECES AND KEEP THEM IN MY JAR.
YOU'RE BLEEDING. USE THIS TO HEAL YOUR WOUNDS.
OKAY, THANKS.
...
IF THE ROCKS STOP GLOWING, THE 1,000-YEAR-OLD MAMODO WILL BE TRAPPED INSIDE THE TABLETS AGAIN...
THAT'S WHY THEY GO BACK TO THE CASTLE AND OBEY MILORDO-Z...
MUMBLE
BUT NOBODY KNOWS WHAT IT ACTUALLY IS, OR WHAT IT'S MADE OF.

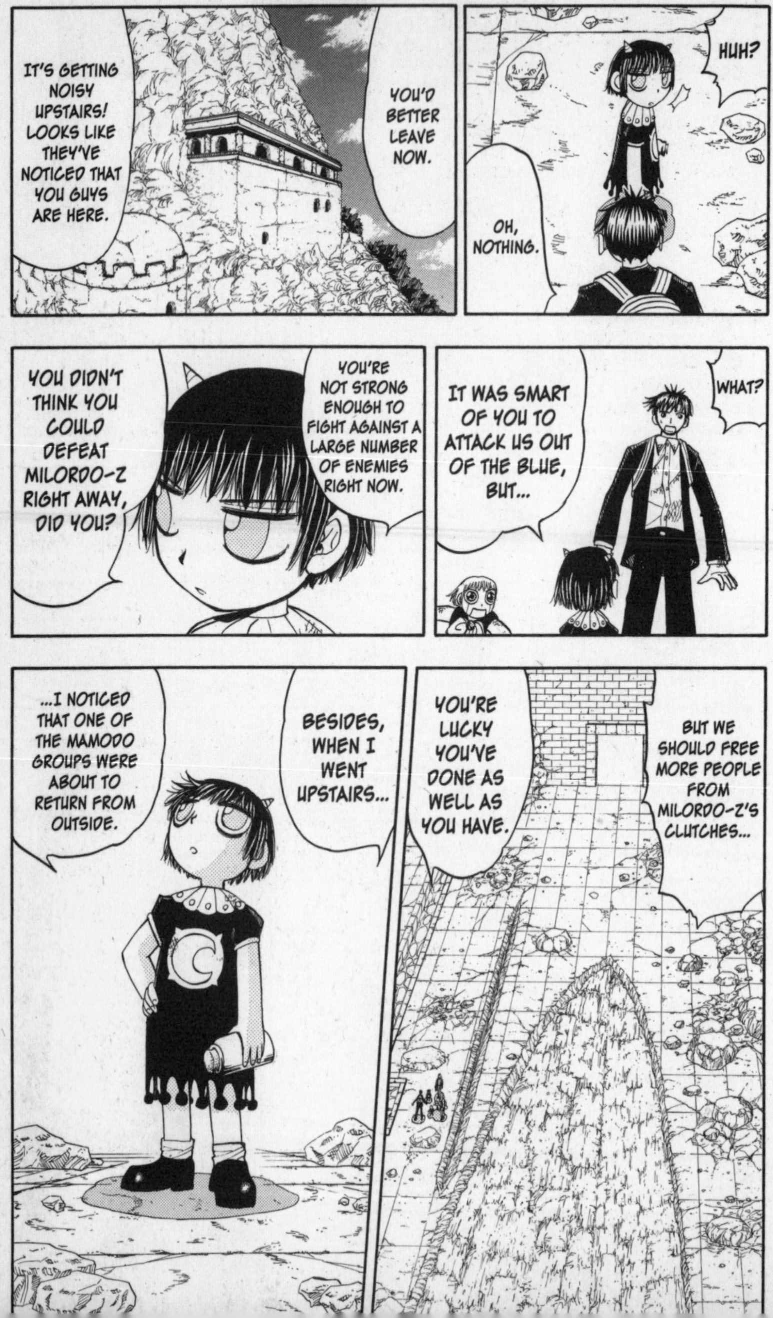
HUH?
OH, NOTHING.
YOU'D BETTER LEAVE NOW.
IT'S GETTING NOISY UPSTAIRS! LOOKS LIKE THEY'VE NOTICED THAT YOU GUYS ARE HERE.
WHAT?
IT WAS SMART OF YOU TO ATTACK US OUT OF THE BLUE, BUT...
YOU'RE NOT STRONG ENOUGH TO FIGHT AGAINST A LARGE NUMBER OF ENEMIES RIGHT NOW.
YOU DIDN'T THINK YOU COULD DEFEAT MILORDO-Z RIGHT AWAY, DID YOU?
BUT WE SHOULD FREE MORE PEOPLE FROM MILORDO-Z'S CLUTCHES...
YOU'RE LUCKY YOU'VE DONE AS WELL AS YOU HAVE.
BESIDES, WHEN I WENT UPSTAIRS...
...I NOTICED THAT ONE OF THE MAMODO GROUPS WERE ABOUT TO RETURN FROM OUTSIDE.

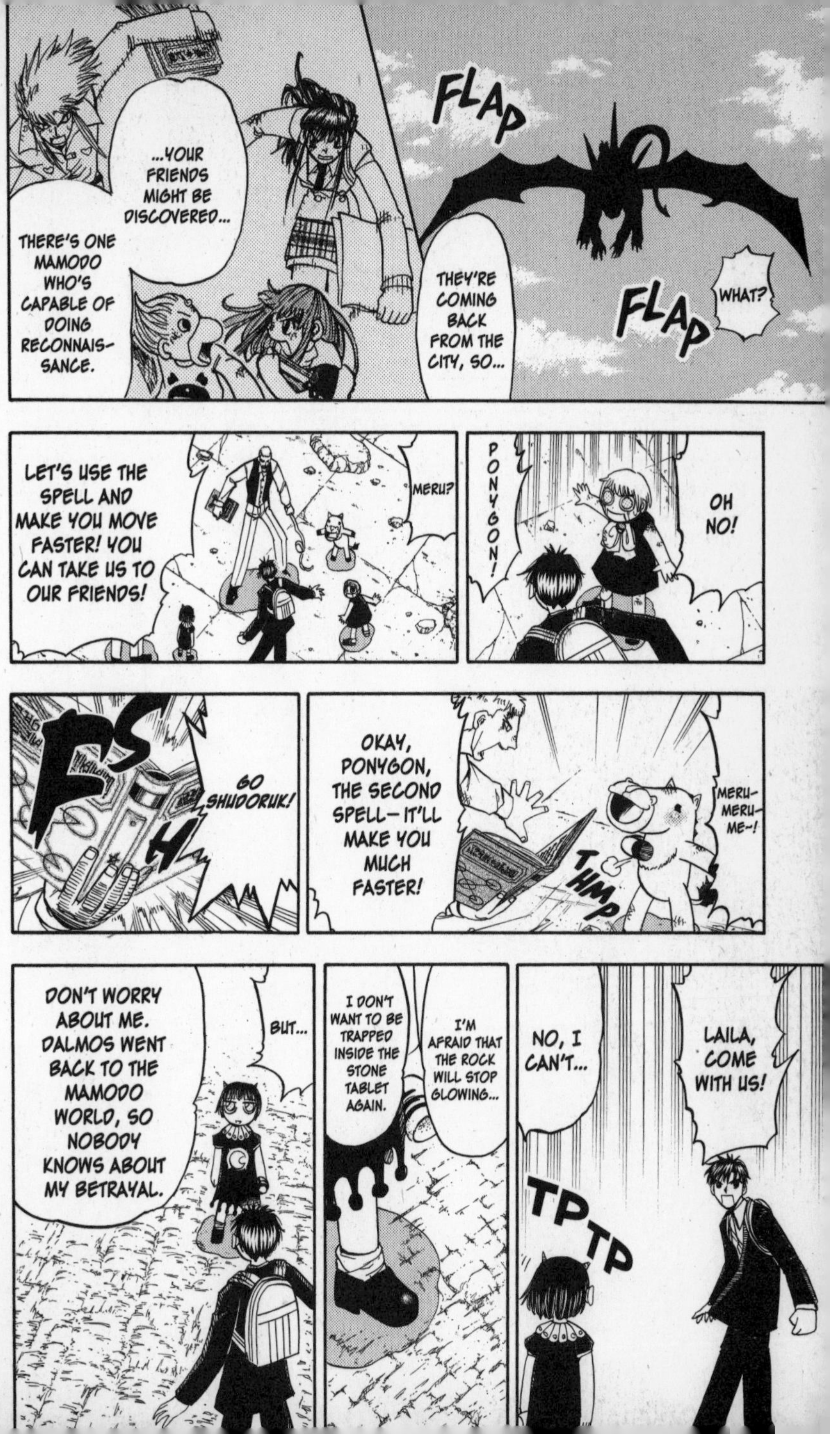
FLAP
WHAT?
FLAP
THEY'RE COMING BACK FROM THE CITY, SO...
...YOUR FRIENDS MIGHT BE DISCOVERED...
THERE'S ONE MAMODO WHO'S CAPABLE OF DOING RECONNAIS-SANCE.
PONYGON!
OH NO!
MERU?
LET'S USE THE SPELL AND MAKE YOU MOVE FASTER! YOU CAN TAKE US TO OUR FRIENDS!
MERU-MERU-ME-!
OKAY, PONYGON, THE SECOND SPELL—IT'LL MAKE YOU MUCH FASTER!
THMP
GO SHUDORUK!
FSSH
LAILA, COME WITH US!
NO, I CAN'T...
TP TP
I'M AFRAID THAT THE ROCK WILL STOP GLOWING...
I DON'T WANT TO BE TRAPPED INSIDE THE STONE TABLET AGAIN.
BUT...
DON'T WORRY ABOUT ME. DALMOS WENT BACK TO THE MAMODO WORLD, SO NOBODY KNOWS ABOUT MY BETRAYAL.

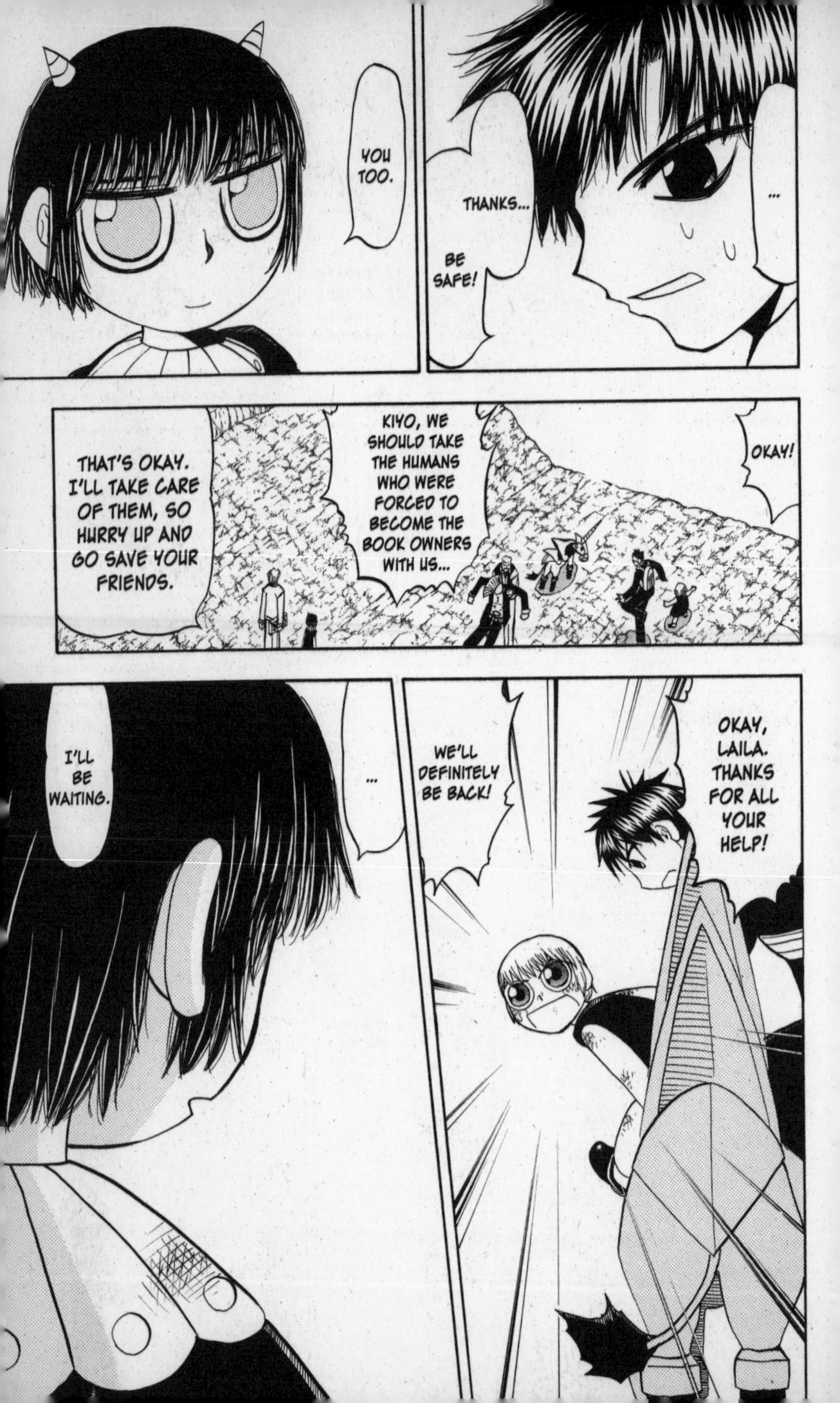
...
THANKS...
BE SAFE!
YOU TOO.
OKAY!
KIYO, WE SHOULD TAKE THE HUMANS WHO WERE FORCED TO BECOME THE BOOK OWNERS WITH US...
THAT'S OKAY. I'LL TAKE CARE OF THEM, SO HURRY UP AND GO SAVE YOUR FRIENDS.
OKAY, LAILA. THANKS FOR ALL YOUR HELP!
WE'LL DEFINITELY BE BACK!
...
I'LL BE WAITING.

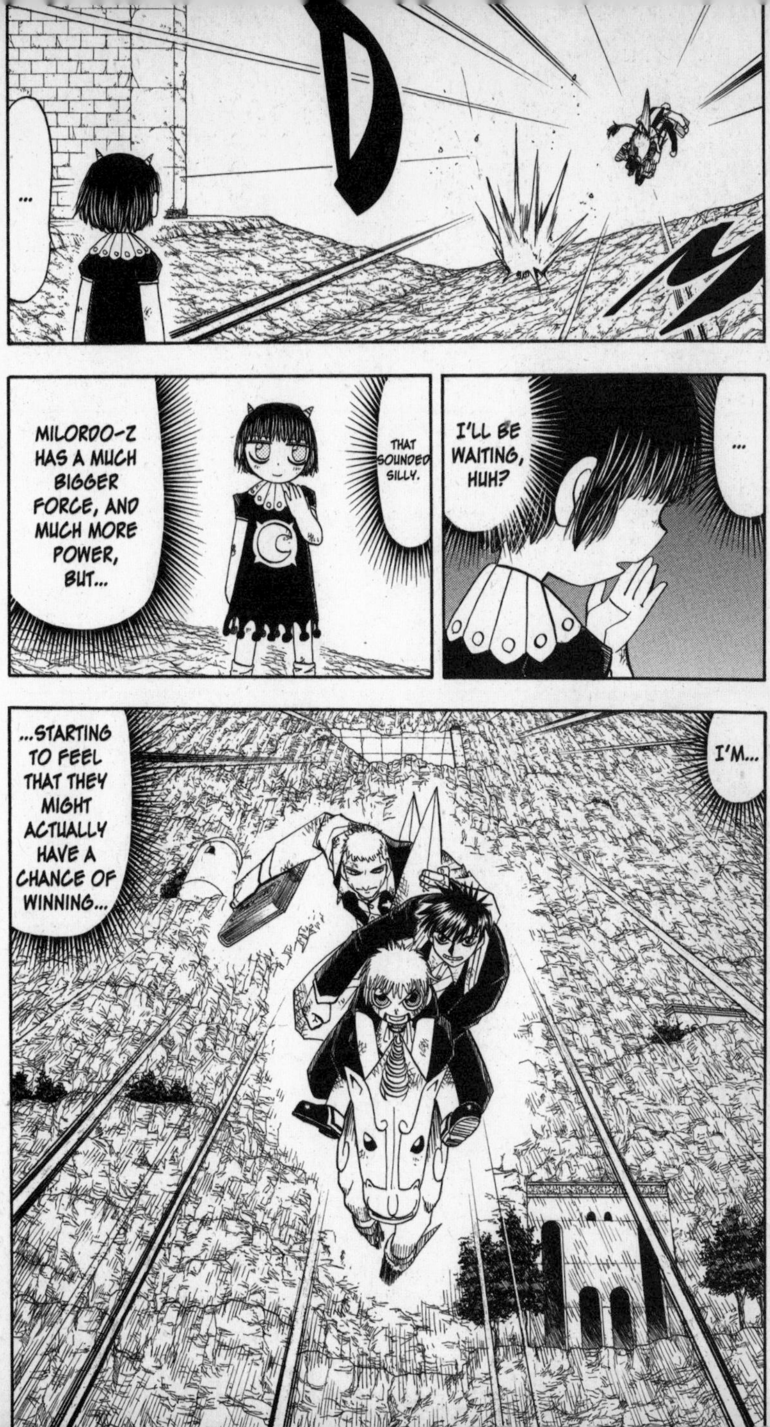
...
...
I'LL BE WAITING, HUH?
THAT SOUNDED SILLY.
MILORDO-Z HAS A MUCH BIGGER FORCE, AND MUCH MORE POWER, BUT...
I'M...
...STARTING TO FEEL THAT THEY MIGHT ACTUALLY HAVE A CHANCE OF WINNING...

LEVEL 125: The Entrusted Book

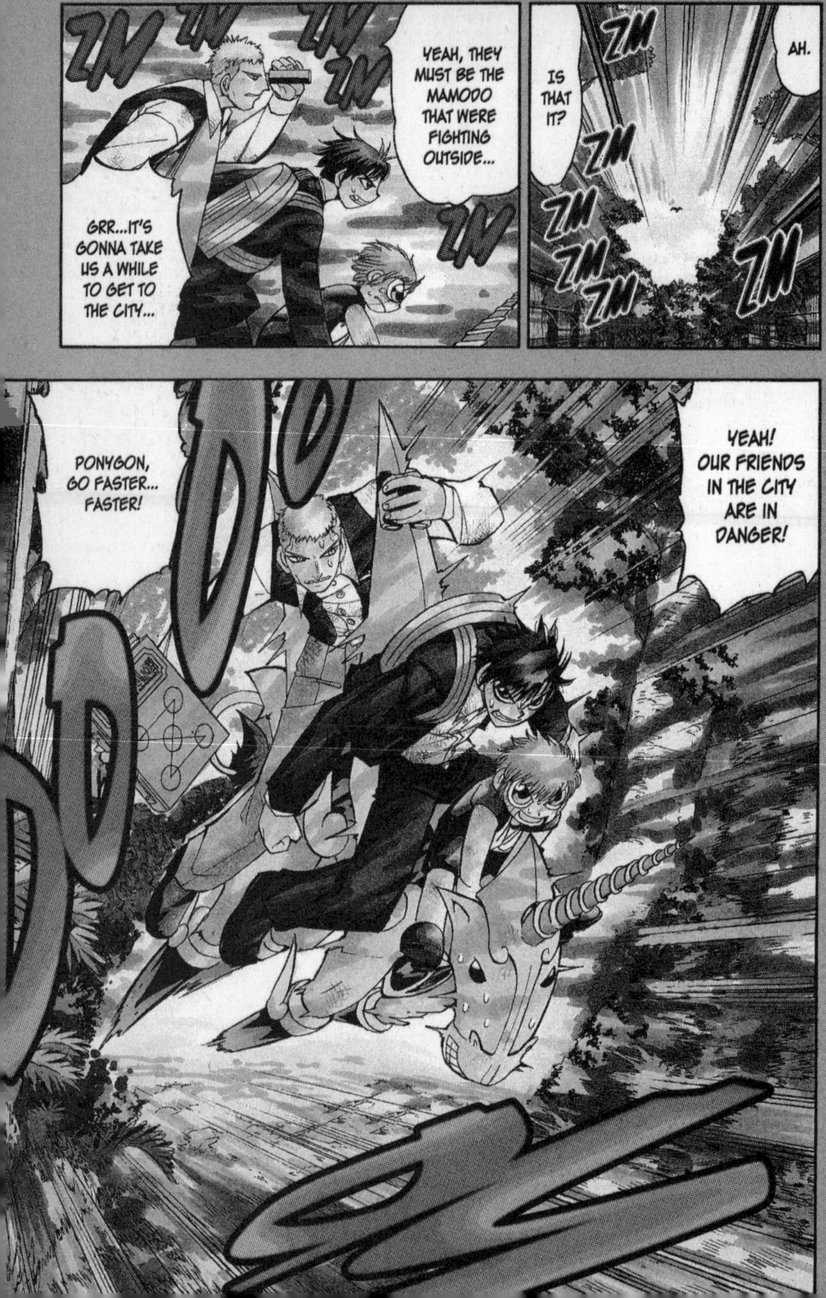
AH.
IS THAT IT?
ZM
ZM
ZM
ZM
ZM
ZM
YEAH, THEY MUST BE THE MAMODO THAT WERE FIGHTING OUTSIDE...
GRR...IT'S GONNA TAKE US A WHILE TO GET TO THE CITY...
ZM
ZM
ZM
ZM
ZM
YEAH! OUR FRIENDS IN THE CITY ARE IN DANGER!
PONYGON, GO FASTER... FASTER!

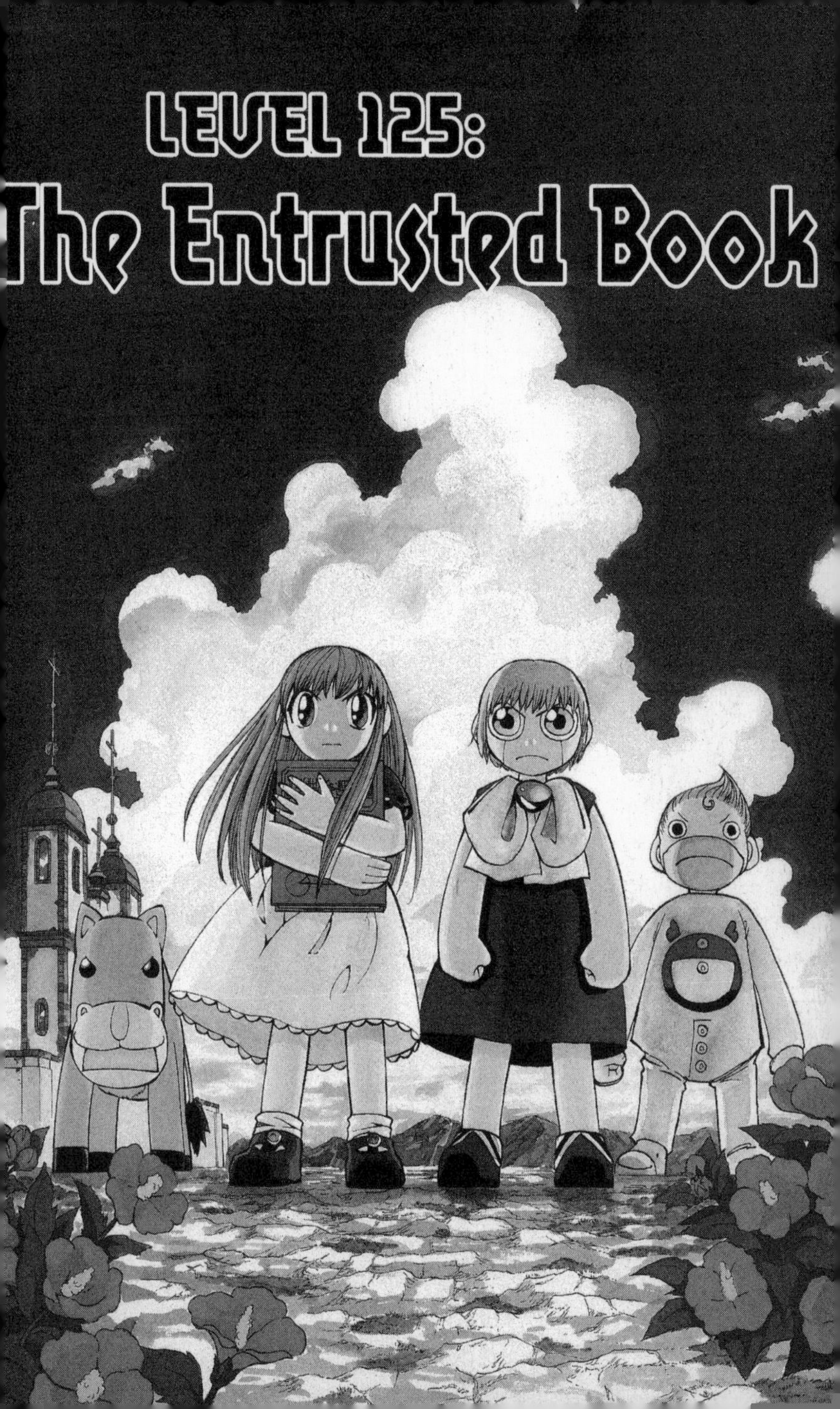
LEVEL 125:
The Entrusted Book

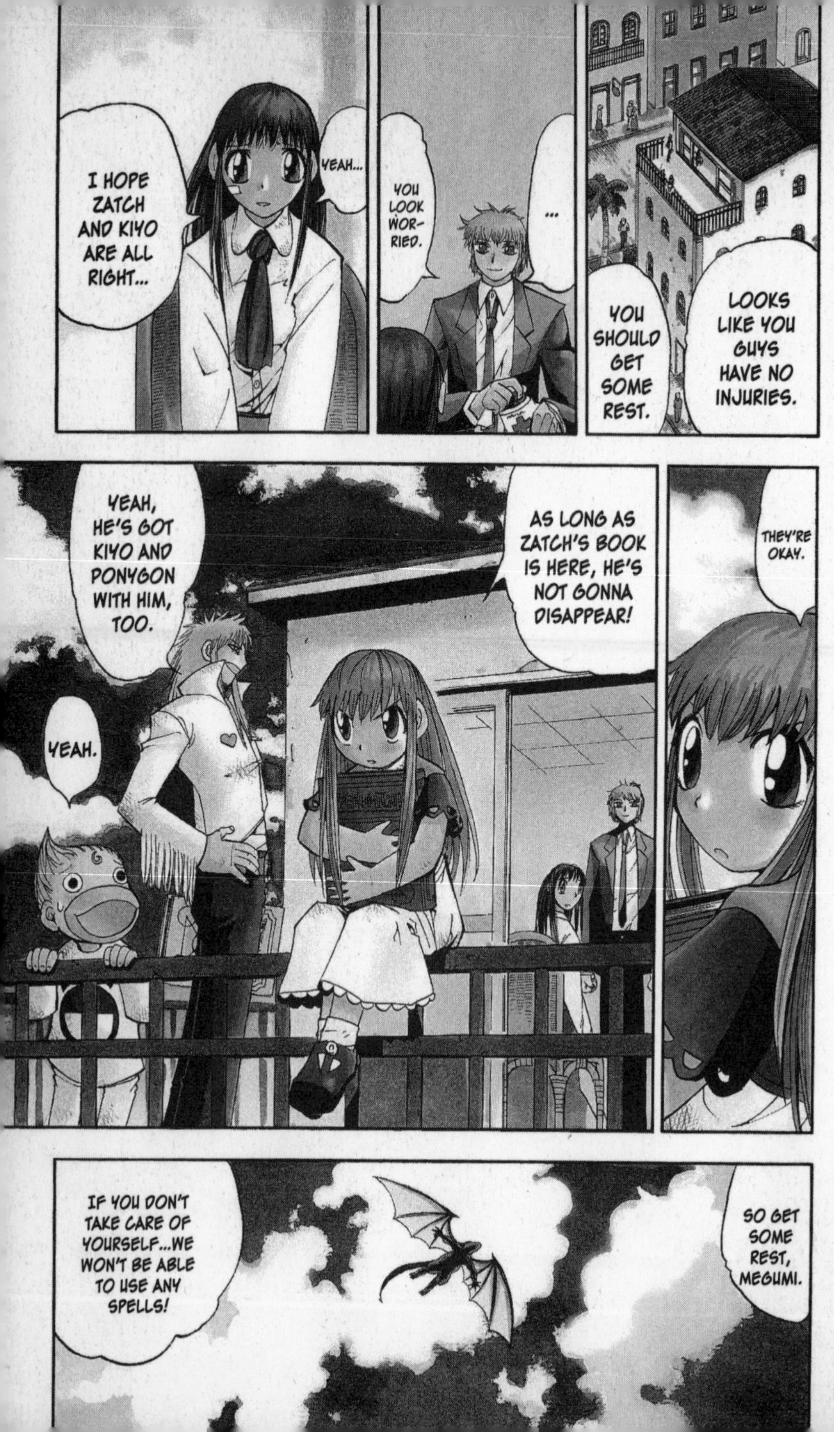
LOOKS LIKE YOU GUYS HAVE NO INJURIES.
YOU SHOULD GET SOME REST.
...
YOU LOOK WORRIED.
YEAH...
I HOPE ZATCH AND KIYO ARE ALL RIGHT...
THEY'RE OKAY.
AS LONG AS ZATCH'S BOOK IS HERE, HE'S NOT GONNA DISAPPEAR!
YEAH, HE'S GOT KIYO AND PONYGON WITH HIM, TOO.
YEAH.
SO GET SOME REST, MEGUMI.
IF YOU DON'T TAKE CARE OF YOURSELF...WE WON'T BE ABLE TO USE ANY SPELLS!

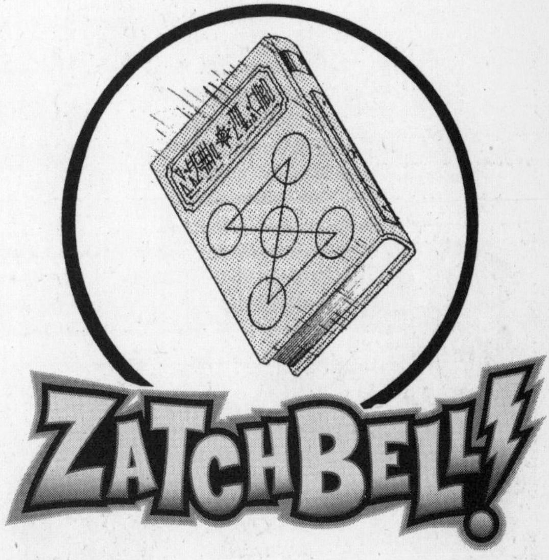

ZATCHBELL!

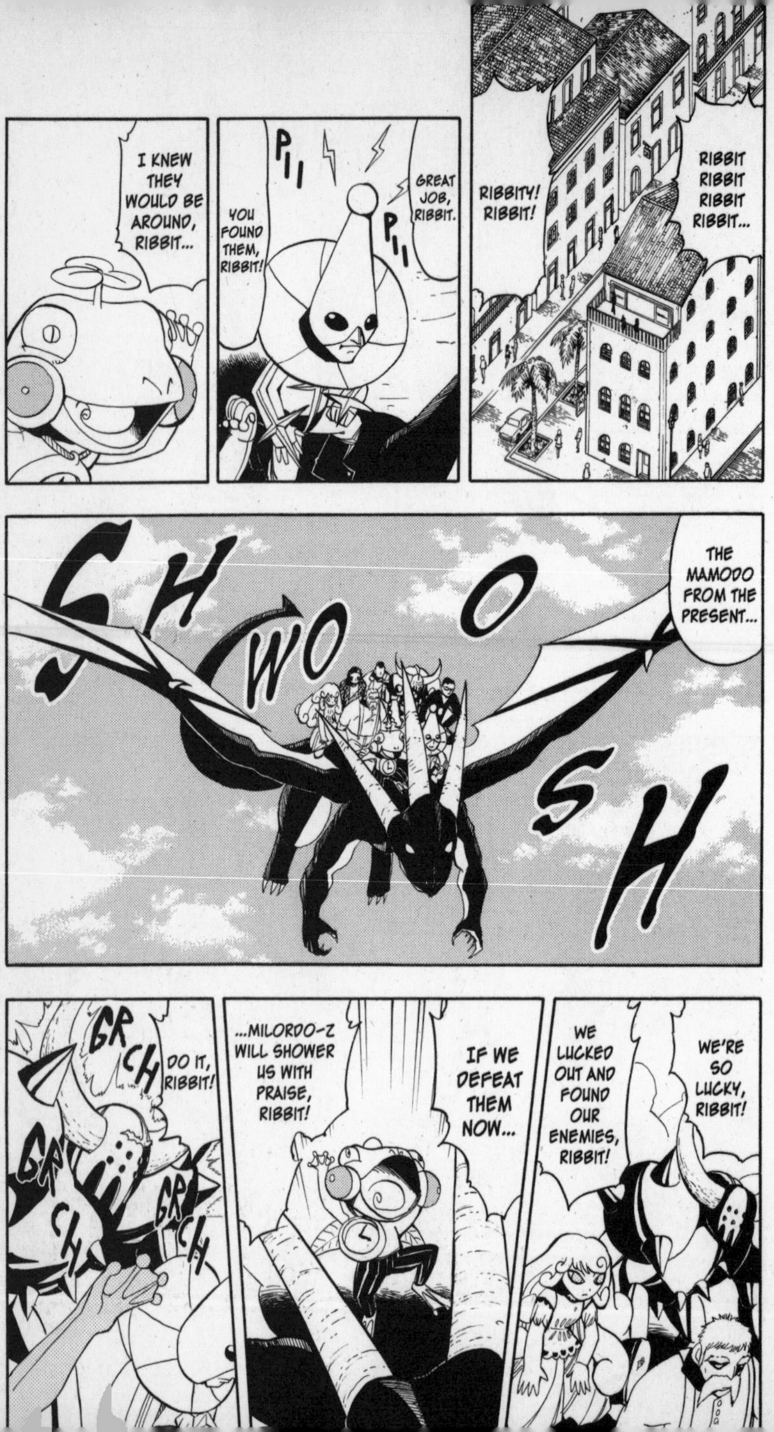
RIBBIT RIBBIT RIBBIT RIBBIT...
RIBBITY! RIBBIT!
GREAT JOB, RIBBIT.
PII
PII
YOU FOUND THEM, RIBBIT!
I KNEW THEY WOULD BE AROUND, RIBBIT...
THE MAMODO FROM THE PRESENT...
SHWOOSH
WE'RE SO LUCKY, RIBBIT!
WE LUCKED OUT AND FOUND OUR ENEMIES, RIBBIT!
IF WE DEFEAT THEM NOW...
...MILORDO-Z WILL SHOWER US WITH PRAISE, RIBBIT!
DO IT, RIBBIT!
GRCH
GRCH
GRCH
GRCH

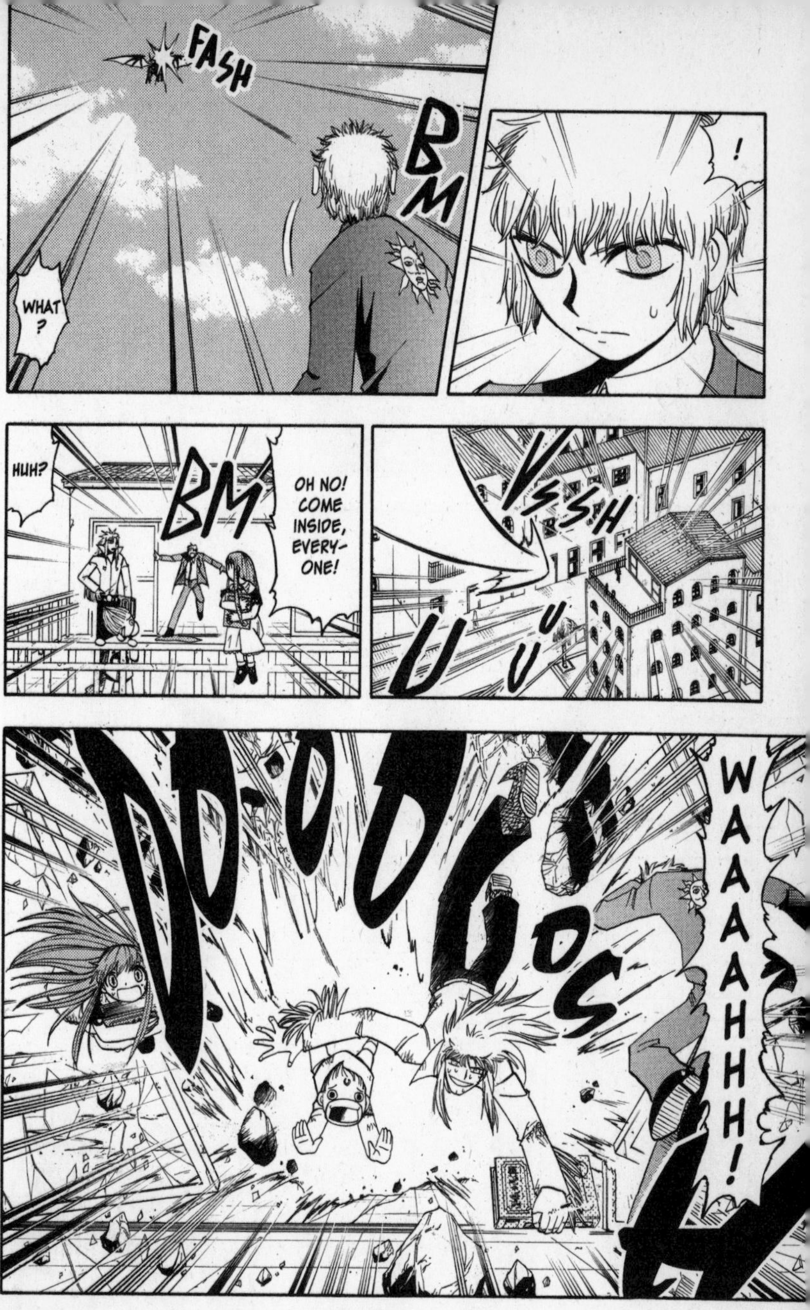
!
FASH
BM
WHAT?
VSSH
UUU
OH NO! COME INSIDE, EVERY-ONE!
BM
HUH?
WAAAAHHH!

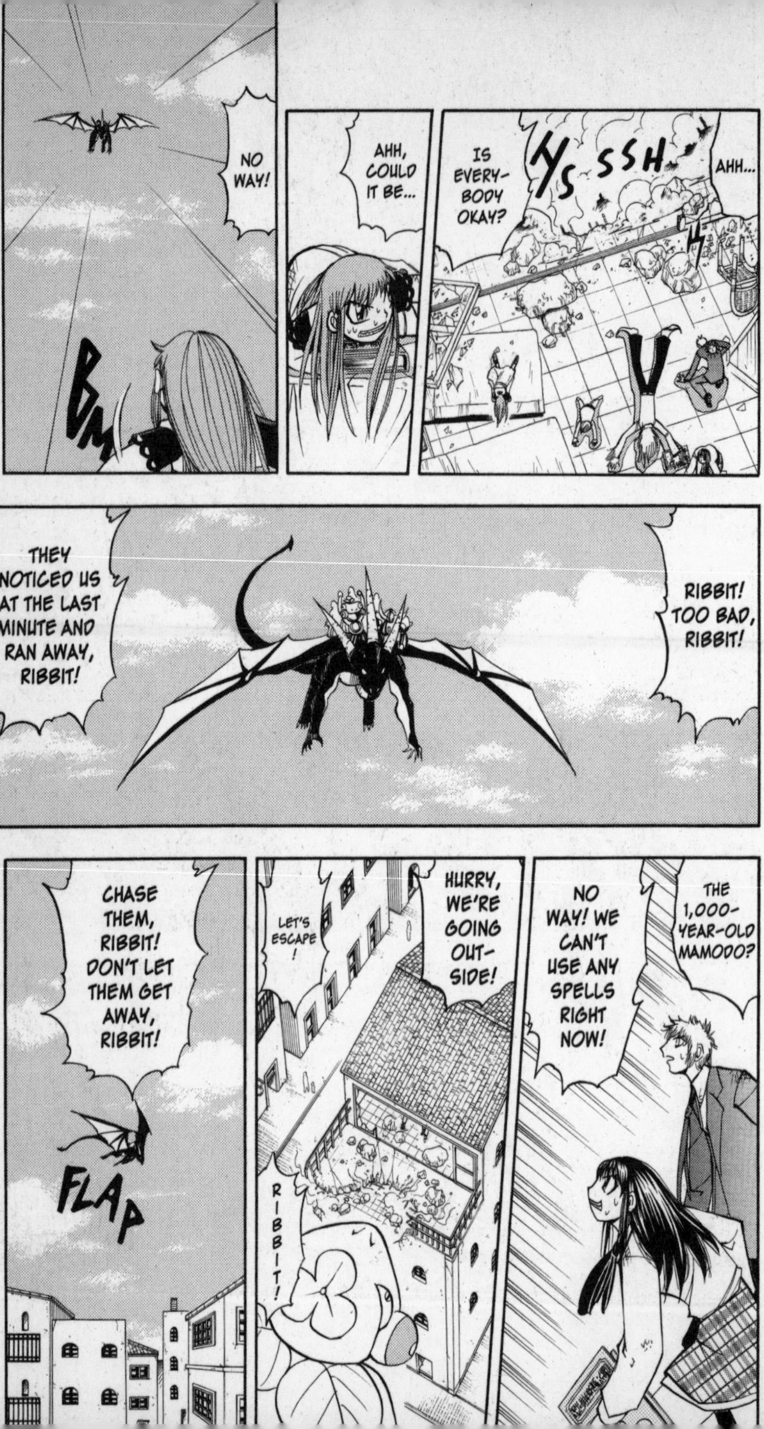
AHH...
HYSSSH
IS EVERY-BODY OKAY?
AHH, COULD IT BE...
NO WAY!
BM
RIBBIT! TOO BAD, RIBBIT!
THEY NOTICED US AT THE LAST MINUTE AND RAN AWAY, RIBBIT!
THE 1,000-YEAR-OLD MAMODO?
NO WAY! WE CAN'T USE ANY SPELLS RIGHT NOW!
HURRY, WE'RE GOING OUT-SIDE!
LET'S ESCAPE!
RIBBIT!
CHASE THEM, RIBBIT! DON'T LET THEM GET AWAY, RIBBIT!
FLAP

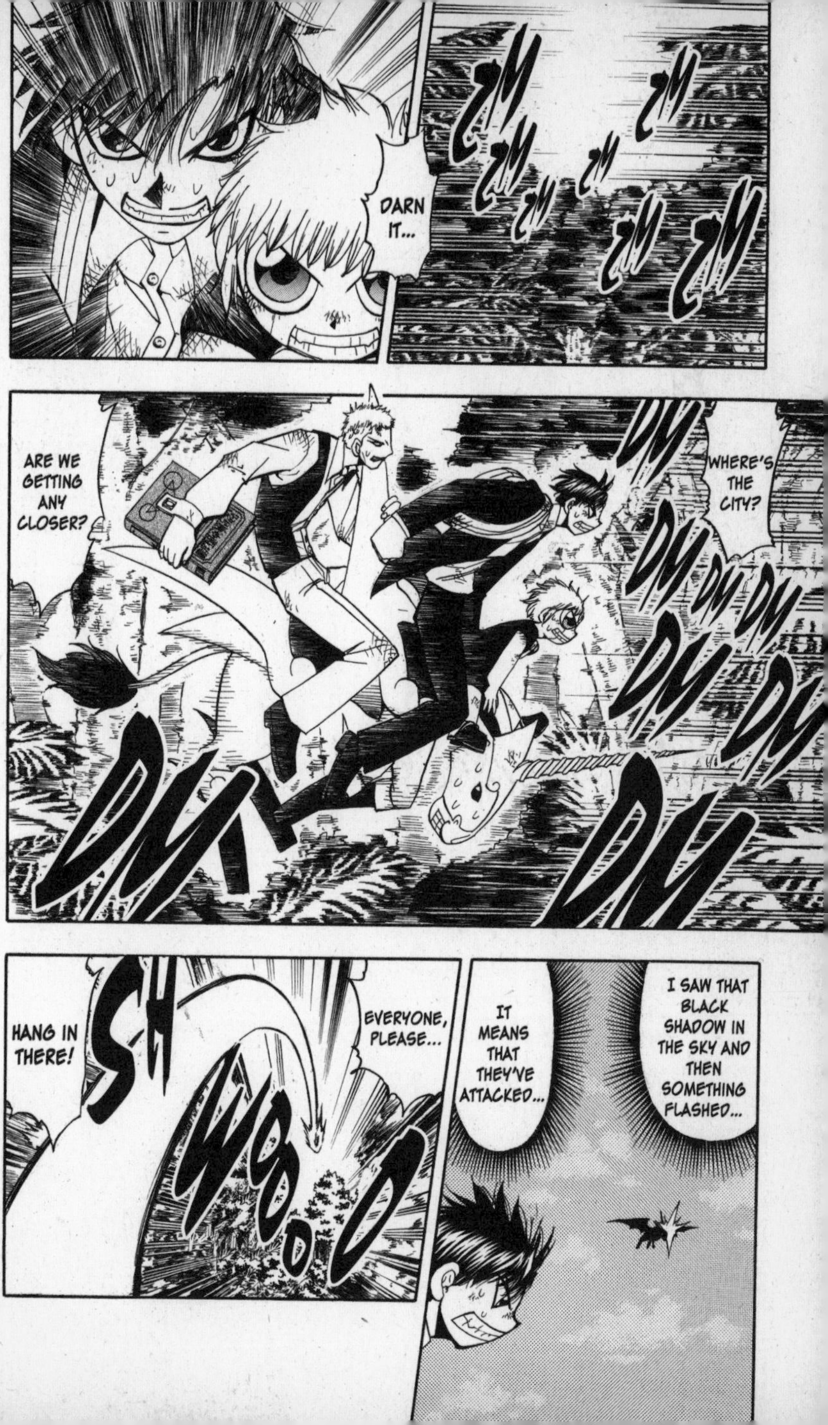
DARN IT...
WHERE'S THE CITY?
ARE WE GETTING ANY CLOSER?
I SAW THAT BLACK SHADOW IN THE SKY AND THEN SOMETHING FLASHED...
IT MEANS THAT THEY'VE ATTACKED...
EVERYONE, PLEASE...
HANG IN THERE!

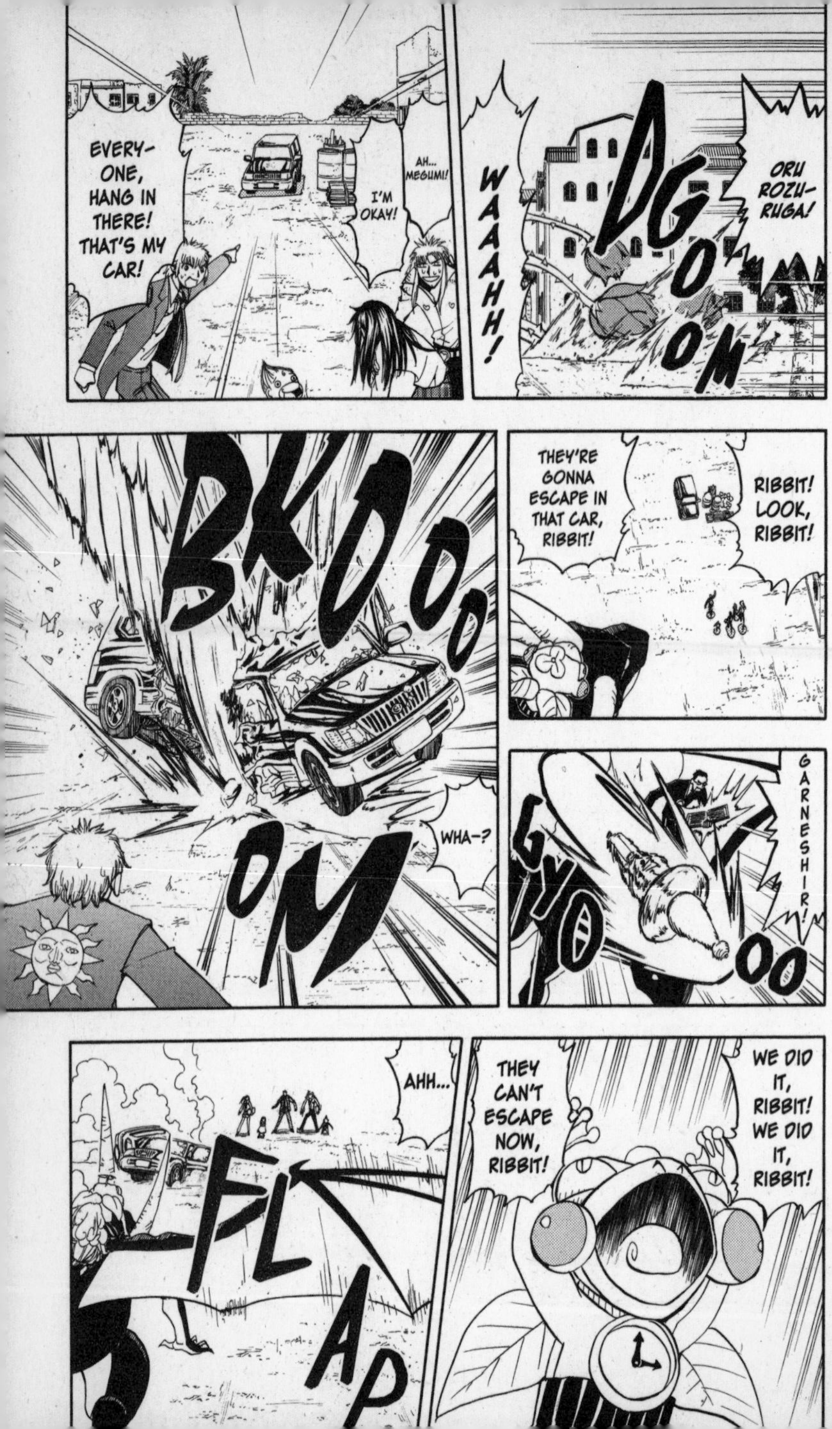
ORU ROZURUGA!
WAAAAHH!
DGOOM
AH... MEGUMI!
I'M OKAY!
EVERYONE, HANG IN THERE! THAT'S MY CAR!
RIBBIT! LOOK, RIBBIT!
THEY'RE GONNA ESCAPE IN THAT CAR, RIBBIT!
GARNESHIR!
GYOOO
BKOOOOOM
WHA-?
WE DID IT, RIBBIT! WE DID IT, RIBBIT!
THEY CAN'T ESCAPE NOW, RIBBIT!
AHH...
FLAP

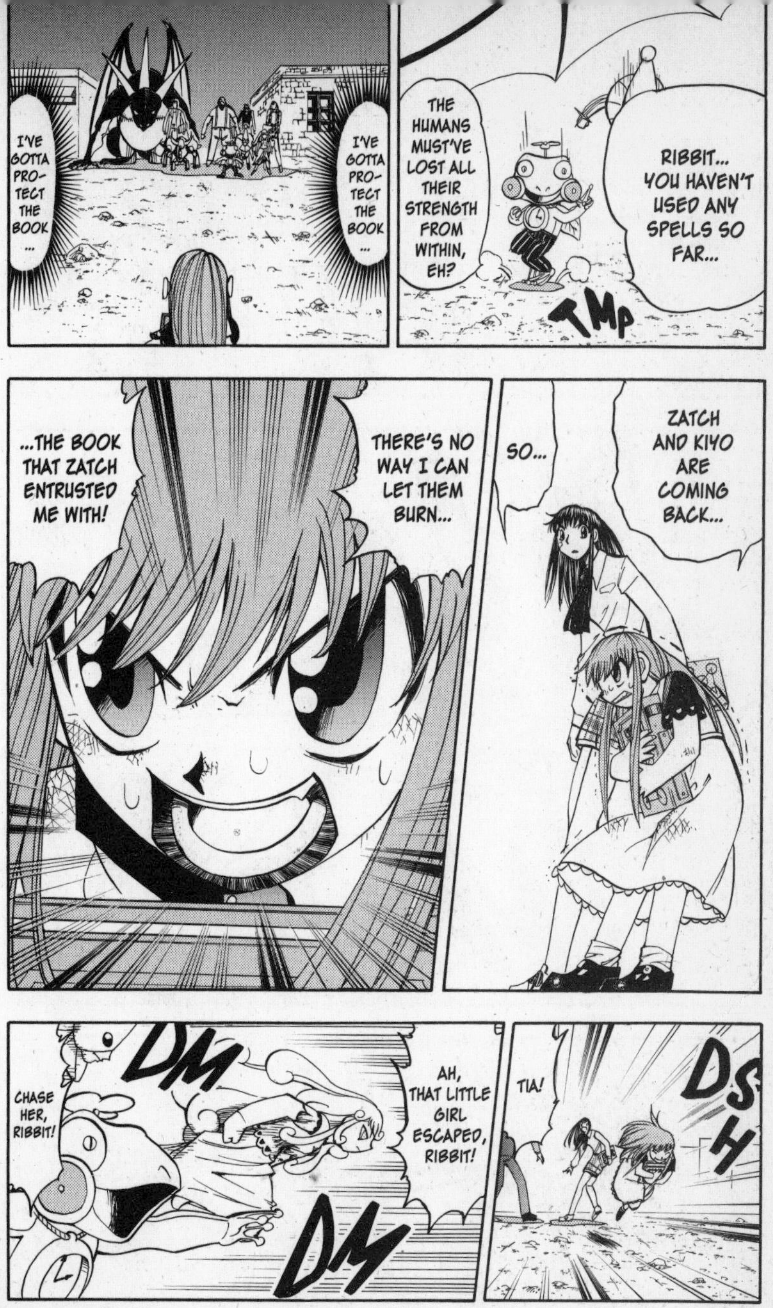
RIBBIT... YOU HAVEN'T USED ANY SPELLS SO FAR...
THE HUMANS MUST'VE LOST ALL THEIR STRENGTH FROM WITHIN, EH?
TMP
I'VE GOTTA PROTECT THE BOOK...
I'VE GOTTA PROTECT THE BOOK...
ZATCH AND KIYO ARE COMING BACK...
SO...
THERE'S NO WAY I CAN LET THEM BURN...
...THE BOOK THAT ZATCH ENTRUSTED ME WITH!
DSH
TIA!
DM
AH, THAT LITTLE GIRL ESCAPED, RIBBIT!
CHASE HER, RIBBIT!
DM

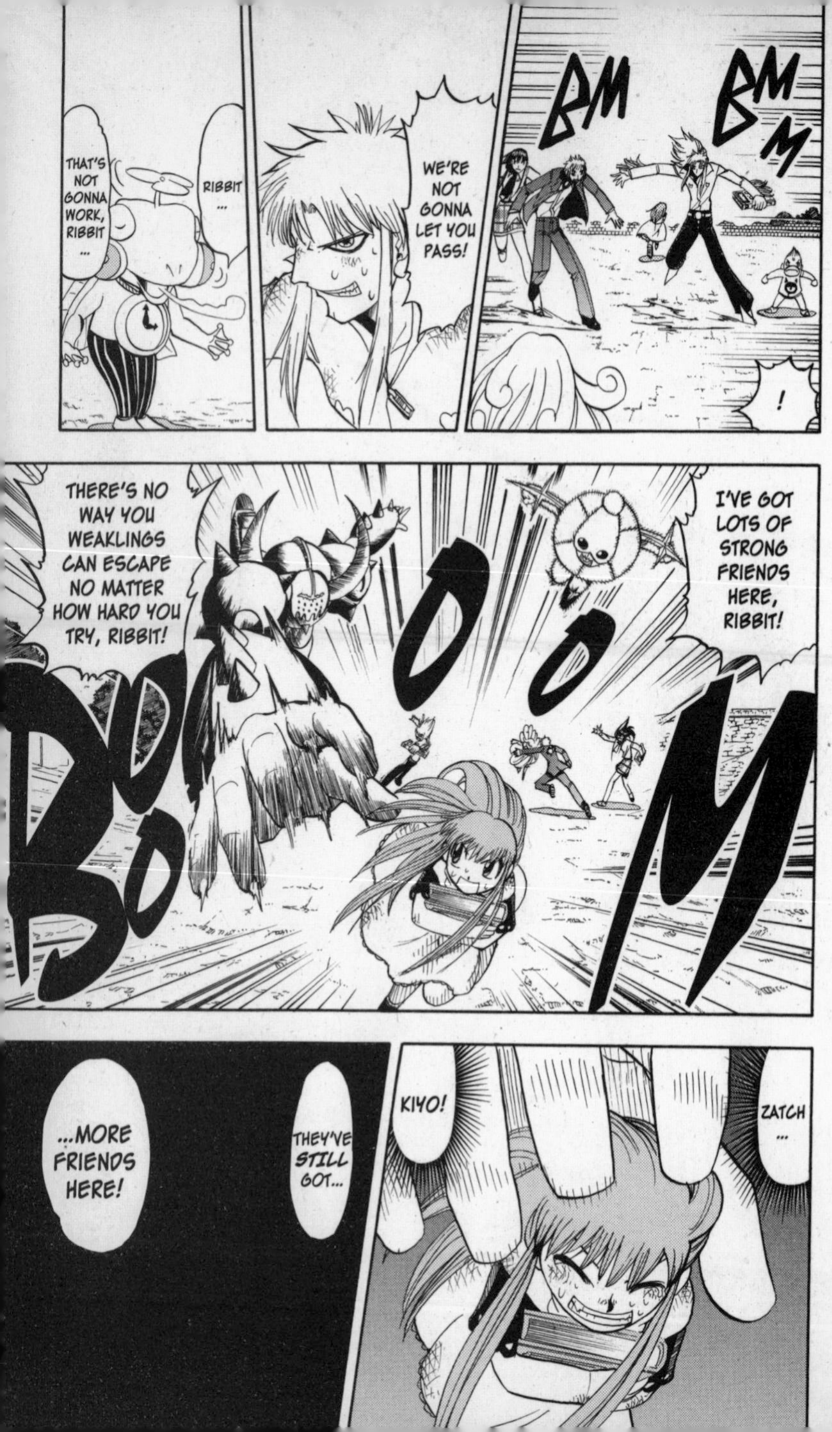
BMM BMM M
!
WE'RE NOT GONNA LET YOU PASS!
RIBBIT ...
THAT'S NOT GONNA WORK, RIBBIT ...
I'VE GOT LOTS OF STRONG FRIENDS HERE, RIBBIT!
THERE'S NO WAY YOU WEAKLINGS CAN ESCAPE NO MATTER HOW HARD YOU TRY, RIBBIT!
BOOOOM
ZATCH ...
KIYO!
THEY'VE STILL GOT...
...MORE FRIENDS HERE!

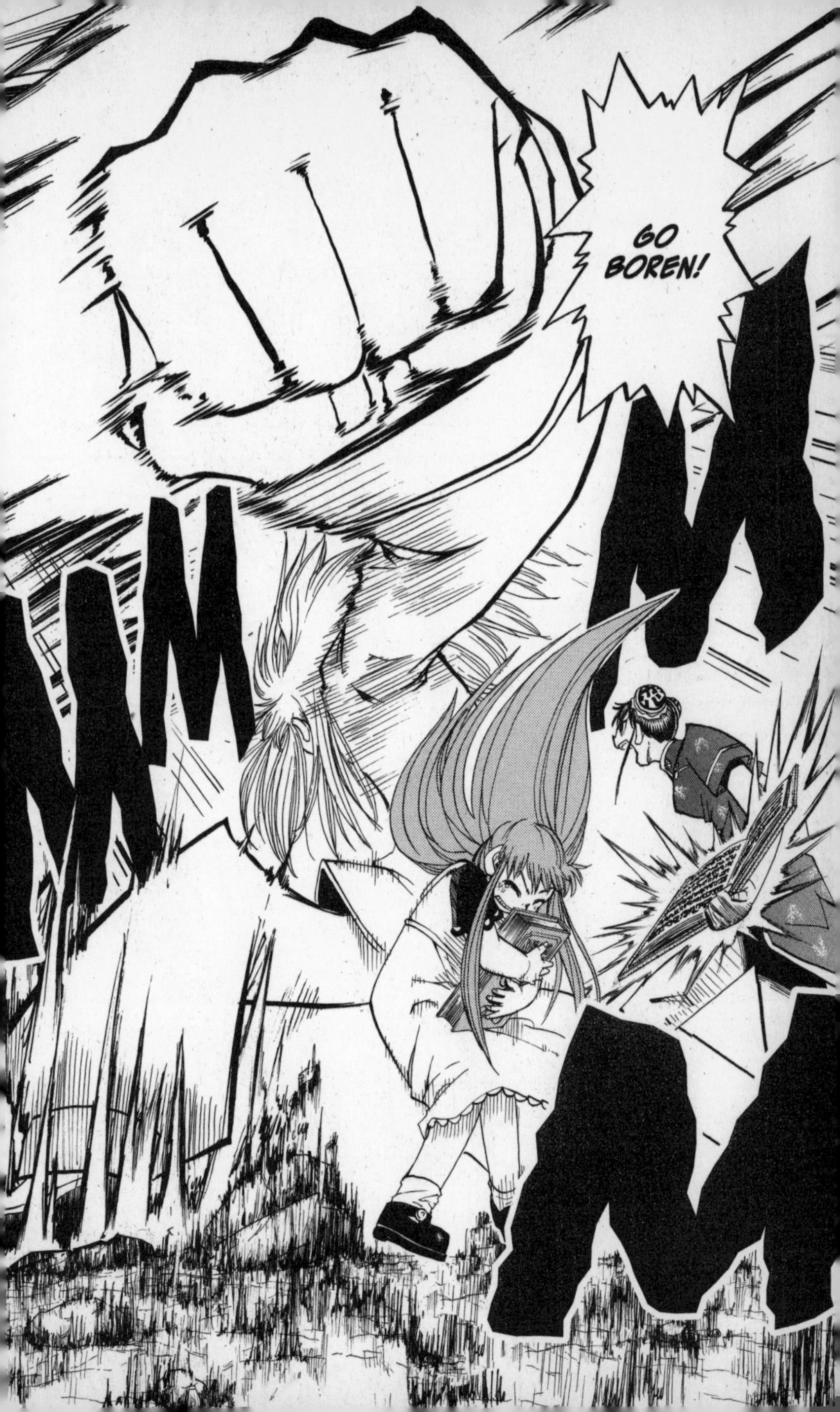
GO BOREN!

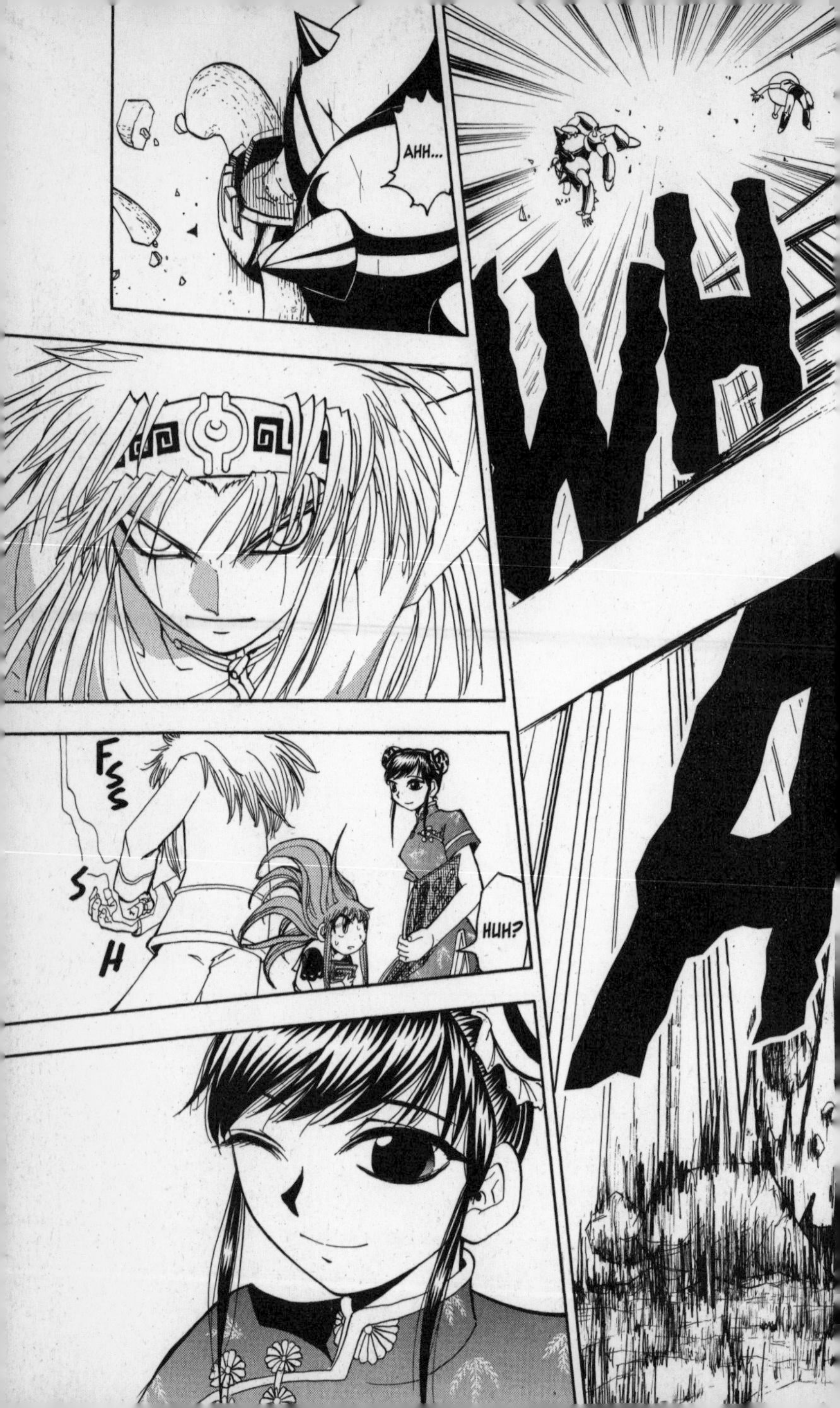
WHA
AHH...
FSSSH
HUH?

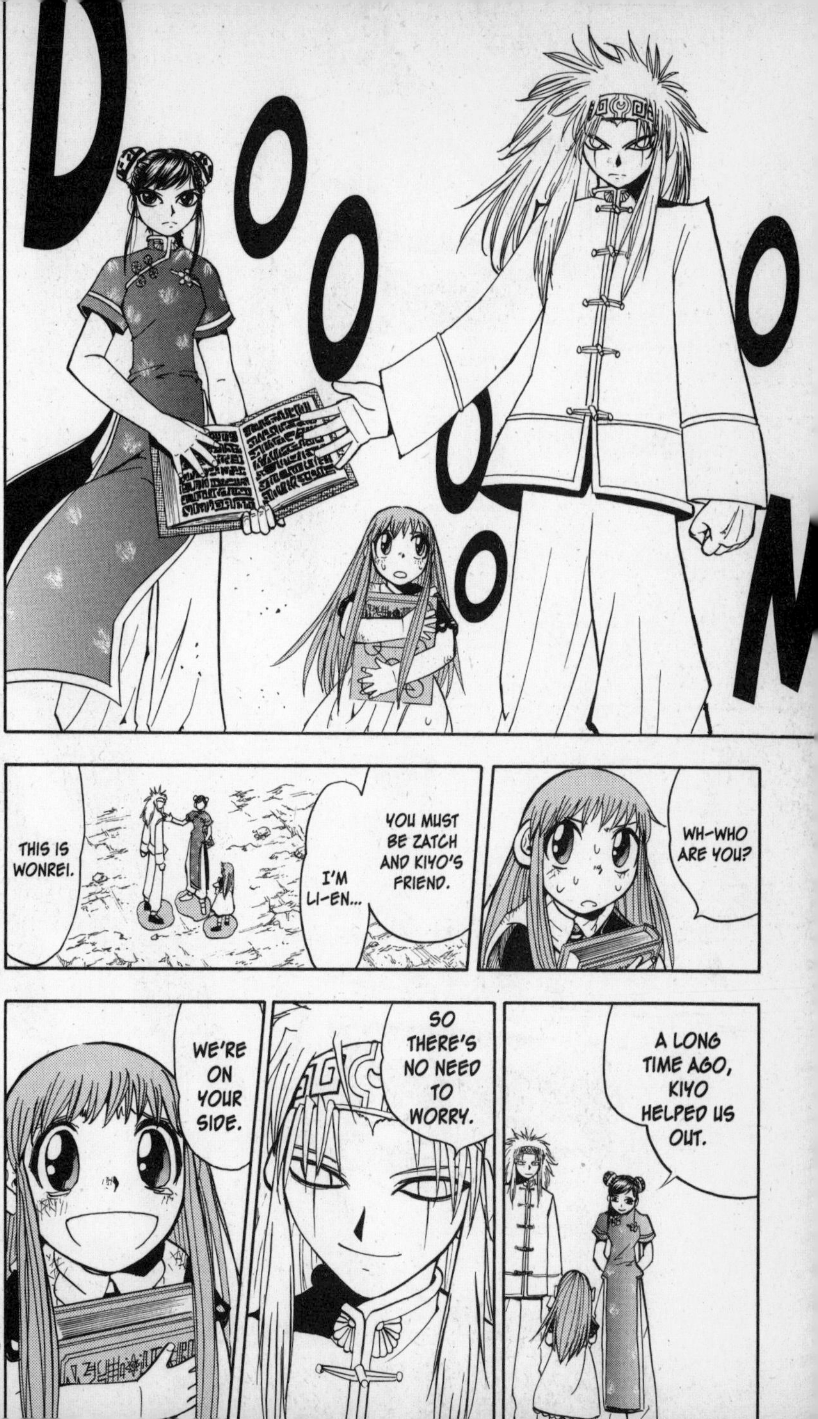
DOOOOON
WH-WHO ARE YOU?
YOU MUST BE ZATCH AND KIYO'S FRIEND.
I'M LI-EN...
THIS IS WONREI.
A LONG TIME AGO, KIYO HELPED US OUT.
SO THERE'S NO NEED TO WORRY.
WE'RE ON YOUR SIDE.

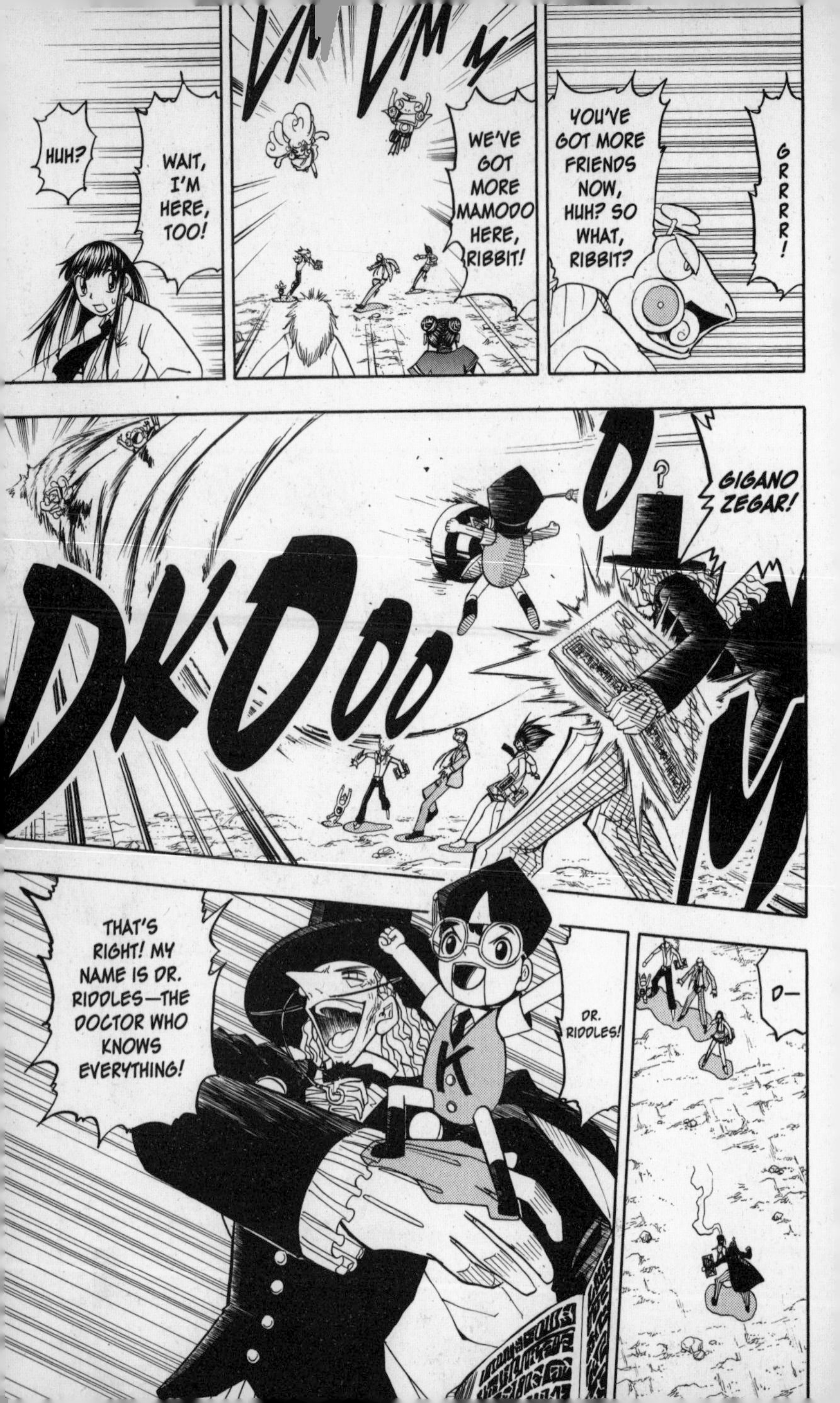
GRRRRR!
YOU'VE GOT MORE FRIENDS NOW, HUH? SO WHAT, RIBBIT?
WE'VE GOT MORE MAMODO HERE, RIBBIT!
WAIT, I'M HERE, TOO!
HUH?
GIGANO ZEGAR!
D—
DR. RIDDLES!
THAT'S RIGHT! MY NAME IS DR. RIDDLES—THE DOCTOR WHO KNOWS EVERYTHING!

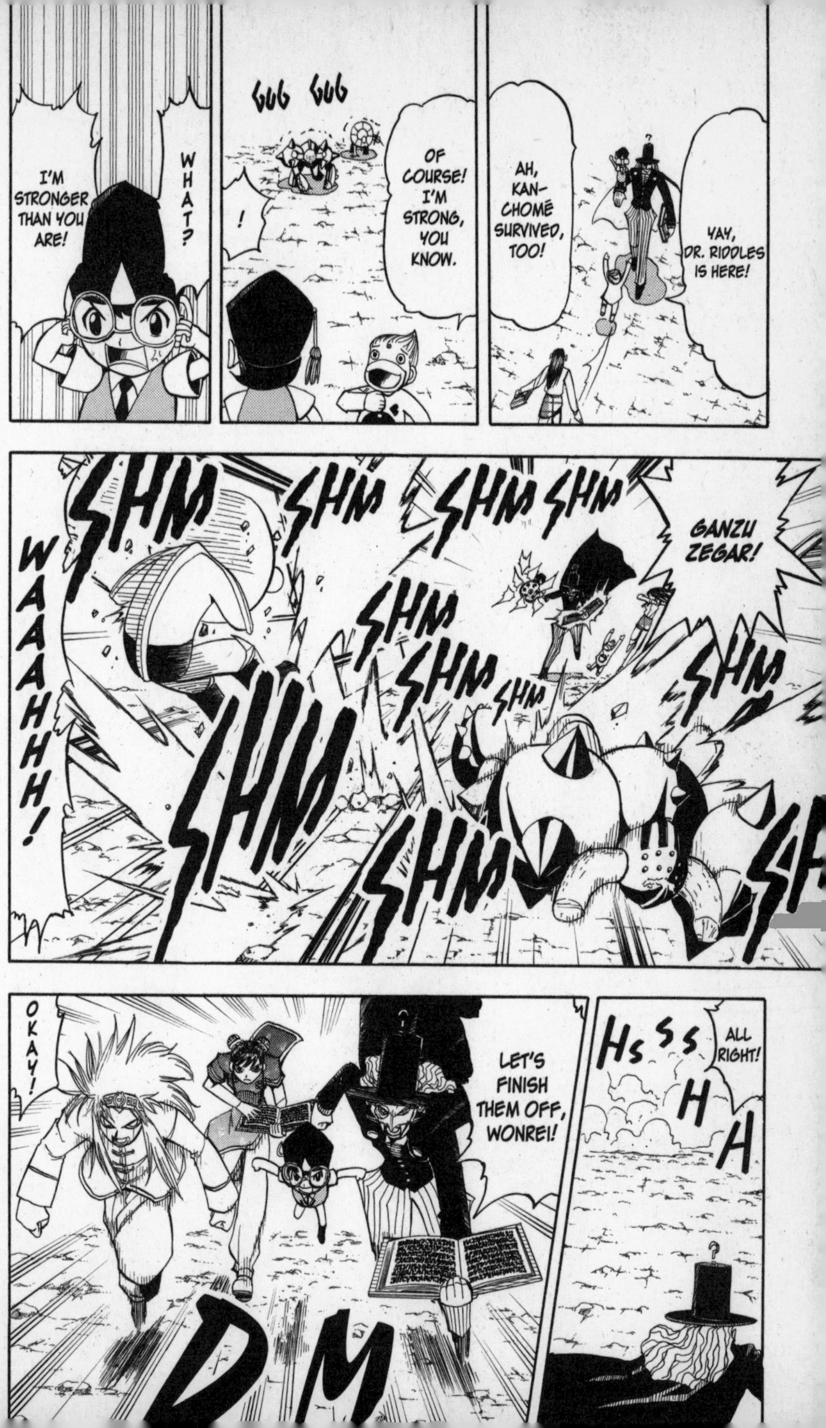
YAY, DR. RIDDLES IS HERE!
AH, KAN-CHOME SURVIVED, TOO!
GUG GUG
OF COURSE! I'M STRONG, YOU KNOW.
!
WHAT?
I'M STRONGER THAN YOU ARE!
GANZU ZEGAR!
SHM SHM SHM SHM
SHM SHM SHM SHM SHM SHM SHM
WAAAAHHHH!
ALL RIGHT!
HSSS HA
LET'S FINISH THEM OFF, WONREI!
OKAY!
DM

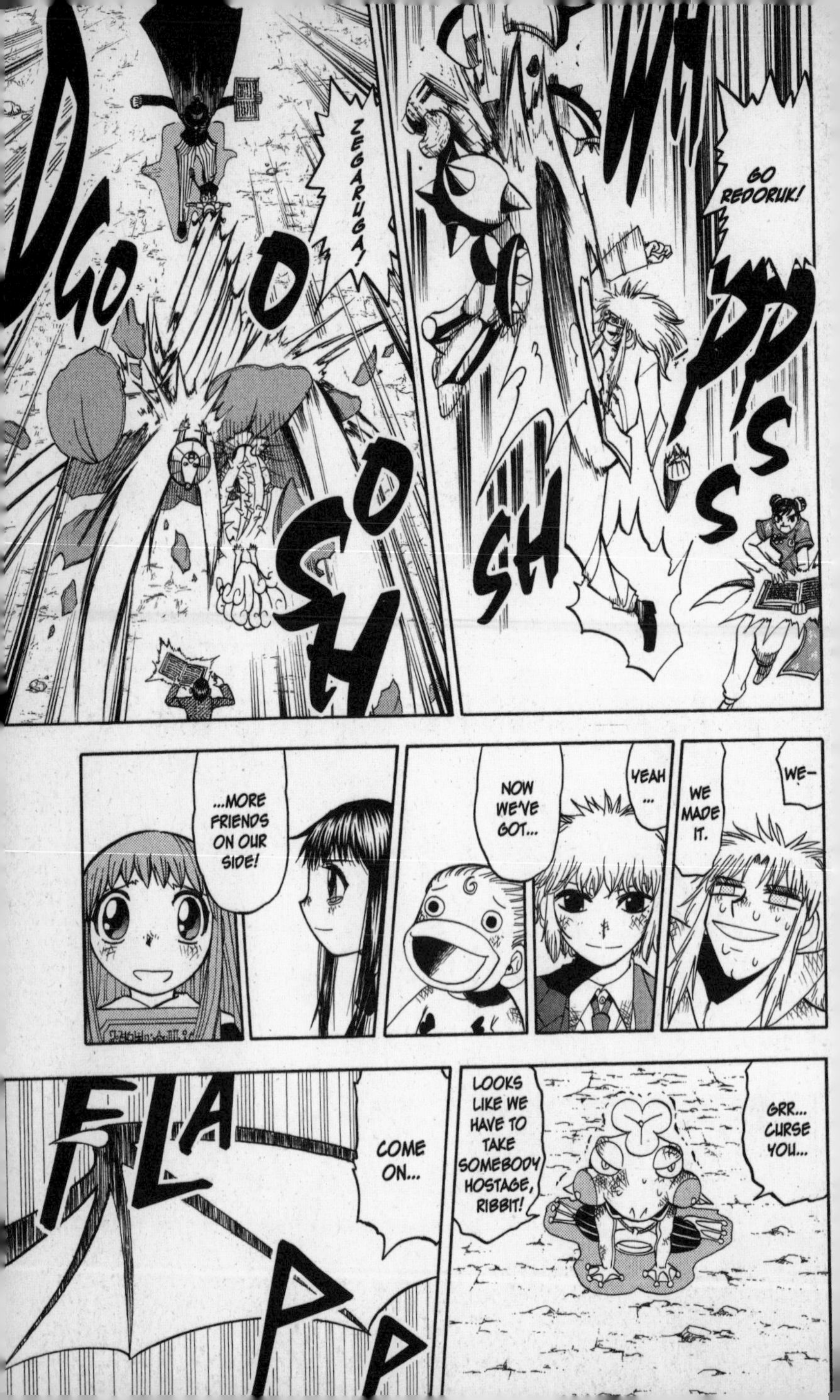
GO REDORUK!
ZEGARUGA!
WE-
WE MADE IT.
YEAH ...
NOW WE'VE GOT...
...MORE FRIENDS ON OUR SIDE!
GRR... CURSE YOU...
LOOKS LIKE WE HAVE TO TAKE SOMEBODY HOSTAGE, RIBBIT!
COME ON...
FLAPP

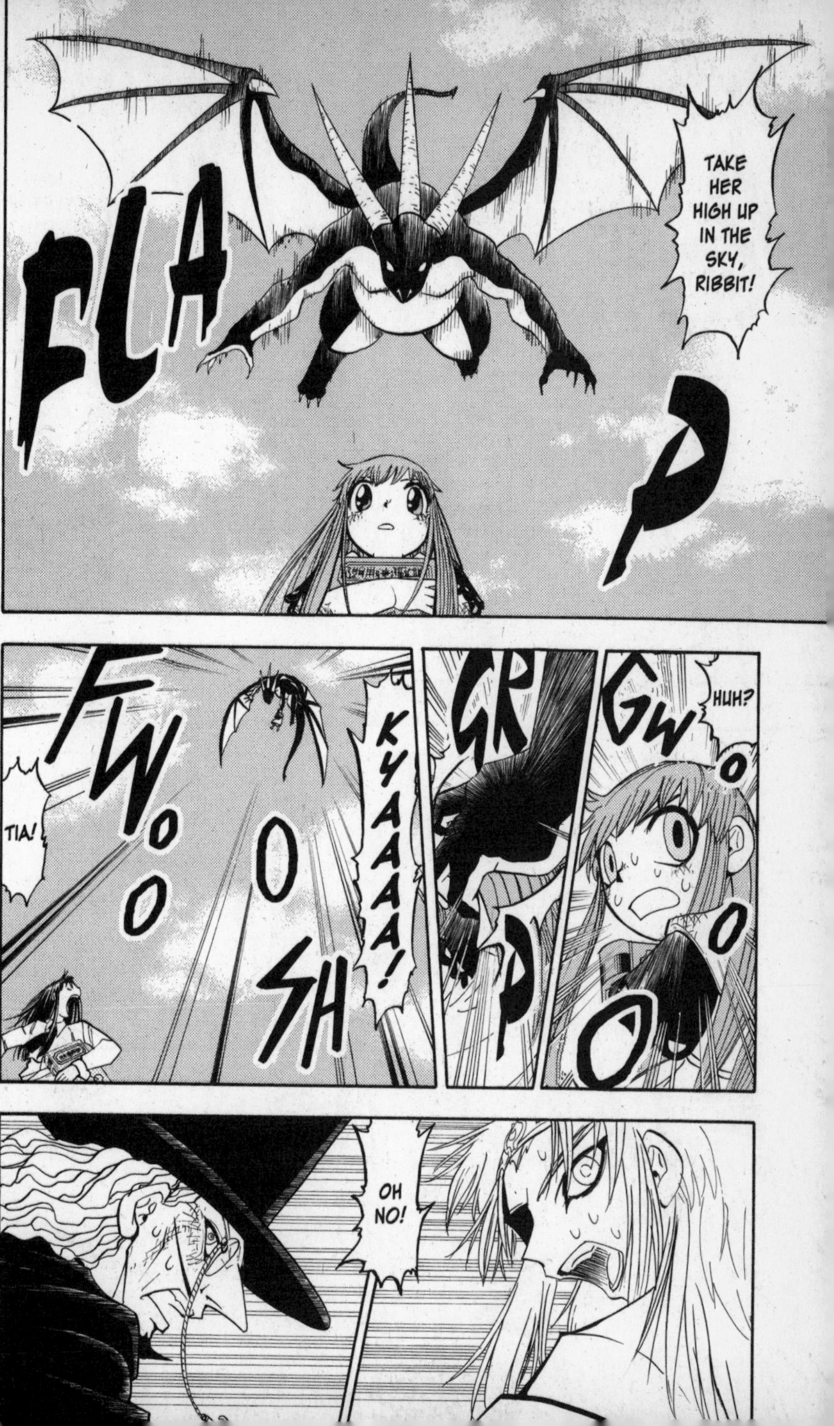
TAKE HER HIGH UP IN THE SKY, RIBBIT!
FLA
P
HUH?
GWOOOO
GR
P
KYAAAAA!
FWOOOSH
TIA!
OH NO!

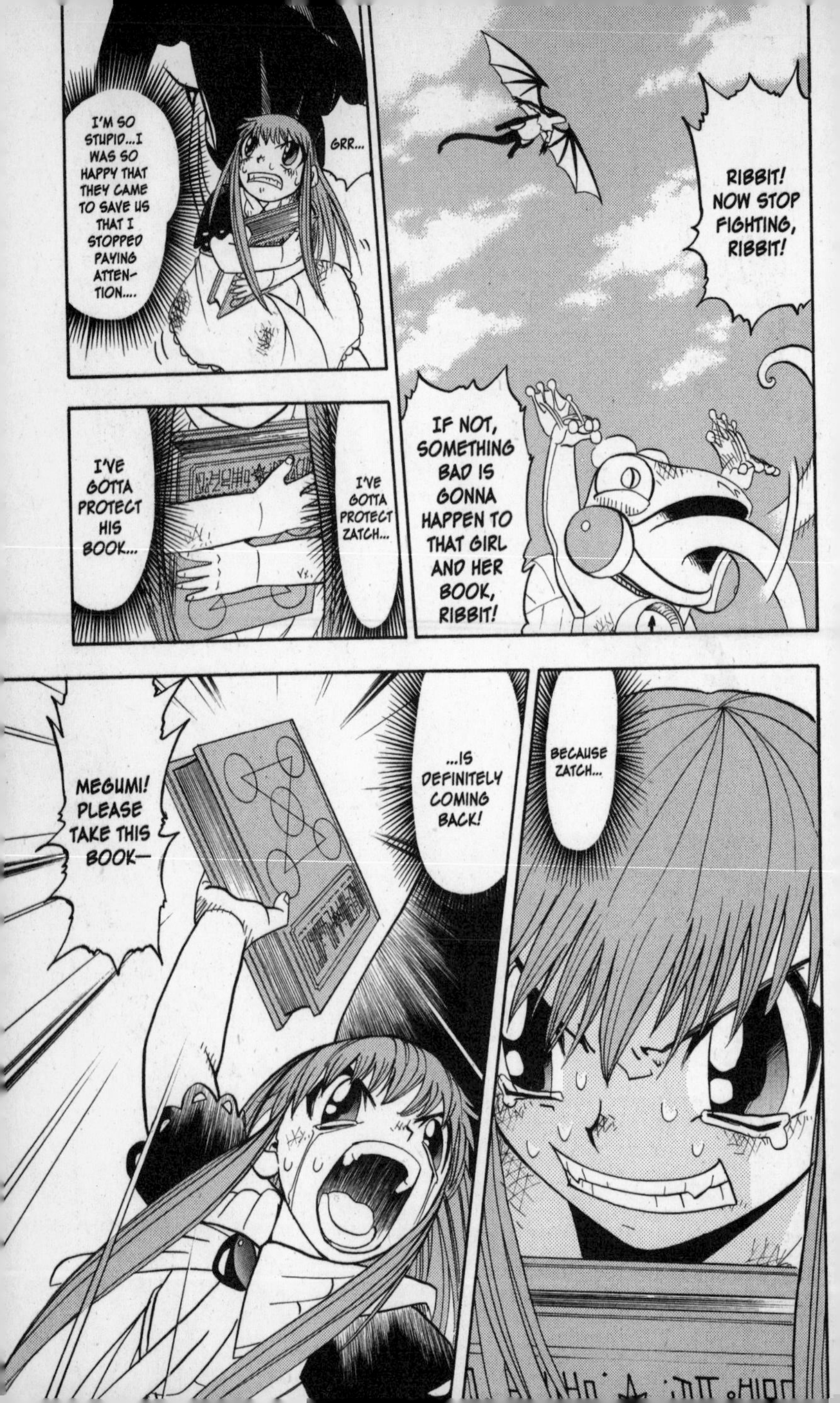
RIBBIT! NOW STOP FIGHTING, RIBBIT!
IF NOT, SOMETHING BAD IS GONNA HAPPEN TO THAT GIRL AND HER BOOK, RIBBIT!
GRR...
I'M SO STUPID...I WAS SO HAPPY THAT THEY CAME TO SAVE US THAT I STOPPED PAYING ATTEN-TION....
I'VE GOTTA PROTECT ZATCH...
I'VE GOTTA PROTECT HIS BOOK...
BECAUSE ZATCH...
...IS DEFINITELY COMING BACK!
MEGUMI! PLEASE TAKE THIS BOOK—

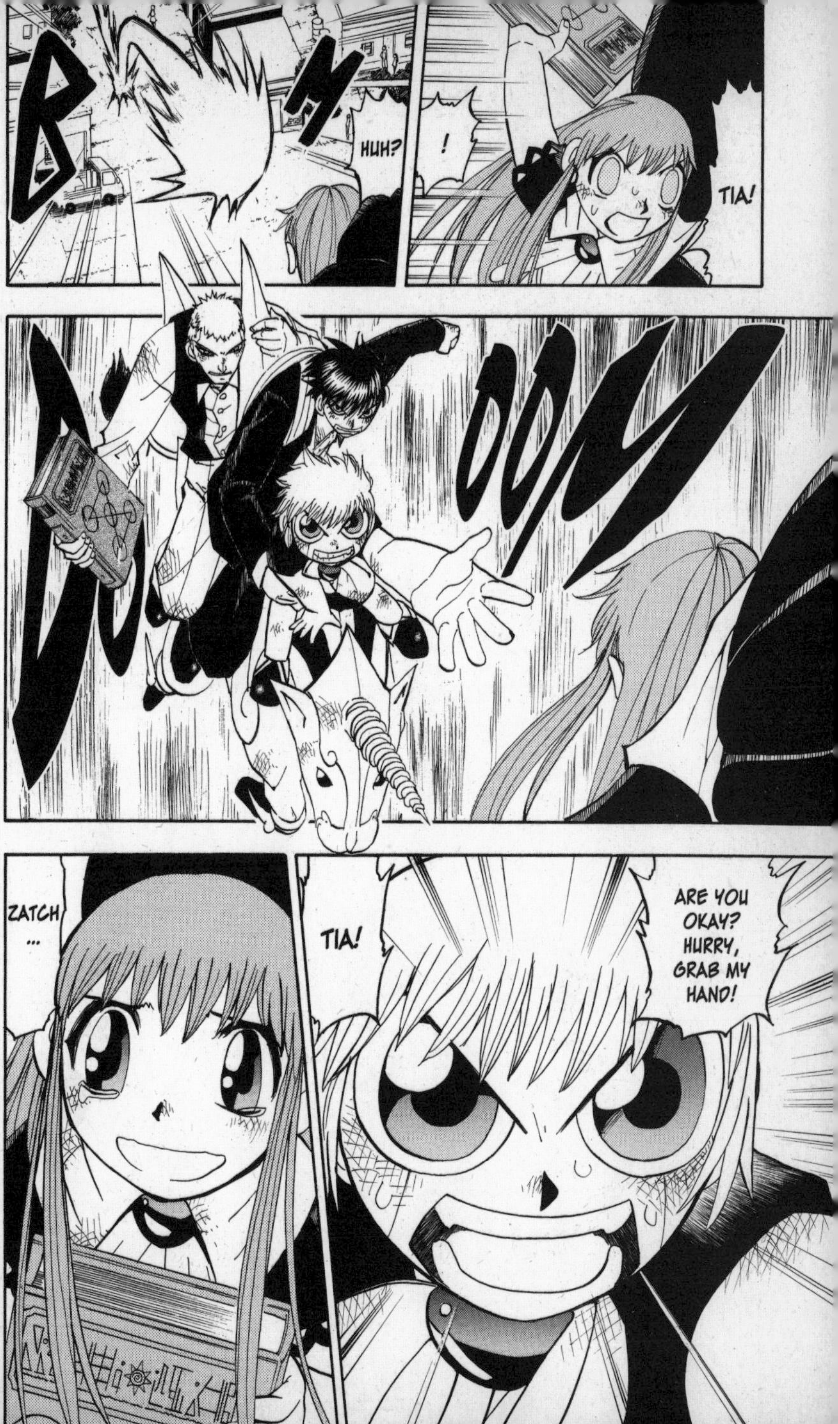
!
TIA!
HUH?
DOOM
ARE YOU OKAY? HURRY, GRAB MY HAND!
TIA!
ZATCH ...

LEVEL 126: Fighting Together

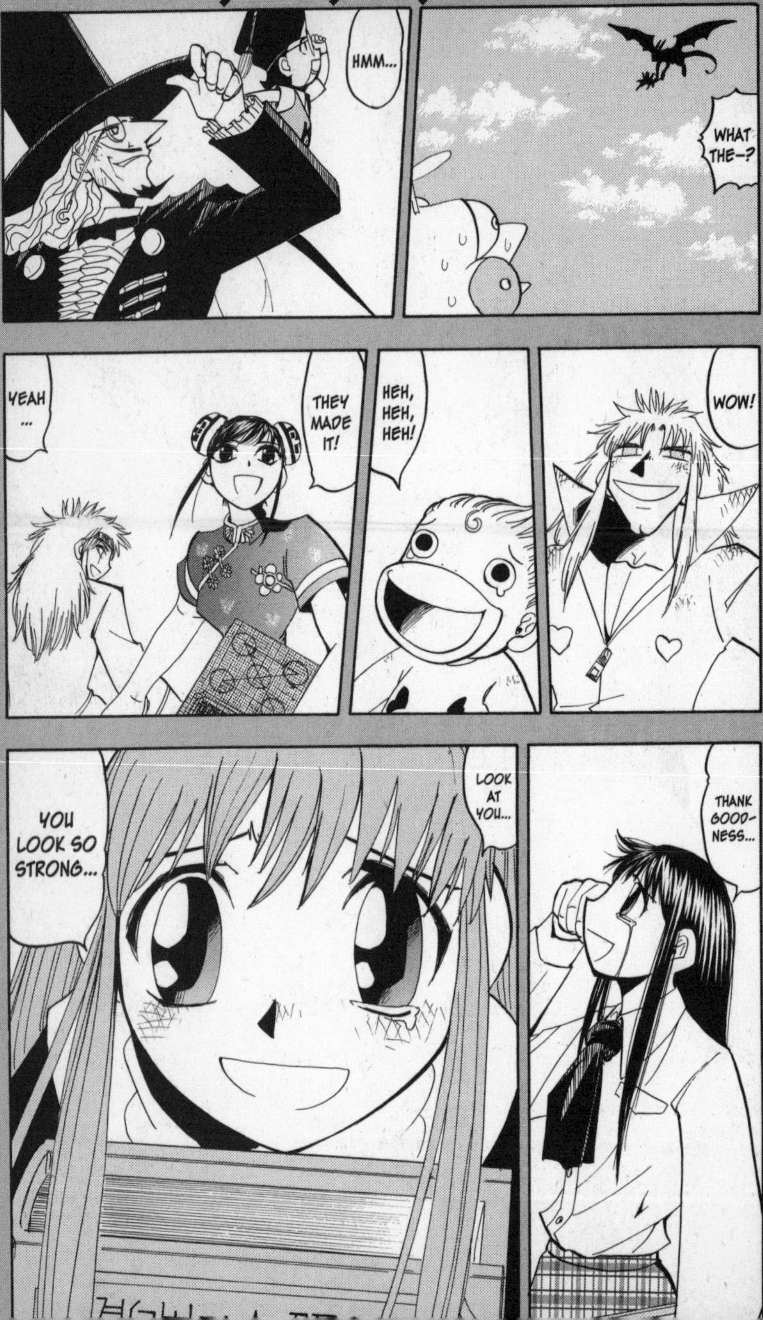
WHAT THE—?
HMM...
WOW!
HEH, HEH, HEH!
THEY MADE IT!
YEAH ...
THANK GOOD-NESS...
LOOK AT YOU...
YOU LOOK SO STRONG...

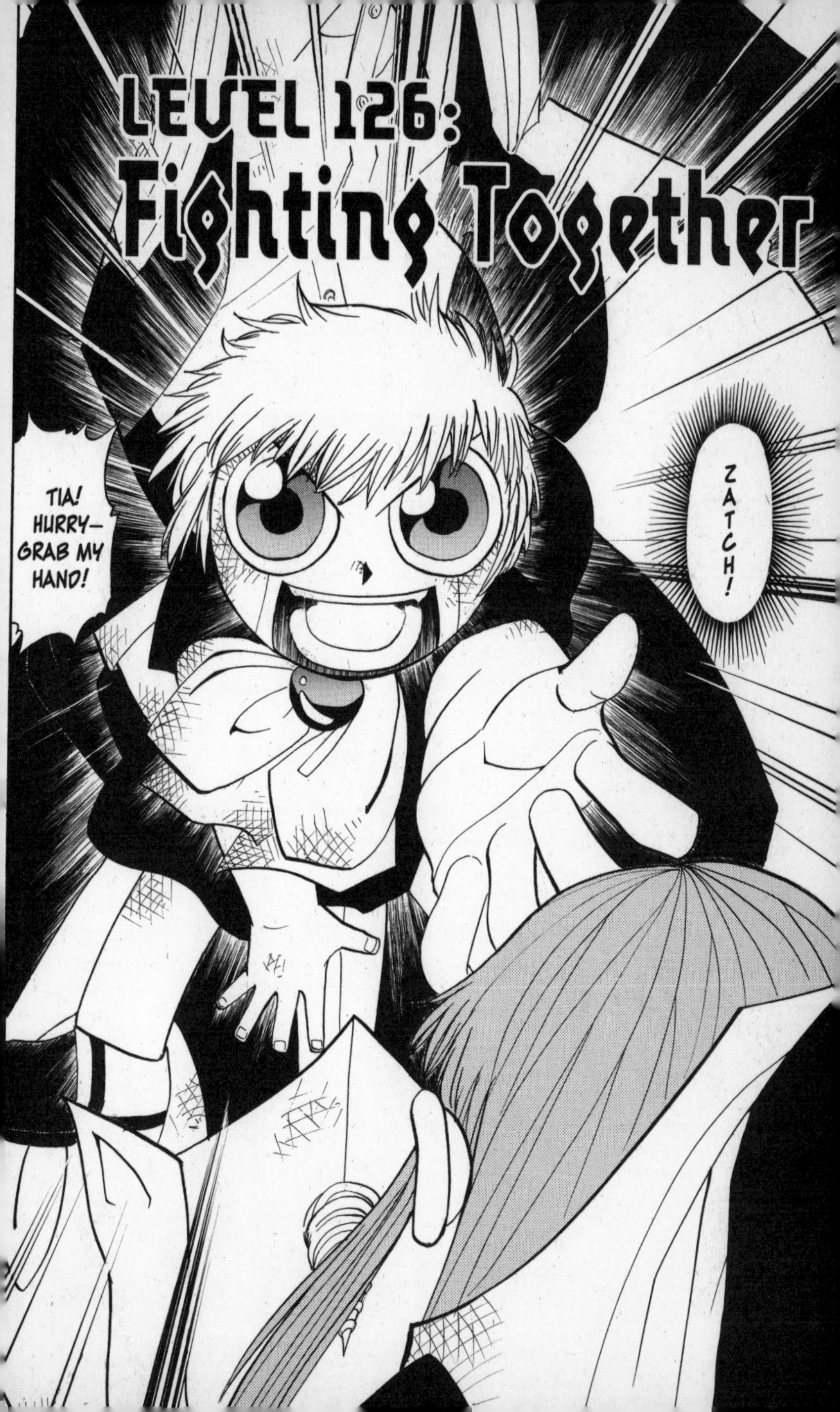
LEVEL 126:
Fighting Together
ZATCH!
TIA! HURRY— GRAB MY HAND!

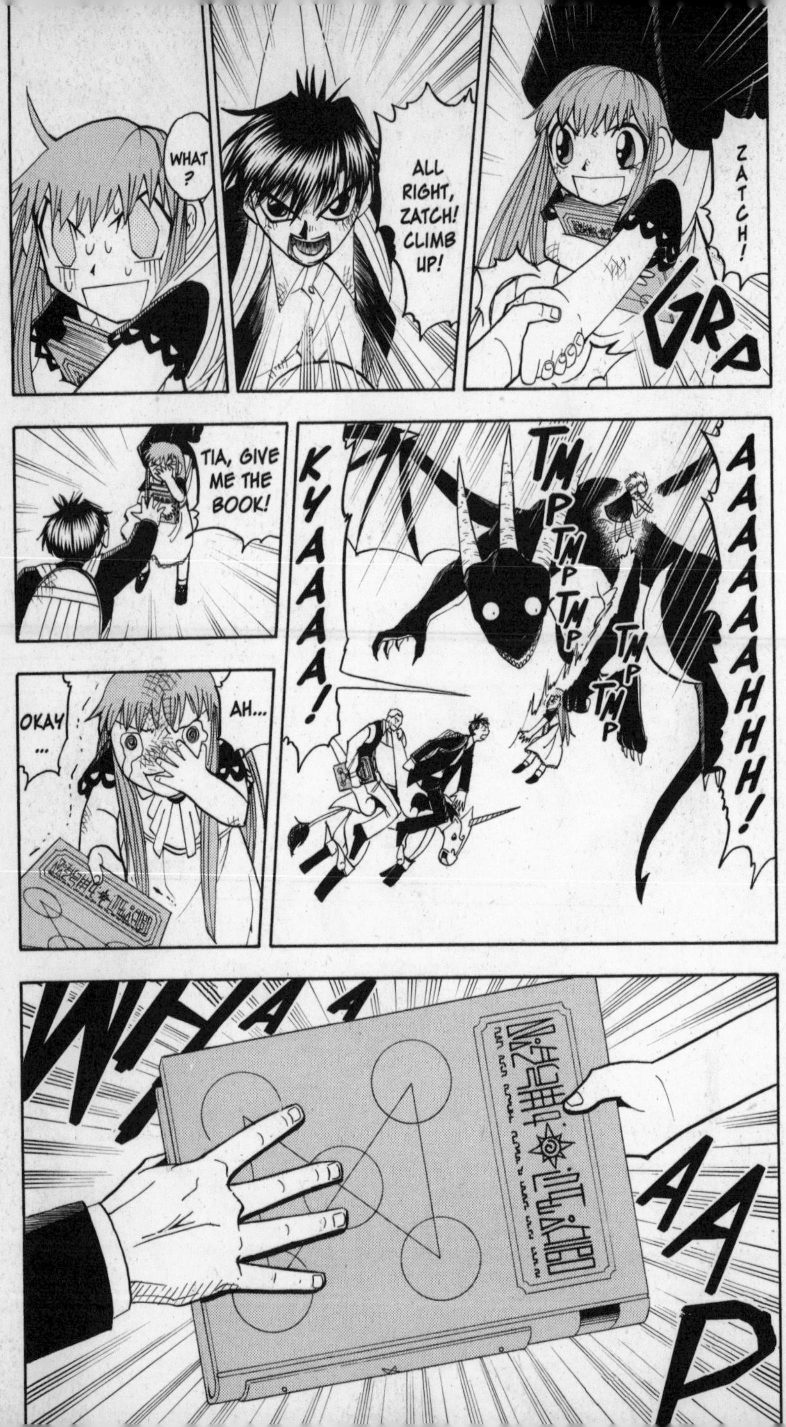

ZATCH!
GRP
ALL RIGHT, ZATCH! CLIMB UP!
WHAT?
AAAAAAAAAHHH!
TMP TMP TMP TMP
TMP TMP TMP
KYAAAAA!
TIA, GIVE ME THE BOOK!
AH...
OKAY...
WHAAAAAP

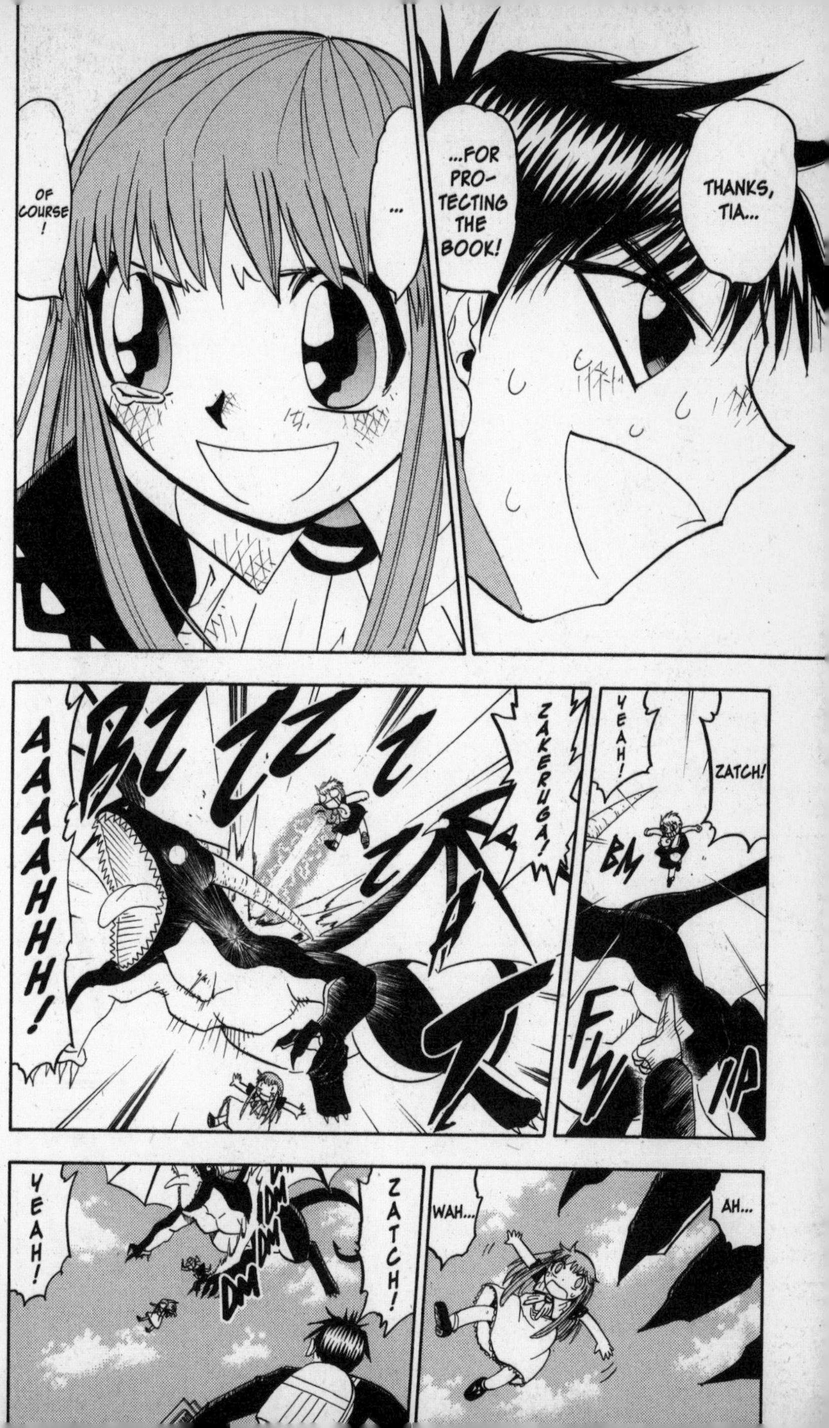
THANKS, TIA...
...FOR PRO-TECTING THE BOOK!
...
OF COURSE!
ZATCH!
YEAH!
BM
FWIP
ZAKERUGA!
AAAAAHHHHH!
AH...
WAH...
ZATCH!
DM DM DM
YEAH!

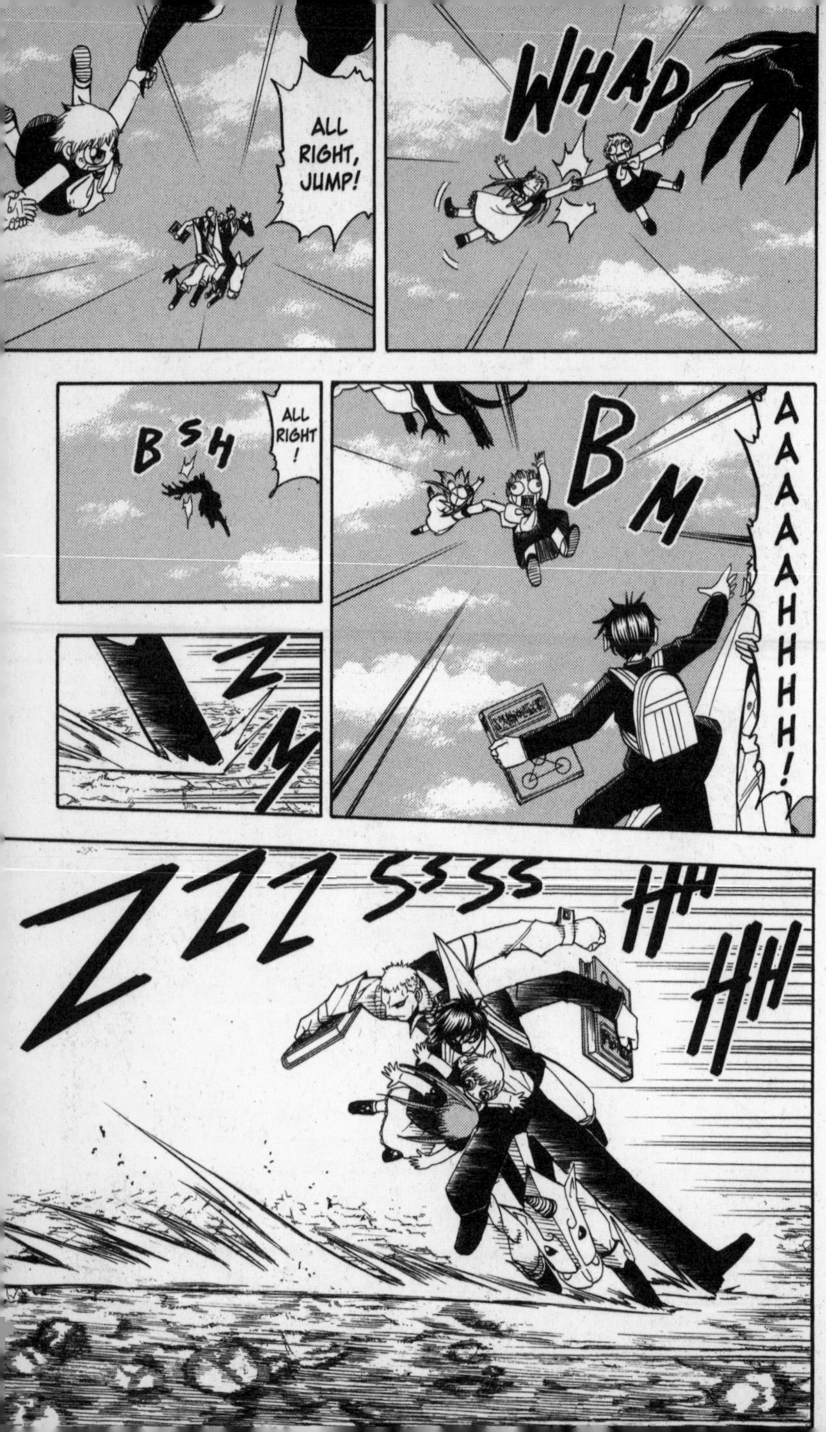
WHAP
ALL RIGHT, JUMP!
BM
AAAAAHHHHH!
ALL RIGHT!
BSH
ZM
ZZZZ
SSSSS
HHHH

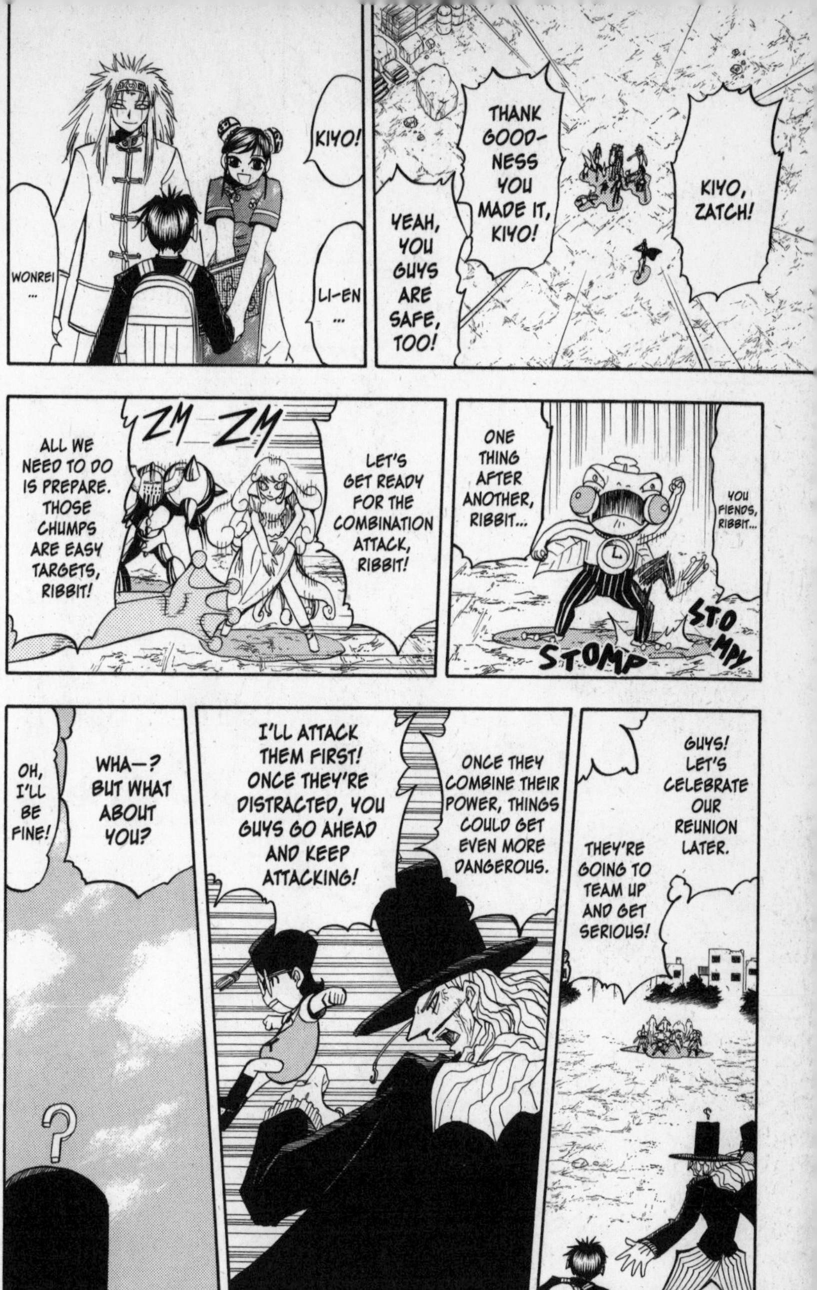
KIYO, ZATCH!
THANK GOODNESS YOU MADE IT, KIYO!
YEAH, YOU GUYS ARE SAFE, TOO!
KIYO!
LI-EN ...
WONREI ...
YOU FIENDS, RIBBIT...
ONE THING AFTER ANOTHER, RIBBIT...
STOMPY
STOMP
LET'S GET READY FOR THE COMBINATION ATTACK, RIBBIT!
ZM ZM
ALL WE NEED TO DO IS PREPARE. THOSE CHUMPS ARE EASY TARGETS, RIBBIT!
GUYS! LET'S CELEBRATE OUR REUNION LATER.
THEY'RE GOING TO TEAM UP AND GET SERIOUS!
ONCE THEY COMBINE THEIR POWER, THINGS COULD GET EVEN MORE DANGEROUS.
I'LL ATTACK THEM FIRST! ONCE THEY'RE DISTRACTED, YOU GUYS GO AHEAD AND KEEP ATTACKING!
WHA—? BUT WHAT ABOUT YOU?
OH, I'LL BE FINE!
?

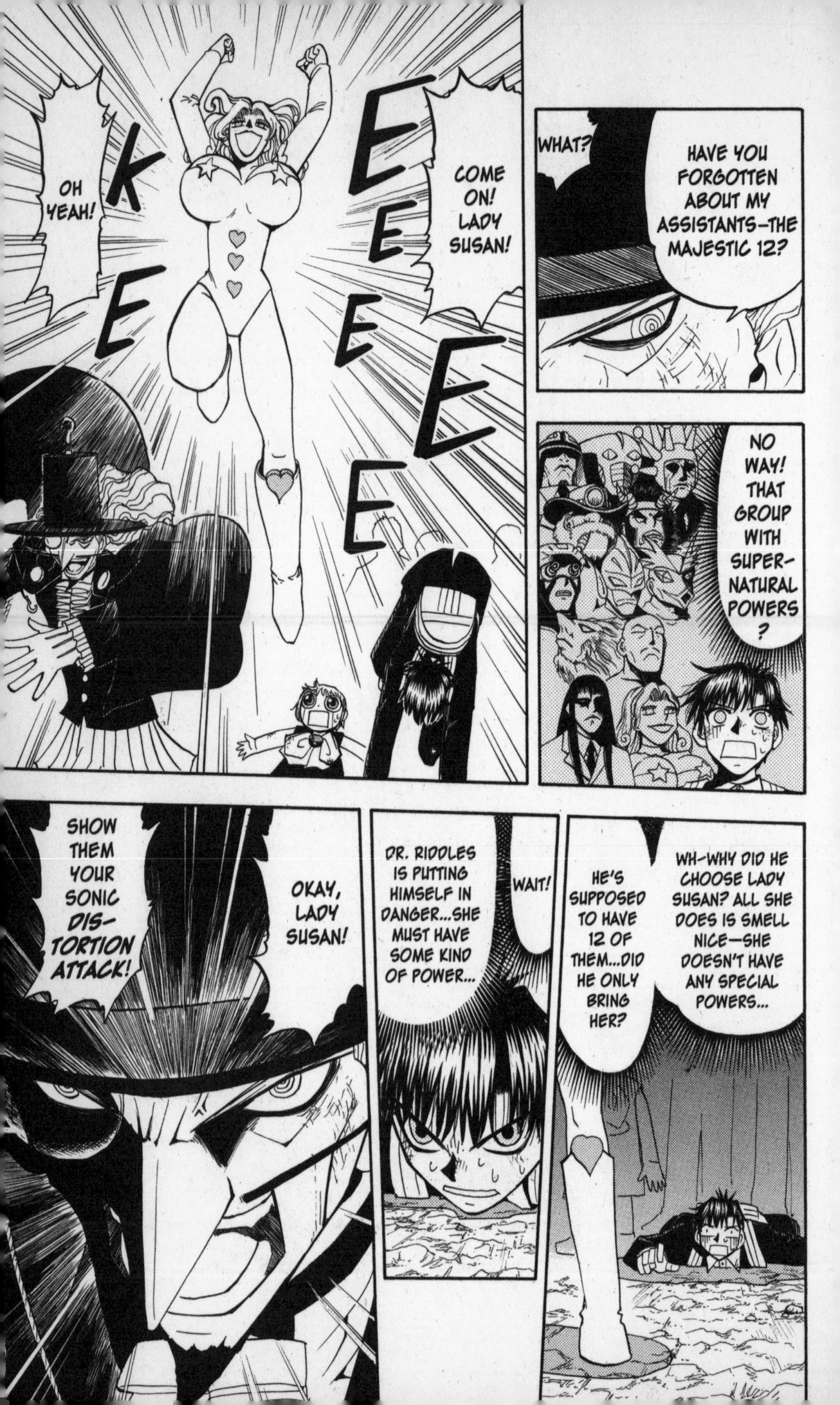
HAVE YOU FORGOTTEN ABOUT MY ASSISTANTS—THE MAJESTIC 12?
WHAT?
NO WAY! THAT GROUP WITH SUPER-NATURAL POWERS?
COME ON! LADY SUSAN!
KEEEEEE
OH YEAH!
WH-WHY DID HE CHOOSE LADY SUSAN? ALL SHE DOES IS SMELL NICE—SHE DOESN'T HAVE ANY SPECIAL POWERS...
HE'S SUPPOSED TO HAVE 12 OF THEM...DID HE ONLY BRING HER?
WAIT!
DR. RIDDLES IS PUTTING HIMSELF IN DANGER...SHE MUST HAVE SOME KIND OF POWER...
OKAY, LADY SUSAN!
SHOW THEM YOUR SONIC DIS-TORTION ATTACK!

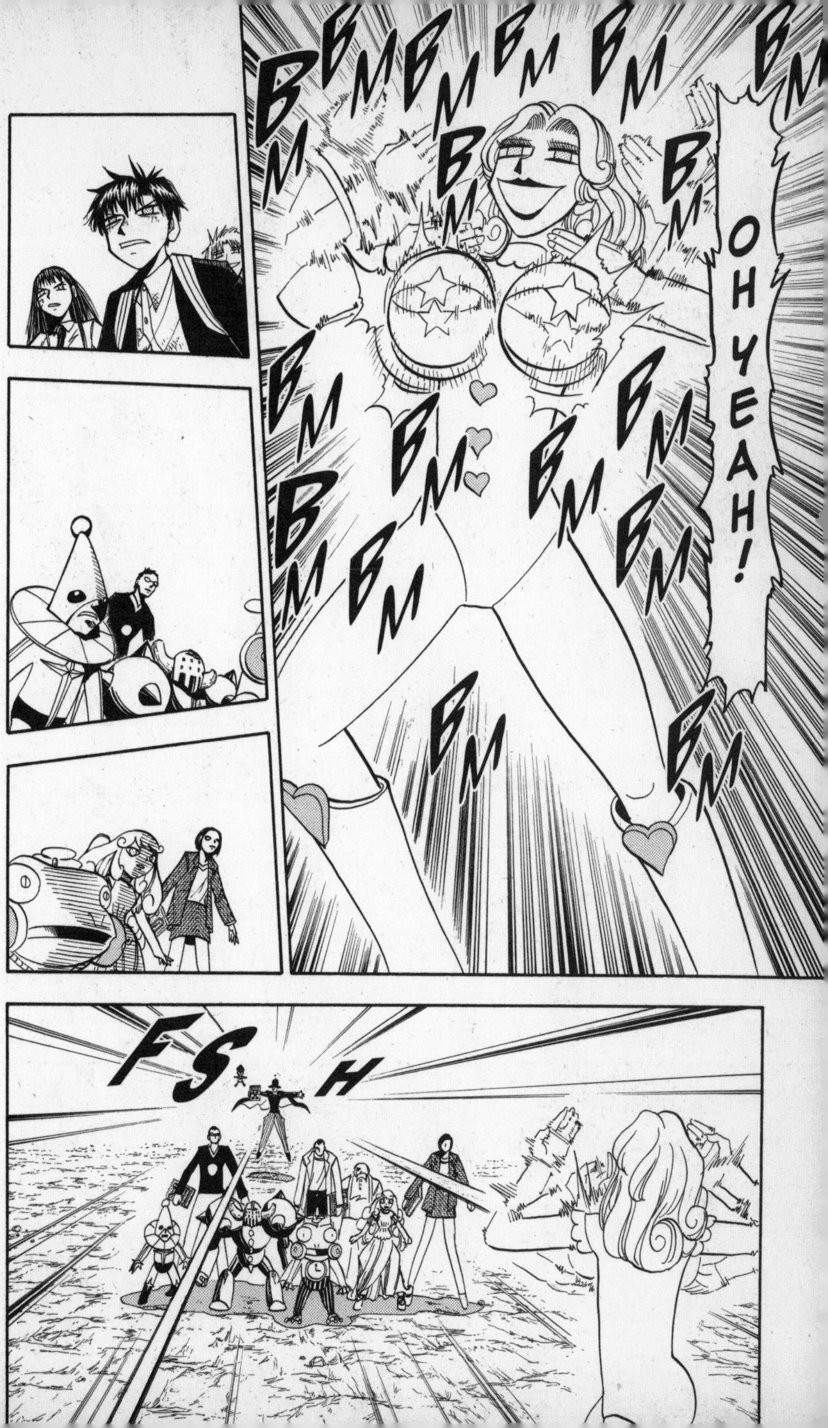
BM BM BM BM BM BM
OH YEAH!
FSH

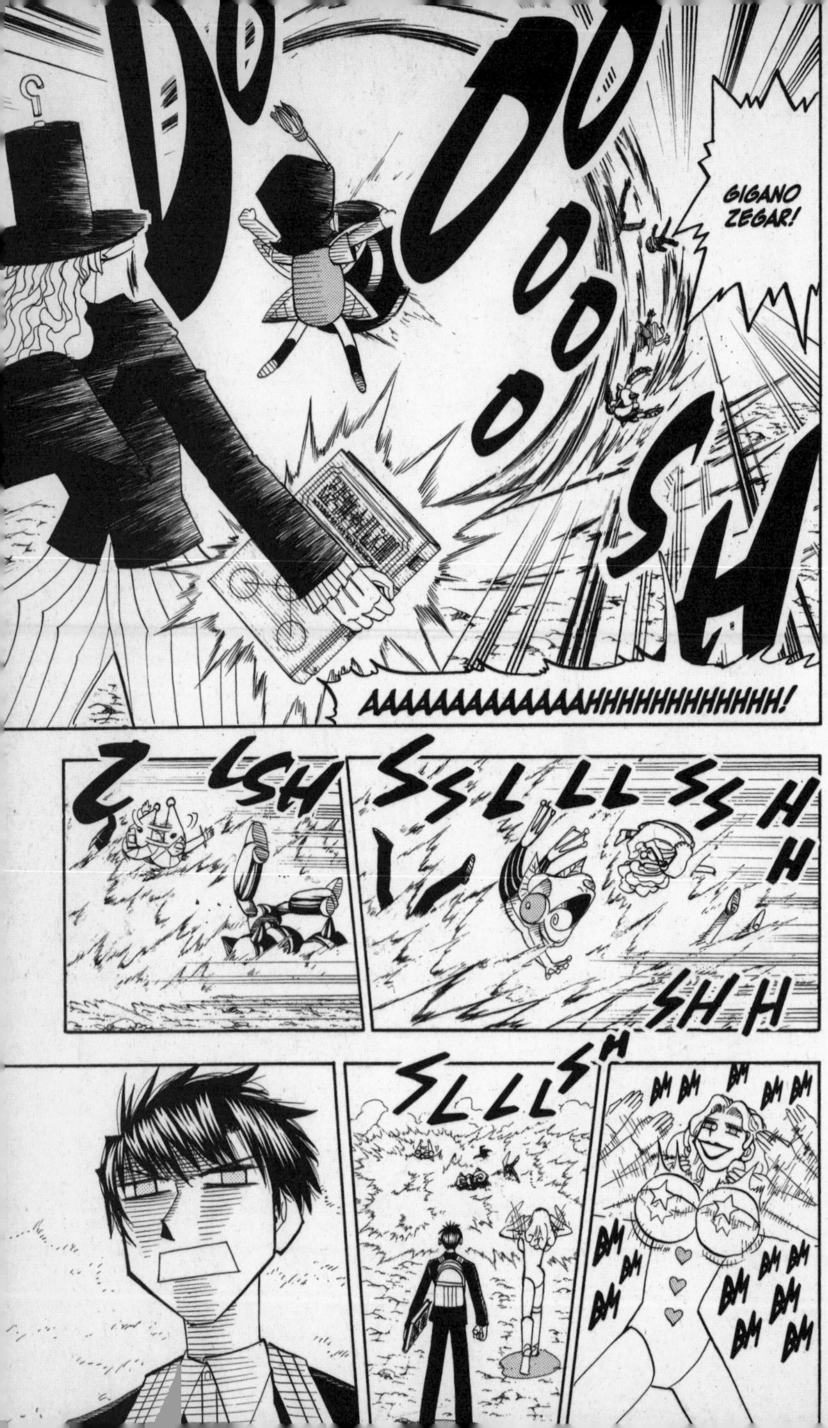

GIGANO ZEGAR!
DODOOOOOSH
AAAAAAAAAAAAAHHHHHHHHHHHH!
SSLLLLSSHHH
SHH
ZISH
BM BM BM BM BM
BM BM BM BM BM BM BM BM BM BM
SLLLSH

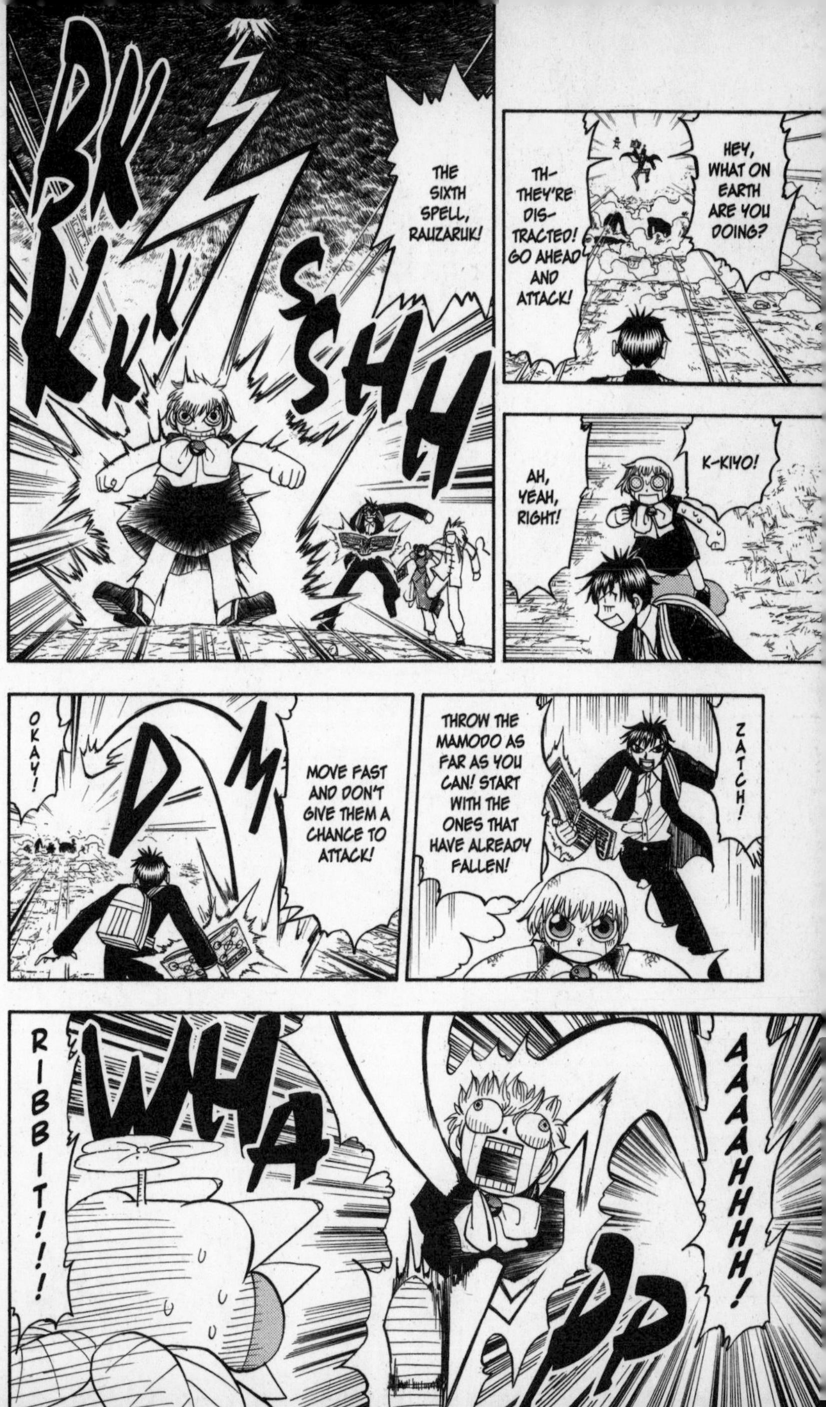
HEY, WHAT ON EARTH ARE YOU DOING?
TH-THEY'RE DIS-TRACTED! GO AHEAD AND ATTACK!
K-KIYO!
AH, YEAH, RIGHT!
THE SIXTH SPELL, RAUZARUK!
SHH
ZATCH!
THROW THE MAMODO AS FAR AS YOU CAN! START WITH THE ONES THAT HAVE ALREADY FALLEN!
OKAY!
MOVE FAST AND DON'T GIVE THEM A CHANCE TO ATTACK!
DM
AAAAHHHH!
WHA
RIBBIT!!!!

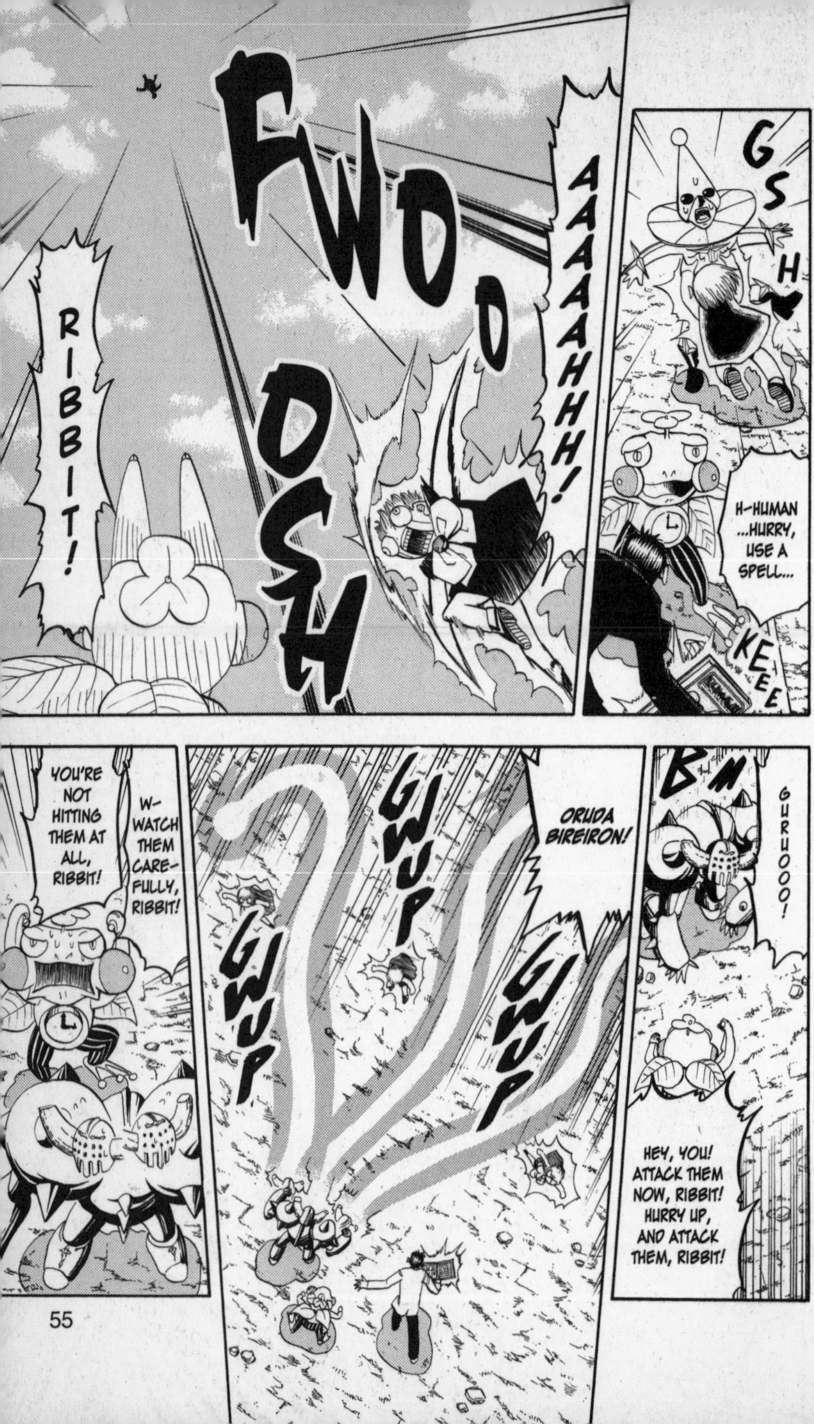
GSH
H-HUMAN ...HURRY, USE A SPELL...
KEEE
FWOOOSH
AAAAAAHHHH!
RIBBIT!
BM
GURUOOO!
HEY, YOU! ATTACK THEM NOW, RIBBIT! HURRY UP, AND ATTACK THEM, RIBBIT!
ORUDA BIREIRON!
GWUP
GWUP
GWUP
GWUP
W-WATCH THEM CARE-FULLY, RIBBIT!
YOU'RE NOT HITTING THEM AT ALL, RIBBIT!

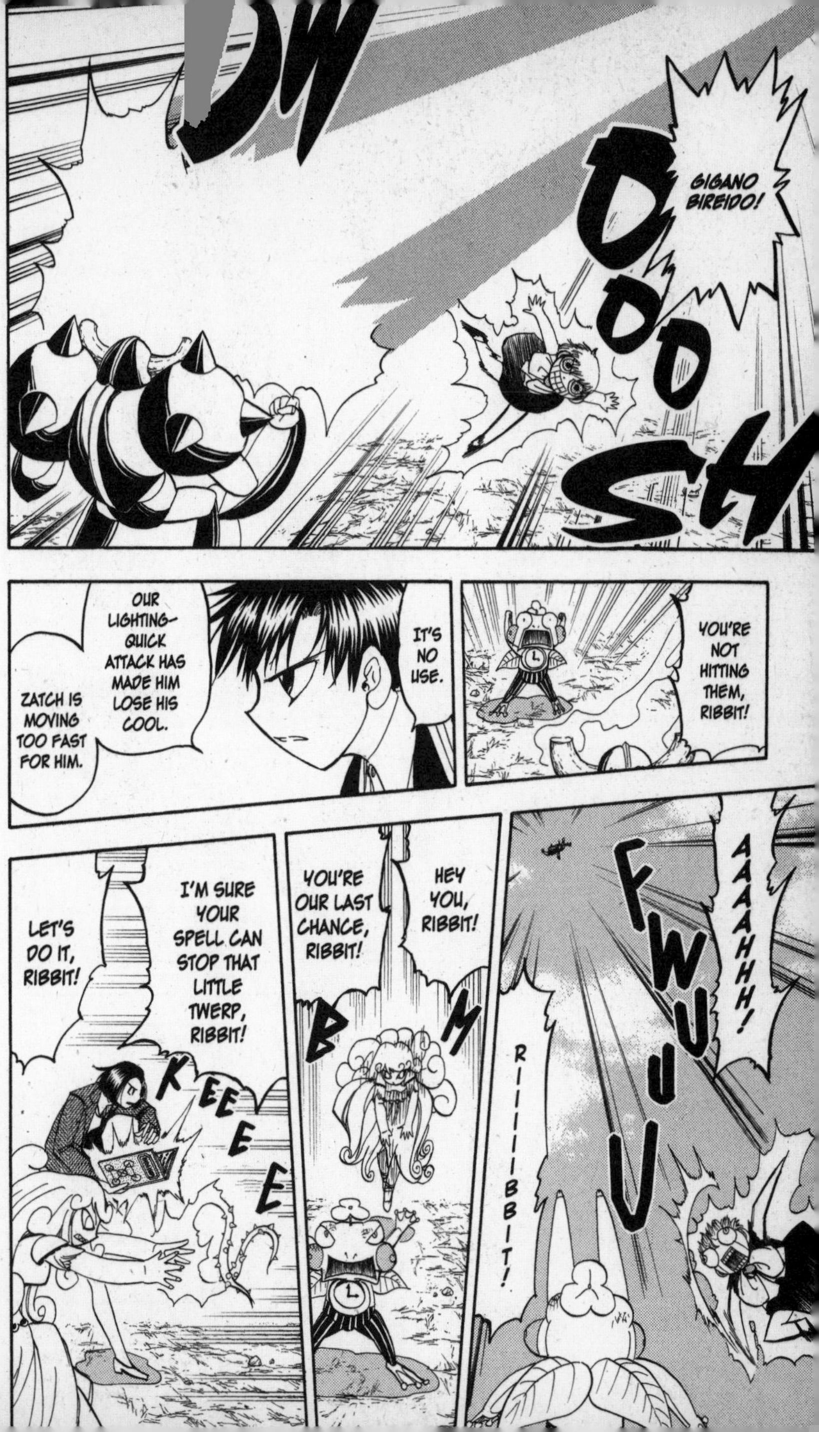
GIGANO BIREIDO!
DOOOSH
DW
YOU'RE NOT HITTING THEM, RIBBIT!
IT'S NO USE.
OUR LIGHTING-QUICK ATTACK HAS MADE HIM LOSE HIS COOL.
ZATCH IS MOVING TOO FAST FOR HIM.
AAAAHHH!
FWUUUU
RIIIIBBIT!
HEY YOU, RIBBIT!
YOU'RE OUR LAST CHANCE, RIBBIT!
BM
I'M SURE YOUR SPELL CAN STOP THAT LITTLE TWERP, RIBBIT!
LET'S DO IT, RIBBIT!
KEEEE

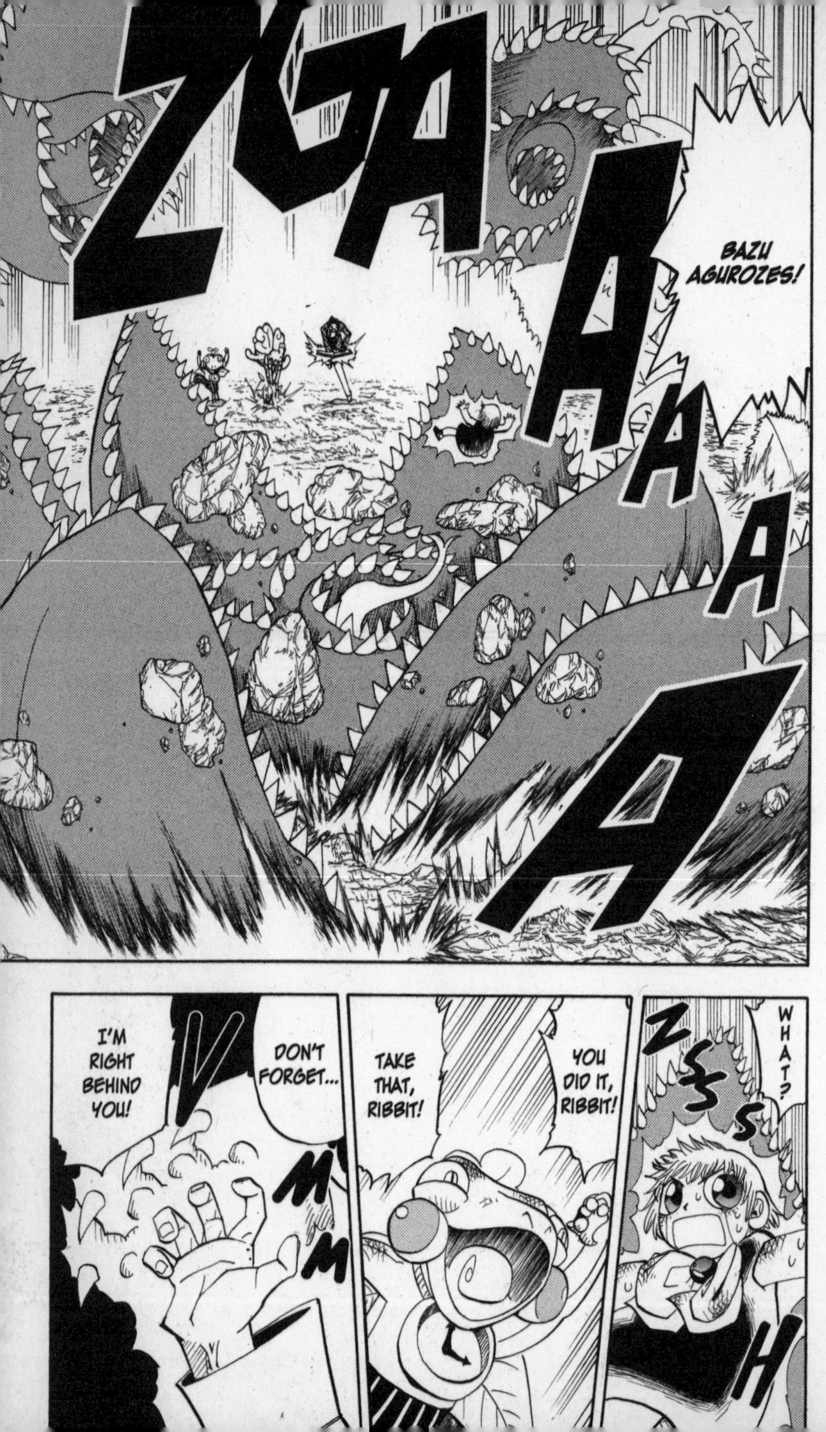
BAZU AGUROZES!
WHAT?
ZSSS
YOU DID IT, RIBBIT!
TAKE THAT, RIBBIT!
DON'T FORGET...
I'M RIGHT BEHIND YOU!

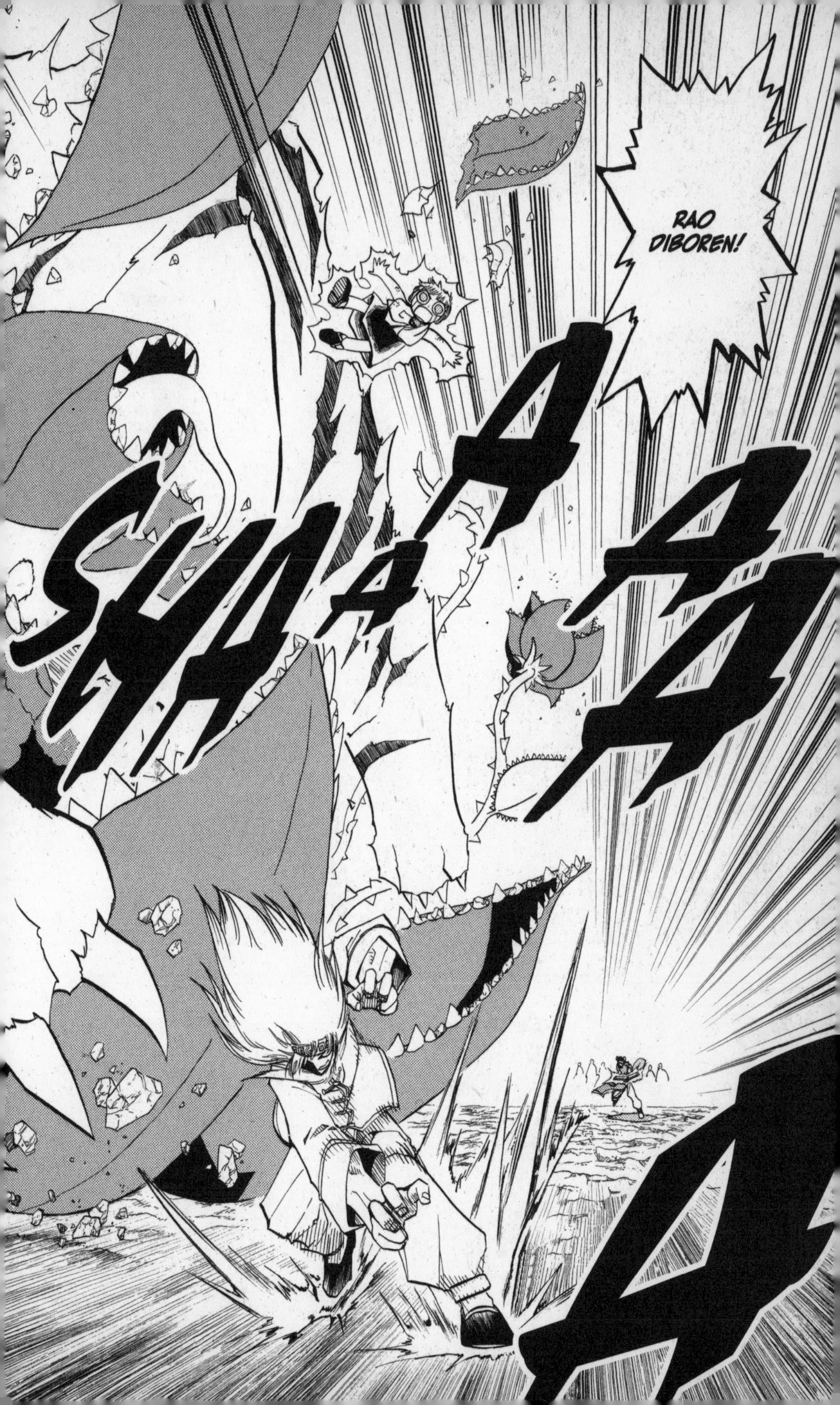
RAO DIBOREN!
SHAAAAAA

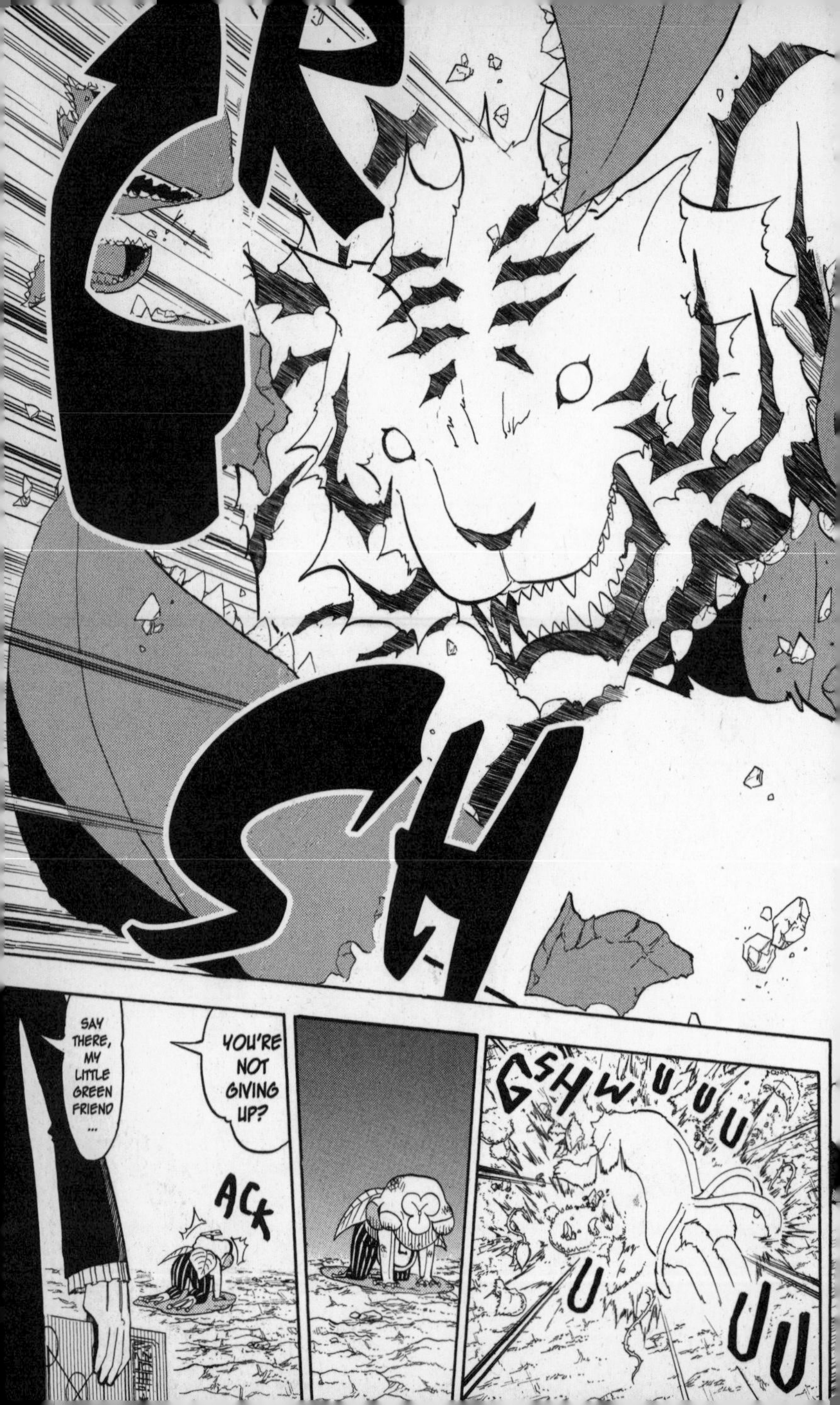
SH
GSHWUUUUUUU
SAY THERE, MY LITTLE GREEN FRIEND...
YOU'RE NOT GIVING UP?
ACK

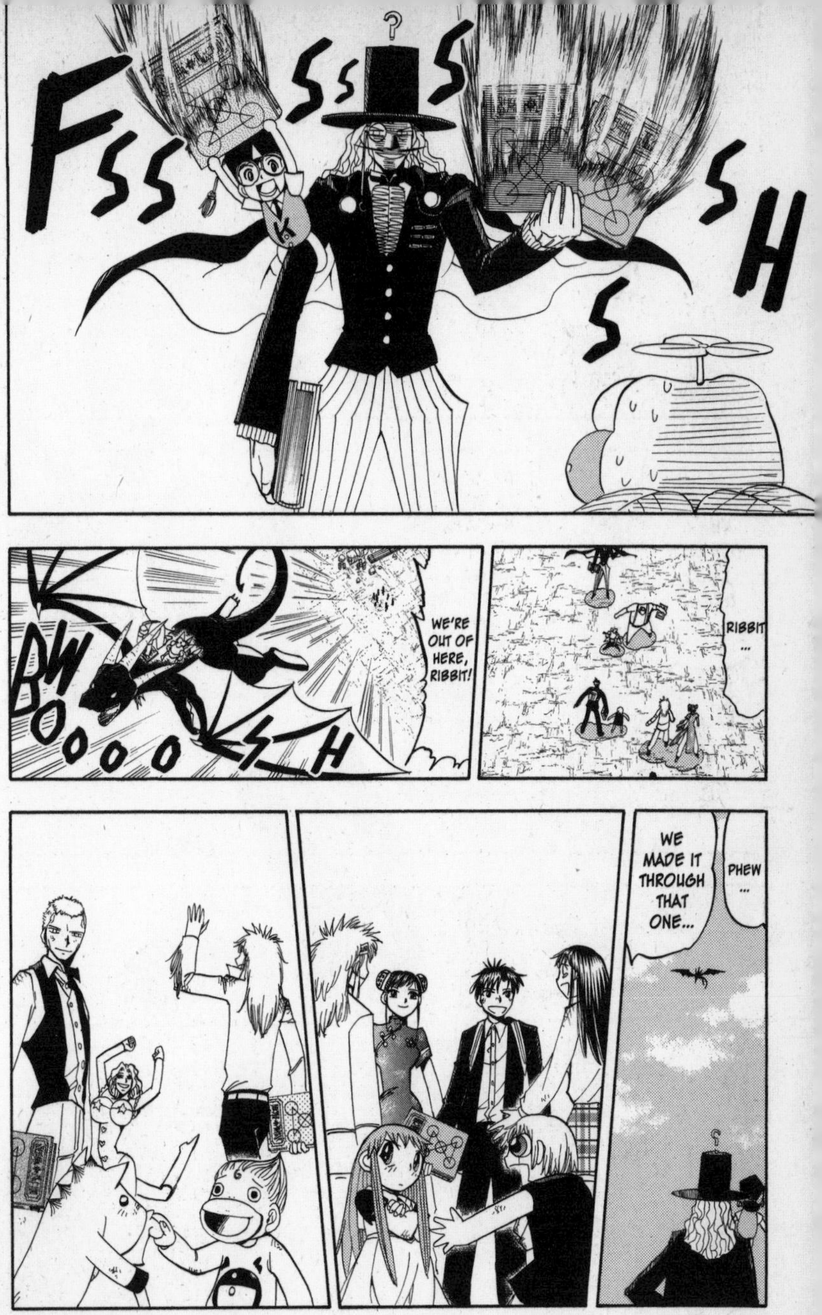
FSSSSSSSH
RIBBIT...
WE'RE OUT OF HERE, RIBBIT!
BWOOOOSH
PHEW...
WE MADE IT THROUGH THAT ONE...

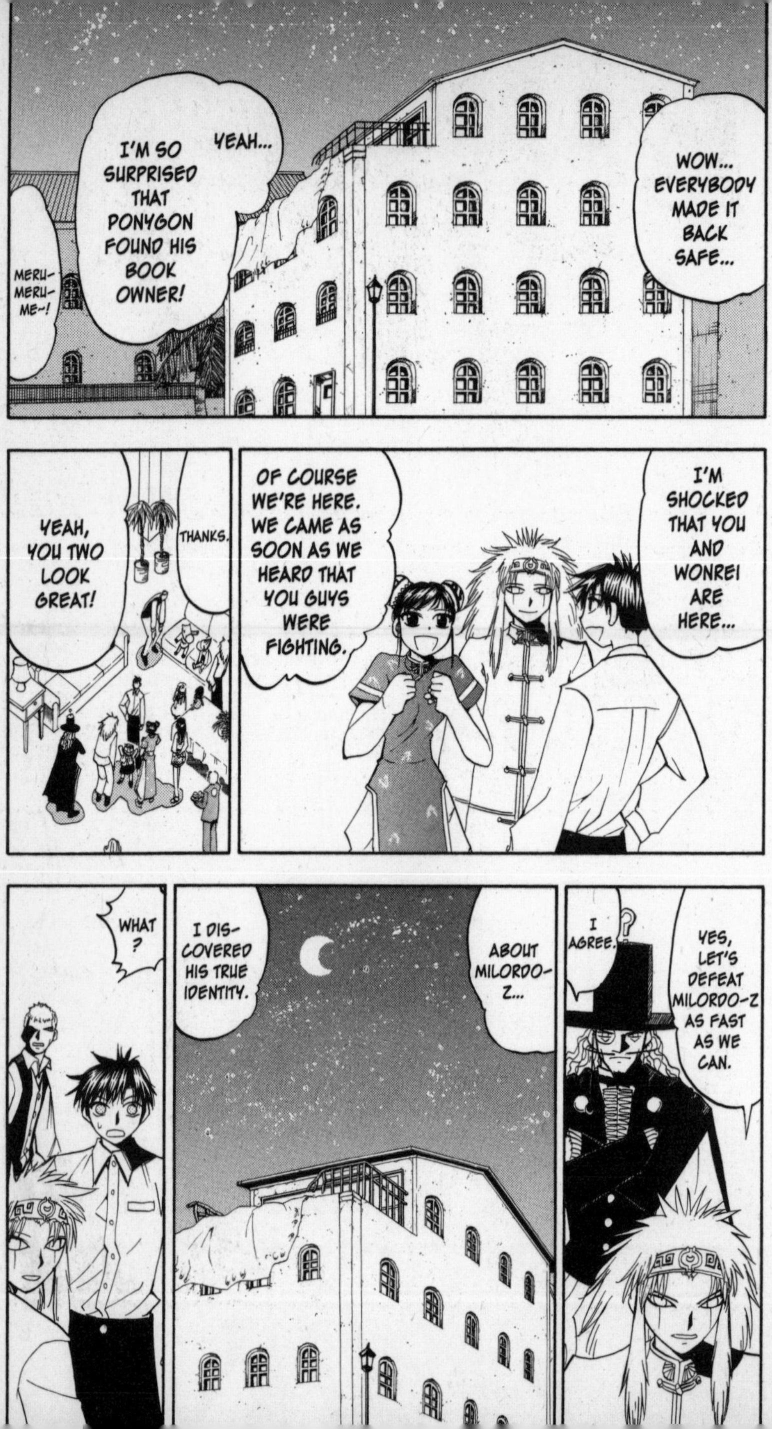
WOW... EVERYBODY MADE IT BACK SAFE...
YEAH...
I'M SO SURPRISED THAT PONYGON FOUND HIS BOOK OWNER!
MERU-MERU-ME~!
I'M SHOCKED THAT YOU AND WONREI ARE HERE...
OF COURSE WE'RE HERE. WE CAME AS SOON AS WE HEARD THAT YOU GUYS WERE FIGHTING.
THANKS.
YEAH, YOU TWO LOOK GREAT!
YES, LET'S DEFEAT MILORDO-Z AS FAST AS WE CAN.
I AGREE.
ABOUT MILORDO-Z...
I DIS-COVERED HIS TRUE IDENTITY.
WHAT?

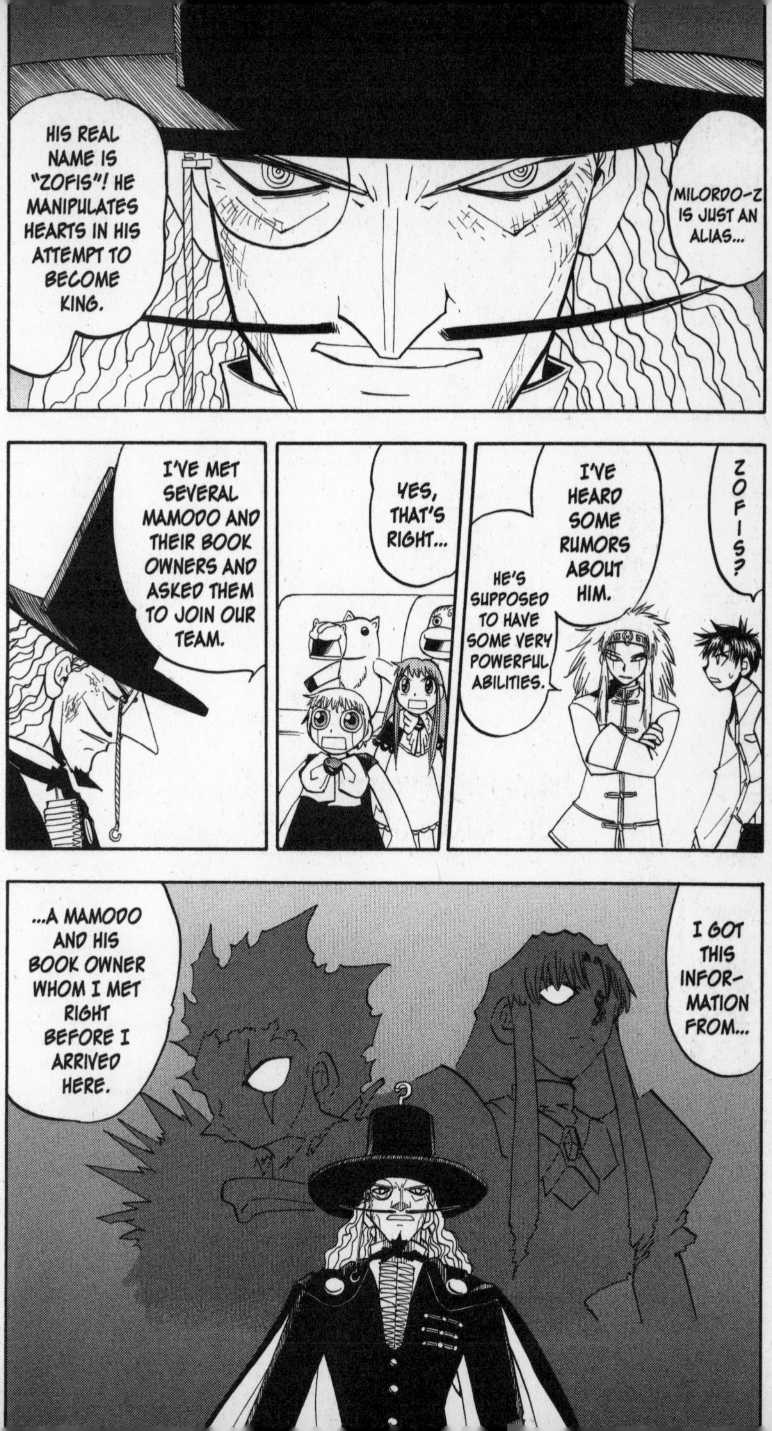
MILORDO-Z IS JUST AN ALIAS...
HIS REAL NAME IS "ZOFIS"! HE MANIPULATES HEARTS IN HIS ATTEMPT TO BECOME KING.
ZOFIS?
I'VE HEARD SOME RUMORS ABOUT HIM.
HE'S SUPPOSED TO HAVE SOME VERY POWERFUL ABILITIES.
YES, THAT'S RIGHT...
I'VE MET SEVERAL MAMODO AND THEIR BOOK OWNERS AND ASKED THEM TO JOIN OUR TEAM.
I GOT THIS INFOR-MATION FROM...
...A MAMODO AND HIS BOOK OWNER WHOM I MET RIGHT BEFORE I ARRIVED HERE.

LEVEL 127: The Most Powerful Mamodo

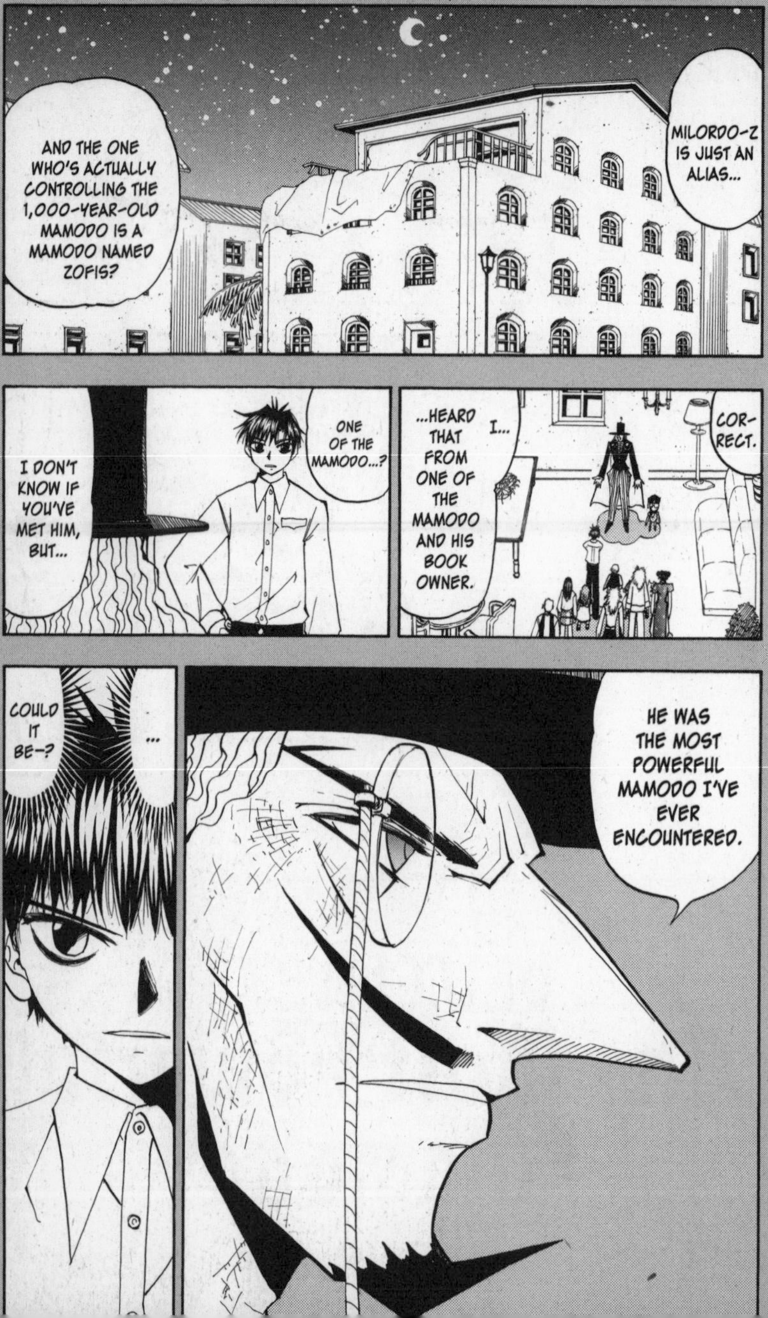

MILORDO-Z IS JUST AN ALIAS...
AND THE ONE WHO'S ACTUALLY CONTROLLING THE 1,000-YEAR-OLD MAMODO IS A MAMODO NAMED ZOFIS?
COR-RECT.
I...
...HEARD THAT FROM ONE OF THE MAMODO AND HIS BOOK OWNER.
ONE OF THE MAMODO...?
I DON'T KNOW IF YOU'VE MET HIM, BUT...
HE WAS THE MOST POWERFUL MAMODO I'VE EVER ENCOUNTERED.
...
COULD IT BE—?

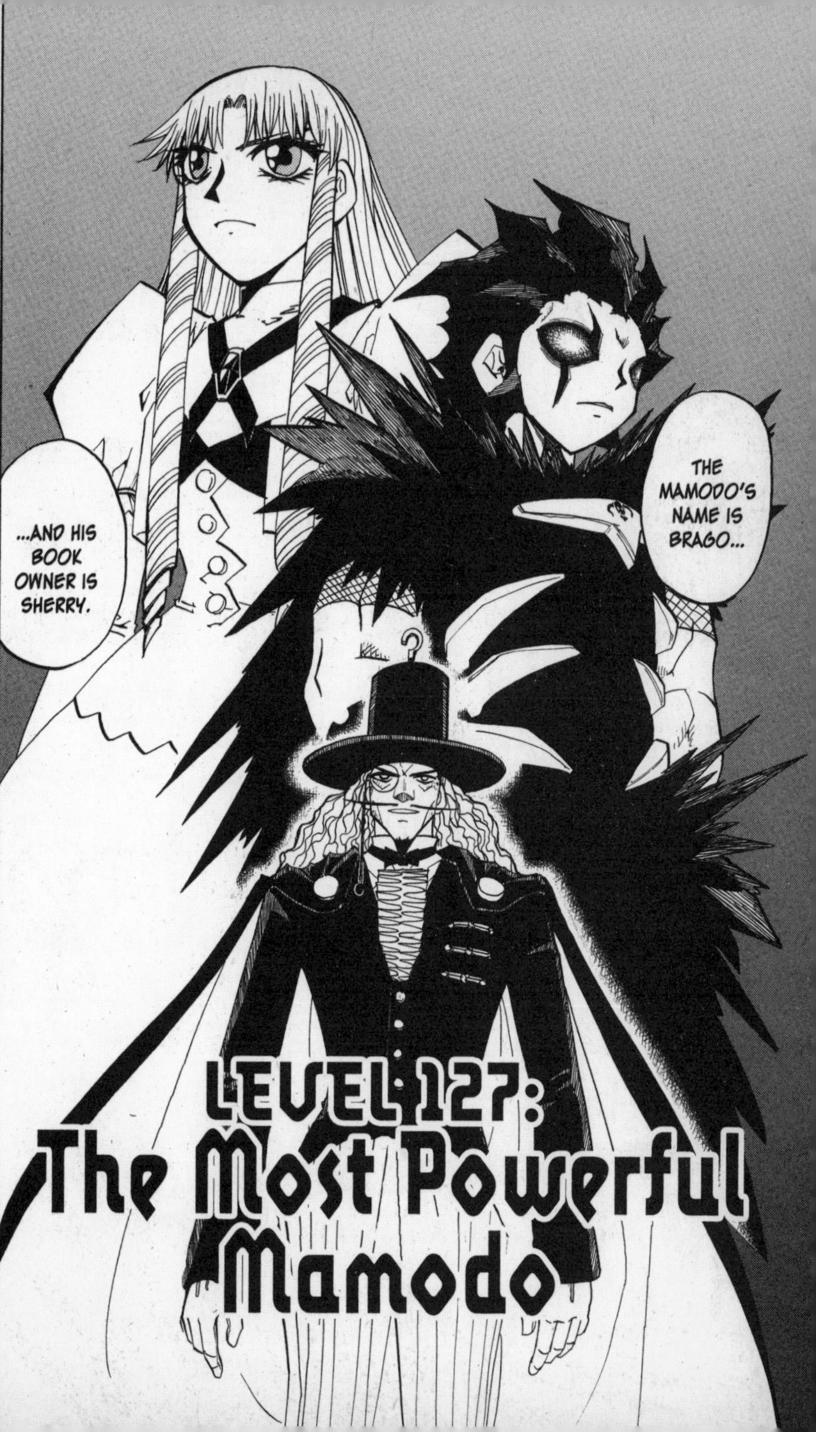
THE MAMODO'S NAME IS BRAGO...
...AND HIS BOOK OWNER IS SHERRY.
LEVEL 127: The Most Powerful Mamodo

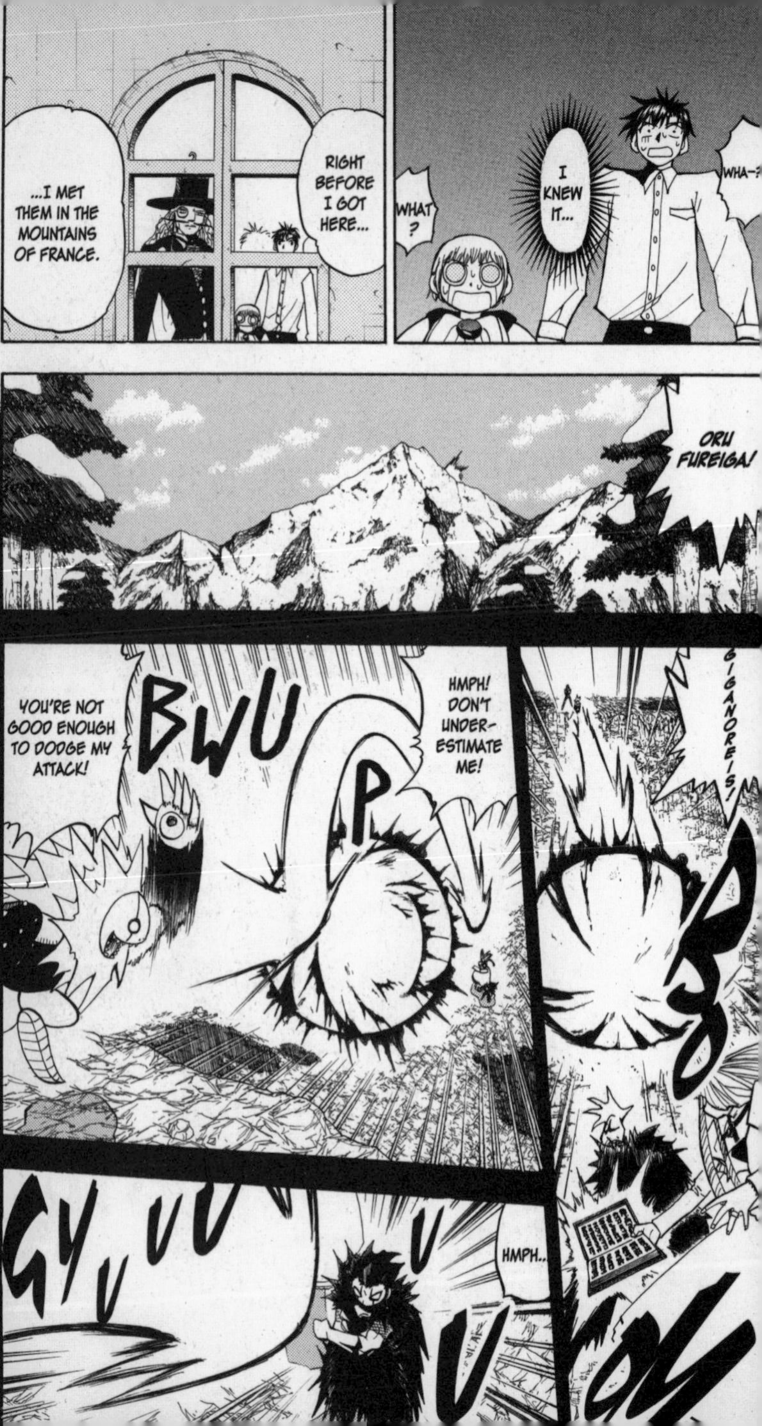
WHA-?
I KNEW IT...
WHAT?
RIGHT BEFORE I GOT HERE...
...I MET THEM IN THE MOUNTAINS OF FRANCE.
ORU FUREIGA!
GIGANOREIS!
HMPH! DON'T UNDER-ESTIMATE ME!
BWUP
YOU'RE NOT GOOD ENOUGH TO DODGE MY ATTACK!
HMPH..

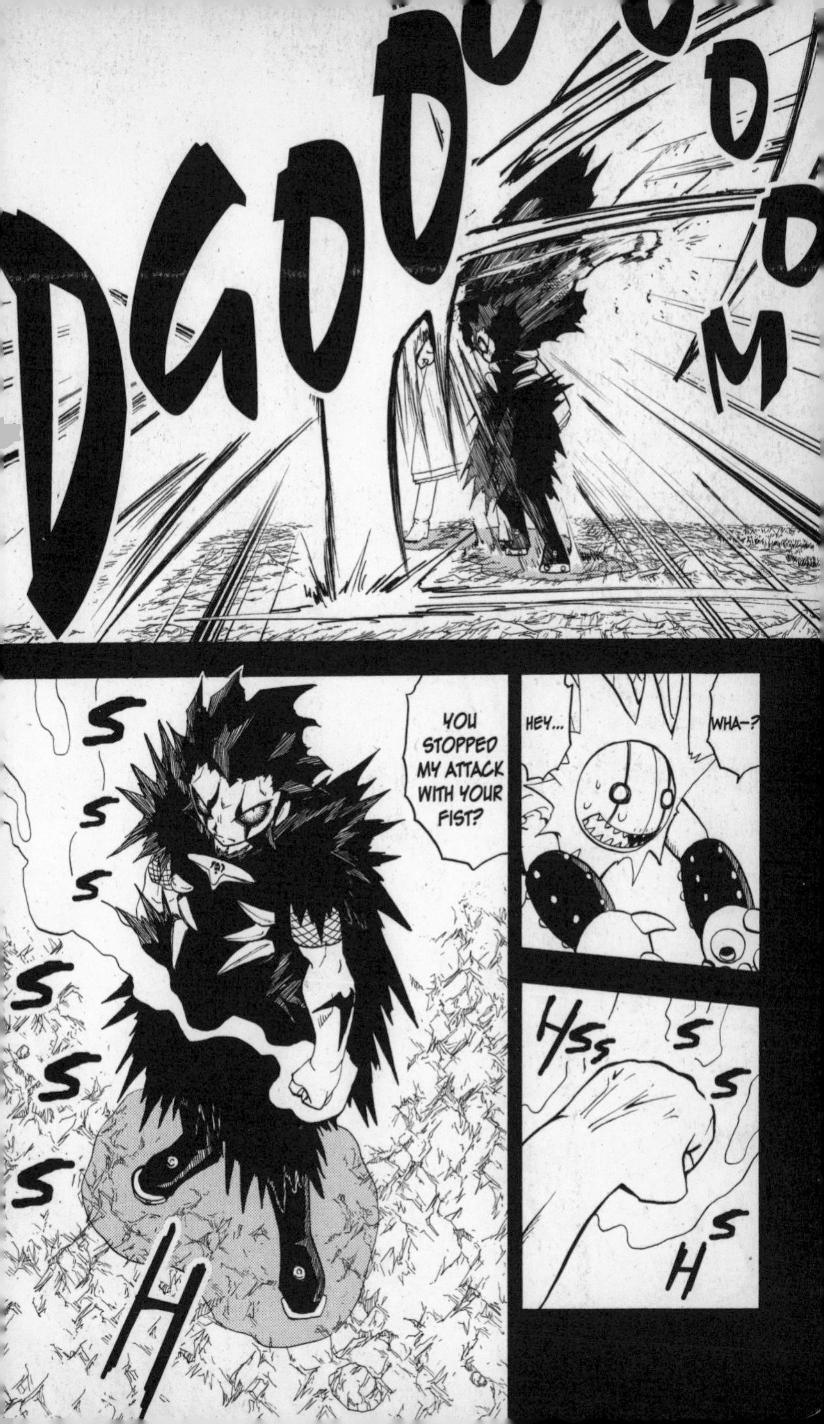
WHA-?
HEY...
HSSS
HSS
YOU STOPPED MY ATTACK WITH YOUR FIST?
SSSSSSH

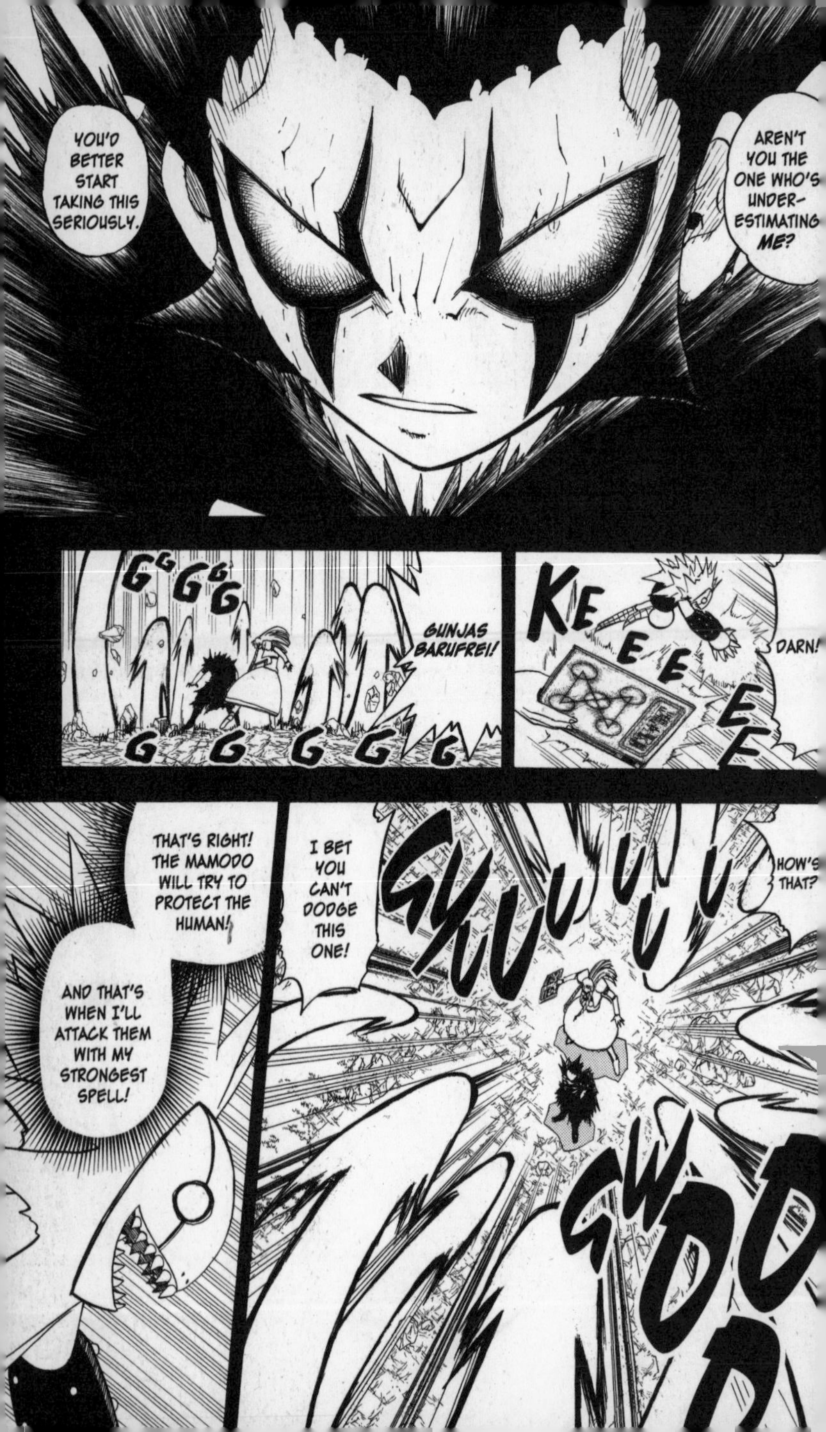
AREN'T YOU THE ONE WHO'S UNDER-ESTIMATING ME?
YOU'D BETTER START TAKING THIS SERIOUSLY.
DARN!
KEEEEE
GUNJAS BARUFREI!
GGGG
GGGGG
HOW'S THAT?
SYUUUUUUU
SWOOOM
I BET YOU CAN'T DODGE THIS ONE!
THAT'S RIGHT! THE MAMODO WILL TRY TO PROTECT THE HUMAN!
AND THAT'S WHEN I'LL ATTACK THEM WITH MY STRONGEST SPELL!

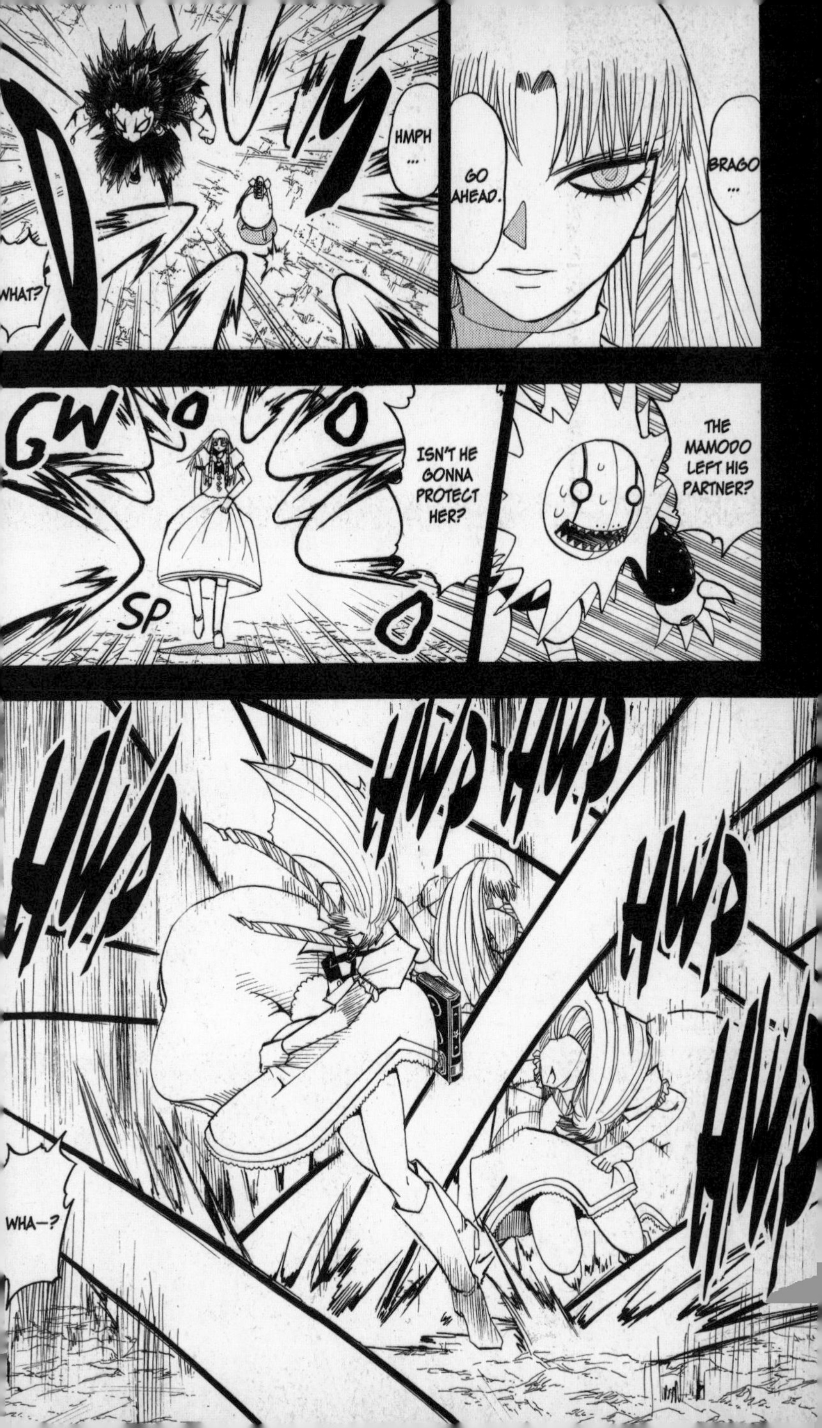
BRAGO ...
GO AHEAD.
HMPH ...
WHAT?
THE MAMODO LEFT HIS PARTNER?
ISN'T HE GONNA PROTECT HER?
WHA-?

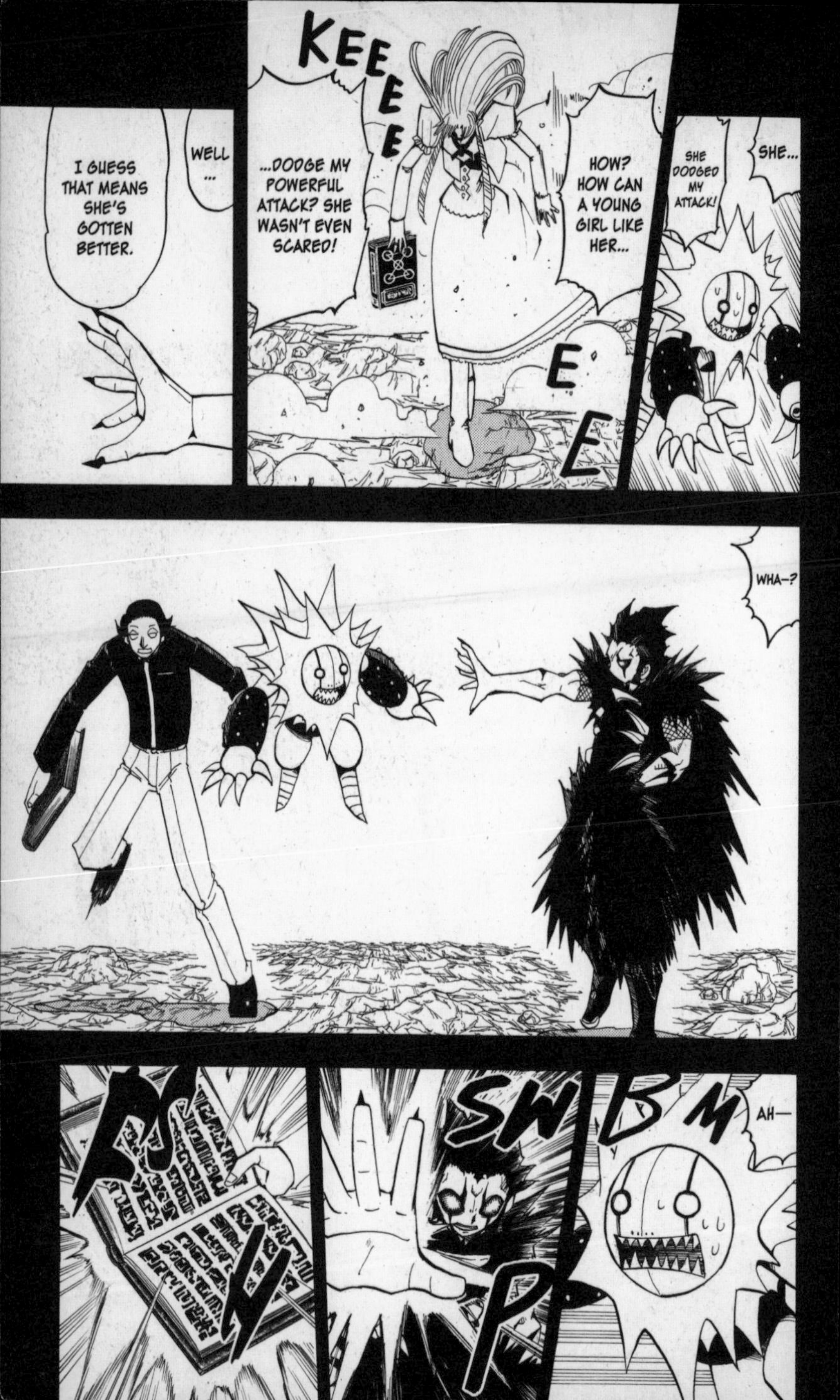
SHE...
SHE DODGED MY ATTACK!
HOW? HOW CAN A YOUNG GIRL LIKE HER...
KEEEEEEE
...DODGE MY POWERFUL ATTACK? SHE WASN'T EVEN SCARED!
WELL ...
I GUESS THAT MEANS SHE'S GOTTEN BETTER.
WHA-?
AH—

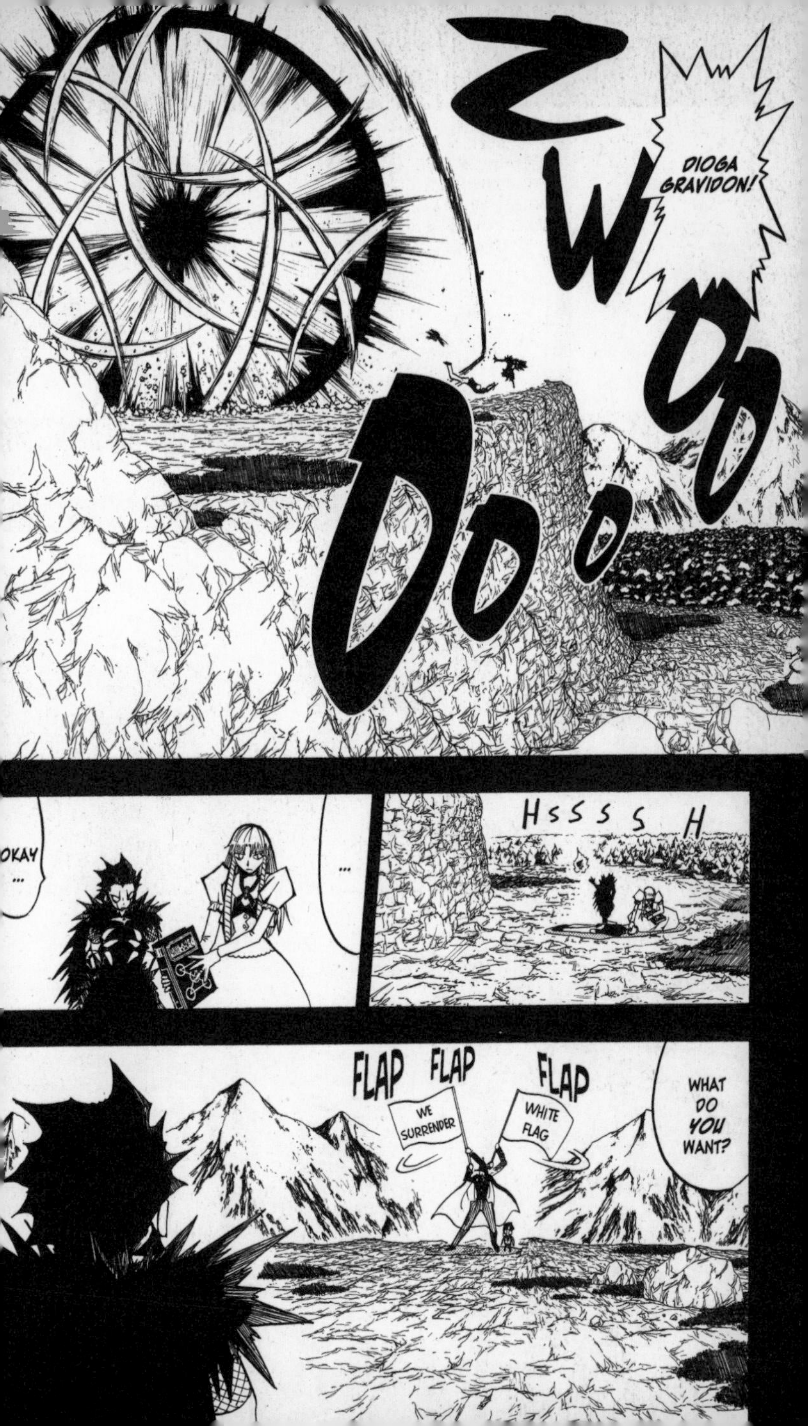
DIOGA GRAVIDON!
ZWOO
DOOO
H S S S S H
...
OKAY ...
WHAT DO YOU WANT?
FLAP FLAP FLAP
WHITE FLAG
WE SURRENDER

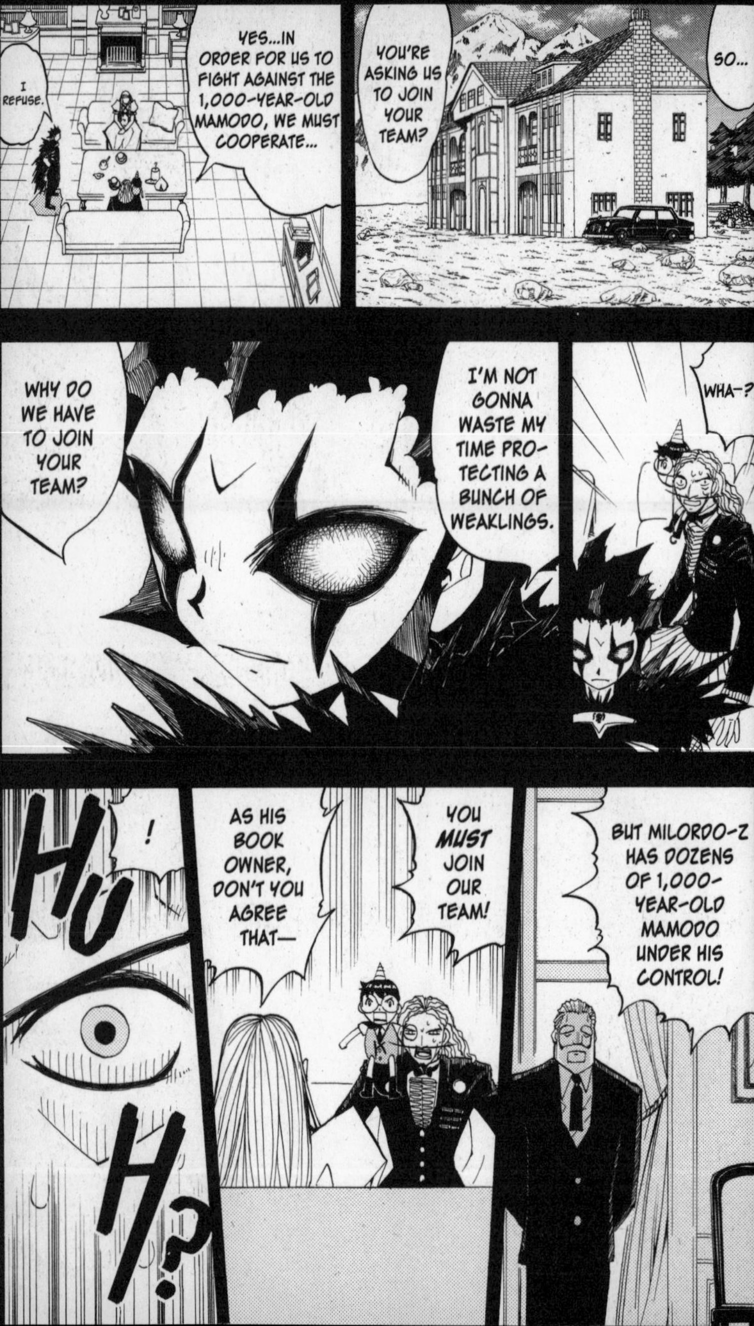
SO...
YOU'RE ASKING US TO JOIN YOUR TEAM?
YES...IN ORDER FOR US TO FIGHT AGAINST THE 1,000-YEAR-OLD MAMODO, WE MUST COOPERATE...
I REFUSE.
WHA-?
I'M NOT GONNA WASTE MY TIME PROTECTING A BUNCH OF WEAKLINGS.
WHY DO WE HAVE TO JOIN YOUR TEAM?
BUT MILORDO-Z HAS DOZENS OF 1,000-YEAR-OLD MAMODO UNDER HIS CONTROL!
YOU **MUST** JOIN OUR TEAM!
AS HIS BOOK OWNER, DON'T YOU AGREE THAT—
!
HUH?

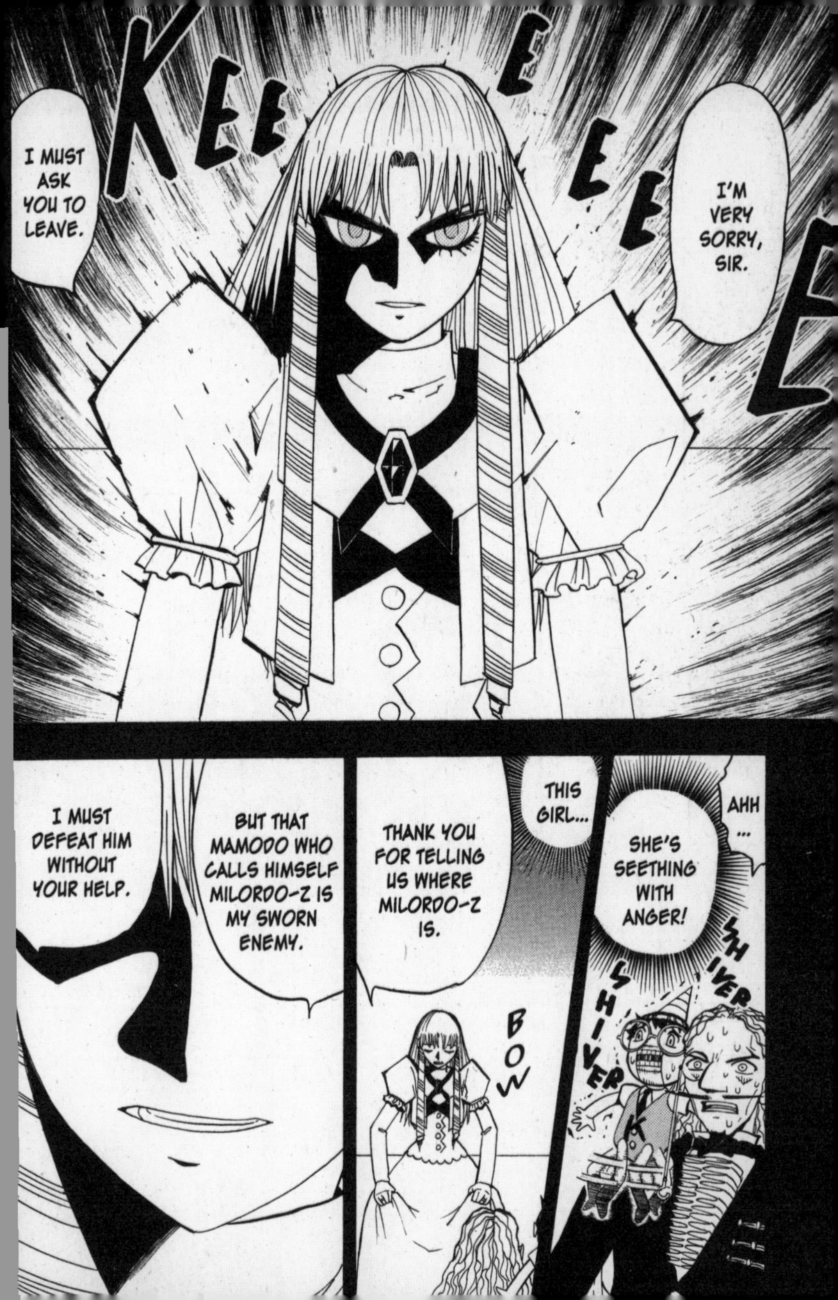
I'M VERY SORRY, SIR.
I MUST ASK YOU TO LEAVE.
KEEEEEEE
AHH ...
THIS GIRL...
SHE'S SEETHING WITH ANGER!
SHIVER
SHIVER
THANK YOU FOR TELLING US WHERE MILORDO-Z IS.
BOW
BUT THAT MAMODO WHO CALLS HIMSELF MILORDO-Z IS MY SWORN ENEMY.
I MUST DEFEAT HIM WITHOUT YOUR HELP.

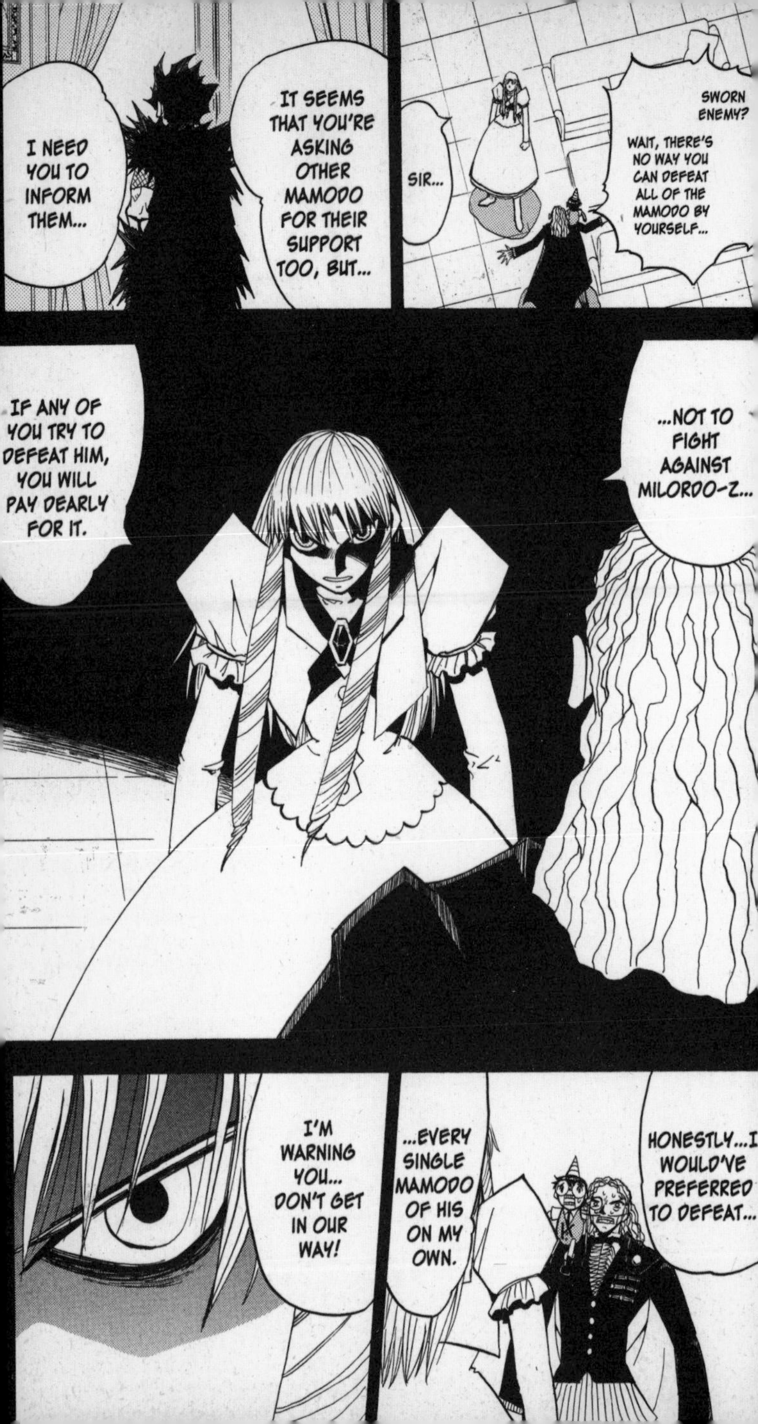
SWORN ENEMY?
WAIT, THERE'S NO WAY YOU CAN DEFEAT ALL OF THE MAMODO BY YOURSELF...
SIR...
IT SEEMS THAT YOU'RE ASKING OTHER MAMODO FOR THEIR SUPPORT TOO, BUT...
I NEED YOU TO INFORM THEM...
...NOT TO FIGHT AGAINST MILORDO-Z...
IF ANY OF YOU TRY TO DEFEAT HIM, YOU WILL PAY DEARLY FOR IT.
HONESTLY...I WOULD'VE PREFERRED TO DEFEAT...
...EVERY SINGLE MAMODO OF HIS ON MY OWN.
I'M WARNING YOU... DON'T GET IN OUR WAY!

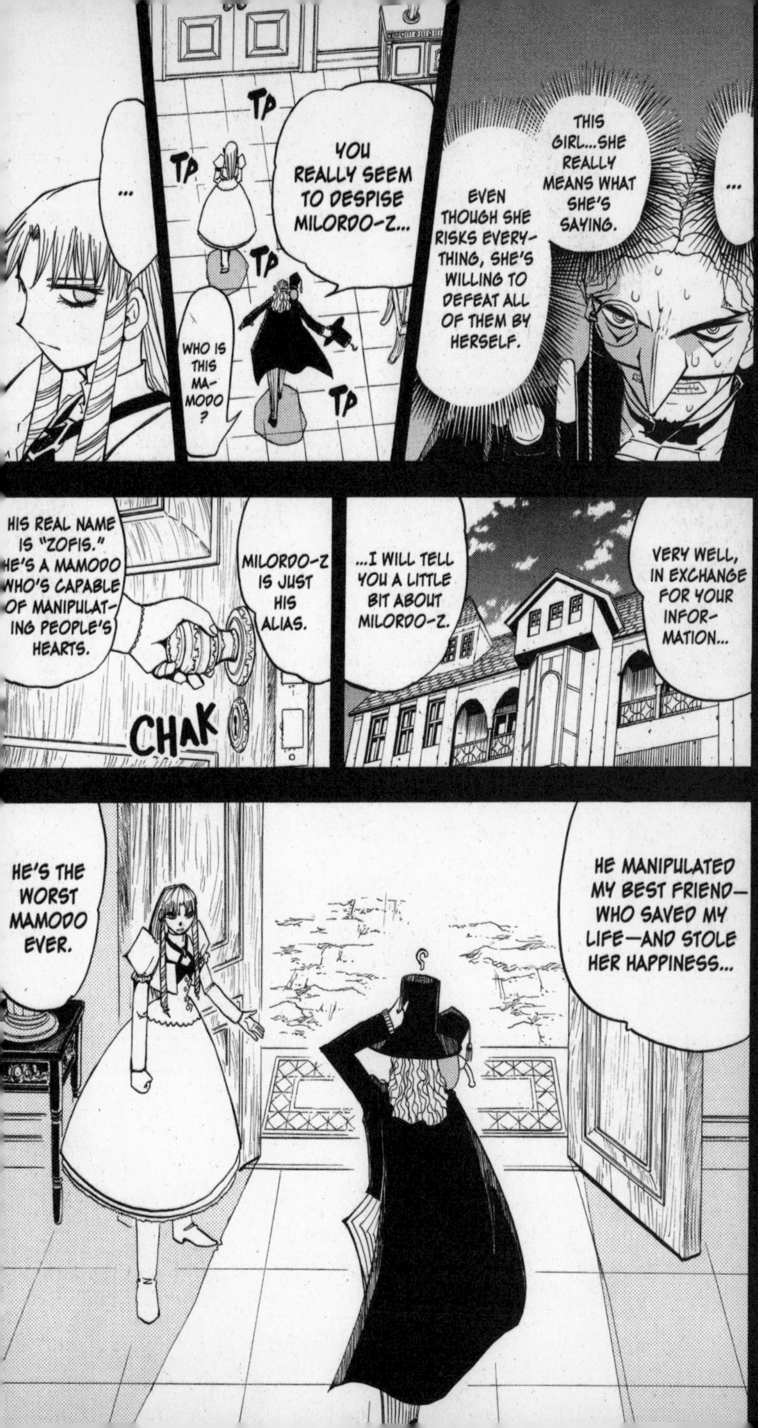
...
THIS GIRL...SHE REALLY MEANS WHAT SHE'S SAYING.
EVEN THOUGH SHE RISKS EVERYTHING, SHE'S WILLING TO DEFEAT ALL OF THEM BY HERSELF.
TP
YOU REALLY SEEM TO DESPISE MILORDO-Z...
TP
TP
WHO IS THIS MAMODO?
TP
...
VERY WELL, IN EXCHANGE FOR YOUR INFORMATION...
...I WILL TELL YOU A LITTLE BIT ABOUT MILORDO-Z.
MILORDO-Z IS JUST HIS ALIAS.
HIS REAL NAME IS "ZOFIS." HE'S A MAMODO WHO'S CAPABLE OF MANIPULATING PEOPLE'S HEARTS.
CHAK
HE MANIPULATED MY BEST FRIEND—WHO SAVED MY LIFE—AND STOLE HER HAPPINESS...
HE'S THE WORST MAMODO EVER.

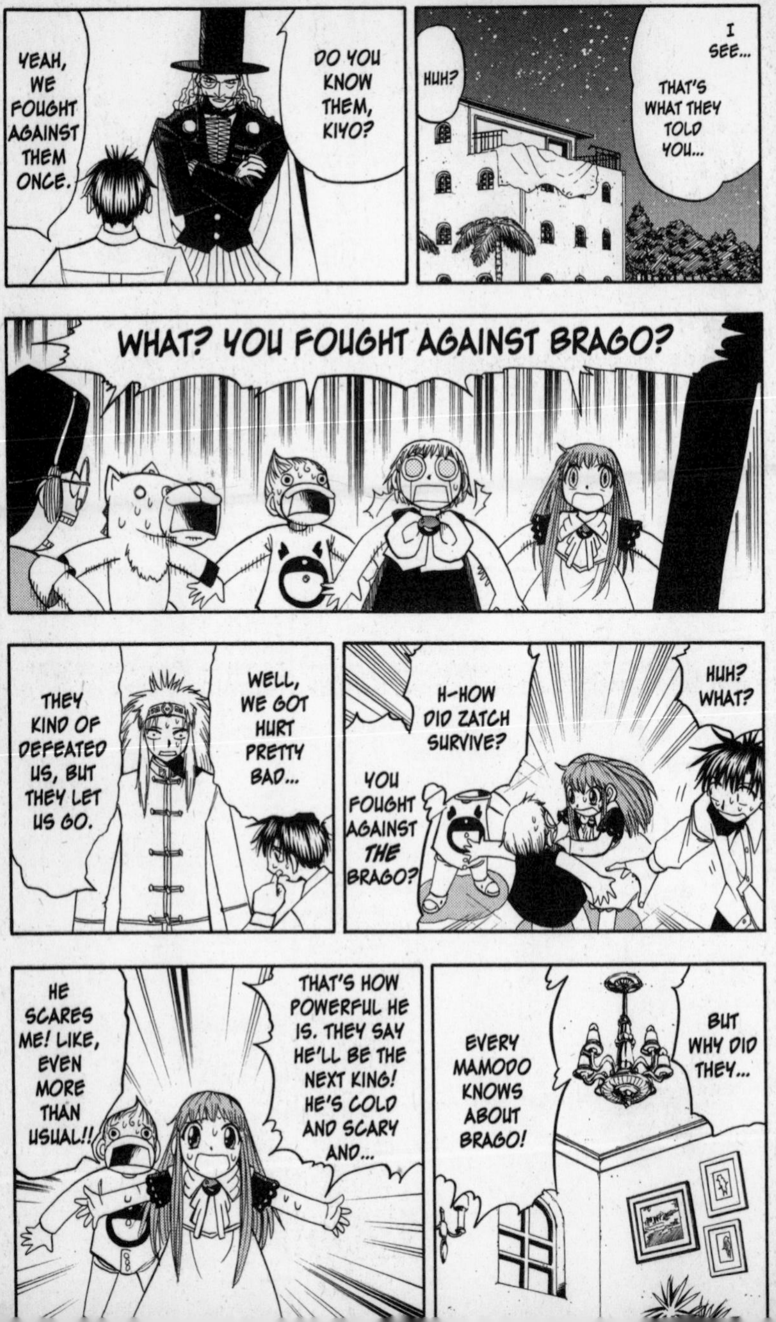
I SEE... THAT'S WHAT THEY TOLD YOU...
HUH?
DO YOU KNOW THEM, KIYO?
YEAH, WE FOUGHT AGAINST THEM ONCE.
WHAT? YOU FOUGHT AGAINST BRAGO?
HUH? WHAT?
H-HOW DID ZATCH SURVIVE?
YOU FOUGHT AGAINST *THE* BRAGO?
WELL, WE GOT HURT PRETTY BAD...
THEY KIND OF DEFEATED US, BUT THEY LET US GO.
BUT WHY DID THEY...
EVERY MAMODO KNOWS ABOUT BRAGO!
THAT'S HOW POWERFUL HE IS. THEY SAY HE'LL BE THE NEXT KING! HE'S COLD AND SCARY AND...
HE SCARES ME! LIKE, EVEN MORE THAN USUAL!!

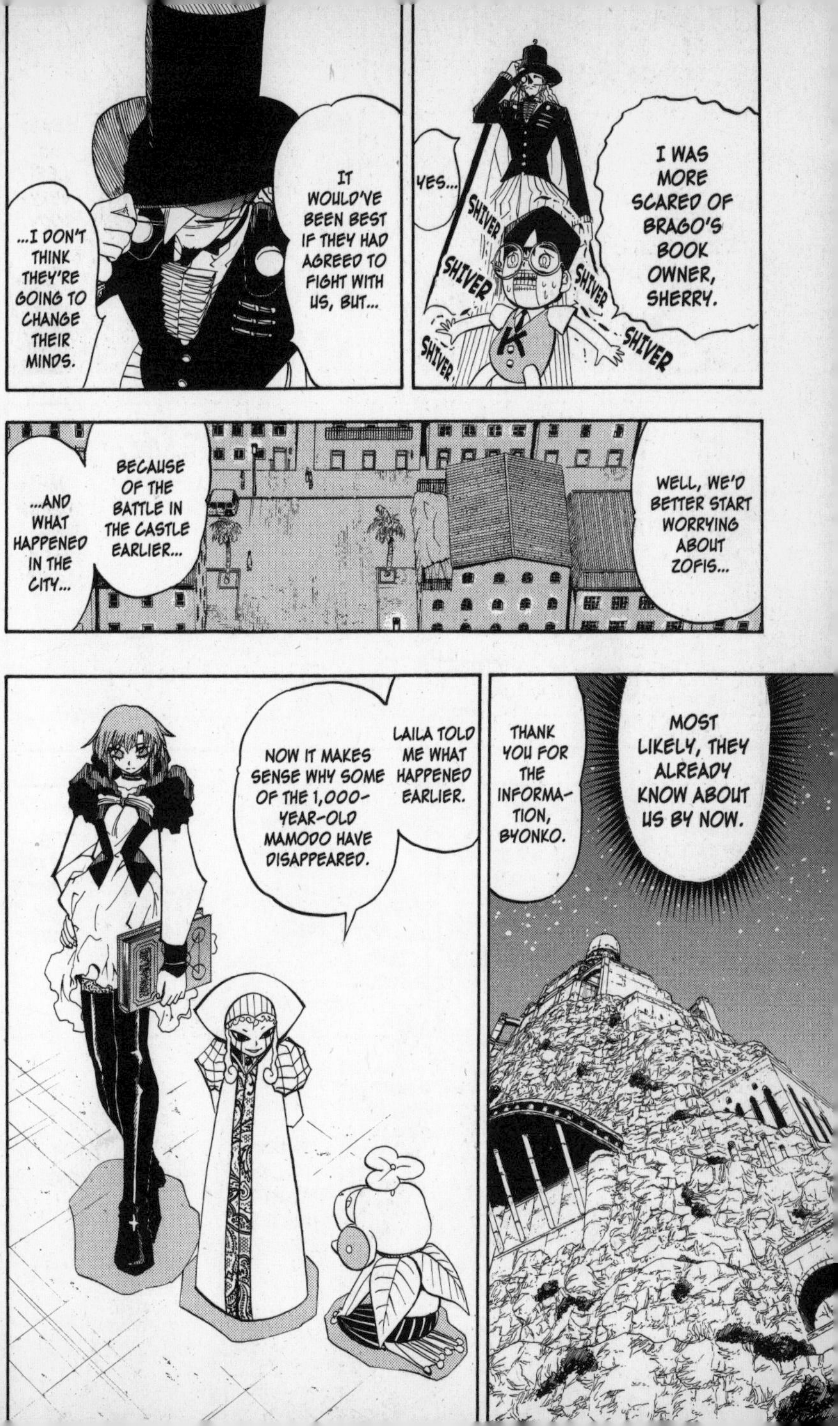
I WAS MORE SCARED OF BRAGO'S BOOK OWNER, SHERRY.
YES...
SHIVER
SHIVER
SHIVER
SHIVER
SHIVER
IT WOULD'VE BEEN BEST IF THEY HAD AGREED TO FIGHT WITH US, BUT...
...I DON'T THINK THEY'RE GOING TO CHANGE THEIR MINDS.
WELL, WE'D BETTER START WORRYING ABOUT ZOFIS...
BECAUSE OF THE BATTLE IN THE CASTLE EARLIER...
...AND WHAT HAPPENED IN THE CITY...
MOST LIKELY, THEY ALREADY KNOW ABOUT US BY NOW.
THANK YOU FOR THE INFORMATION, BYONKO.
LAILA TOLD ME WHAT HAPPENED EARLIER.
NOW IT MAKES SENSE WHY SOME OF THE 1,000-YEAR-OLD MAMODO HAVE DISAPPEARED.

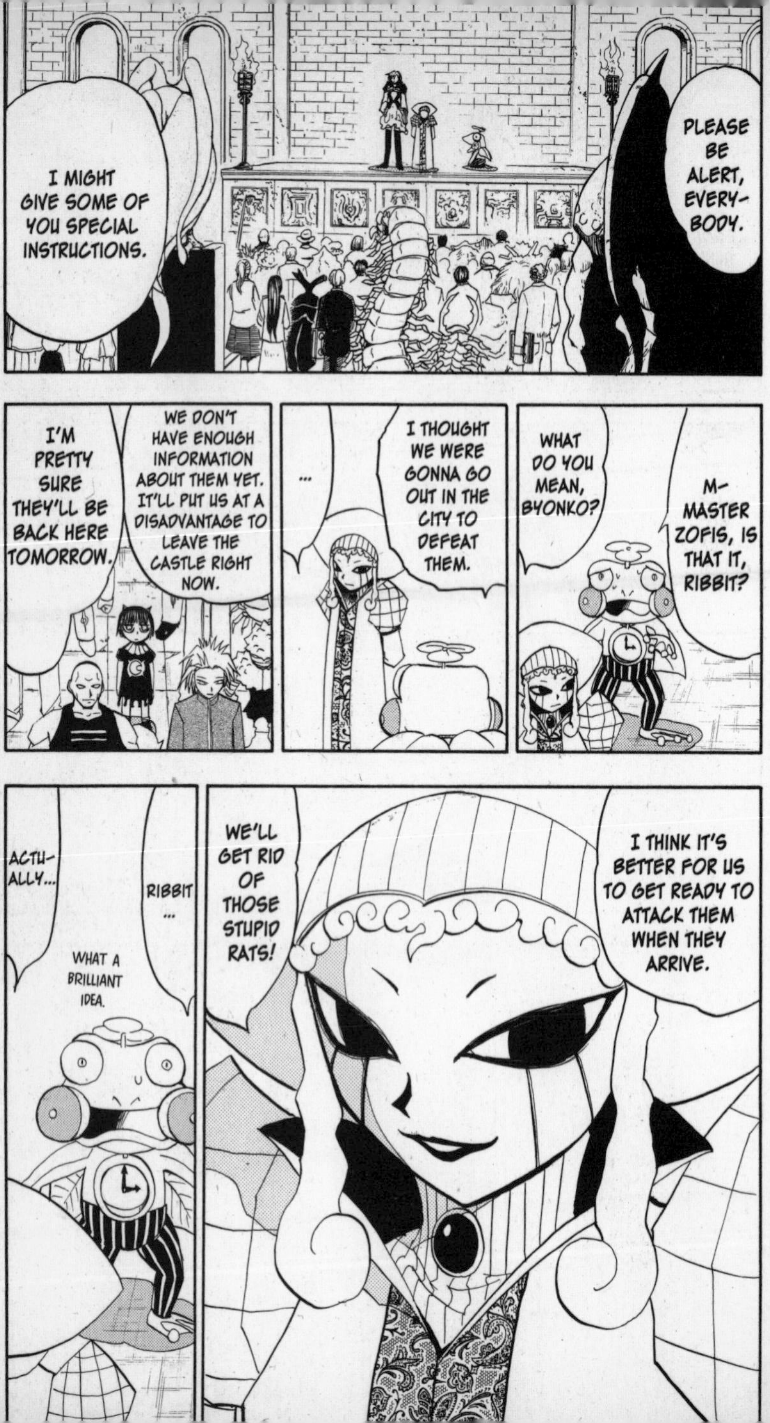
PLEASE BE ALERT, EVERYBODY.
I MIGHT GIVE SOME OF YOU SPECIAL INSTRUCTIONS.
M-MASTER ZOFIS, IS THAT IT, RIBBIT?
WHAT DO YOU MEAN, BYONKO?
I THOUGHT WE WERE GONNA GO OUT IN THE CITY TO DEFEAT THEM.
...
WE DON'T HAVE ENOUGH INFORMATION ABOUT THEM YET. IT'LL PUT US AT A DISADVANTAGE TO LEAVE THE CASTLE RIGHT NOW.
I'M PRETTY SURE THEY'LL BE BACK HERE TOMORROW.
I THINK IT'S BETTER FOR US TO GET READY TO ATTACK THEM WHEN THEY ARRIVE.
WE'LL GET RID OF THOSE STUPID RATS!
RIBBIT...
ACTU-ALLY...
WHAT A BRILLIANT IDEA.

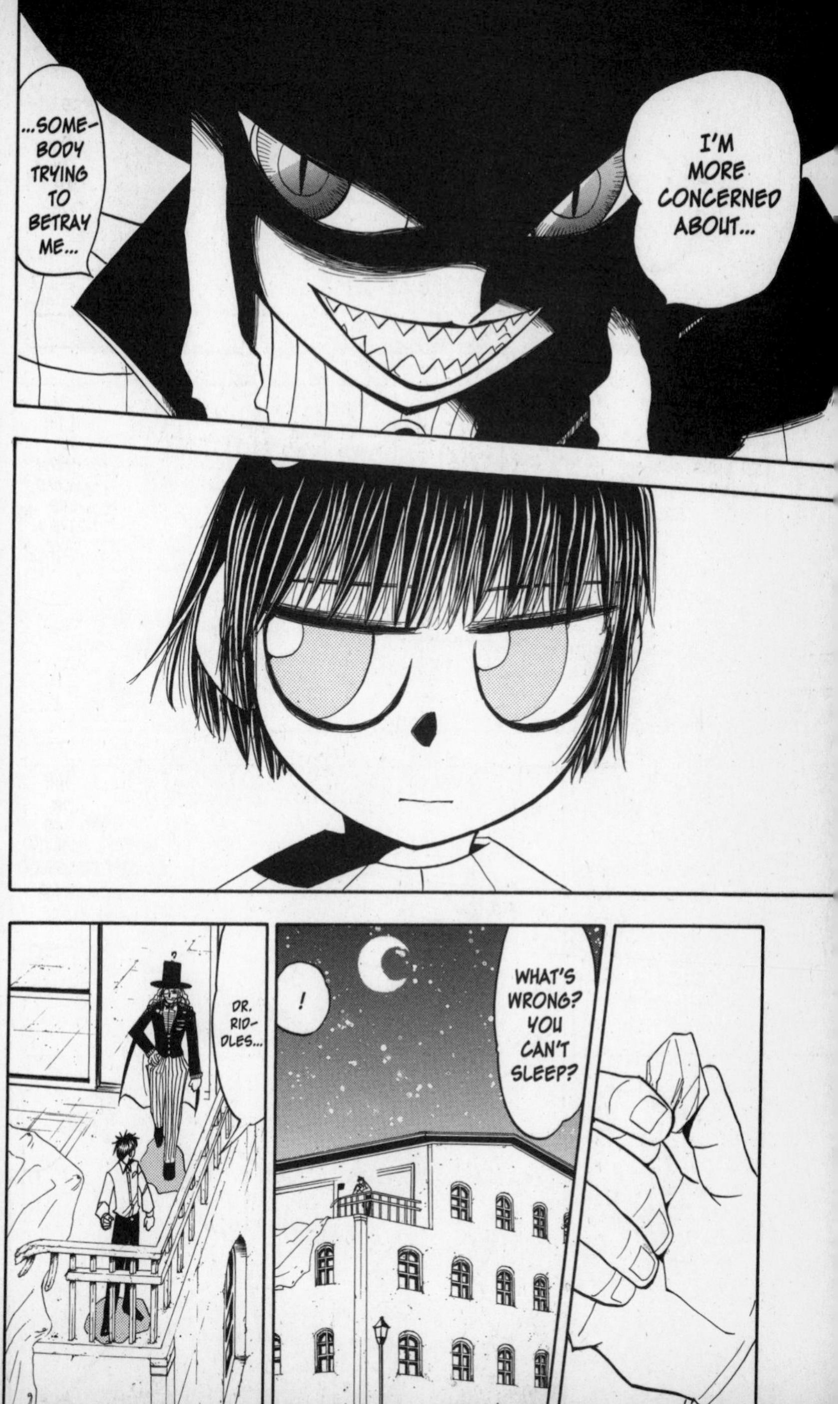
I'M MORE CONCERNED ABOUT...
...SOME-BODY TRYING TO BETRAY ME...
WHAT'S WRONG? YOU CAN'T SLEEP?
!
DR. RID-DLES...

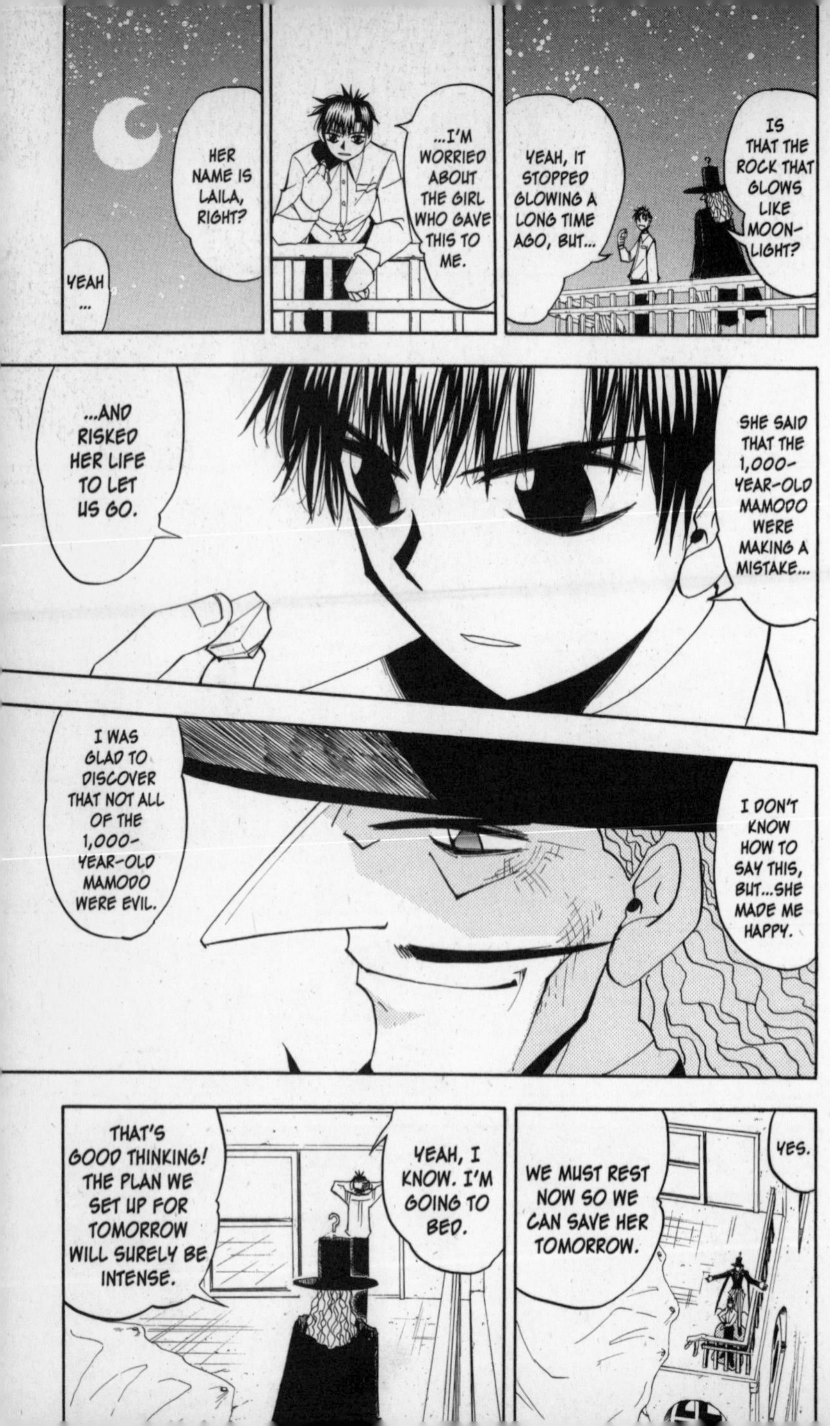
IS THAT THE ROCK THAT GLOWS LIKE MOON-LIGHT?
YEAH, IT STOPPED GLOWING A LONG TIME AGO, BUT...
...I'M WORRIED ABOUT THE GIRL WHO GAVE THIS TO ME.
HER NAME IS LAILA, RIGHT?
YEAH...
SHE SAID THAT THE 1,000-YEAR-OLD MAMODO WERE MAKING A MISTAKE...
...AND RISKED HER LIFE TO LET US GO.
I DON'T KNOW HOW TO SAY THIS, BUT...SHE MADE ME HAPPY.
I WAS GLAD TO DISCOVER THAT NOT ALL OF THE 1,000-YEAR-OLD MAMODO WERE EVIL.
YES.
WE MUST REST NOW SO WE CAN SAVE HER TOMORROW.
YEAH, I KNOW. I'M GOING TO BED.
THAT'S GOOD THINKING! THE PLAN WE SET UP FOR TOMORROW WILL SURELY BE INTENSE.

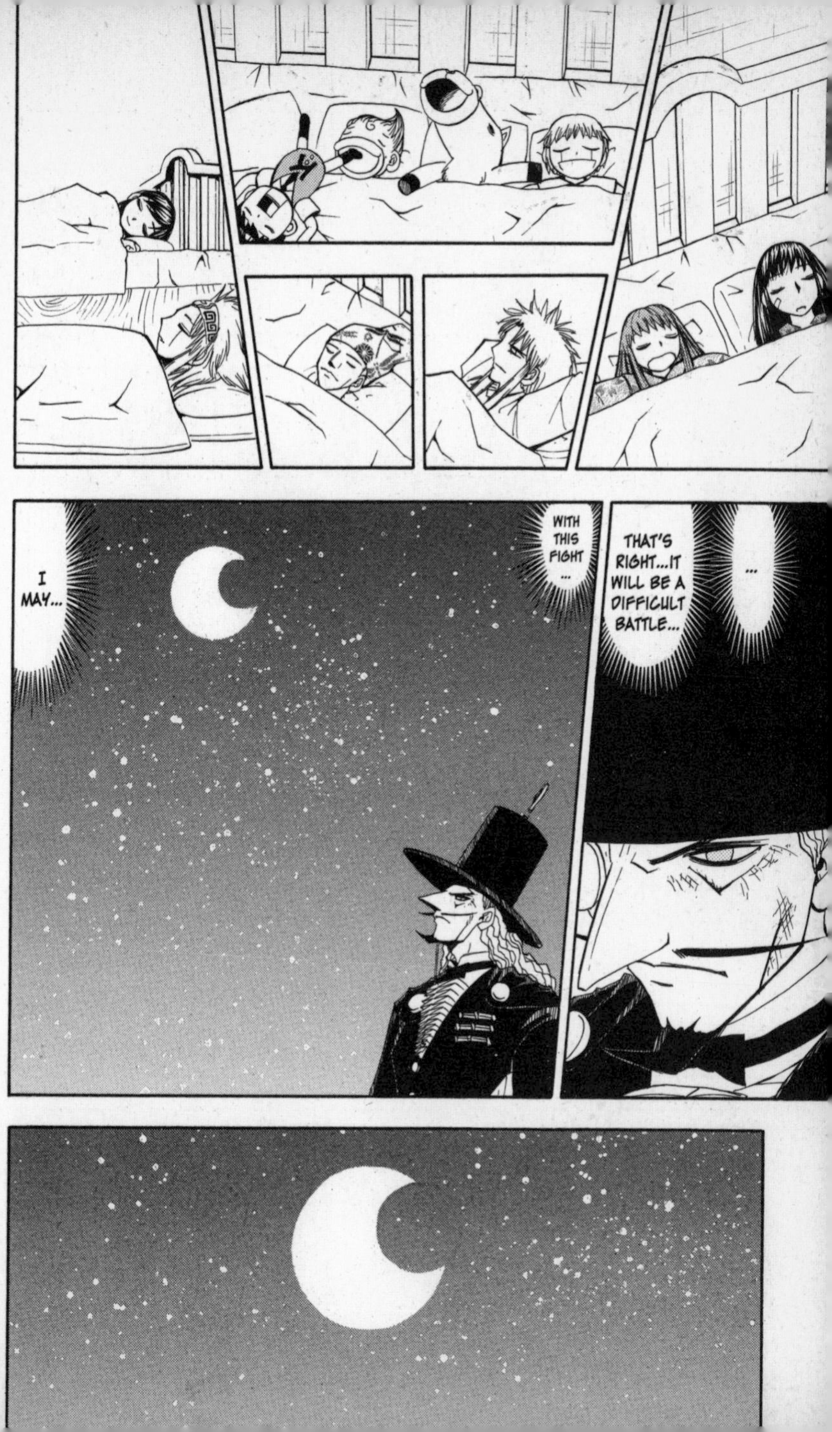
...
THAT'S RIGHT...IT WILL BE A DIFFICULT BATTLE...
WITH THIS FIGHT ...
I MAY...

LEVEL 128: A Single Path

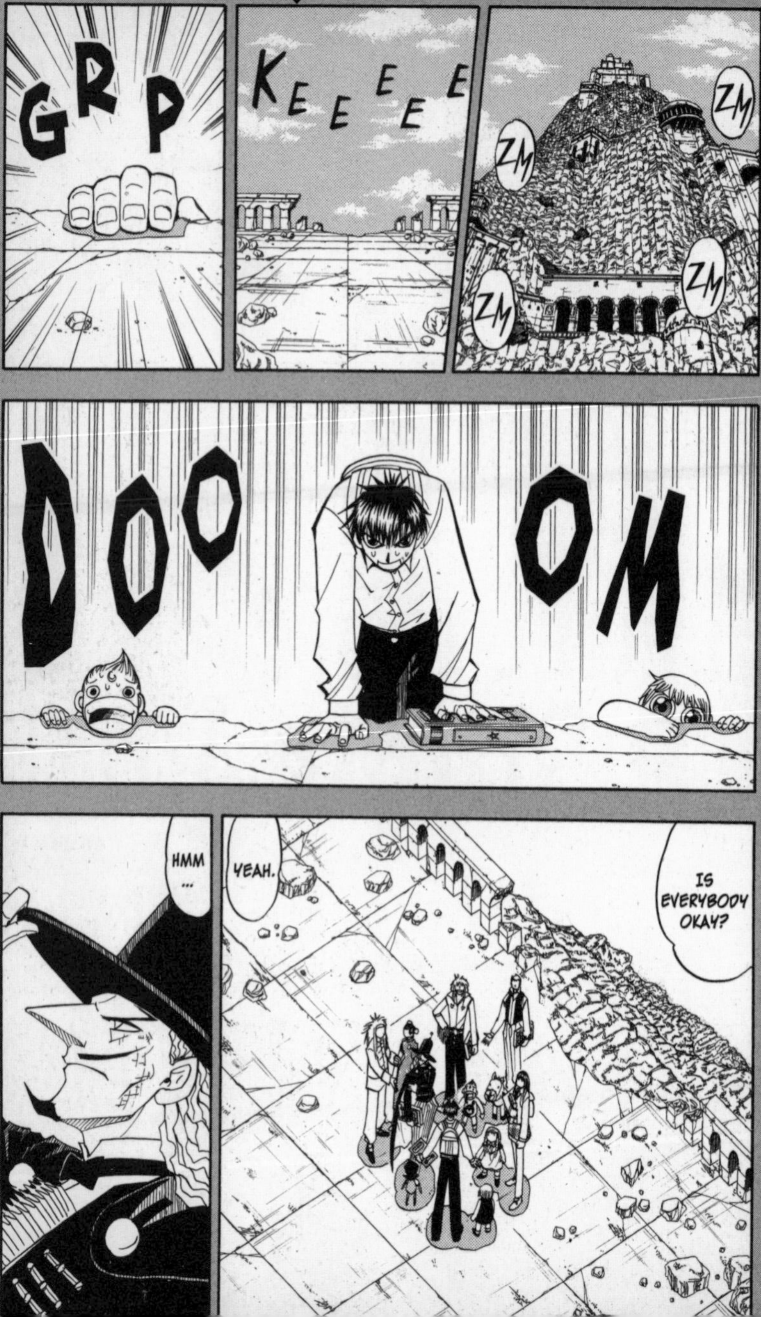

ZM
ZM
ZM
ZM
KEEEEE
GRP
DOOOM
IS EVERYBODY OKAY?
YEAH.
HMM ...

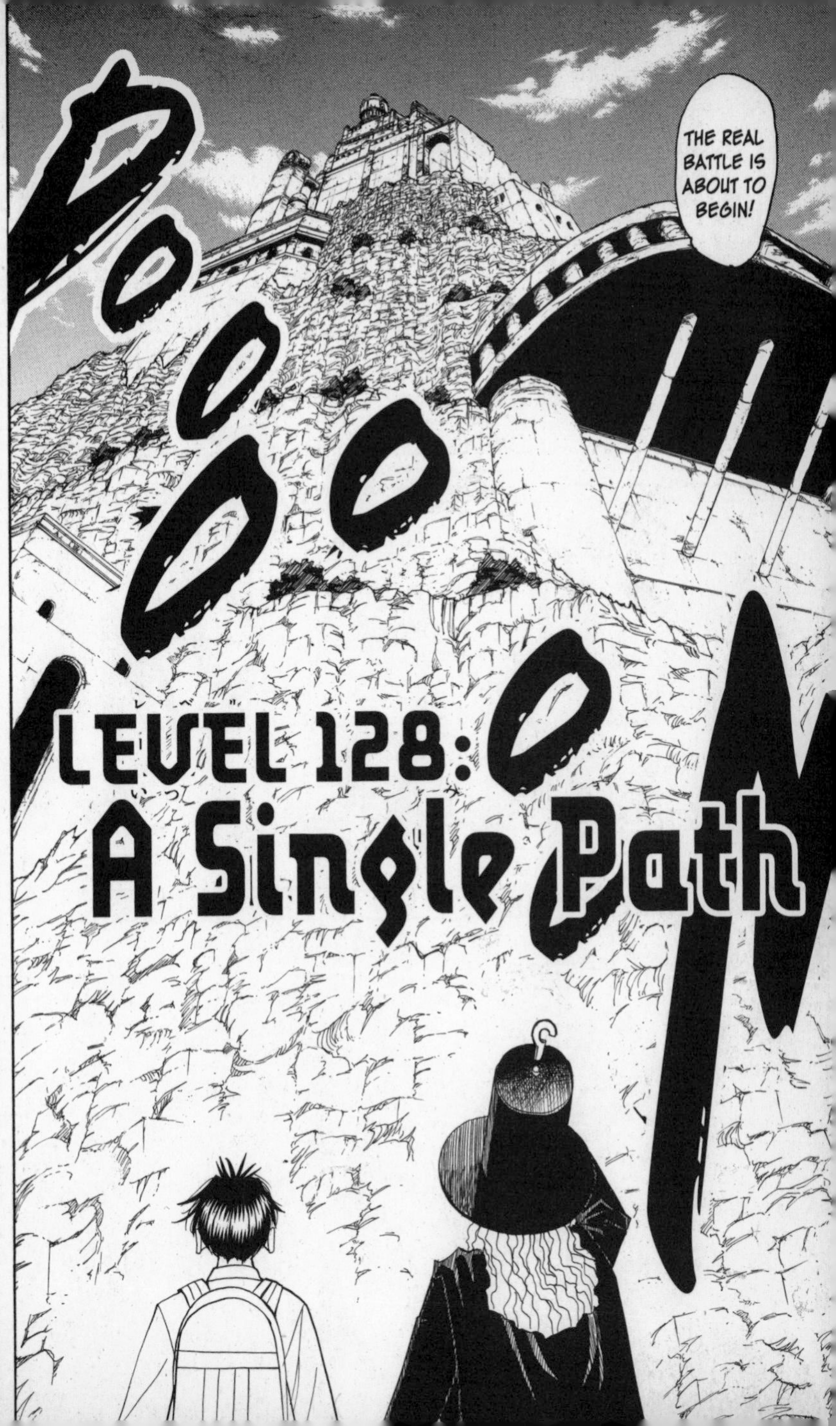
THE REAL BATTLE IS ABOUT TO BEGIN!
LEVEL 128:
A Single Path

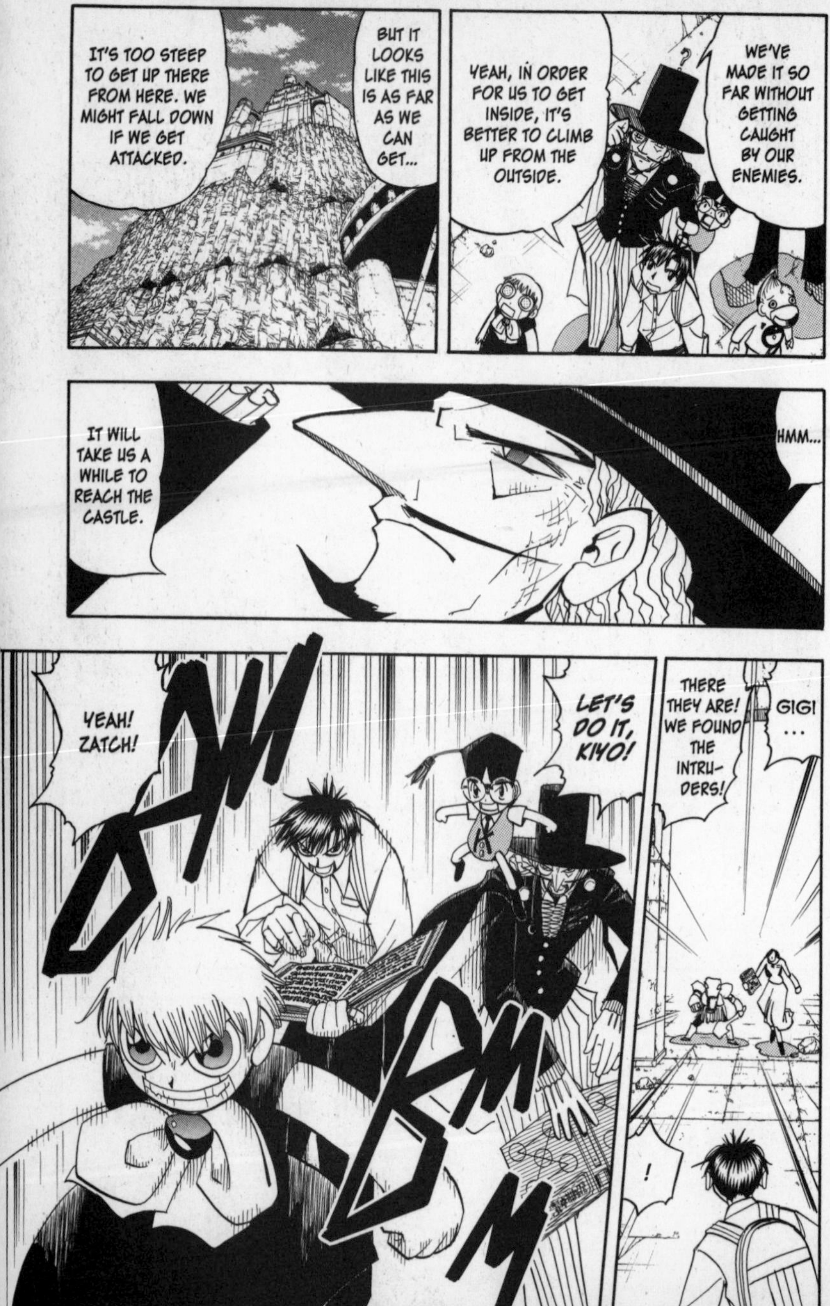
WE'VE MADE IT SO FAR WITHOUT GETTING CAUGHT BY OUR ENEMIES.
YEAH, IN ORDER FOR US TO GET INSIDE, IT'S BETTER TO CLIMB UP FROM THE OUTSIDE.
BUT IT LOOKS LIKE THIS IS AS FAR AS WE CAN GET...
IT'S TOO STEEP TO GET UP THERE FROM HERE. WE MIGHT FALL DOWN IF WE GET ATTACKED.
HMM...
IT WILL TAKE US A WHILE TO REACH THE CASTLE.
GIGI ...
THERE THEY ARE! WE FOUND THE INTRU-DERS!
!
LET'S DO IT, KIYO!
YEAH! ZATCH!

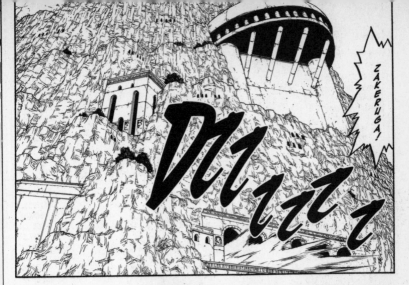

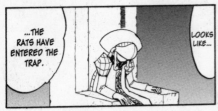

...THE RATS HAVE ENTERED THE TRAP.

LOOKS LIKE...

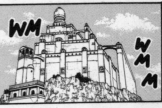

WM

WMM

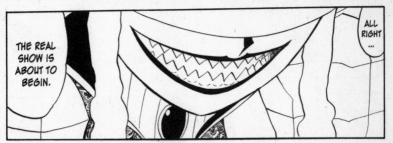

THE REAL SHOW IS ABOUT TO BEGIN.

ALL RIGHT...

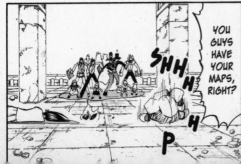

YOU GUYS HAVE YOUR MAPS, RIGHT?

SHH H H P

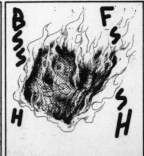

BSS

FSS

SH H

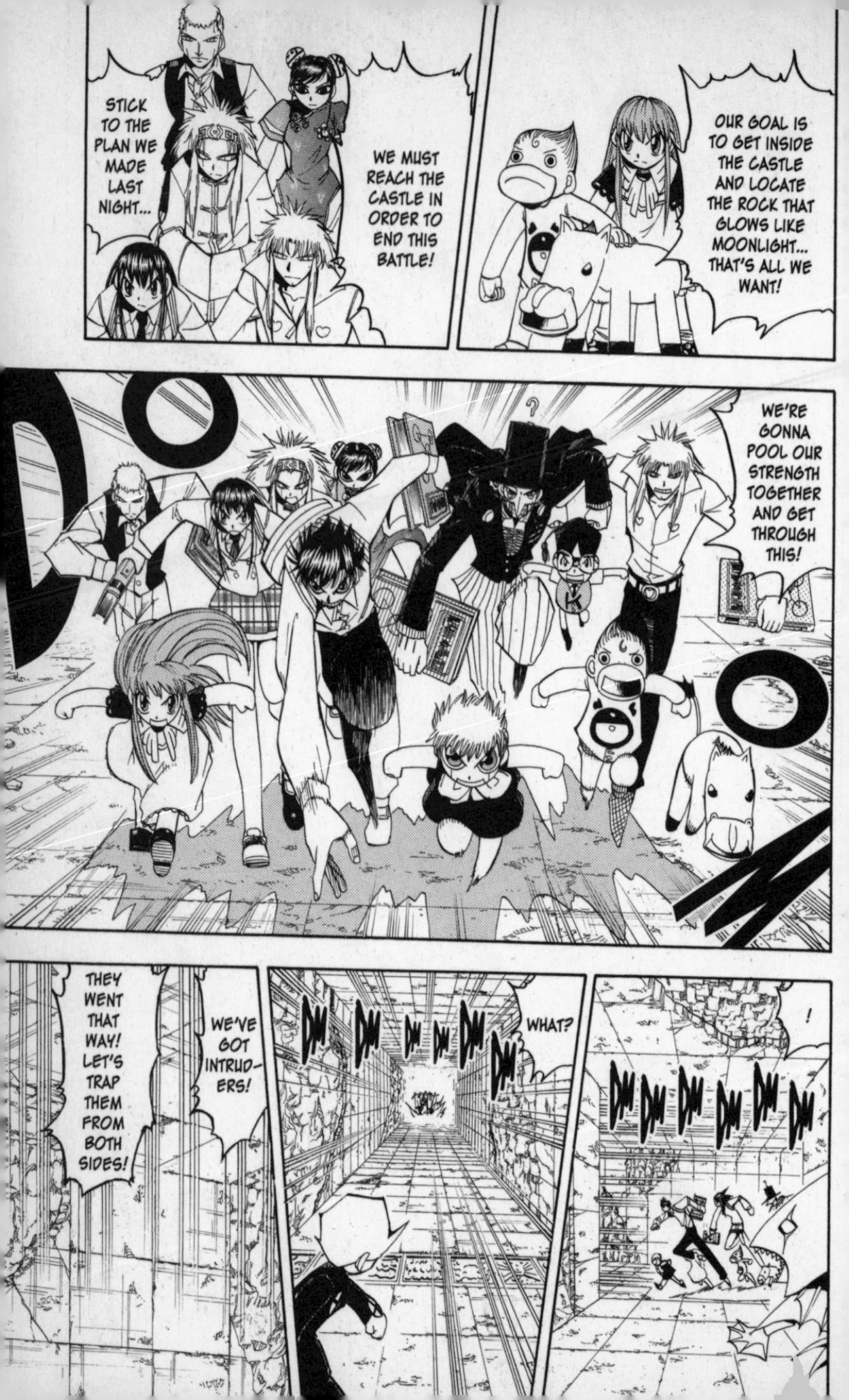
OUR GOAL IS TO GET INSIDE THE CASTLE AND LOCATE THE ROCK THAT GLOWS LIKE MOONLIGHT... THAT'S ALL WE WANT!
WE MUST REACH THE CASTLE IN ORDER TO END THIS BATTLE!
STICK TO THE PLAN WE MADE LAST NIGHT...
WE'RE GONNA POOL OUR STRENGTH TOGETHER AND GET THROUGH THIS!
?
DOOM
!
DM DM DM DM DM DM
WHAT?
DM DM DM DM DM DM
WE'VE GOT INTRUDERS!
THEY WENT THAT WAY! LET'S TRAP THEM FROM BOTH SIDES!

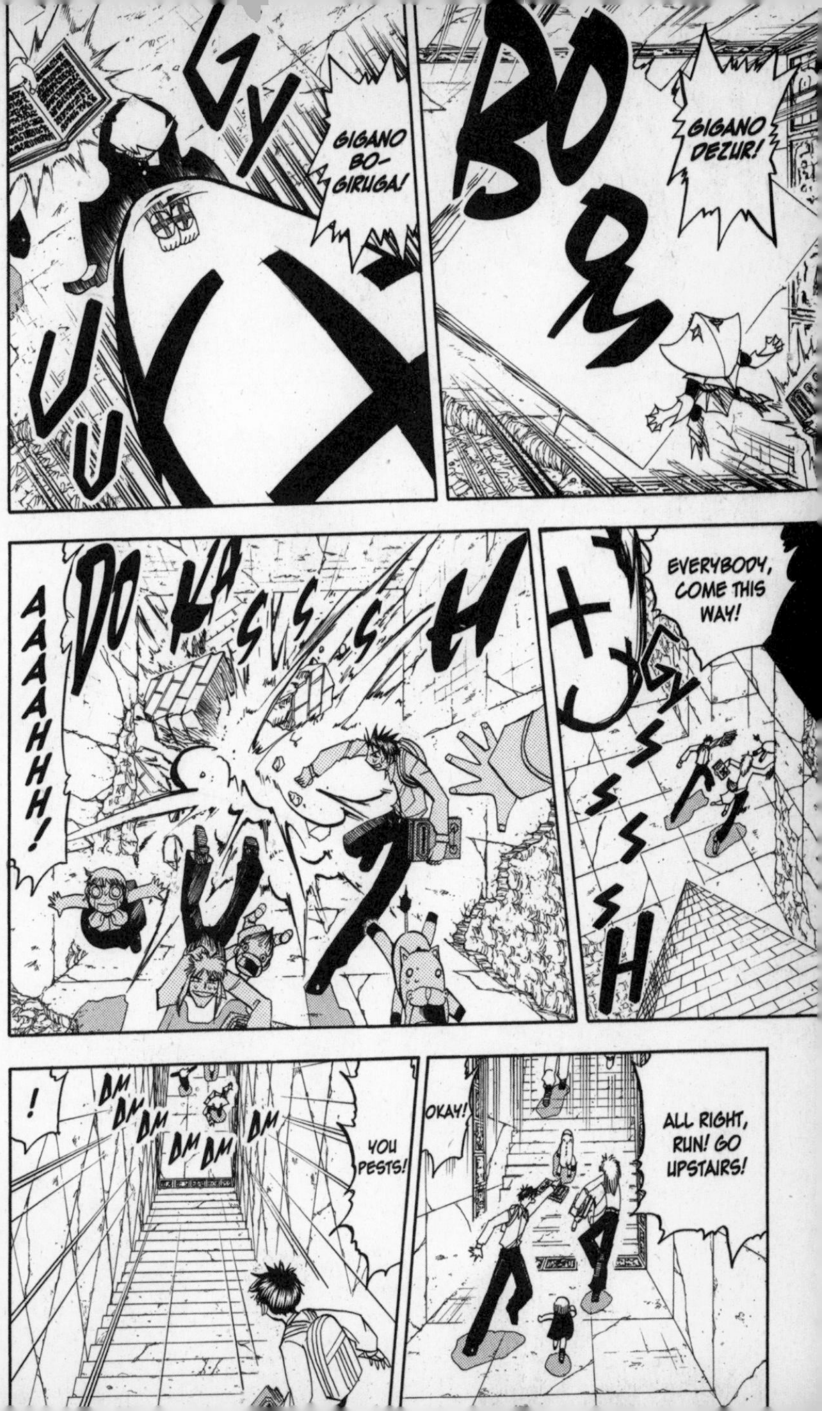
BOOM
GIGANO DEZUR!
GIGANO BO-GIRUGA!
EVERYBODY, COME THIS WAY!
DOKASSSSH
AAAAAHHH!
ALL RIGHT, RUN! GO UPSTAIRS!
OKAY!
YOU PESTS!
!
DM DM DM DM DM DM

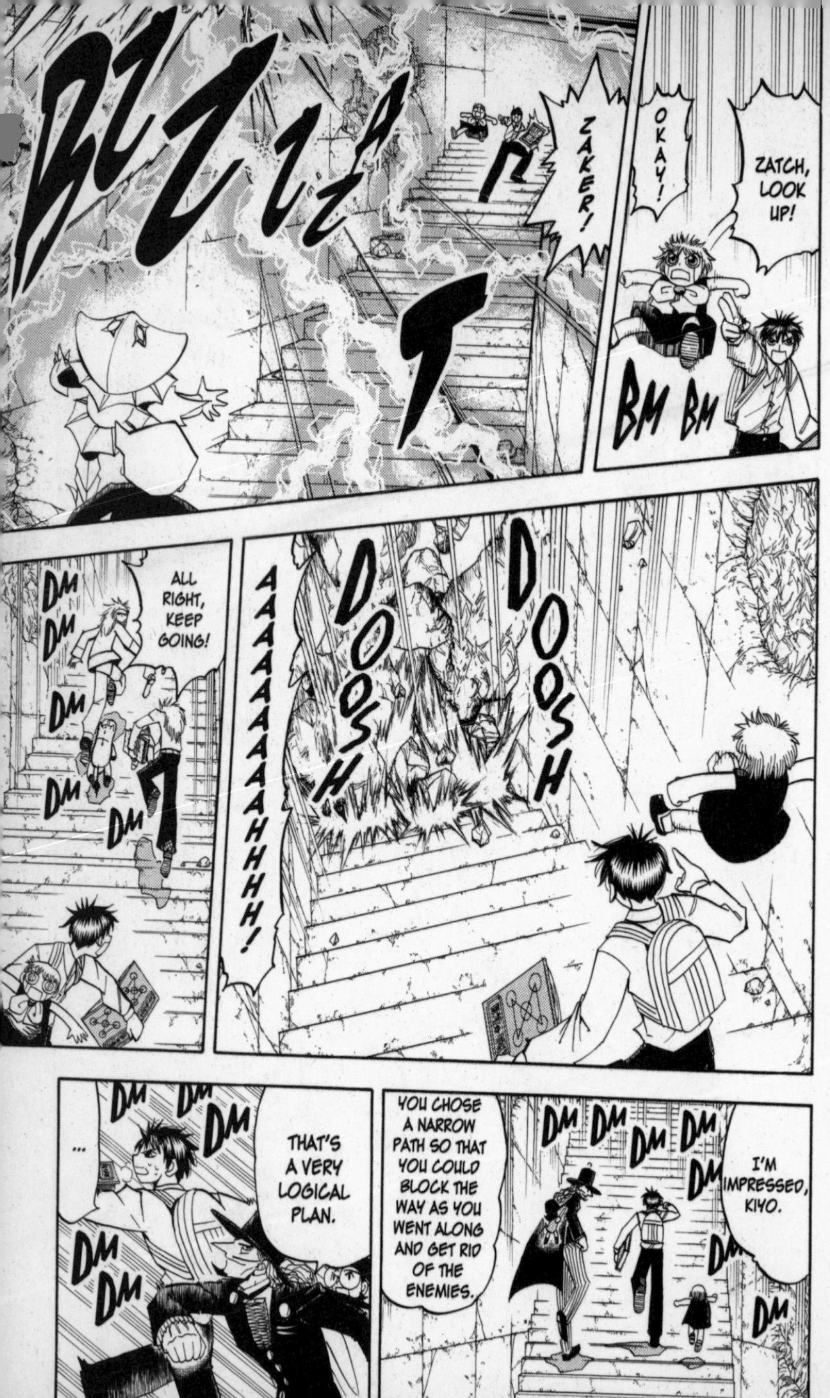
ZATCH, LOOK UP!
OKAY!
BM BM
ZAKER!
DOOSH
DOOSH
AAAAAAAAAAHHHHHH!
ALL RIGHT, KEEP GOING!
DM DM DM DM DM
DM DM DM DM DM DM
I'M IMPRESSED, KIYO.
YOU CHOSE A NARROW PATH SO THAT YOU COULD BLOCK THE WAY AS YOU WENT ALONG AND GET RID OF THE ENEMIES.
DM DM DM
THAT'S A VERY LOGICAL PLAN.
...

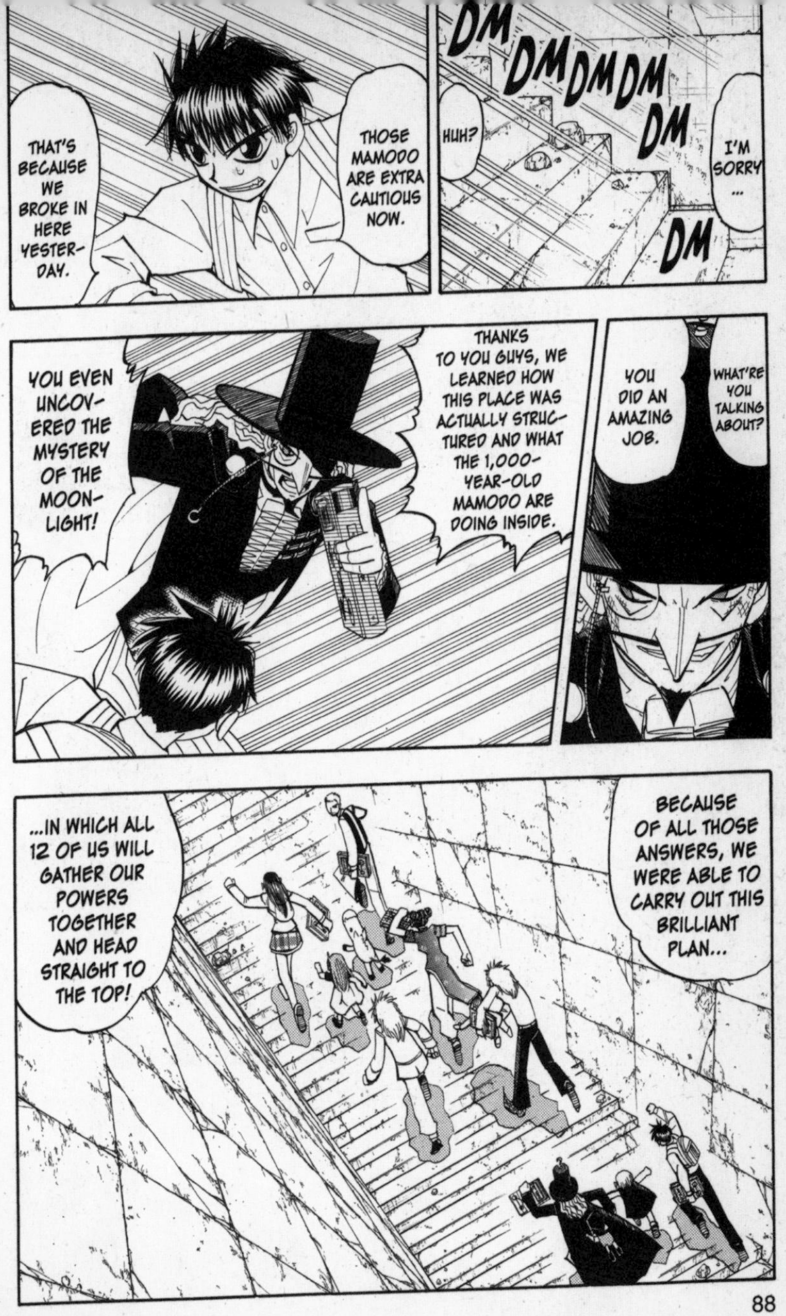
I'M SORRY ...
DM DM DM DM DM DM DM
HUH?
THOSE MAMODO ARE EXTRA CAUTIOUS NOW.
THAT'S BECAUSE WE BROKE IN HERE YESTERDAY.
WHAT'RE YOU TALKING ABOUT?
YOU DID AN AMAZING JOB.
THANKS TO YOU GUYS, WE LEARNED HOW THIS PLACE WAS ACTUALLY STRUCTURED AND WHAT THE 1,000-YEAR-OLD MAMODO ARE DOING INSIDE.
YOU EVEN UNCOVERED THE MYSTERY OF THE MOONLIGHT!
BECAUSE OF ALL THOSE ANSWERS, WE WERE ABLE TO CARRY OUT THIS BRILLIANT PLAN...
...IN WHICH ALL 12 OF US WILL GATHER OUR POWERS TOGETHER AND HEAD STRAIGHT TO THE TOP!

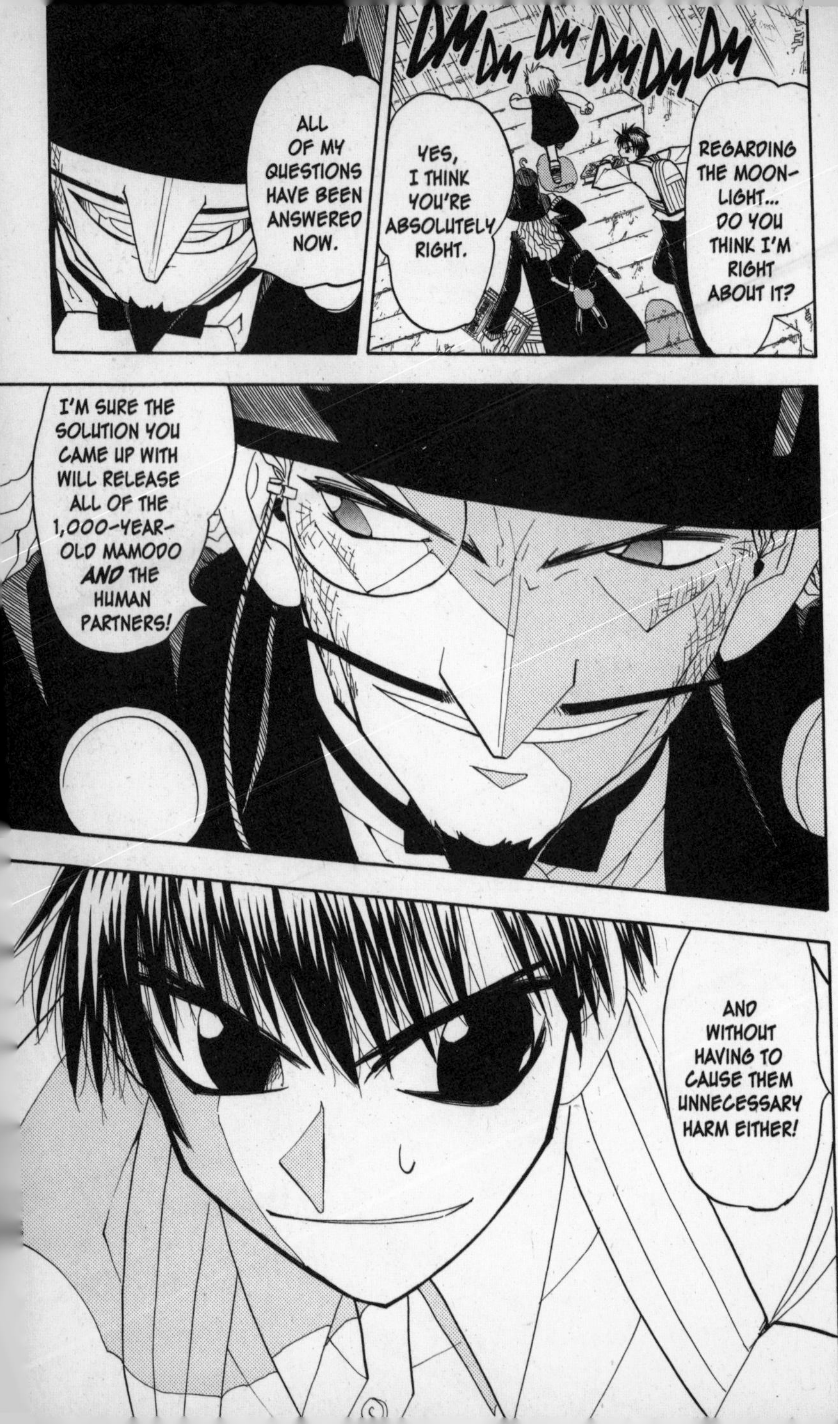
DM DM DM DM DM DM
REGARDING THE MOON-LIGHT... DO YOU THINK I'M RIGHT ABOUT IT?
YES, I THINK YOU'RE ABSOLUTELY RIGHT.
ALL OF MY QUESTIONS HAVE BEEN ANSWERED NOW.
I'M SURE THE SOLUTION YOU CAME UP WITH WILL RELEASE ALL OF THE 1,000-YEAR-OLD MAMODO AND THE HUMAN PARTNERS!
AND WITHOUT HAVING TO CAUSE THEM UNNECESSARY HARM EITHER!

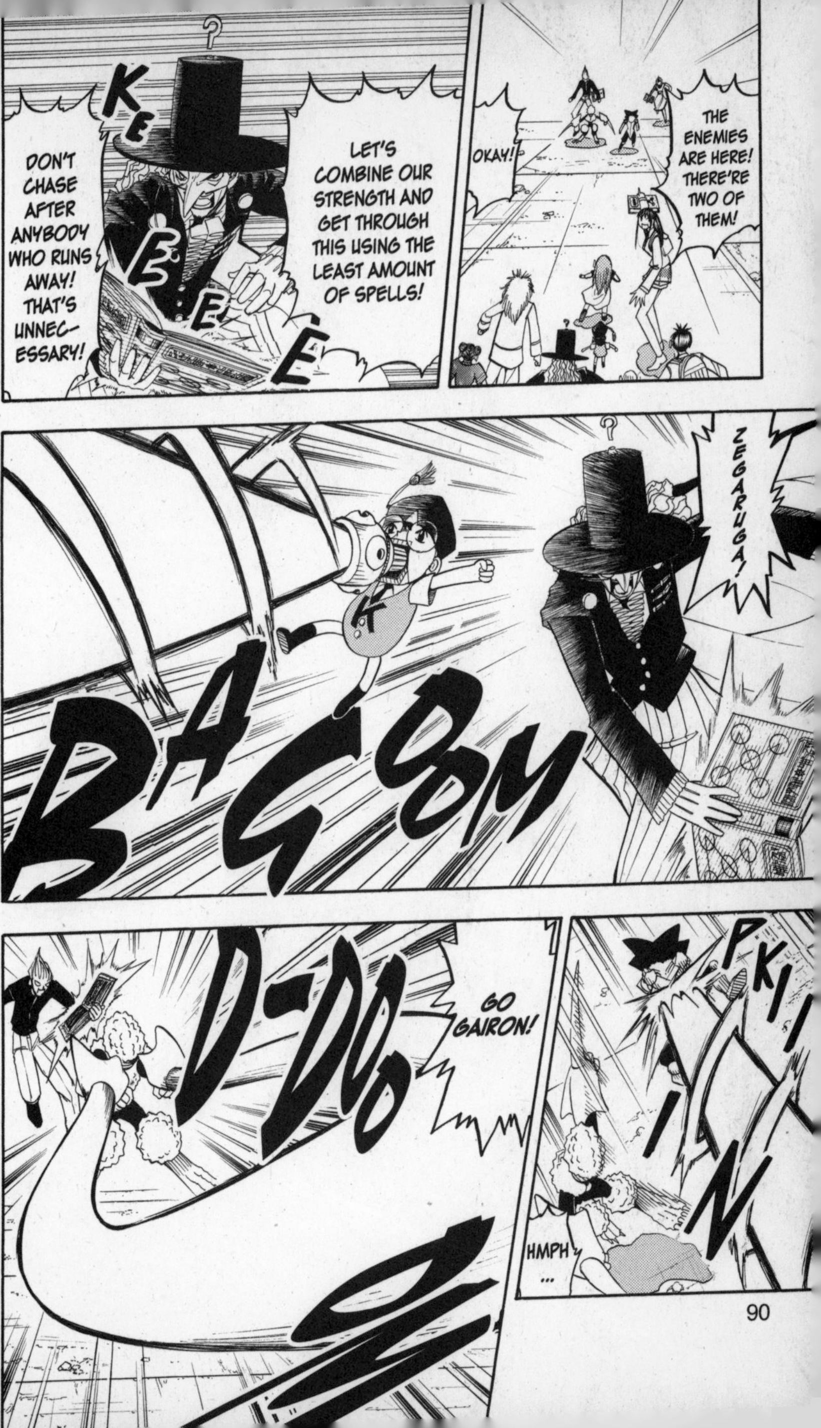
THE ENEMIES ARE HERE! THERE'RE TWO OF THEM!
OKAY!
LET'S COMBINE OUR STRENGTH AND GET THROUGH THIS USING THE LEAST AMOUNT OF SPELLS!
DON'T CHASE AFTER ANYBODY WHO RUNS AWAY! THAT'S UNNECESSARY!
KEEEEE
?
ZEGARUGA!
BAGOOM
PKIIIN
HMPH...
GO GAIRON!
D-DOOOM

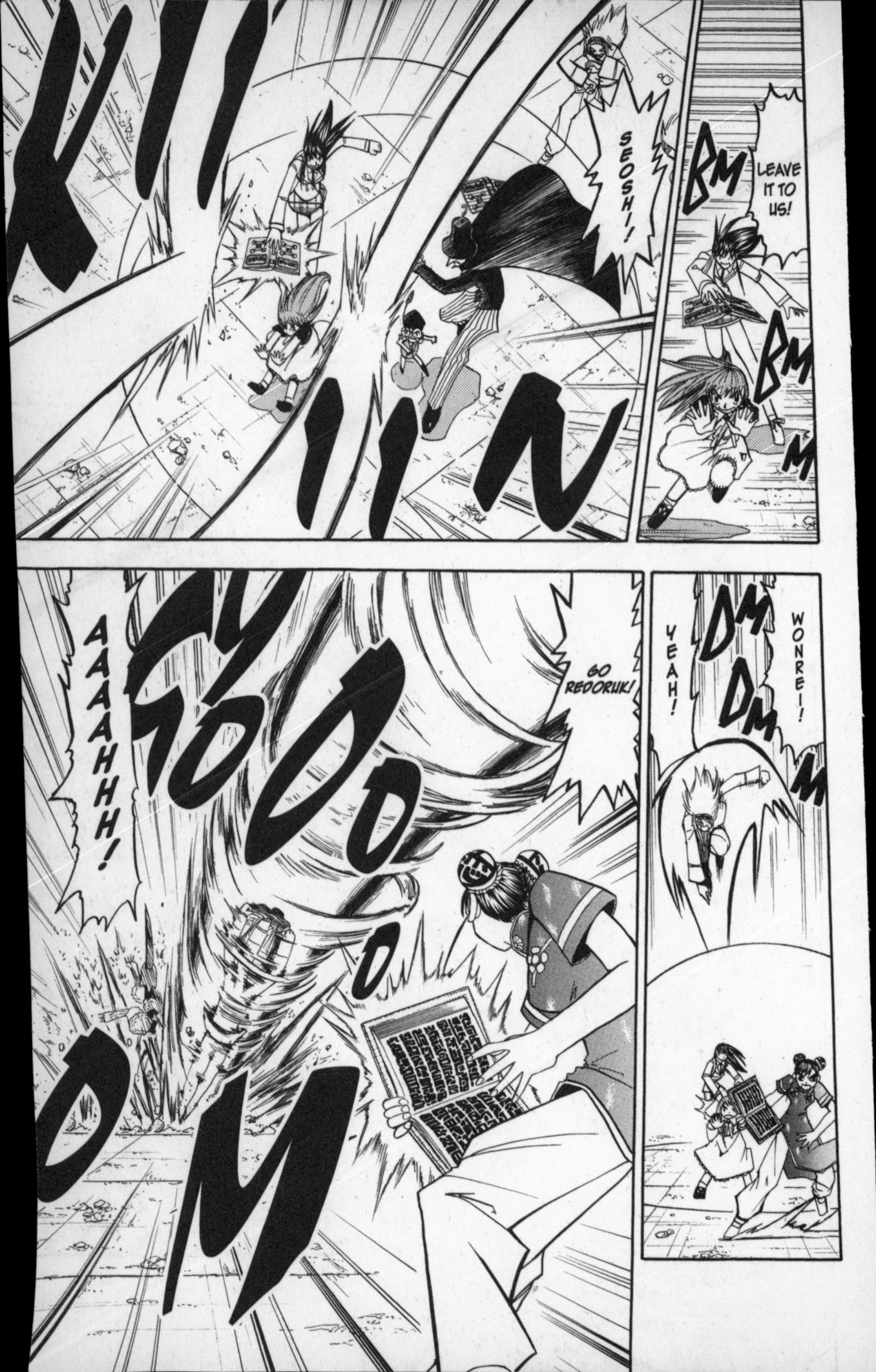
BM
LEAVE IT TO US!
BM BMM
SEOSHI!
DM
WONREI!
YEAH!
DMM
GO REDORUK!
AAAAHHH!

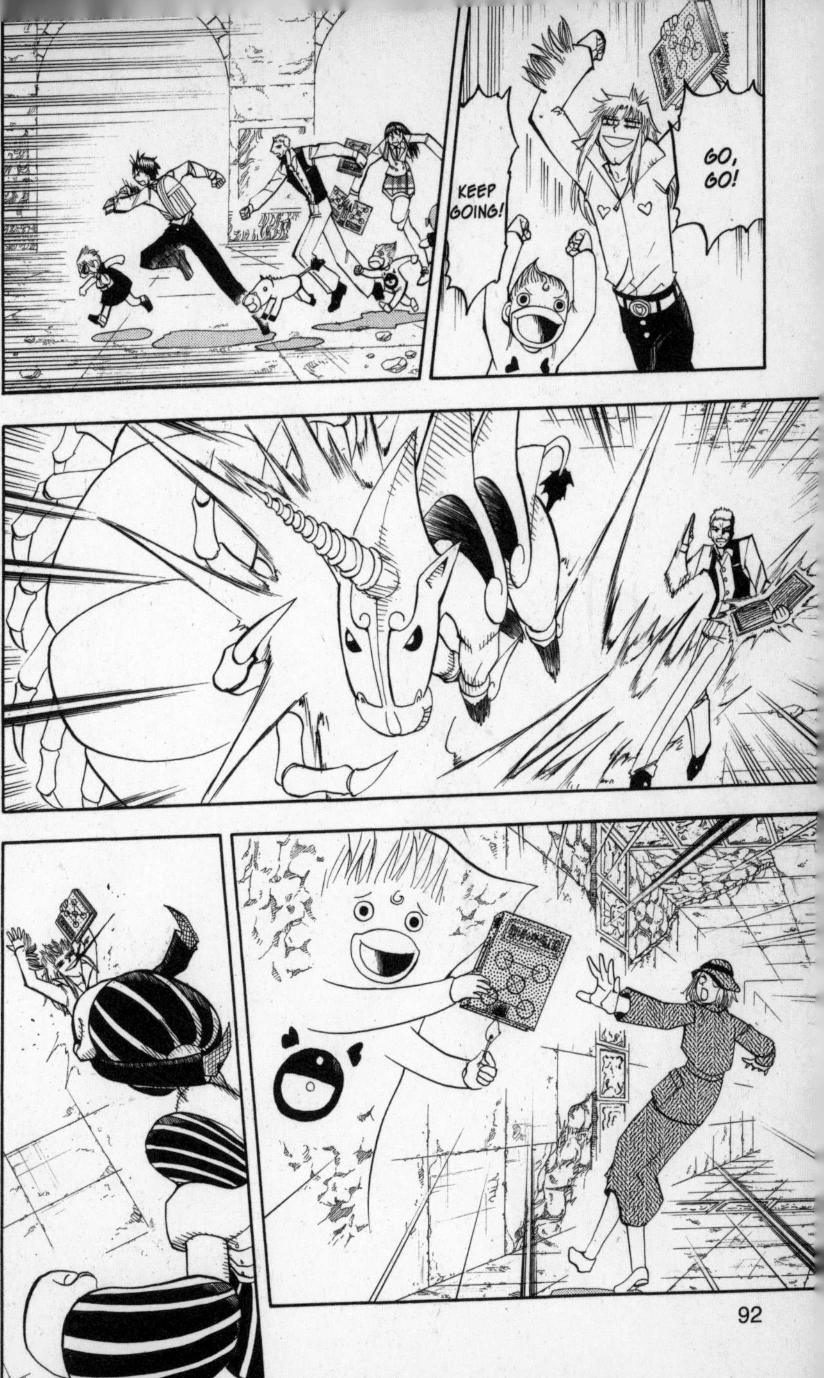
GO, GO!
KEEP GOING!

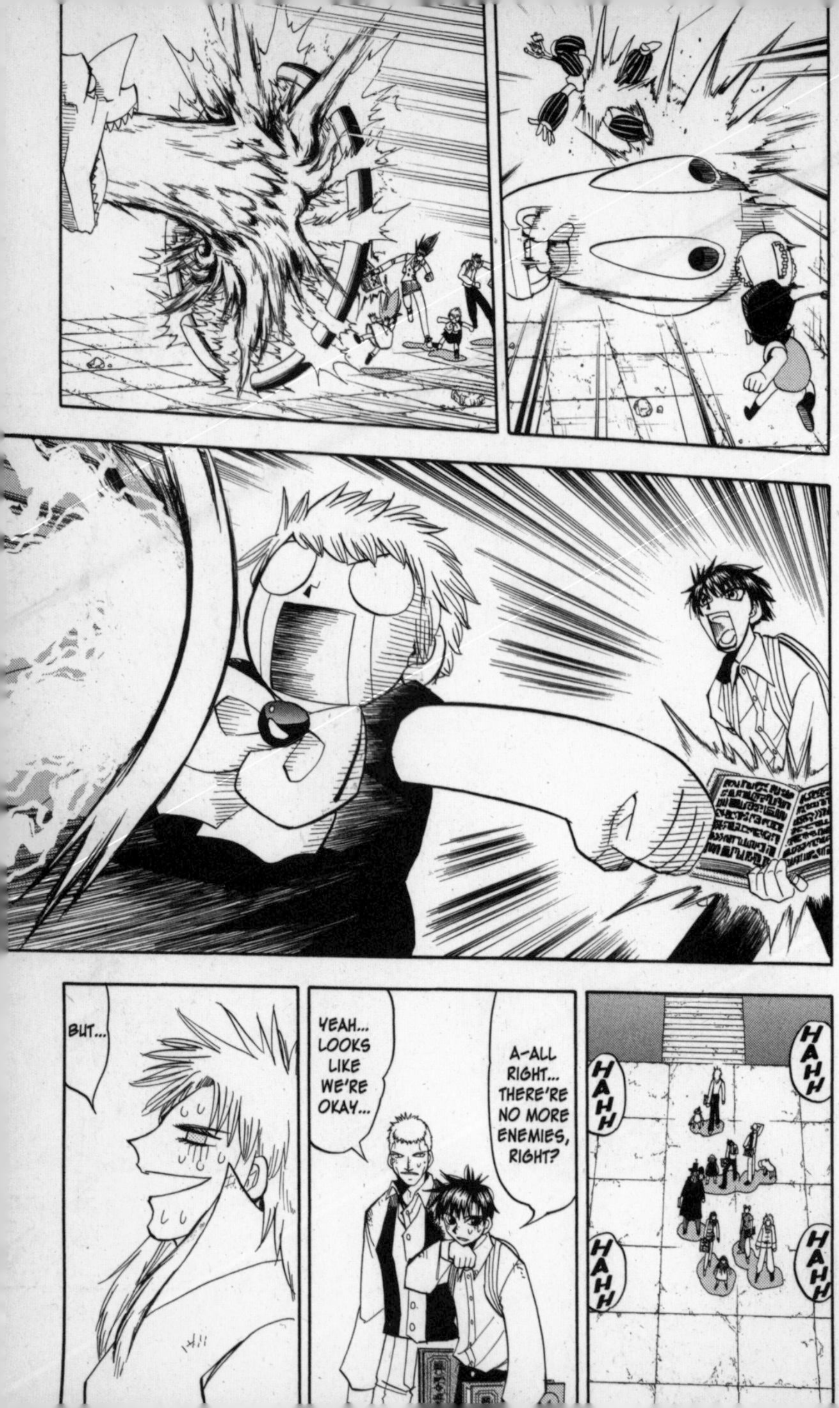
HAHH
HAHH
HAHH
HAHH
A-ALL RIGHT... THERE'RE NO MORE ENEMIES, RIGHT?
YEAH... LOOKS LIKE WE'RE OKAY...
BUT...

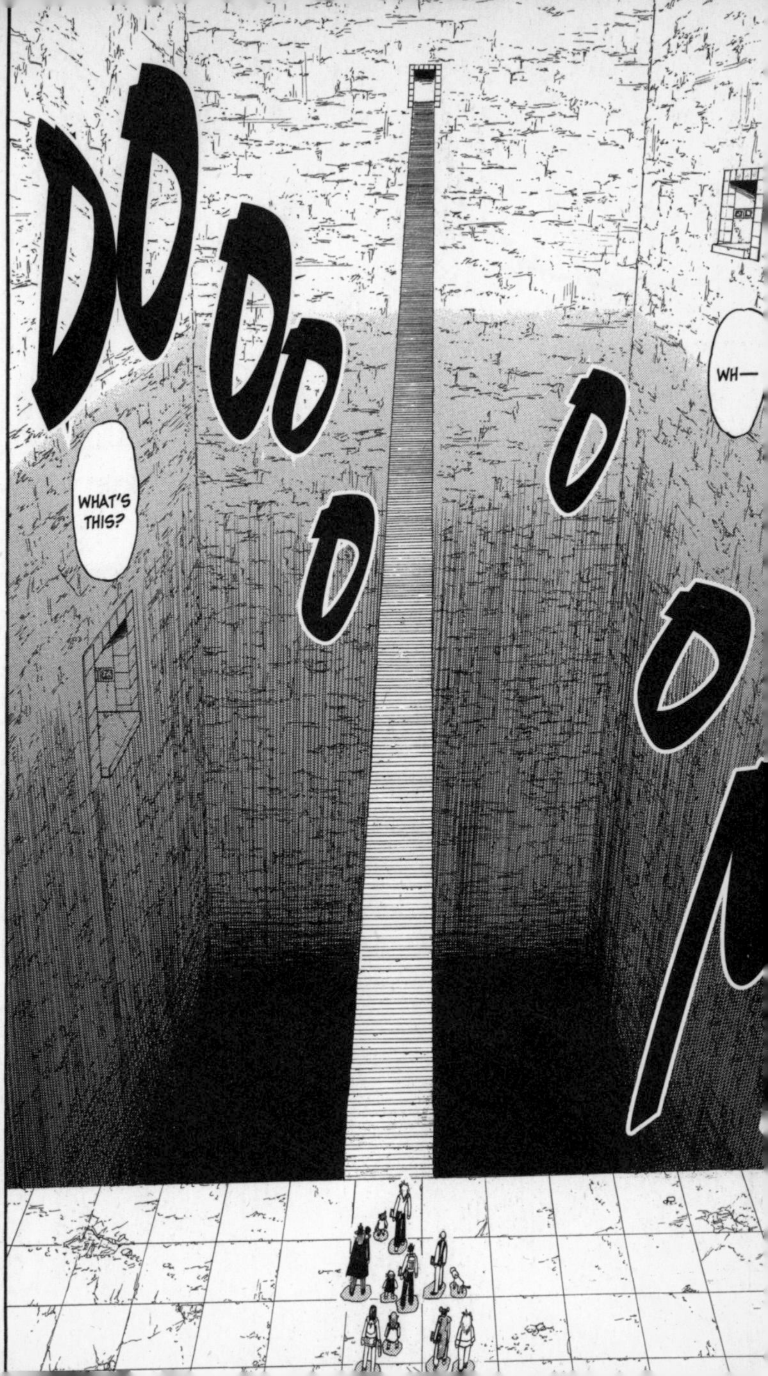
WH—
WHAT'S THIS?

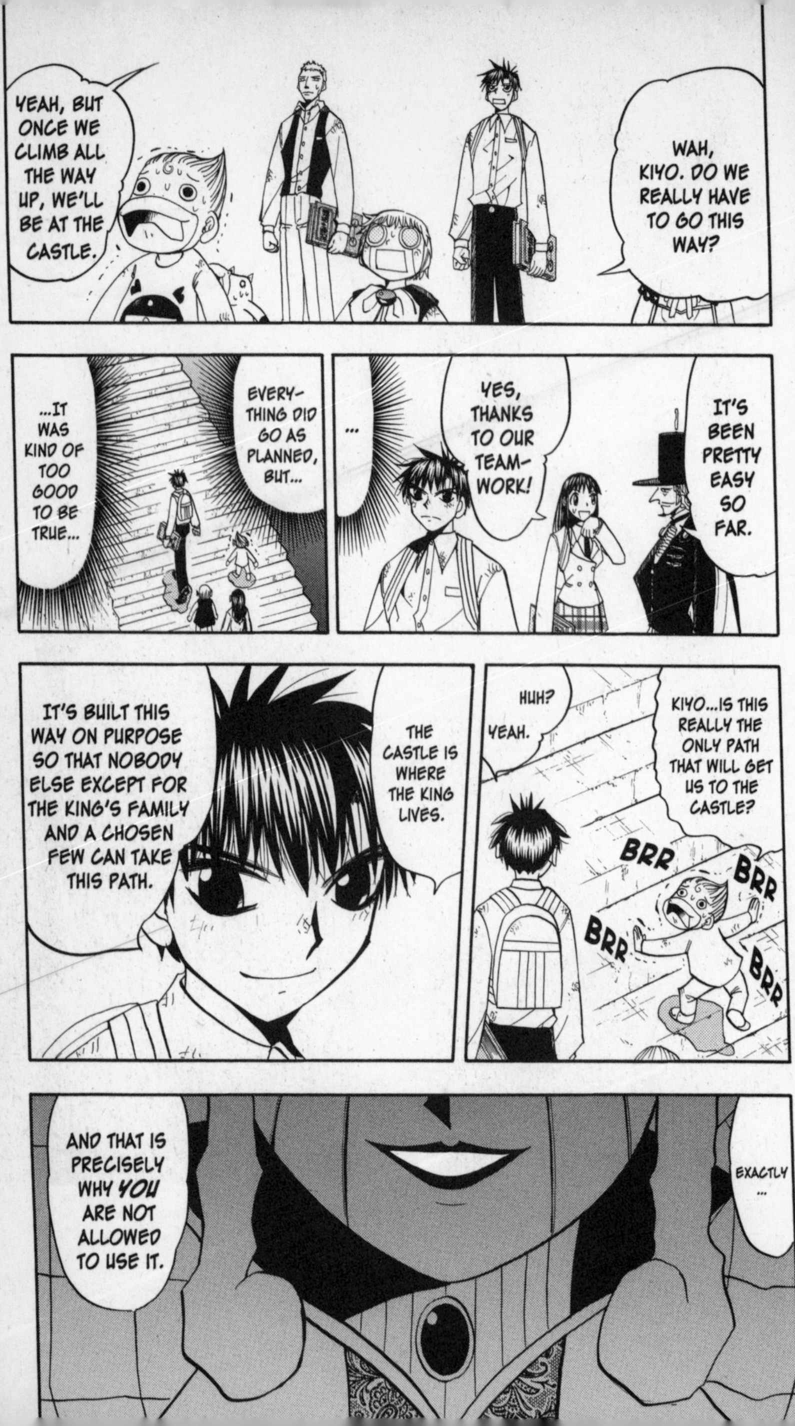
WAH, KIYO. DO WE REALLY HAVE TO GO THIS WAY?
YEAH, BUT ONCE WE CLIMB ALL THE WAY UP, WE'LL BE AT THE CASTLE.
IT'S BEEN PRETTY EASY SO FAR.
YES, THANKS TO OUR TEAM-WORK!
...
EVERY-THING DID GO AS PLANNED, BUT...
...IT WAS KIND OF TOO GOOD TO BE TRUE...
KIYO...IS THIS REALLY THE ONLY PATH THAT WILL GET US TO THE CASTLE?
HUH? YEAH.
BRR BRR BRR BRR
THE CASTLE IS WHERE THE KING LIVES.
IT'S BUILT THIS WAY ON PURPOSE SO THAT NOBODY ELSE EXCEPT FOR THE KING'S FAMILY AND A CHOSEN FEW CAN TAKE THIS PATH.
EXACTLY ...
AND THAT IS PRECISELY WHY *YOU* ARE NOT ALLOWED TO USE IT.

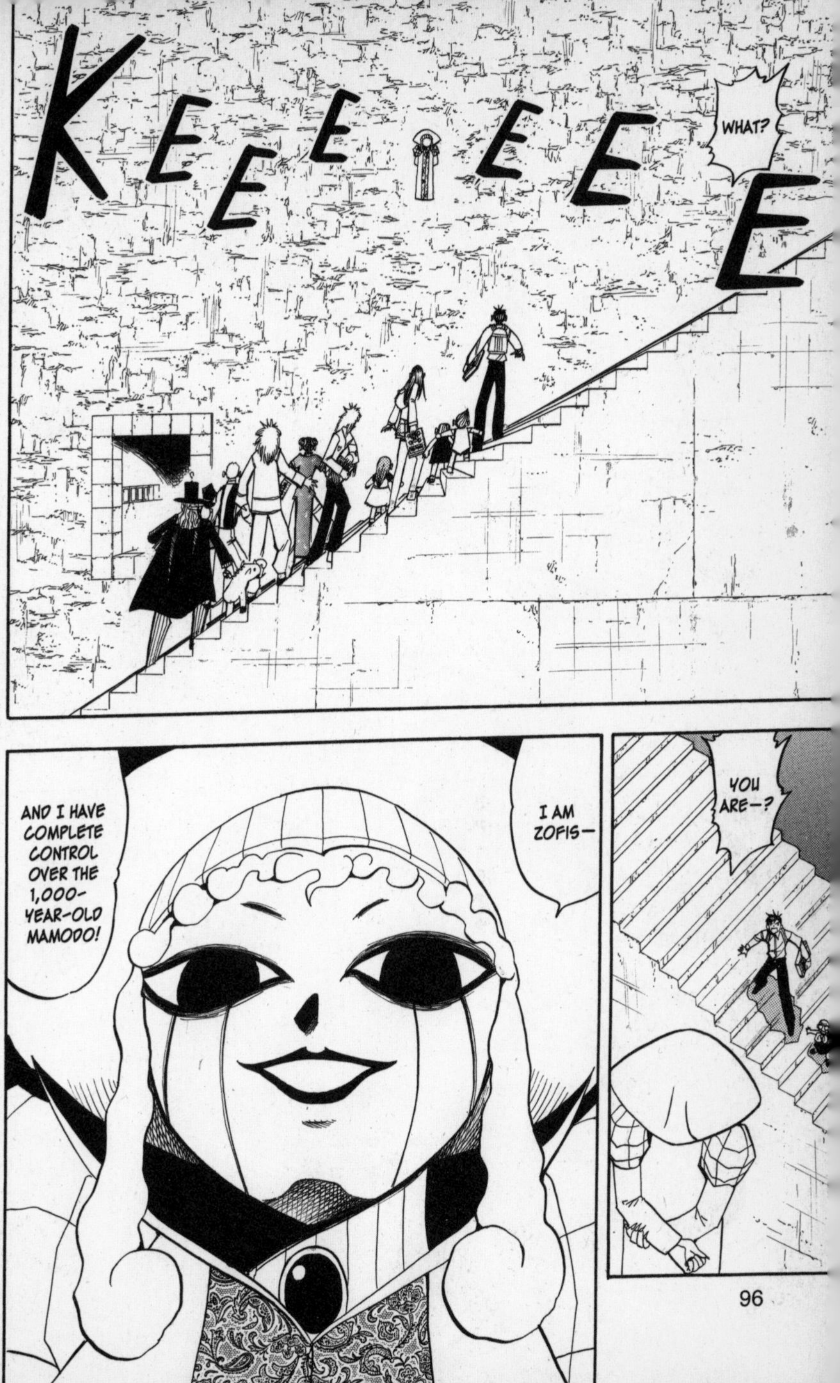
KEEEEEEE
WHAT?
YOU ARE—?
I AM ZOFIS—
AND I HAVE COMPLETE CONTROL OVER THE 1,000-YEAR-OLD MAMODO!

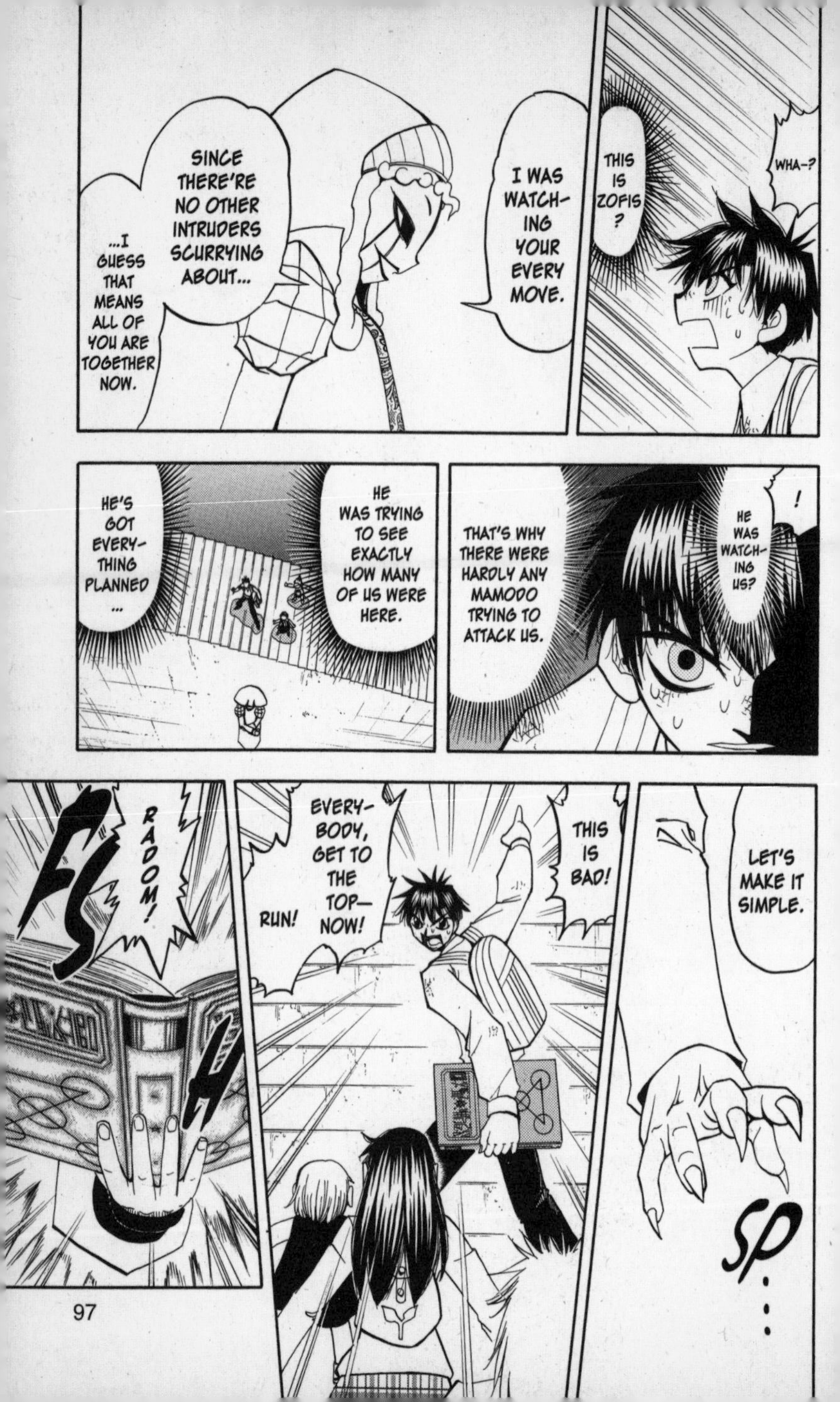
WHA-?
THIS IS ZOFIS?
I WAS WATCHING YOUR EVERY MOVE.
SINCE THERE'RE NO OTHER INTRUDERS SCURRYING ABOUT...
...I GUESS THAT MEANS ALL OF YOU ARE TOGETHER NOW.
!
HE WAS WATCHING US?
THAT'S WHY THERE WERE HARDLY ANY MAMODO TRYING TO ATTACK US.
HE WAS TRYING TO SEE EXACTLY HOW MANY OF US WERE HERE.
HE'S GOT EVERYTHING PLANNED ...
LET'S MAKE IT SIMPLE.
SP...
THIS IS BAD!
EVERYBODY, GET TO THE TOP— NOW!
RUN!
RADOM!
FSH

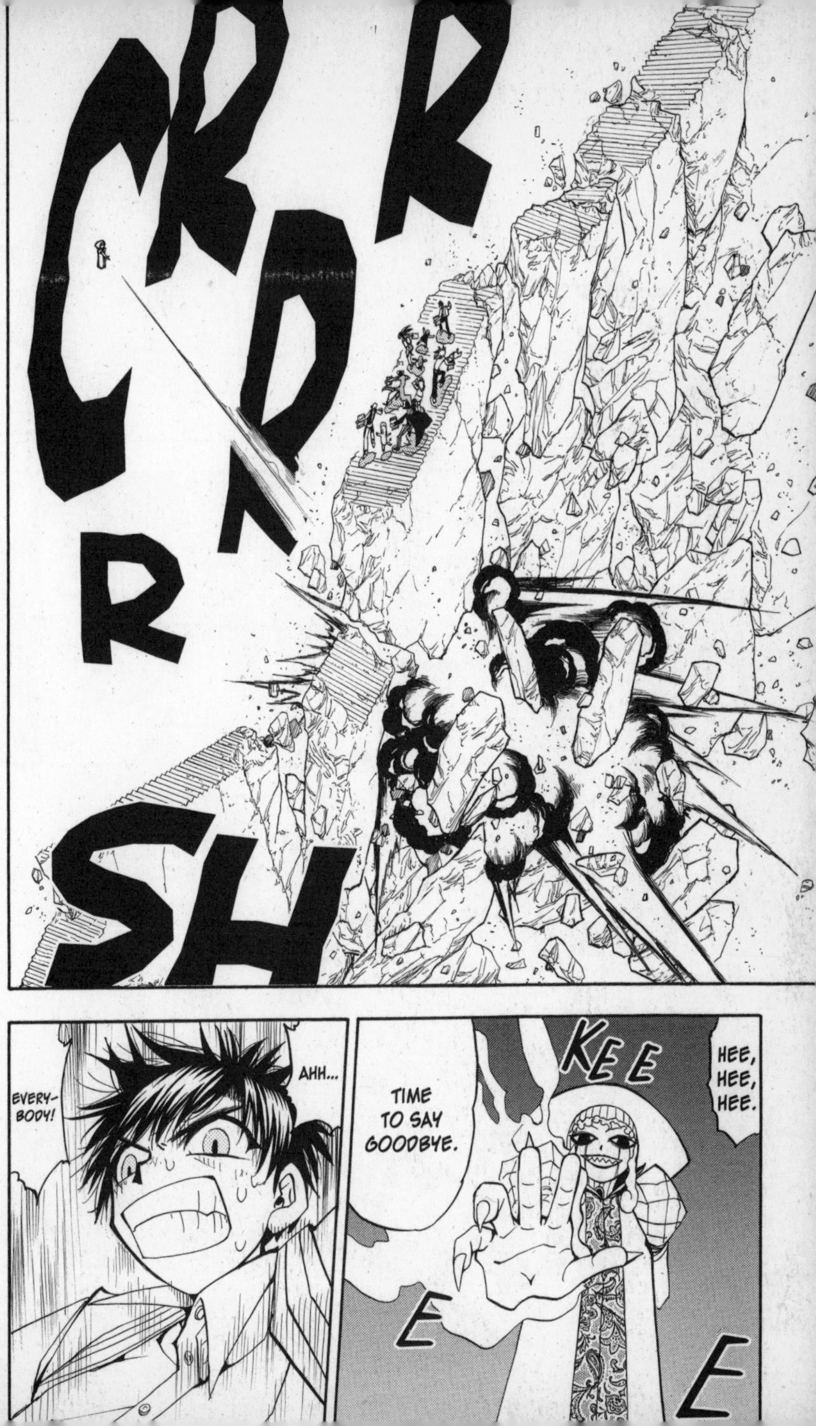
CRRRRSH
HEE, HEE, HEE.
KEE
TIME TO SAY GOODBYE.
E
E
AHH...
EVERY-BODY!

LEVEL 129: Emergency

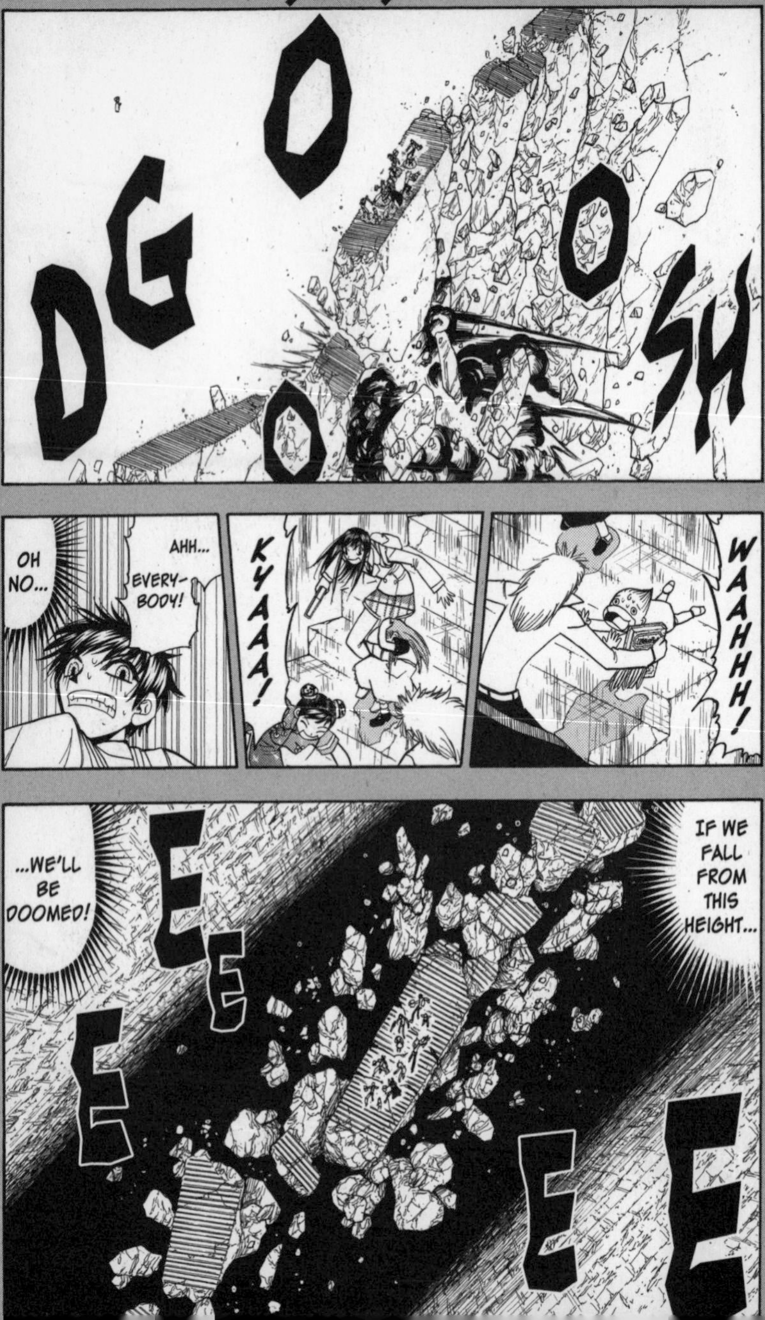
DGOOOSH
WAAAHHH!
KYAAAA!
AHH... EVERY-BODY!
OH NO...
IF WE FALL FROM THIS HEIGHT...
...WE'LL BE DOOMED!
EEEEE

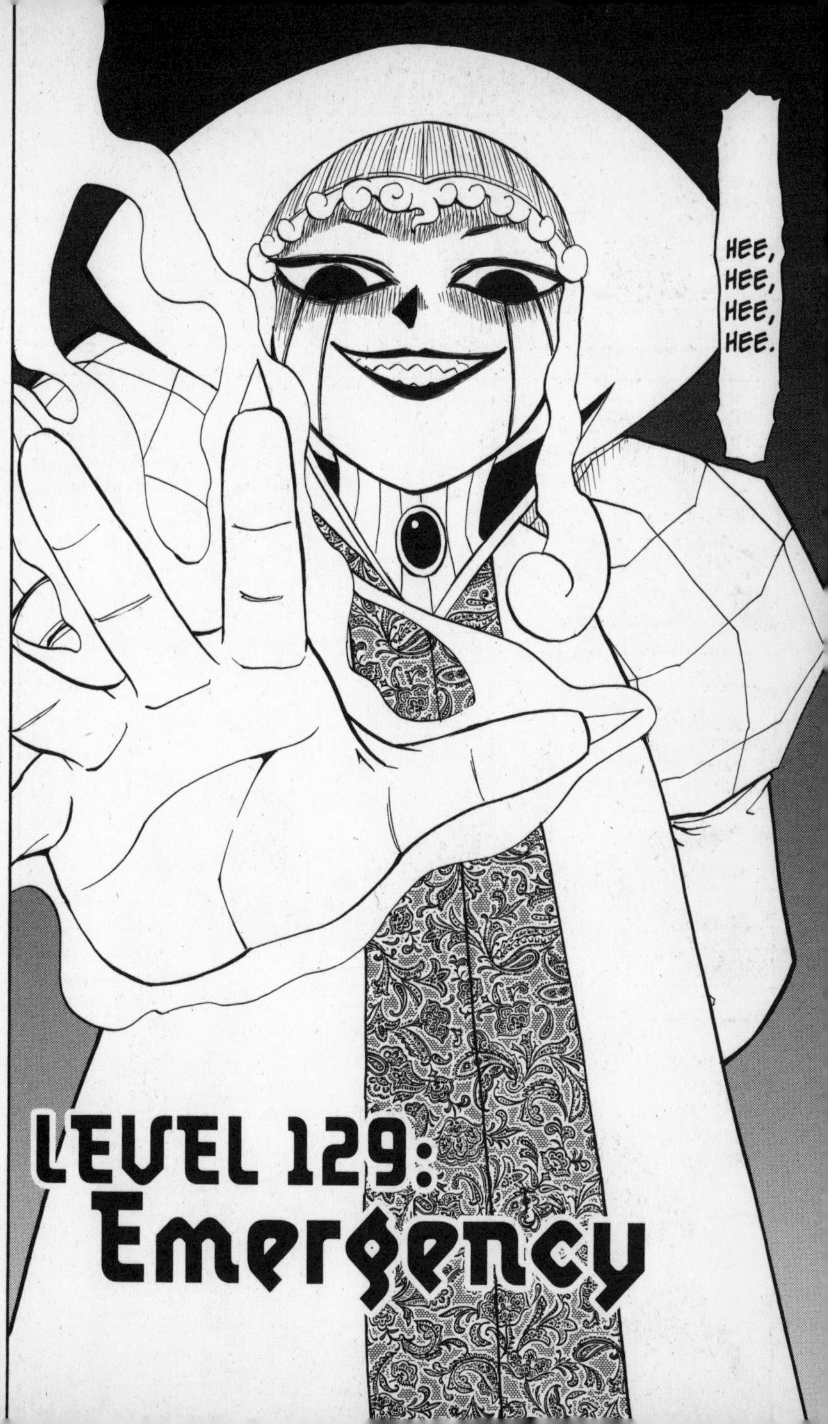
HEE, HEE, HEE, HEE.
LEVEL 129: Emergency

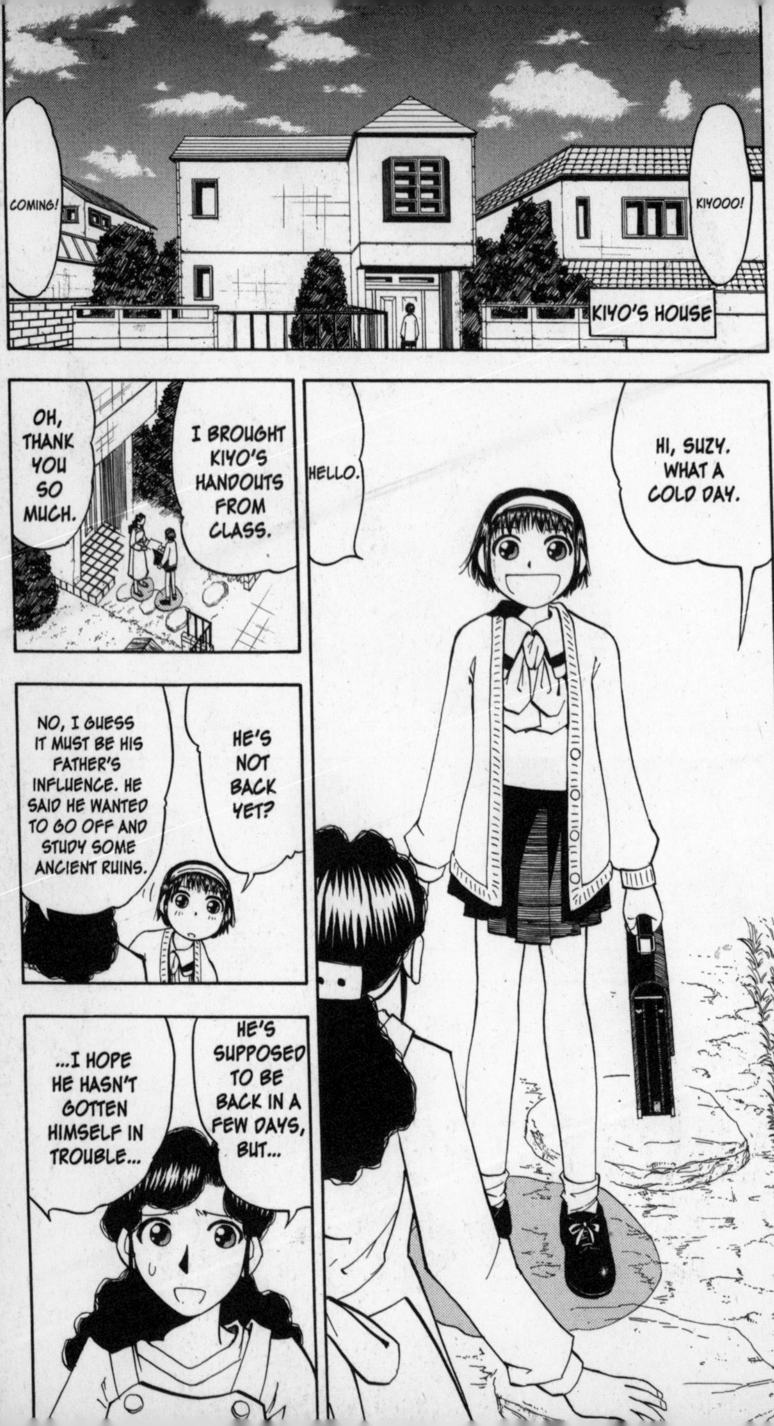
KIYOOO!
COMING!
KIYO'S HOUSE
HI, SUZY. WHAT A COLD DAY.
HELLO.
I BROUGHT KIYO'S HANDOUTS FROM CLASS.
OH, THANK YOU SO MUCH.
HE'S NOT BACK YET?
NO, I GUESS IT MUST BE HIS FATHER'S INFLUENCE. HE SAID HE WANTED TO GO OFF AND STUDY SOME ANCIENT RUINS.
HE'S SUPPOSED TO BE BACK IN A FEW DAYS, BUT...
...I HOPE HE HASN'T GOTTEN HIMSELF IN TROUBLE...

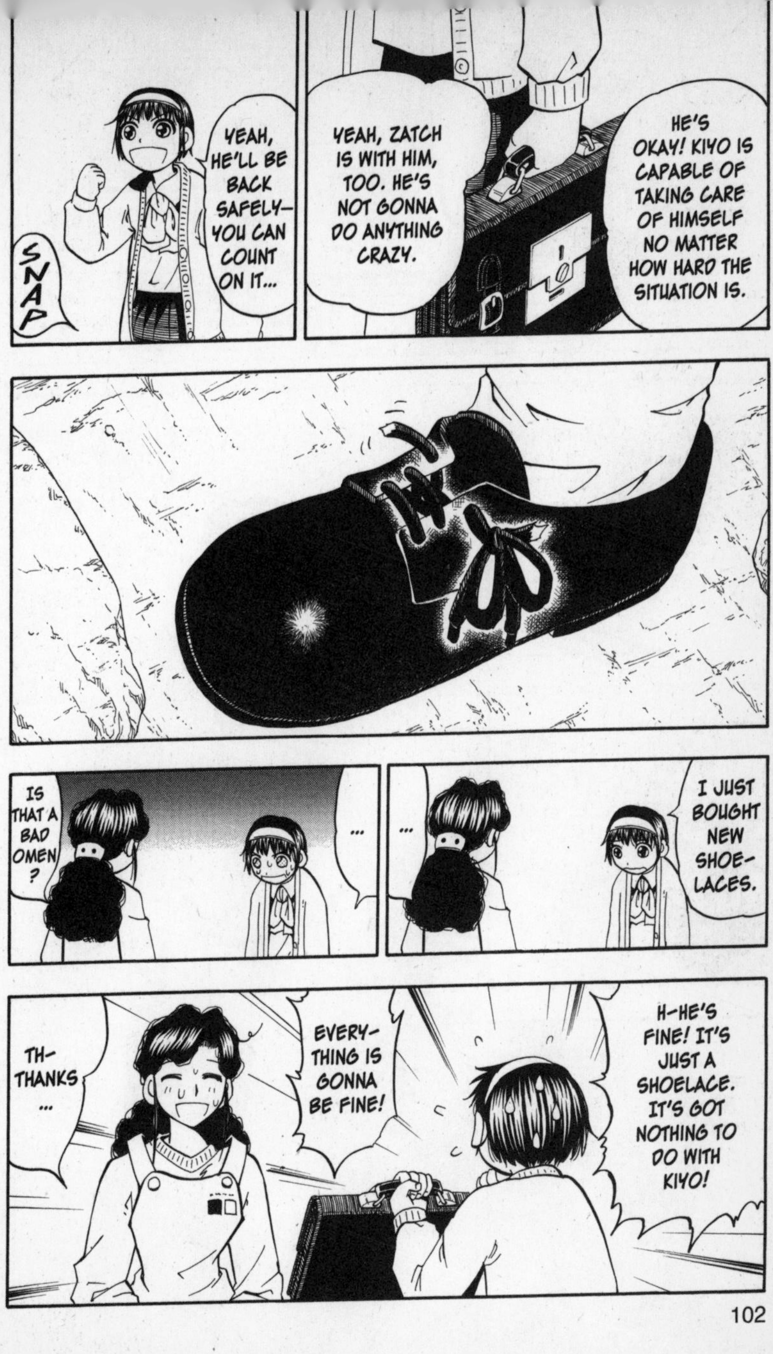
HE'S OKAY! KIYO IS CAPABLE OF TAKING CARE OF HIMSELF NO MATTER HOW HARD THE SITUATION IS.
YEAH, ZATCH IS WITH HIM, TOO. HE'S NOT GONNA DO ANYTHING CRAZY.
YEAH, HE'LL BE BACK SAFELY-YOU CAN COUNT ON IT...
SNAP
I JUST BOUGHT NEW SHOE-LACES.
...
...
IS THAT A BAD OMEN?
H-HE'S FINE! IT'S JUST A SHOELACE. IT'S GOT NOTHING TO DO WITH KIYO!
EVERY-THING IS GONNA BE FINE!
TH-THANKS ...

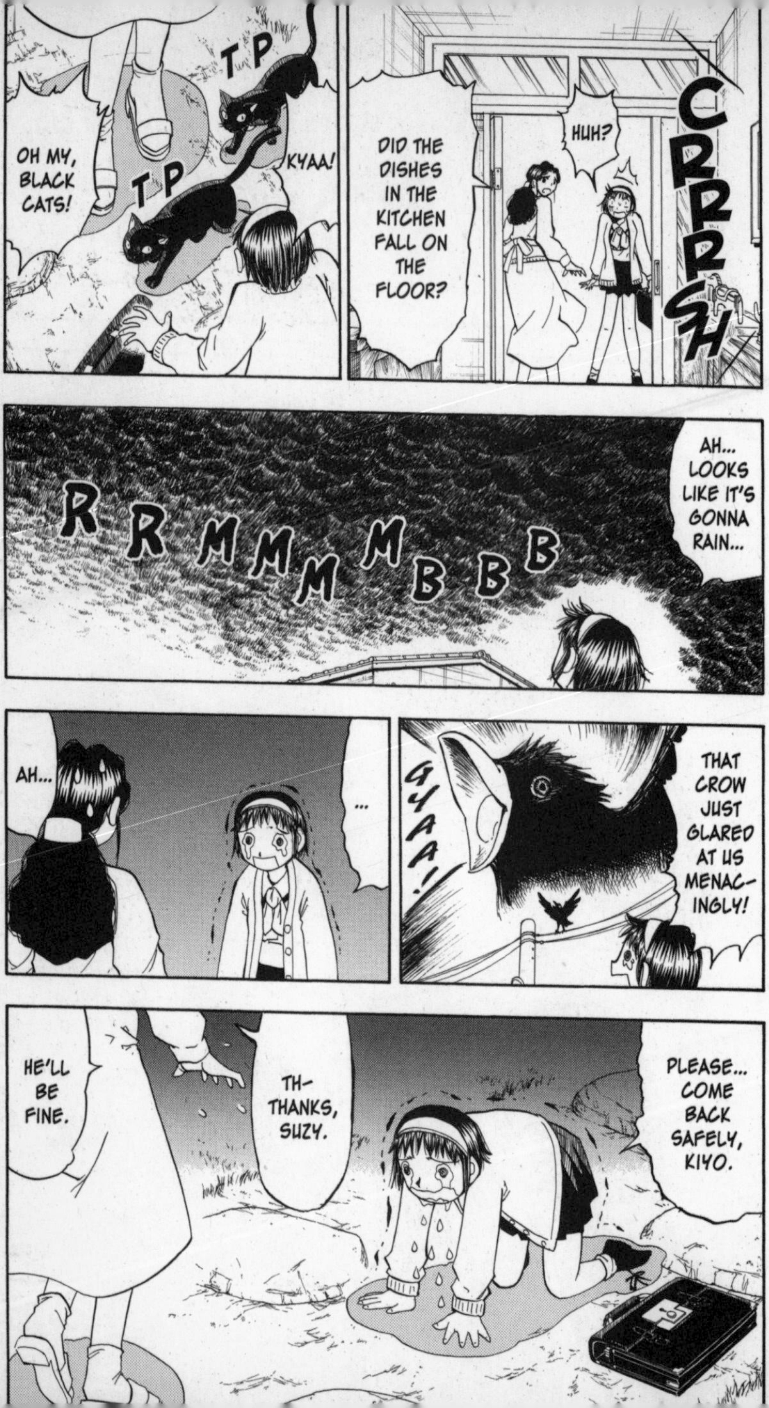
CRRRSH
HUH?
DID THE DISHES IN THE KITCHEN FALL ON THE FLOOR?
TP
KYAA!
TP
OH MY, BLACK CATS!
AH... LOOKS LIKE IT'S GONNA RAIN...
RRMMMMBBB
THAT CROW JUST GLARED AT US MENAC-INGLY!
GYAAA!!
...
AH...
PLEASE... COME BACK SAFELY, KIYO.
TH-THANKS, SUZY.
HE'LL BE FINE.

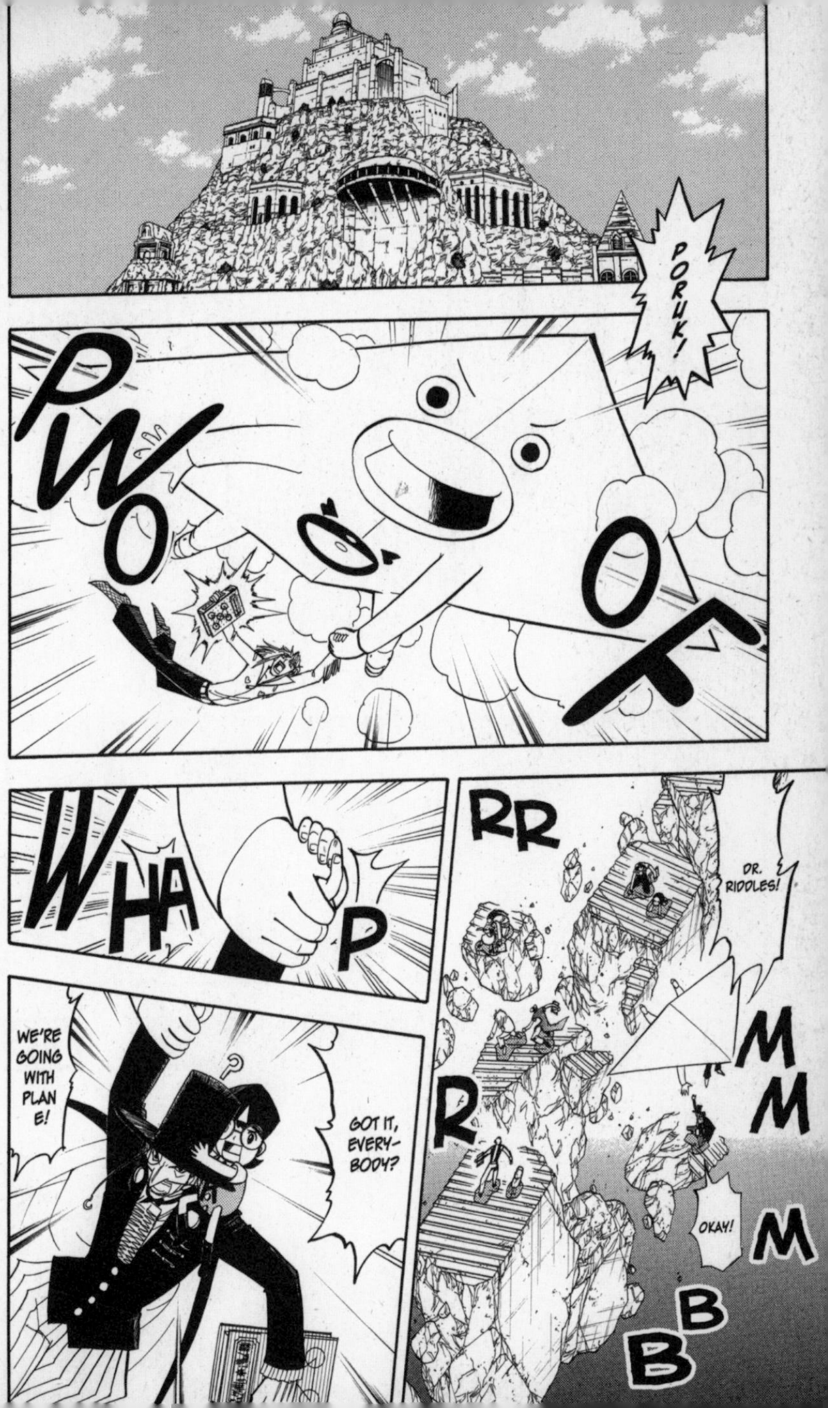
PORUK!
PWOOF
DR. RIDDLES!
RR
MMM
R
OKAY!
BB
WHAP
WE'RE GOING WITH PLAN E!
GOT IT, EVERY-BODY?

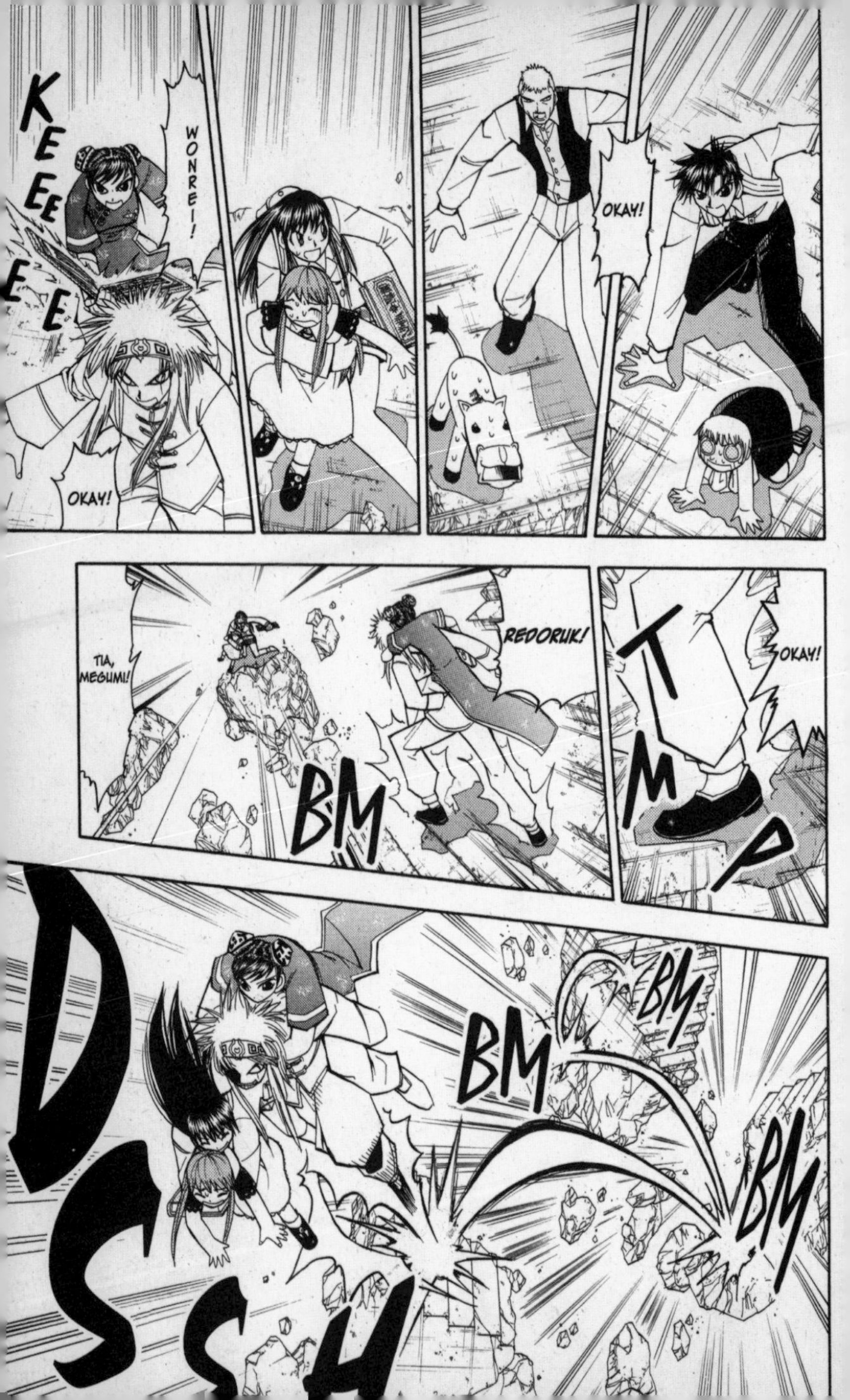
OKAY!
WONREI!
KEEEEE
OKAY!
OKAY!
TMP
REDORUK!
TIA, MEGUMI!
BM
BM
BM
BM
DSSH

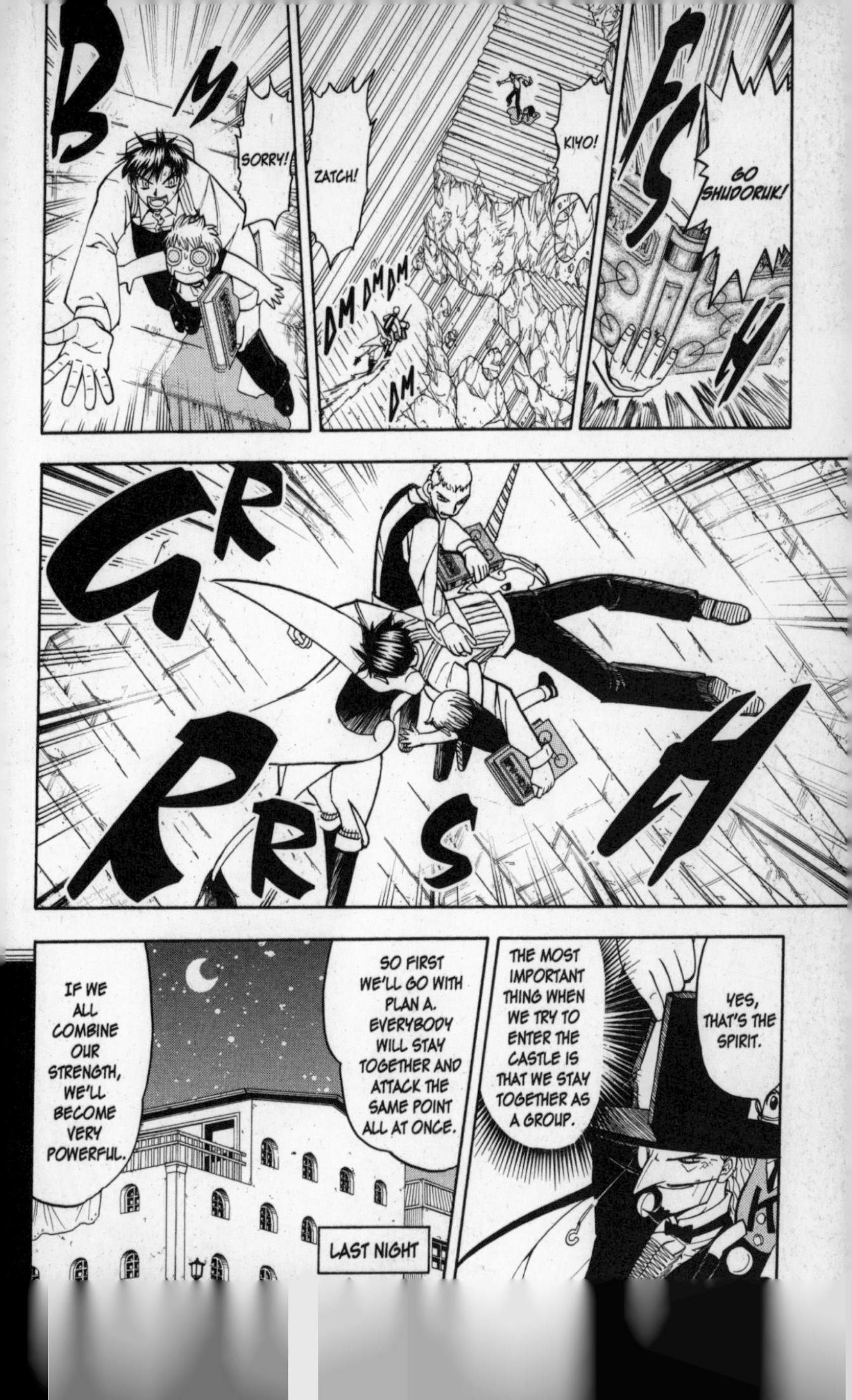
GO SHUDORUK!
FSSH
KIYO!
ZATCH!
DM DM DM DM
DM
BM
SORRY!
GRRRSH
YES, THAT'S THE SPIRIT.
THE MOST IMPORTANT THING WHEN WE TRY TO ENTER THE CASTLE IS THAT WE STAY TOGETHER AS A GROUP.
SO FIRST WE'LL GO WITH PLAN A. EVERYBODY WILL STAY TOGETHER AND ATTACK THE SAME POINT ALL AT ONCE.
IF WE ALL COMBINE OUR STRENGTH, WE'LL BECOME VERY POWERFUL.
LAST NIGHT

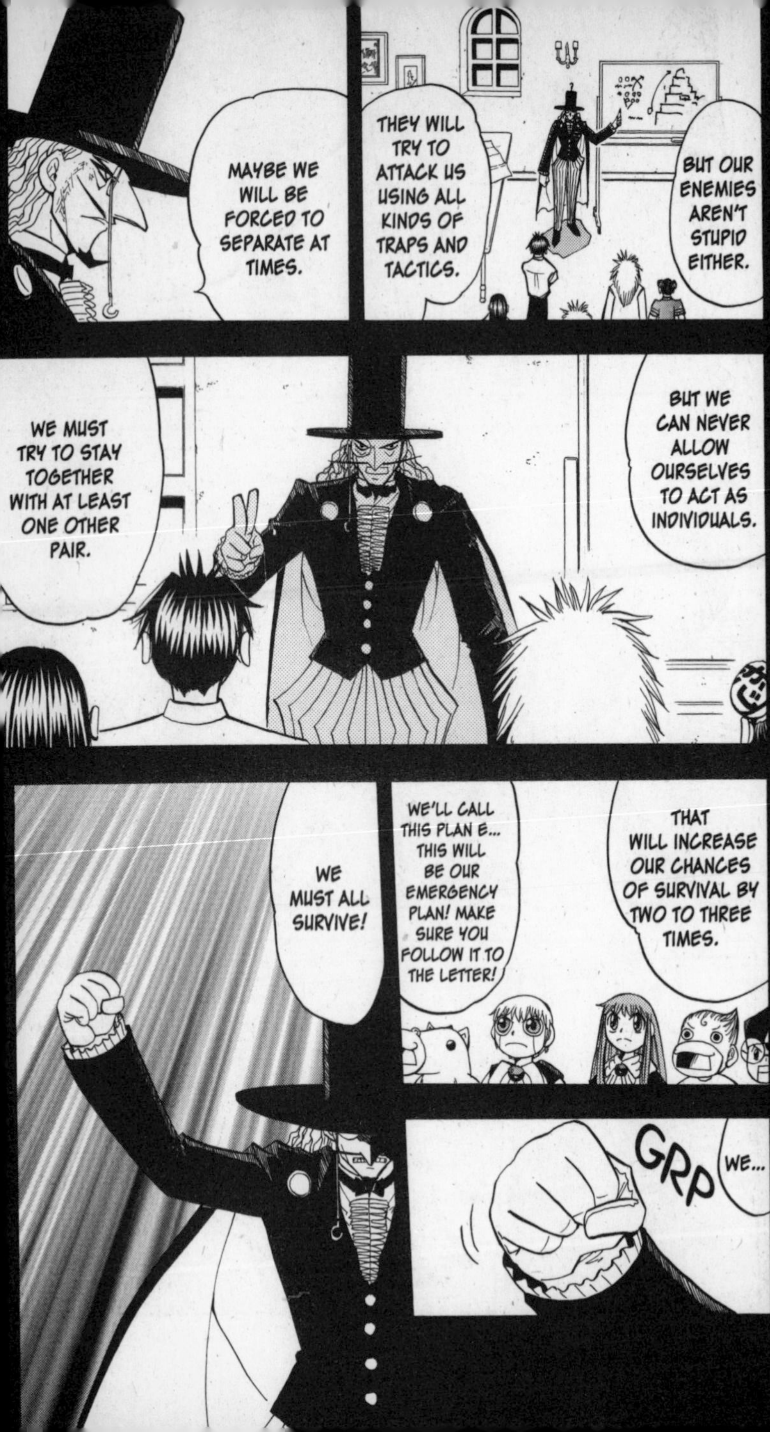

BUT OUR ENEMIES AREN'T STUPID EITHER.
THEY WILL TRY TO ATTACK US USING ALL KINDS OF TRAPS AND TACTICS.
MAYBE WE WILL BE FORCED TO SEPARATE AT TIMES.
BUT WE CAN NEVER ALLOW OURSELVES TO ACT AS INDIVIDUALS.
WE MUST TRY TO STAY TOGETHER WITH AT LEAST ONE OTHER PAIR.
THAT WILL INCREASE OUR CHANCES OF SURVIVAL BY TWO TO THREE TIMES.
WE'LL CALL THIS PLAN E... THIS WILL BE OUR EMERGENCY PLAN! MAKE SURE YOU FOLLOW IT TO THE LETTER!
WE...
GRP
WE MUST ALL SURVIVE!

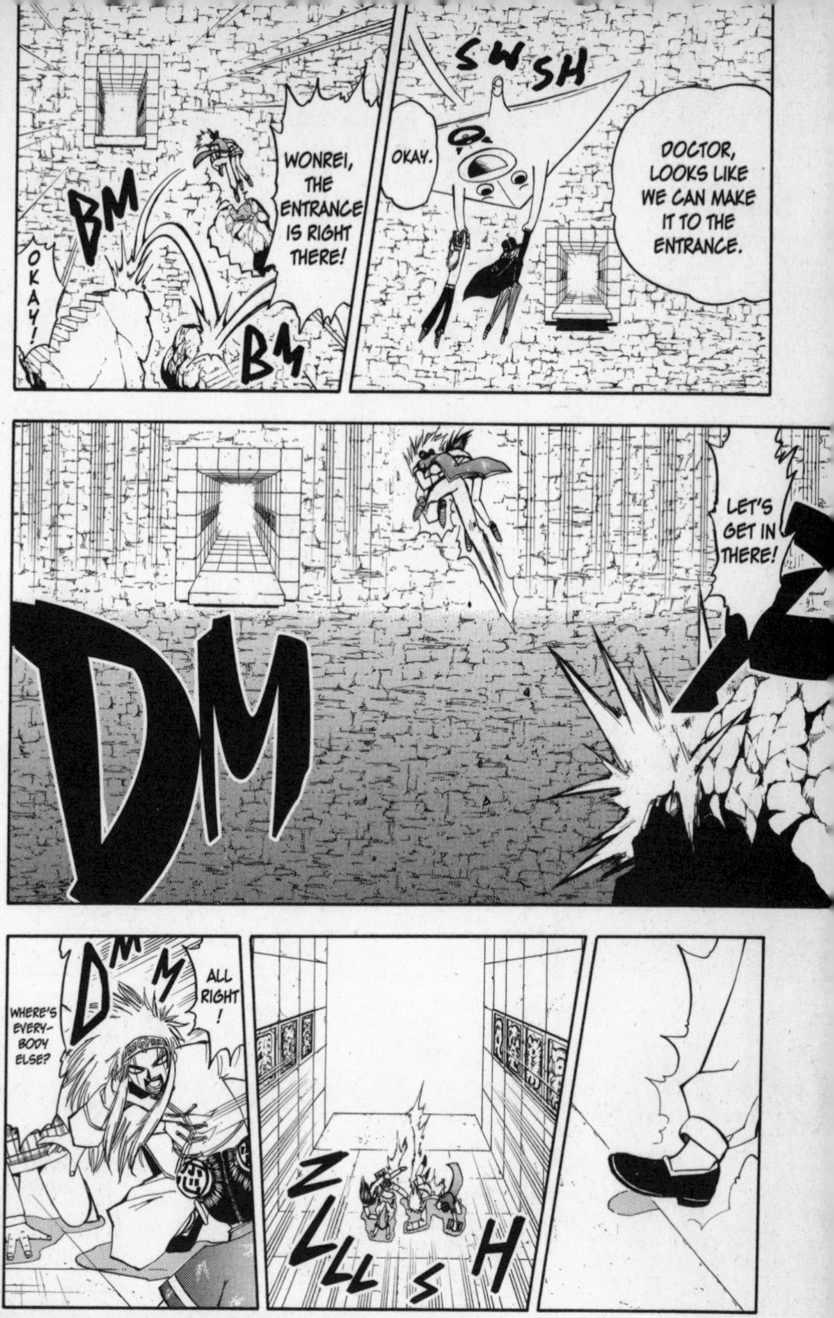
SWSH
DOCTOR, LOOKS LIKE WE CAN MAKE IT TO THE ENTRANCE.
OKAY.
WONREI, THE ENTRANCE IS RIGHT THERE!
BM
OKAY!
BM
LET'S GET IN THERE!
DM
ZLLLSH
DMM
ALL RIGHT!
WHERE'S EVERYBODY ELSE?

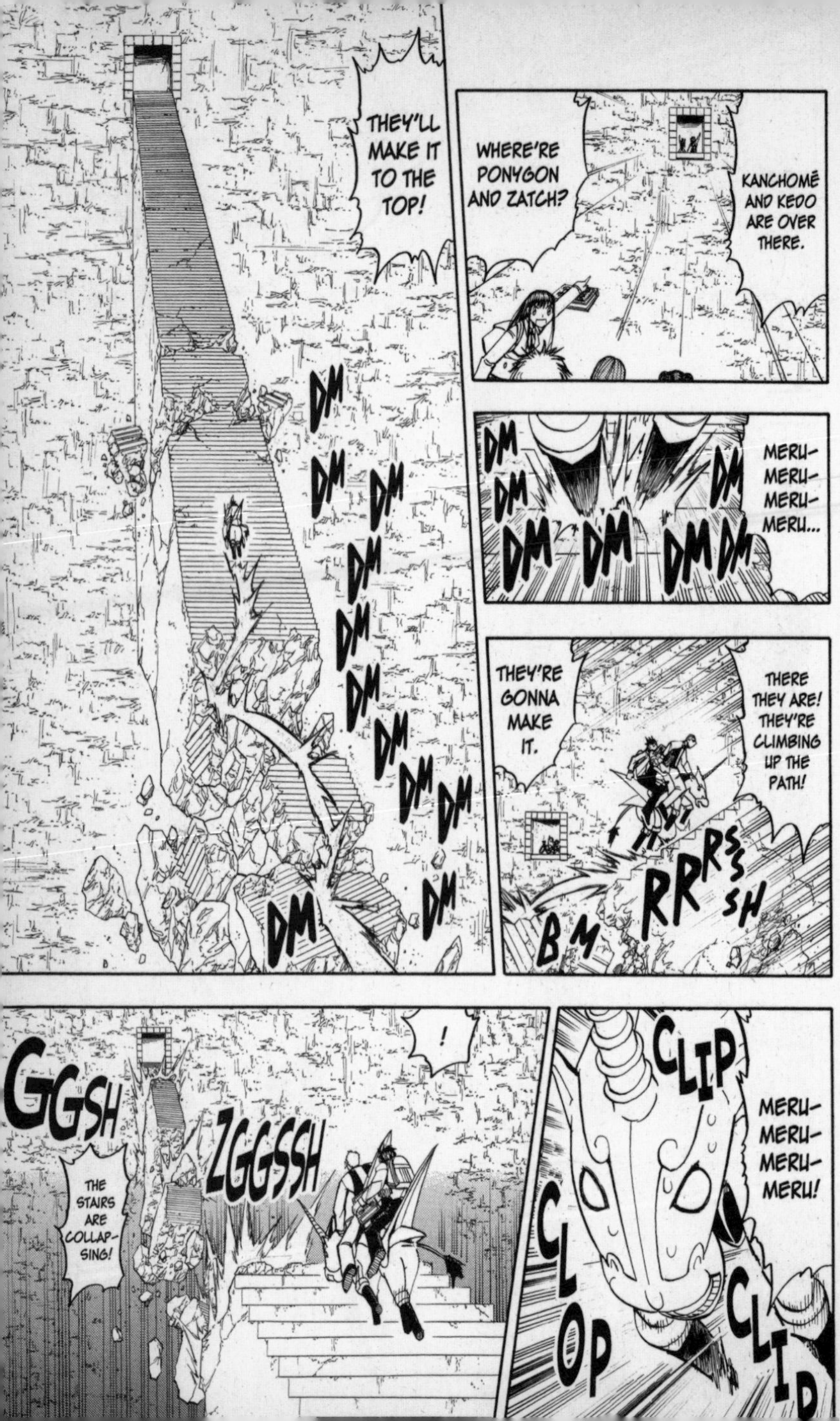
KANCHOMĒ AND KEDO ARE OVER THERE.
WHERE'RE PONYGON AND ZATCH?
MERU-MERU-MERU-MERU...
DM DM DM DM DM DM DM DM
THERE THEY ARE! THEY'RE CLIMBING UP THE PATH!
THEY'RE GONNA MAKE IT.
RRRSSH
BM
THEY'LL MAKE IT TO THE TOP!
DM DM DM DM DM DM DM DM DM DM DM DM
CLIP
MERU-MERU-MERU-MERU!
CLOP
CLIP
!
ZGGSSH
GGSH
THE STAIRS ARE COLLAP-SING!

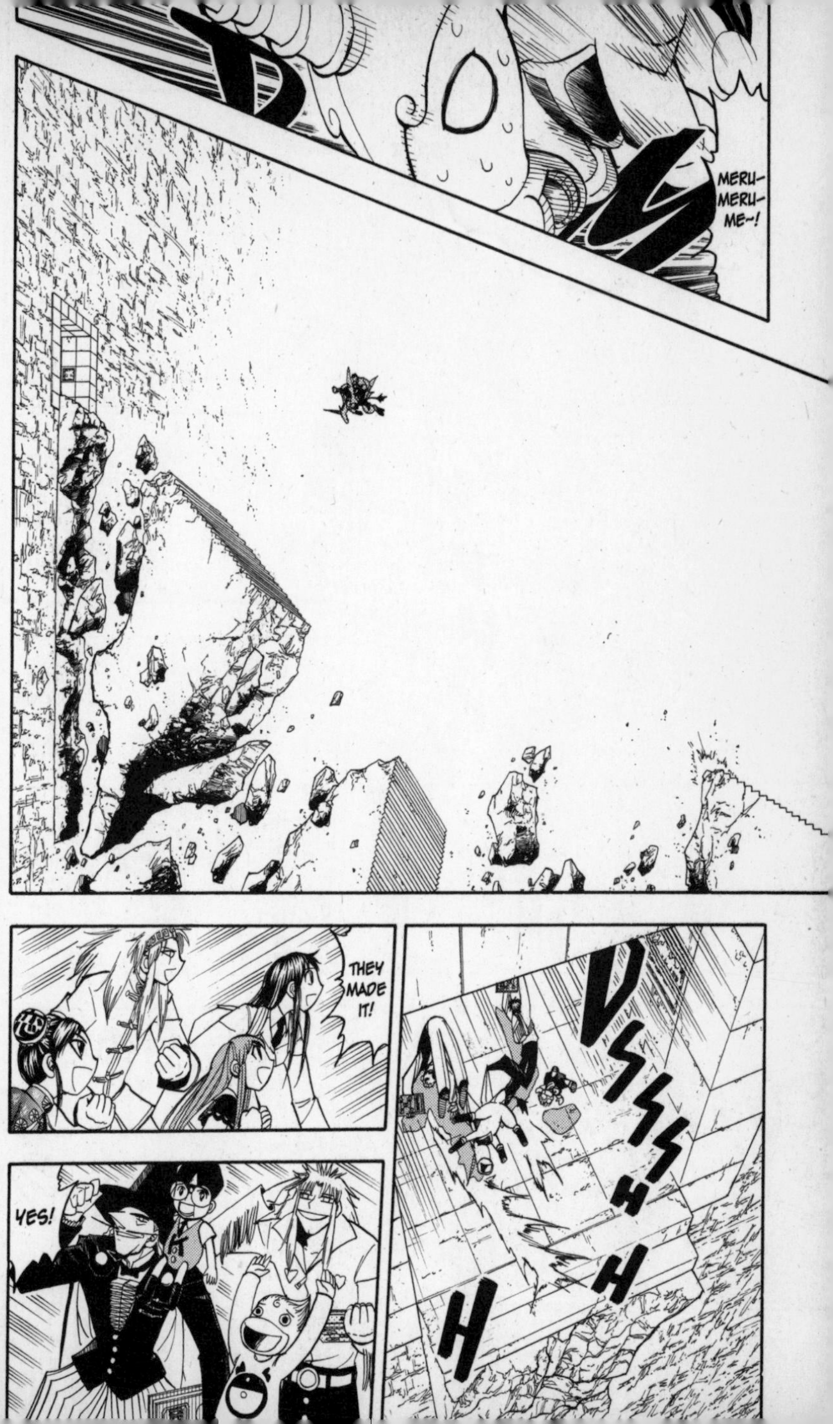
MERU-MERU-ME~!
VSSSHHH
THEY MADE IT!
YES!

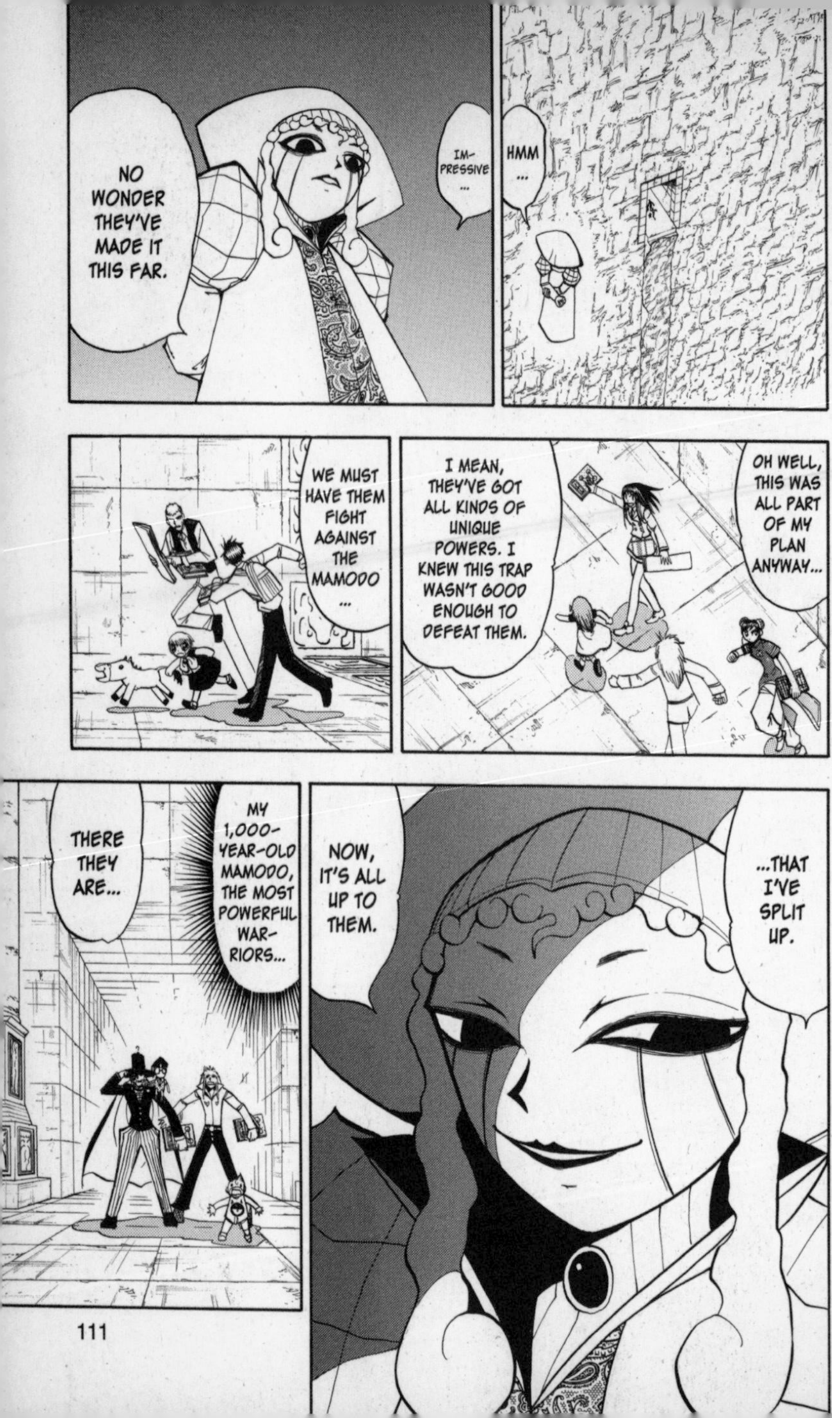
HMM ...
IM-PRESSIVE ...
NO WONDER THEY'VE MADE IT THIS FAR.
OH WELL, THIS WAS ALL PART OF MY PLAN ANYWAY...
I MEAN, THEY'VE GOT ALL KINDS OF UNIQUE POWERS. I KNEW THIS TRAP WASN'T GOOD ENOUGH TO DEFEAT THEM.
WE MUST HAVE THEM FIGHT AGAINST THE MAMODO ...
...THAT I'VE SPLIT UP.
NOW, IT'S ALL UP TO THEM.
MY 1,000-YEAR-OLD MAMODO, THE MOST POWERFUL WAR-RIORS...
THERE THEY ARE...

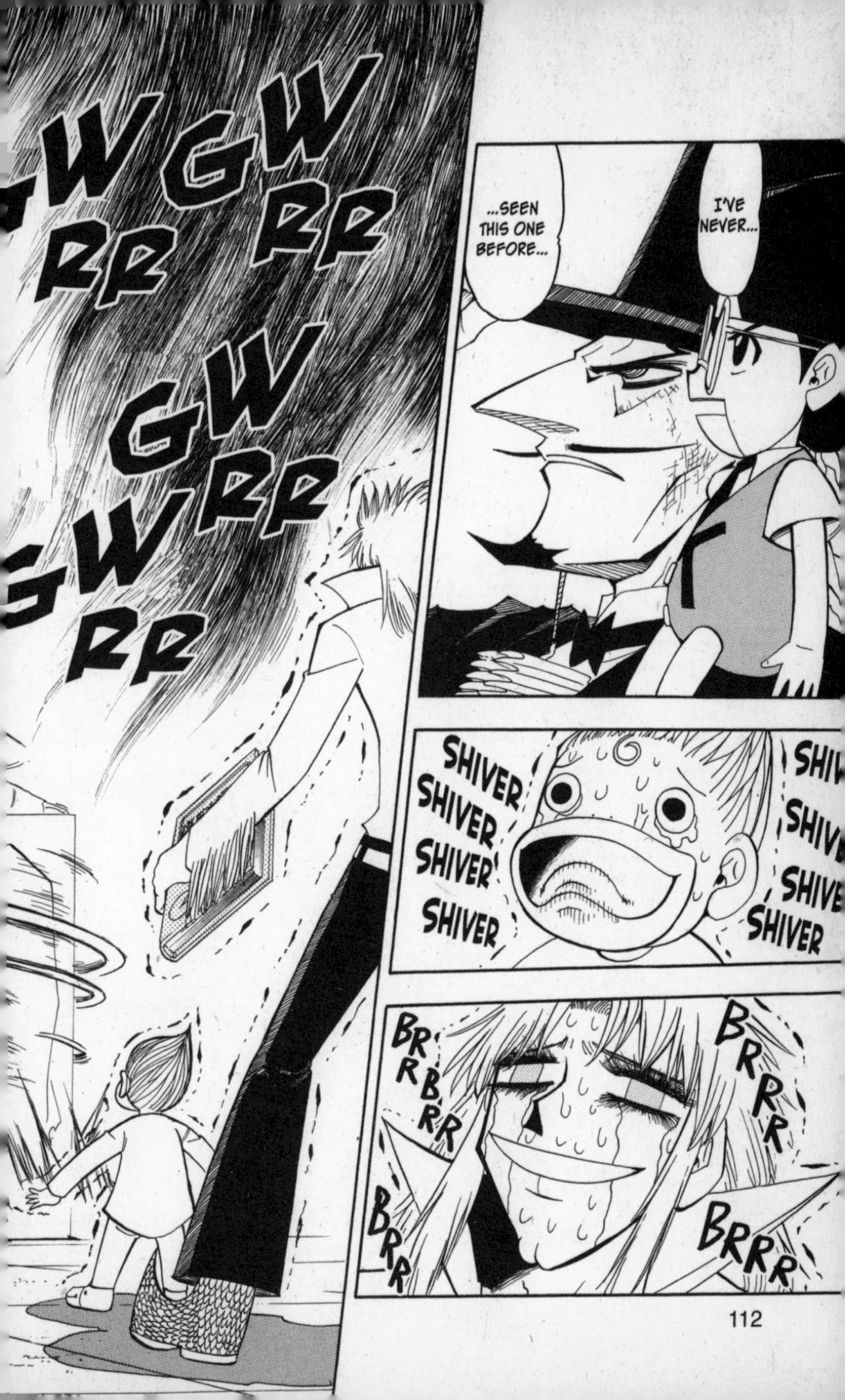
I'VE NEVER...
...SEEN THIS ONE BEFORE...
SHIVER SHIVER SHIVER SHIVER
SHIVER SHIVER SHIVER SHIVER
BRRRR
BRRR
BRR BRRR
BRRR
GWGW RR RR
GW GW RR RR

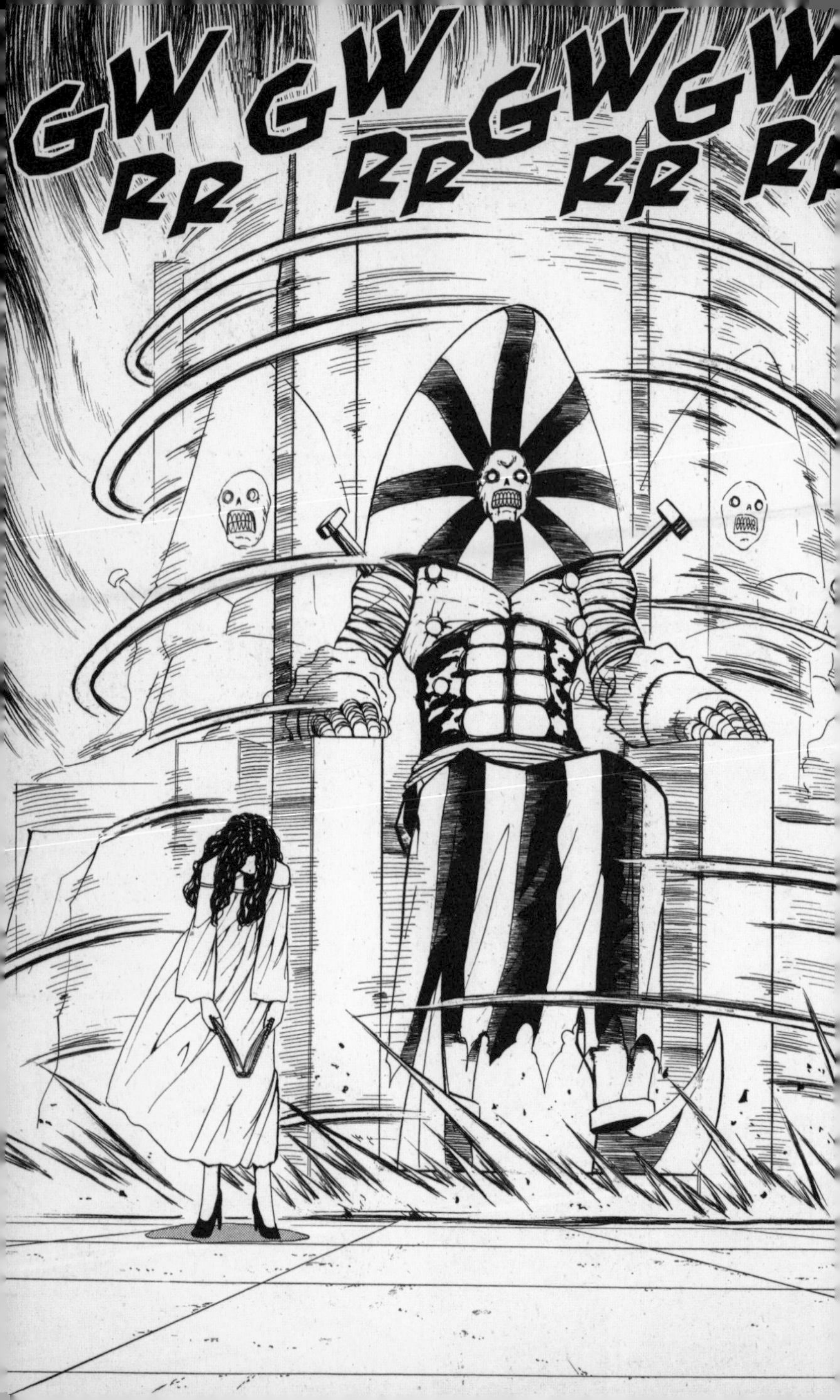

GWGWGWGW
RRRRRRRR

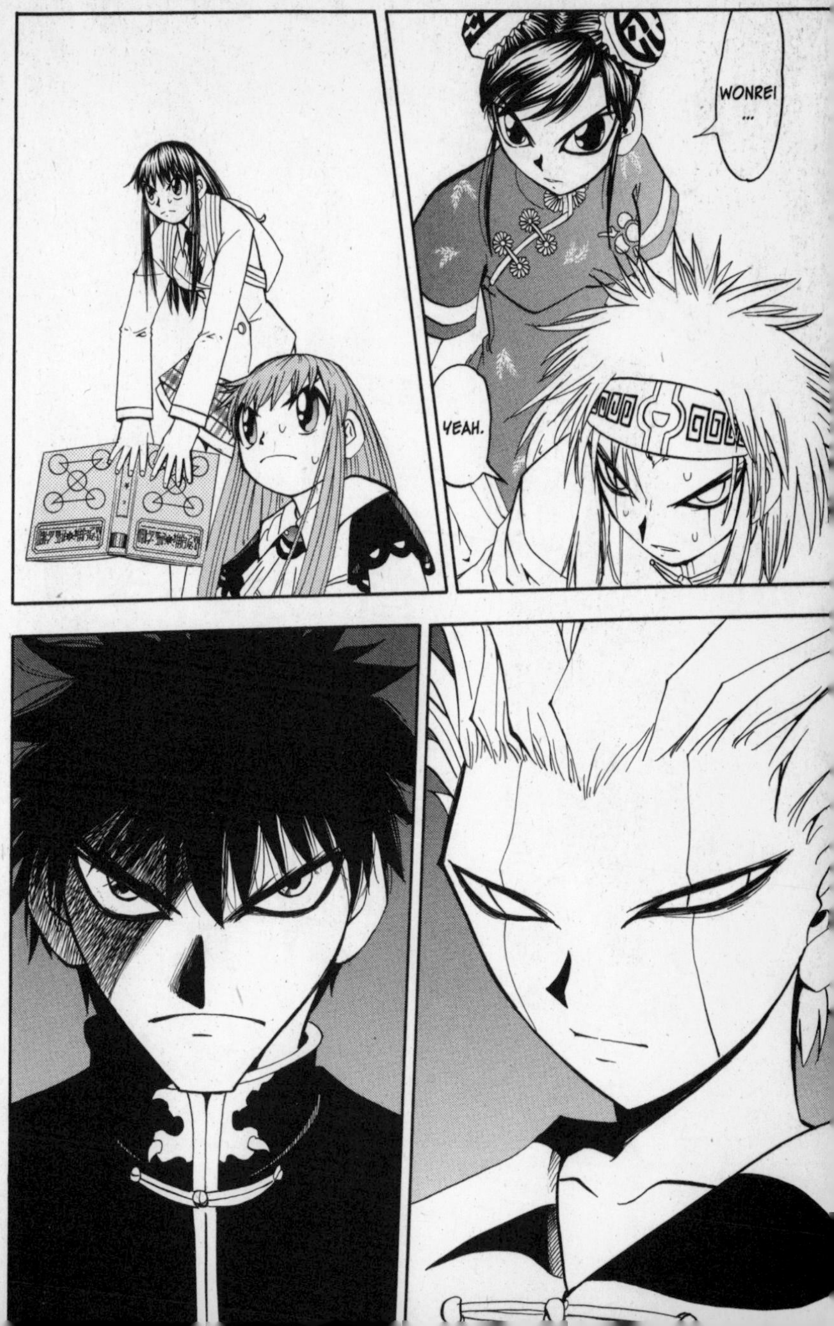
WONREI ...
YEAH.

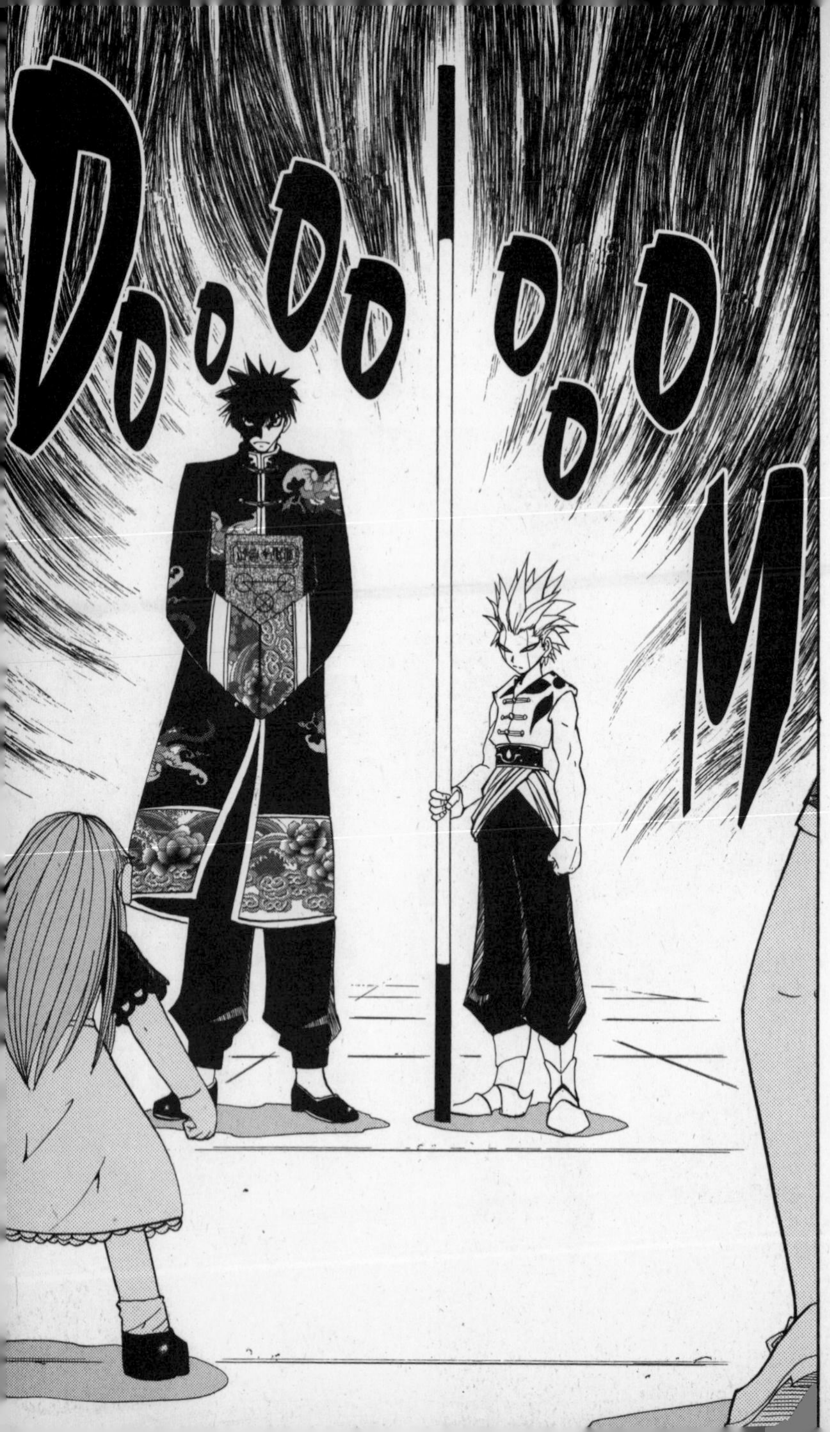
DDDDDDDDM

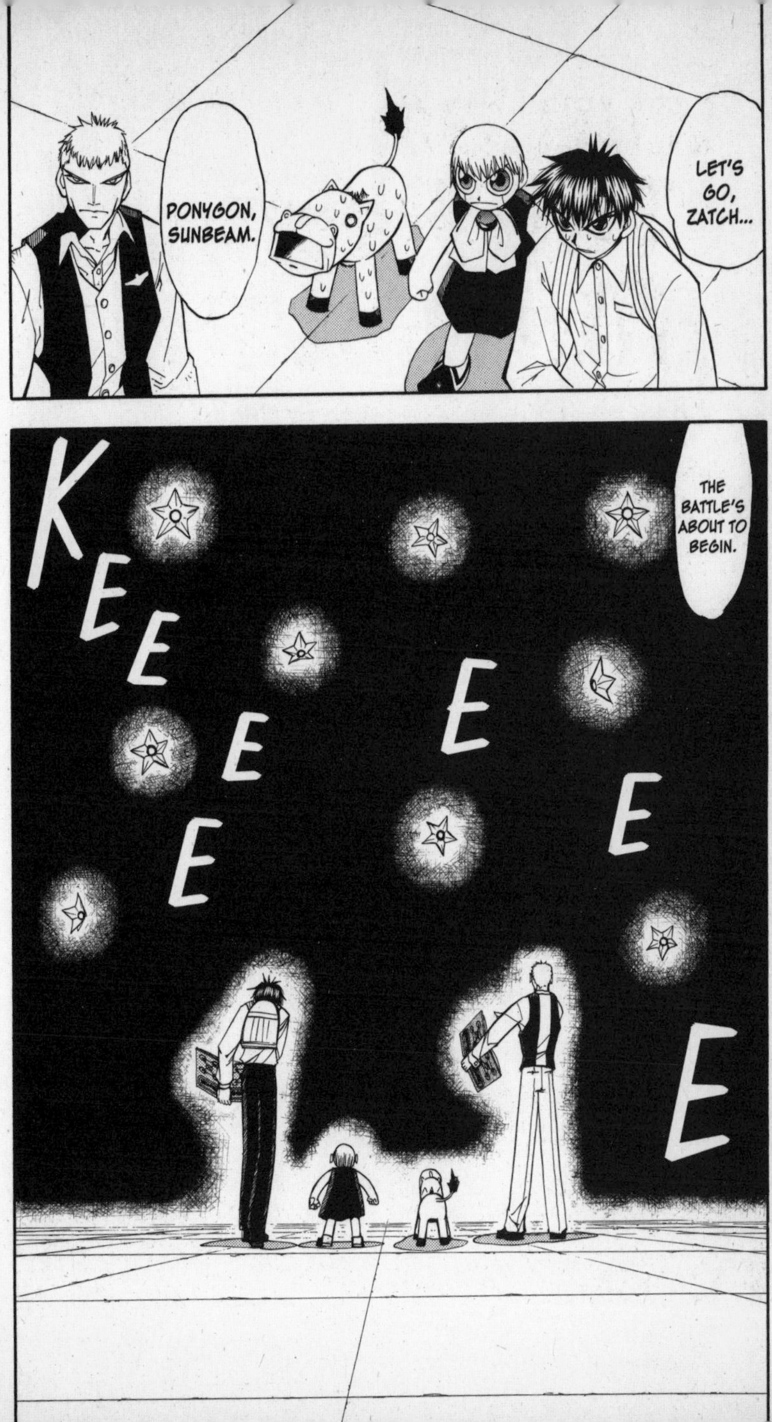
LET'S GO, ZATCH...
PONYGON, SUNBEAM.
THE BATTLE'S ABOUT TO BEGIN.
KEEEEEEEE

LEVEL 130:
The Perfect Martial Art

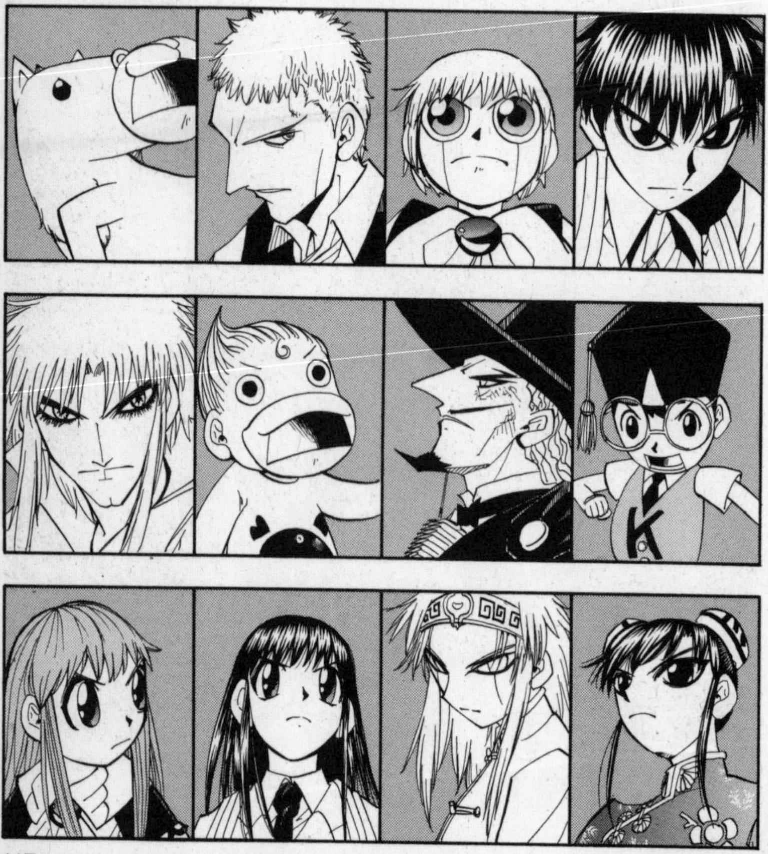

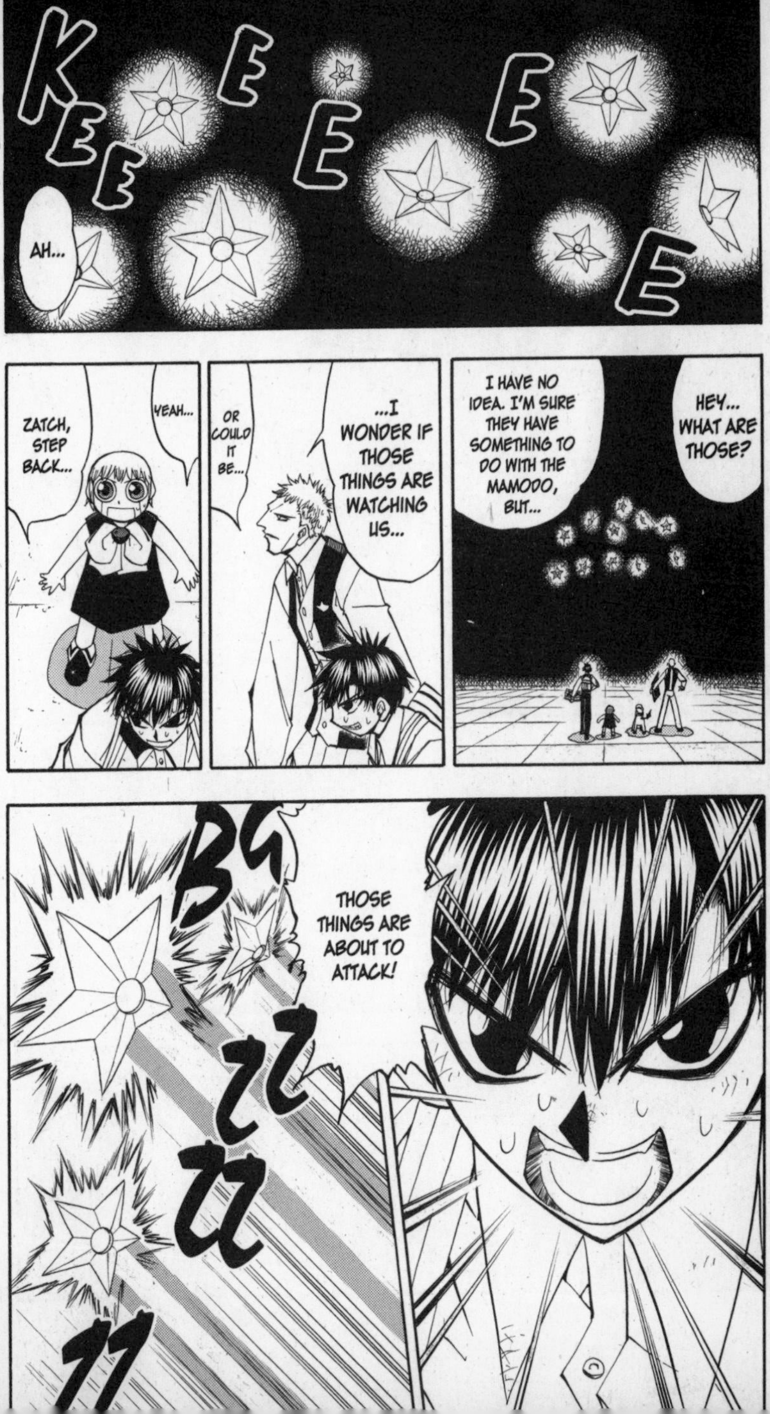
KEEEEEE
AH...
HEY... WHAT ARE THOSE?
I HAVE NO IDEA. I'M SURE THEY HAVE SOMETHING TO DO WITH THE MAMODO, BUT...
...I WONDER IF THOSE THINGS ARE WATCHING US...
OR COULD IT BE...
ZATCH, STEP BACK...
YEAH...
THOSE THINGS ARE ABOUT TO ATTACK!

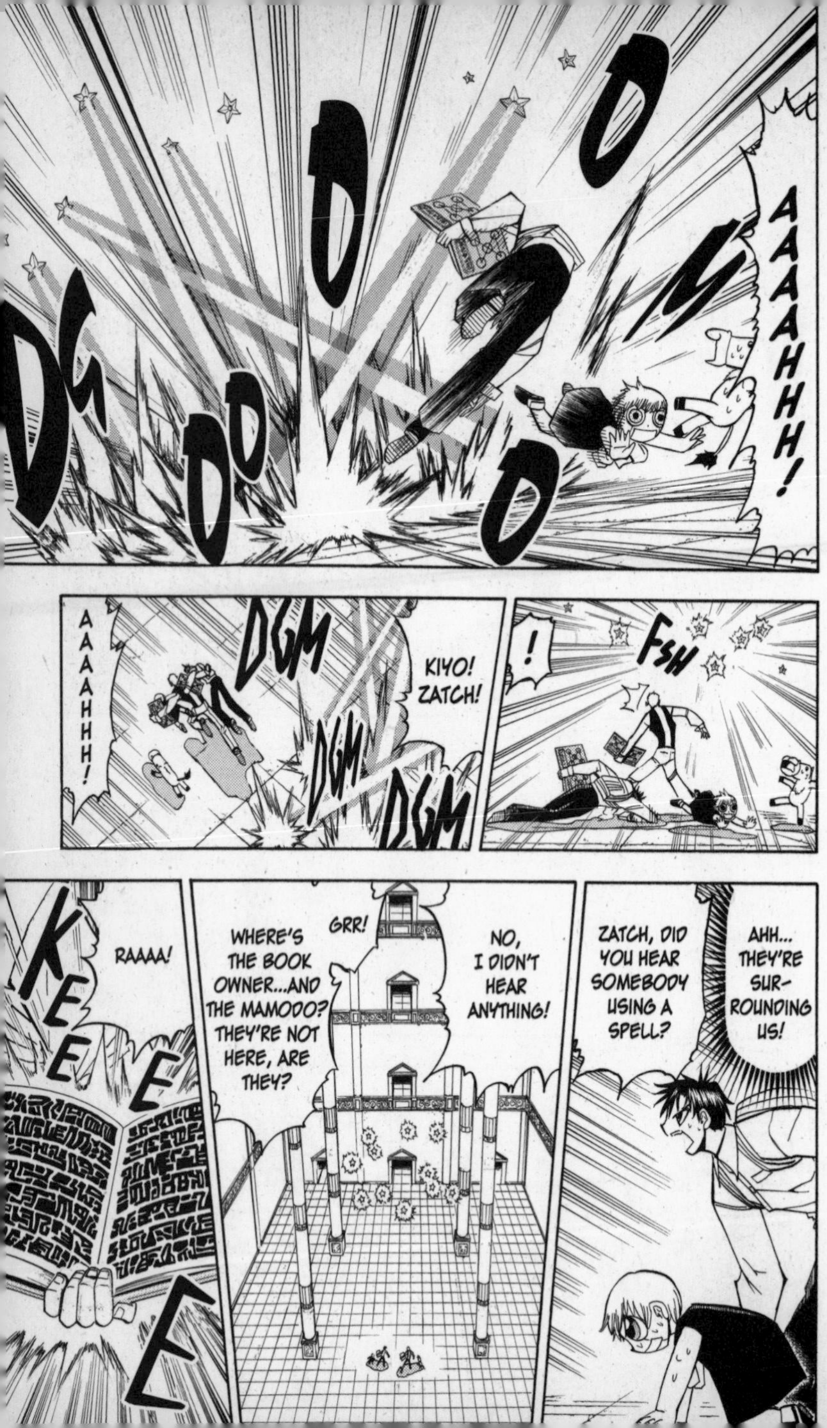
AAAAHHH!
!
FSH
KIYO! ZATCH!
DGM
DGM
DGM
AAAAHHH!
AHH... THEY'RE SUR-ROUNDING US!
ZATCH, DID YOU HEAR SOMEBODY USING A SPELL?
NO, I DIDN'T HEAR ANYTHING!
GRR!
WHERE'S THE BOOK OWNER...AND THE MAMODO? THEY'RE NOT HERE, ARE THEY?
RAAAA!
KEEEE

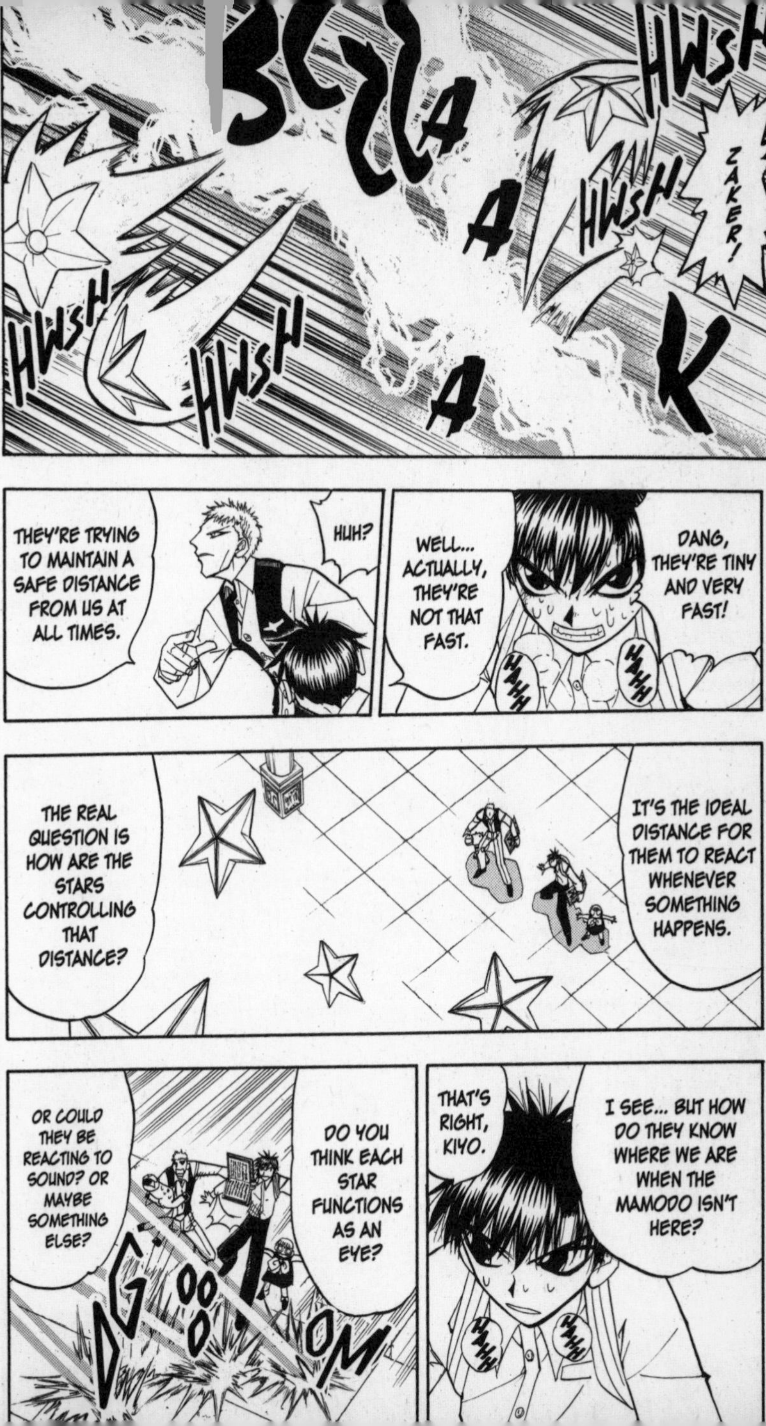
HWSH
ZAKER!
HWSH
HWSH
HWSH
DANG, THEY'RE TINY AND VERY FAST!
WELL... ACTUALLY, THEY'RE NOT THAT FAST.
HUH?
THEY'RE TRYING TO MAINTAIN A SAFE DISTANCE FROM US AT ALL TIMES.
IT'S THE IDEAL DISTANCE FOR THEM TO REACT WHENEVER SOMETHING HAPPENS.
THE REAL QUESTION IS HOW ARE THE STARS CONTROLLING THAT DISTANCE?
I SEE... BUT HOW DO THEY KNOW WHERE WE ARE WHEN THE MAMODO ISN'T HERE?
THAT'S RIGHT, KIYO.
DO YOU THINK EACH STAR FUNCTIONS AS AN EYE?
OR COULD THEY BE REACTING TO SOUND? OR MAYBE SOMETHING ELSE?
DGOOOOM

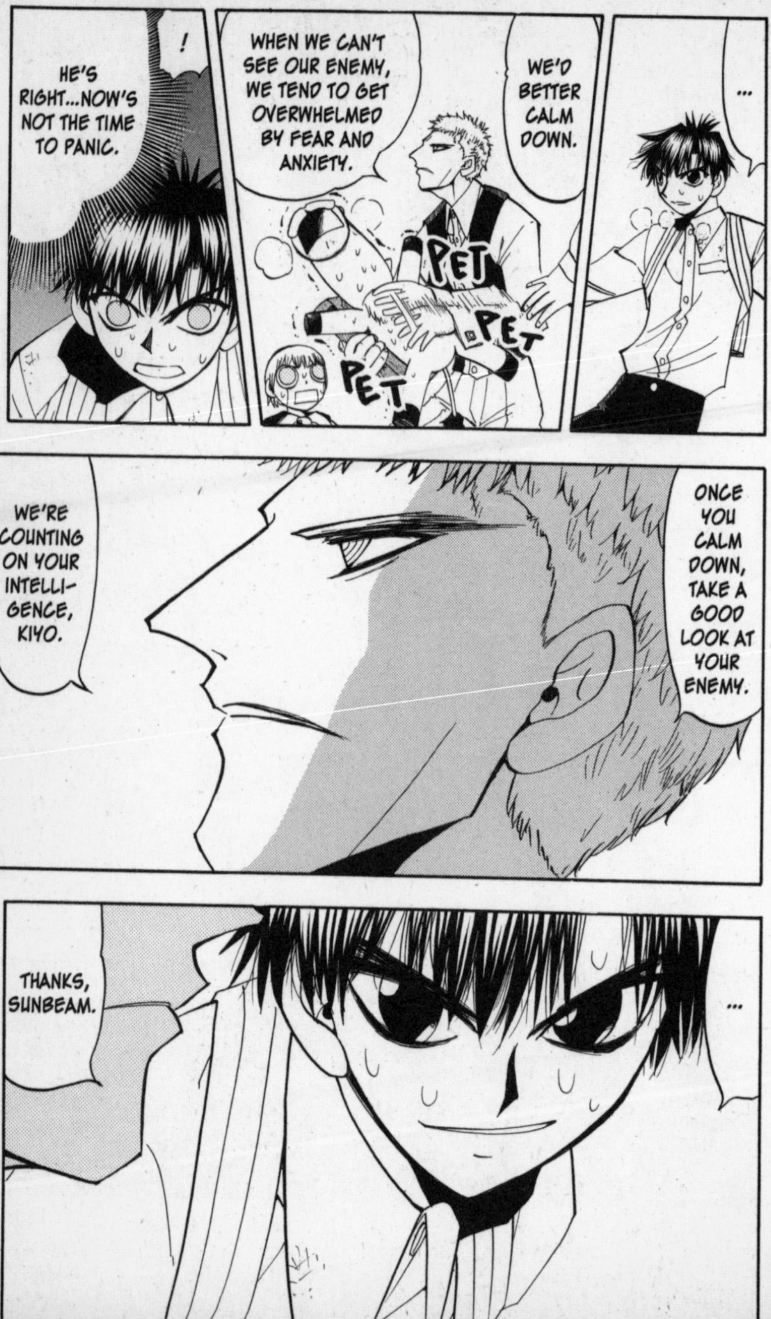
...
WE'D BETTER CALM DOWN.
WHEN WE CAN'T SEE OUR ENEMY, WE TEND TO GET OVERWHELMED BY FEAR AND ANXIETY.
PET
PET
PET
!
HE'S RIGHT...NOW'S NOT THE TIME TO PANIC.
ONCE YOU CALM DOWN, TAKE A GOOD LOOK AT YOUR ENEMY.
WE'RE COUNTING ON YOUR INTELLIGENCE, KIYO.
...
THANKS, SUNBEAM.

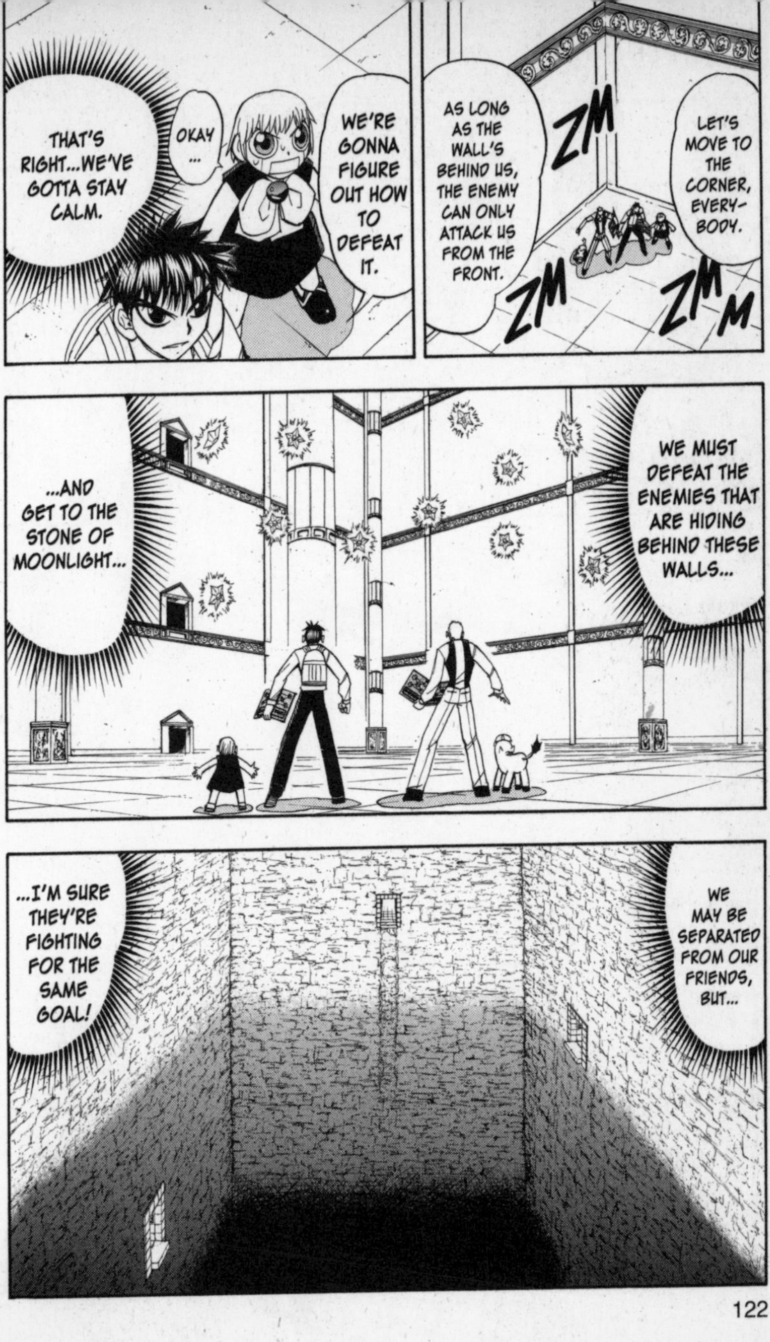
LET'S MOVE TO THE CORNER, EVERYBODY.
ZM
AS LONG AS THE WALL'S BEHIND US, THE ENEMY CAN ONLY ATTACK US FROM THE FRONT.
ZMM
ZM
WE'RE GONNA FIGURE OUT HOW TO DEFEAT IT.
OKAY...
THAT'S RIGHT...WE'VE GOTTA STAY CALM.
WE MUST DEFEAT THE ENEMIES THAT ARE HIDING BEHIND THESE WALLS...
...AND GET TO THE STONE OF MOONLIGHT...
WE MAY BE SEPARATED FROM OUR FRIENDS, BUT...
...I'M SURE THEY'RE FIGHTING FOR THE SAME GOAL!

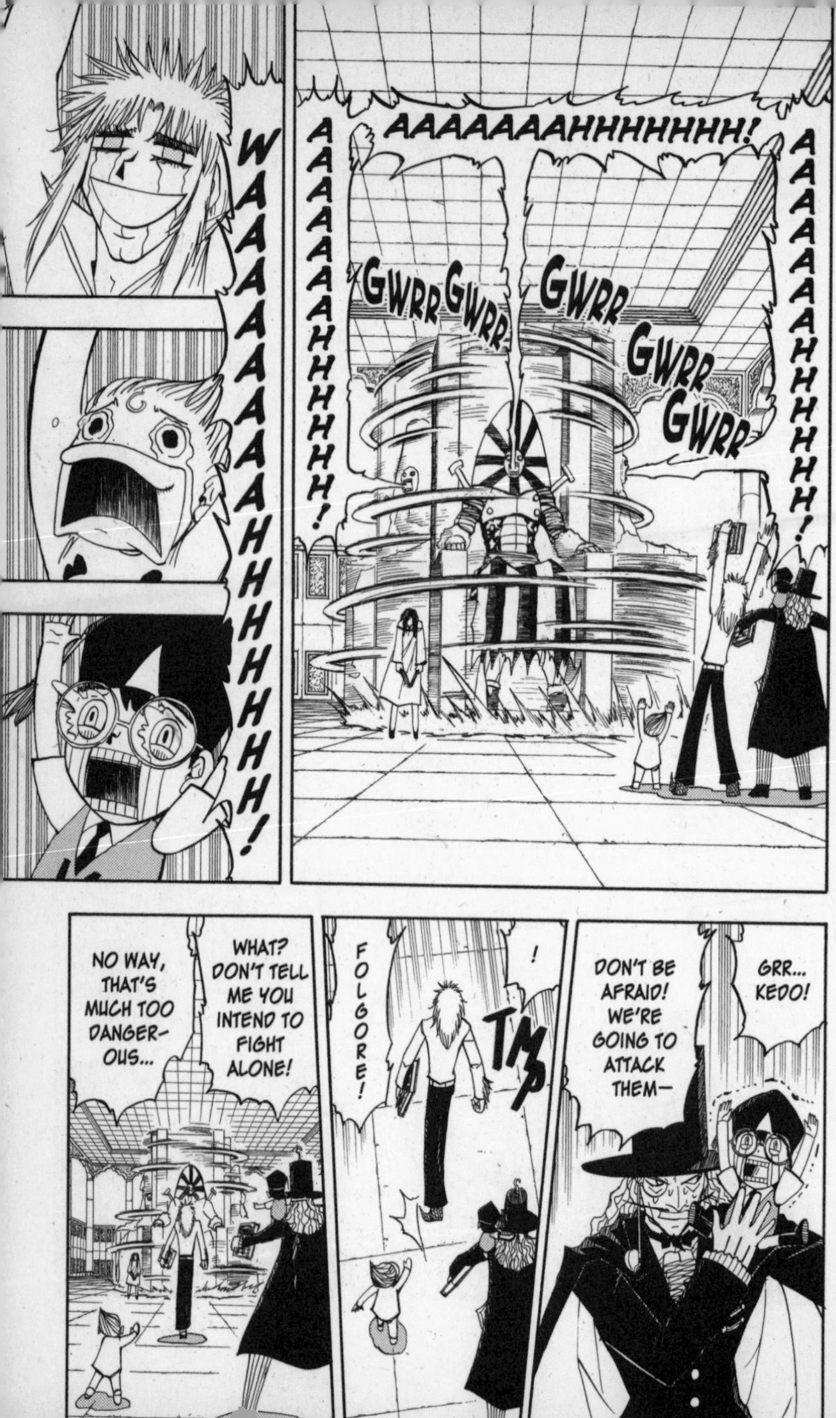
AAAAAAAAHHHHHHH!
AAAAAAAAHHHHHH!
AAAAAAAHHHHHH!
GWRR GWRR
GWRR
GWRR
GWRR
WAAAAAAAAAHHHHHHH!
GRR... KEDO!
DON'T BE AFRAID! WE'RE GOING TO ATTACK THEM—
!
TMP
FOLGORE!
WHAT? DON'T TELL ME YOU INTEND TO FIGHT ALONE!
NO WAY, THAT'S MUCH TOO DANGER-OUS...

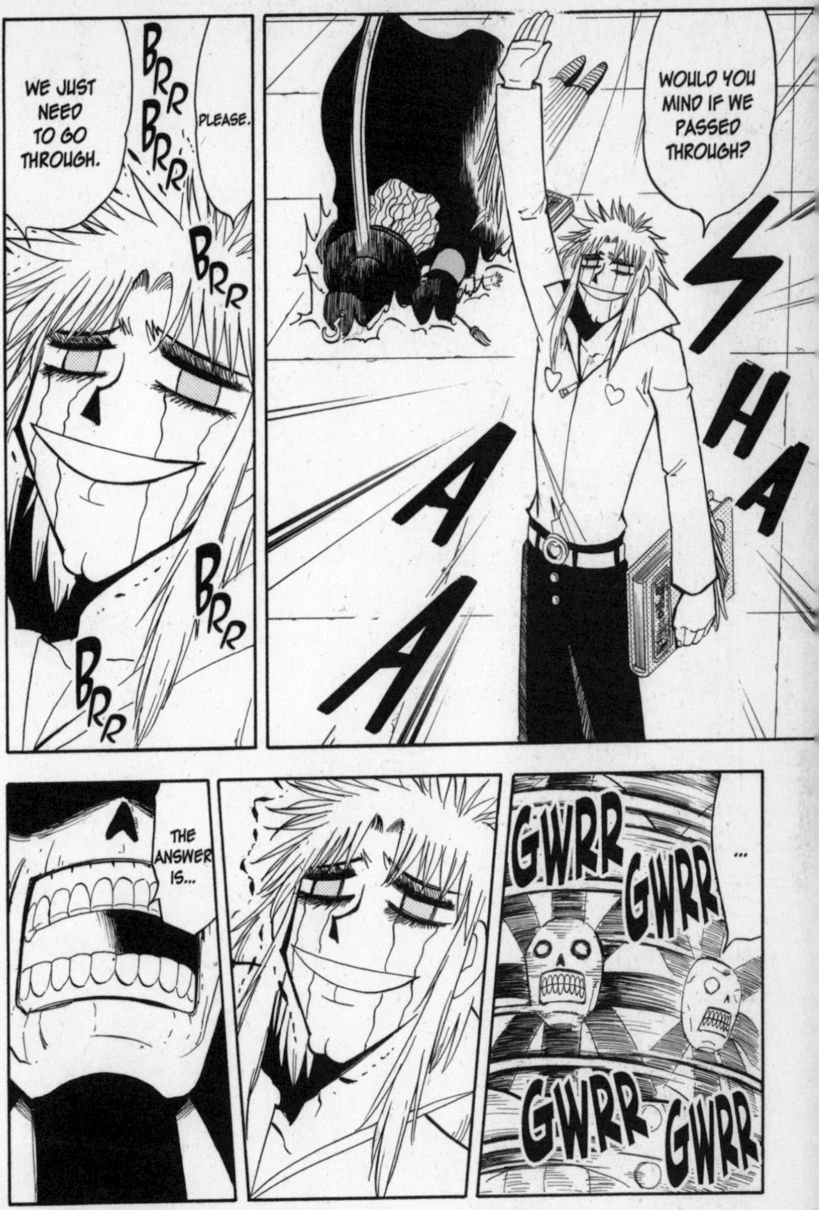
WOULD YOU MIND IF WE PASSED THROUGH?
SHAAA
PLEASE.
WE JUST NEED TO GO THROUGH.
BRR BRR BRR BRR BRR
GWRR GWRR...
GWRR GWRR
THE ANSWER IS...

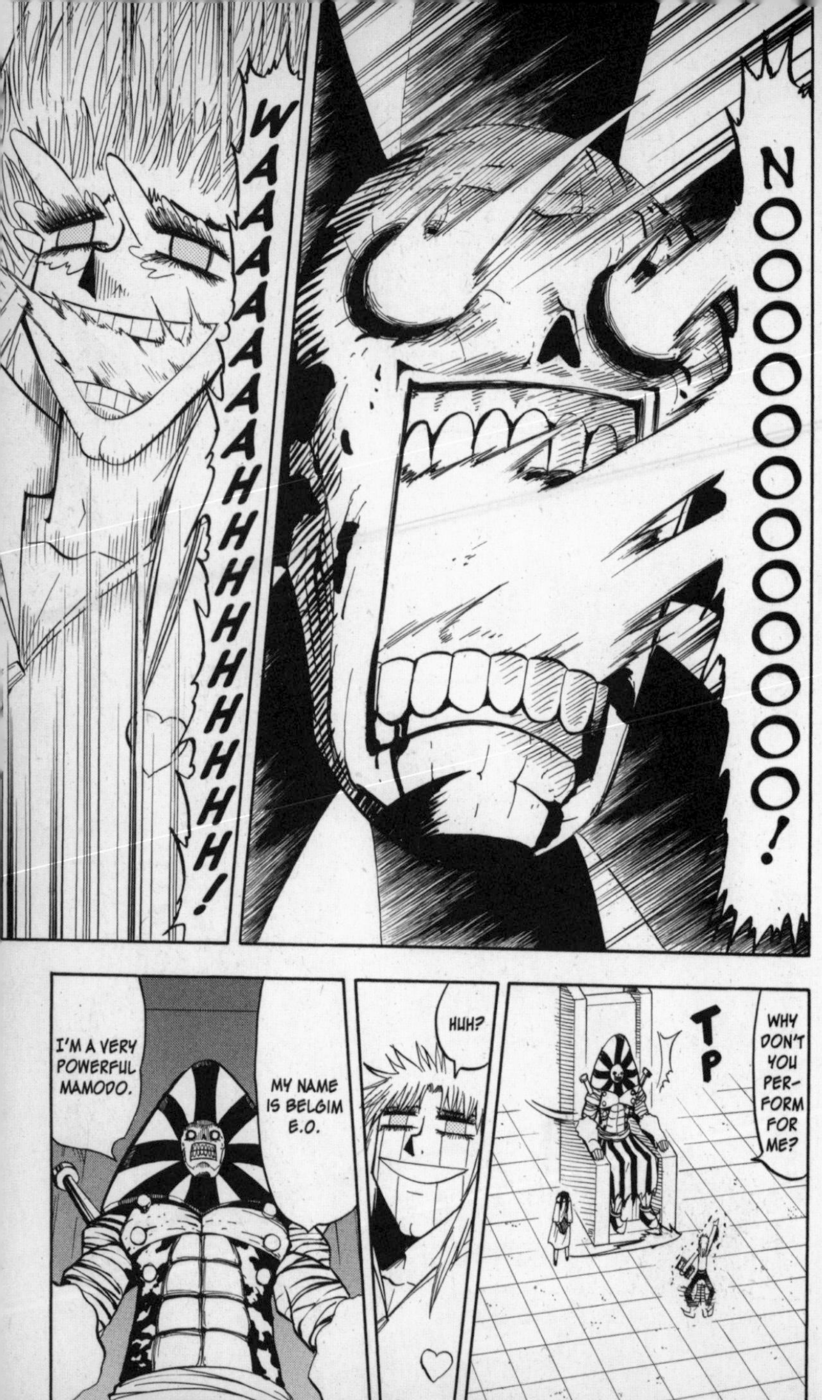

NOOOOOOOOOOOOO!
WAAAAAAAHHHHHHHHHH!
WHY DON'T YOU PER-FORM FOR ME?
TP
!
HUH?
MY NAME IS BELGIM E.O.
I'M A VERY POWERFUL MAMODO.

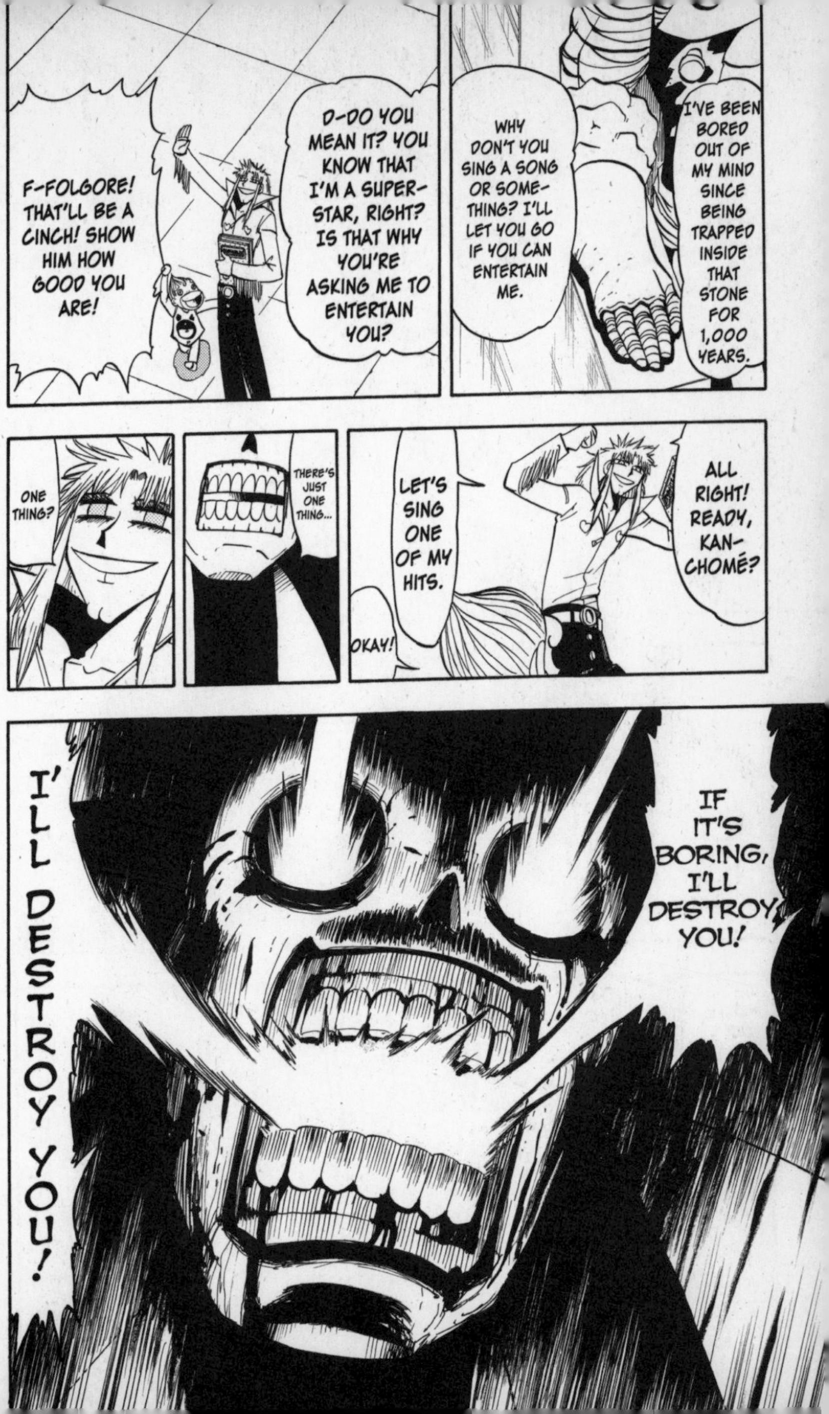
I'VE BEEN BORED OUT OF MY MIND SINCE BEING TRAPPED INSIDE THAT STONE FOR 1,000 YEARS.
WHY DON'T YOU SING A SONG OR SOMETHING? I'LL LET YOU GO IF YOU CAN ENTERTAIN ME.
D-DO YOU MEAN IT? YOU KNOW THAT I'M A SUPERSTAR, RIGHT? IS THAT WHY YOU'RE ASKING ME TO ENTERTAIN YOU?
F-FOLGORE! THAT'LL BE A CINCH! SHOW HIM HOW GOOD YOU ARE!
ALL RIGHT! READY, KANCHOMÉ?
LET'S SING ONE OF MY HITS.
OKAY!
THERE'S JUST ONE THING...
ONE THING?
IF IT'S BORING, I'LL DESTROY YOU!
I'LL DESTROY YOU!

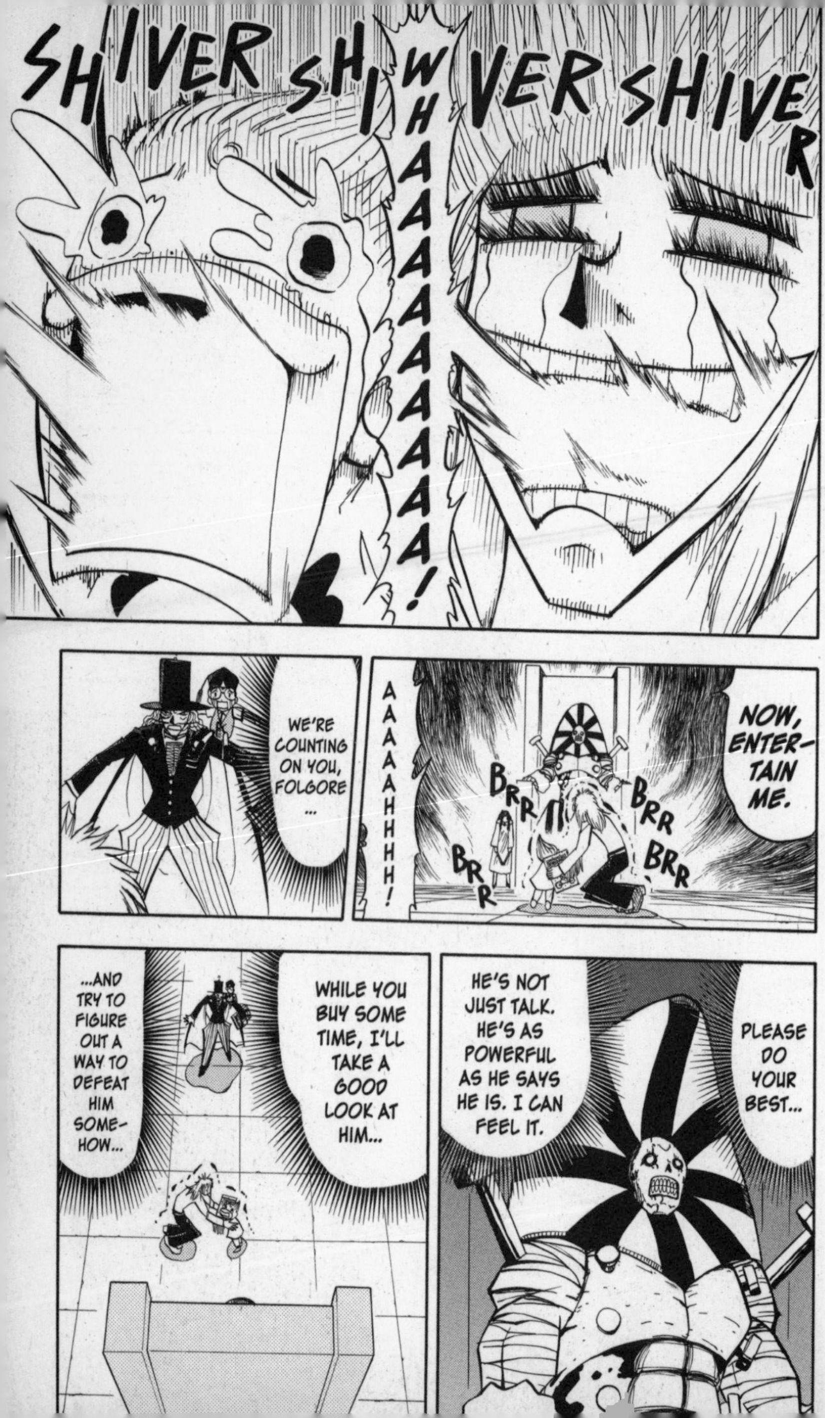
SHIVER SHIVER SHIVER SHIVER
WHAAAAAAAAAAAA!
NOW, ENTERTAIN ME.
AAAAAAHHHH!
BRRR BRRR BRRR BRRR
WE'RE COUNTING ON YOU, FOLGORE...
PLEASE DO YOUR BEST...
HE'S NOT JUST TALK. HE'S AS POWERFUL AS HE SAYS HE IS. I CAN FEEL IT.
WHILE YOU BUY SOME TIME, I'LL TAKE A GOOD LOOK AT HIM...
...AND TRY TO FIGURE OUT A WAY TO DEFEAT HIM SOMEHOW...

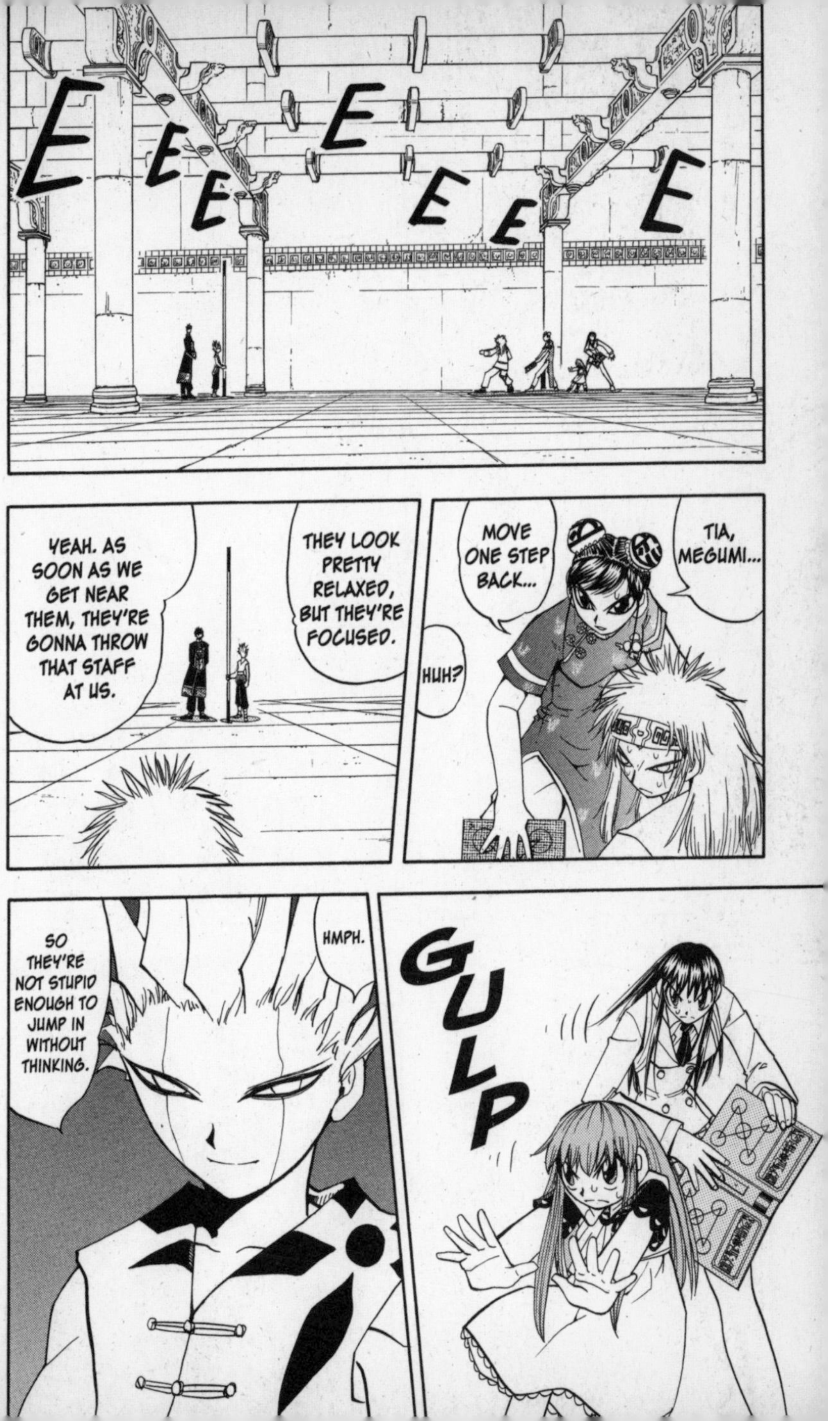
EEEEEEE
TIA, MEGUMI...
MOVE ONE STEP BACK...
HUH?
THEY LOOK PRETTY RELAXED, BUT THEY'RE FOCUSED.
YEAH. AS SOON AS WE GET NEAR THEM, THEY'RE GONNA THROW THAT STAFF AT US.
GULP
HMPH.
SO THEY'RE NOT STUPID ENOUGH TO JUMP IN WITHOUT THINKING.

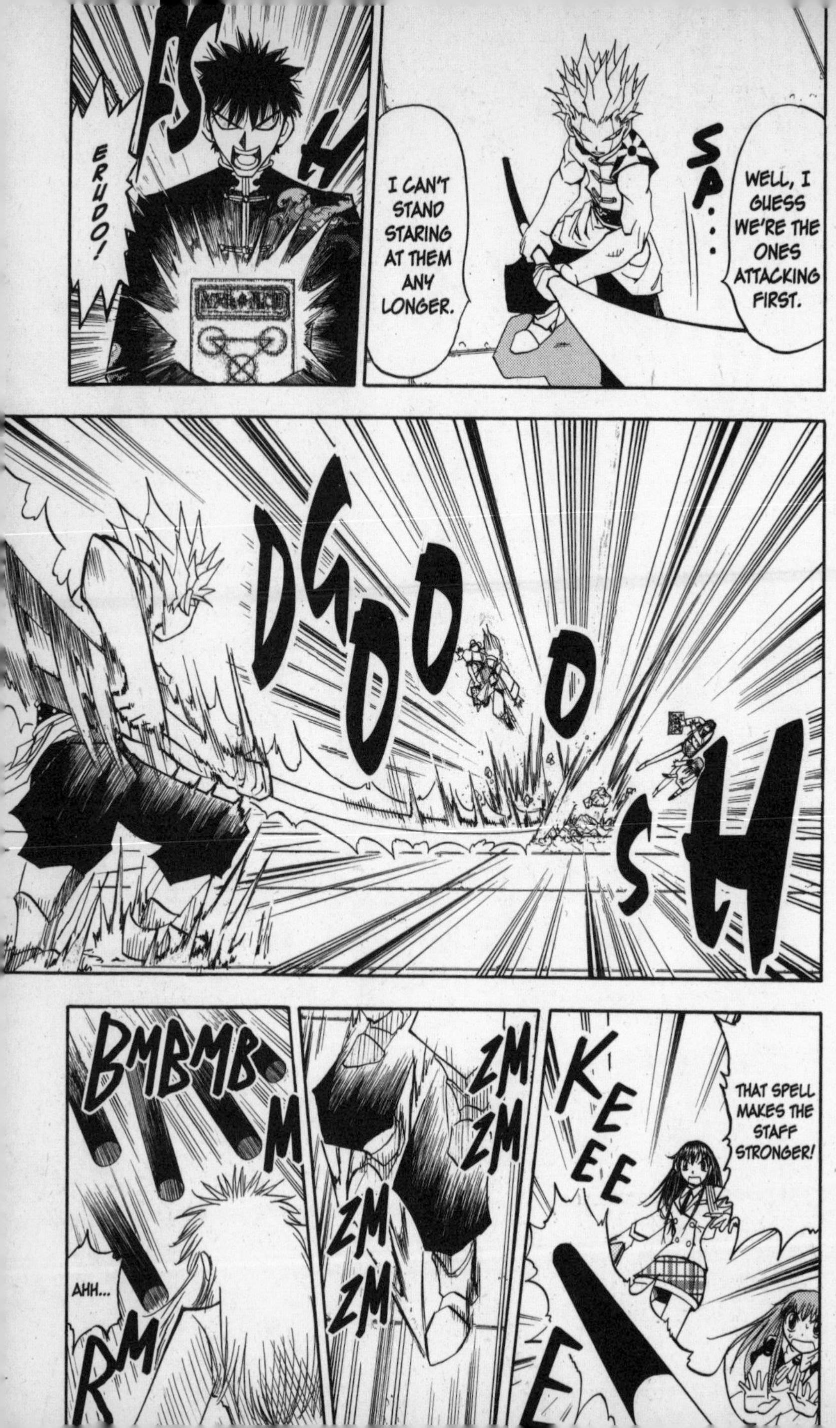
WELL, I GUESS WE'RE THE ONES ATTACKING FIRST.
SP...
I CAN'T STAND STARING AT THEM ANY LONGER.
FSSH
ERUDO!
DGDODOSH
THAT SPELL MAKES THE STAFF STRONGER!
KEEEE
ZMZMZMZMZM
BMBMBM
RM
AHH...

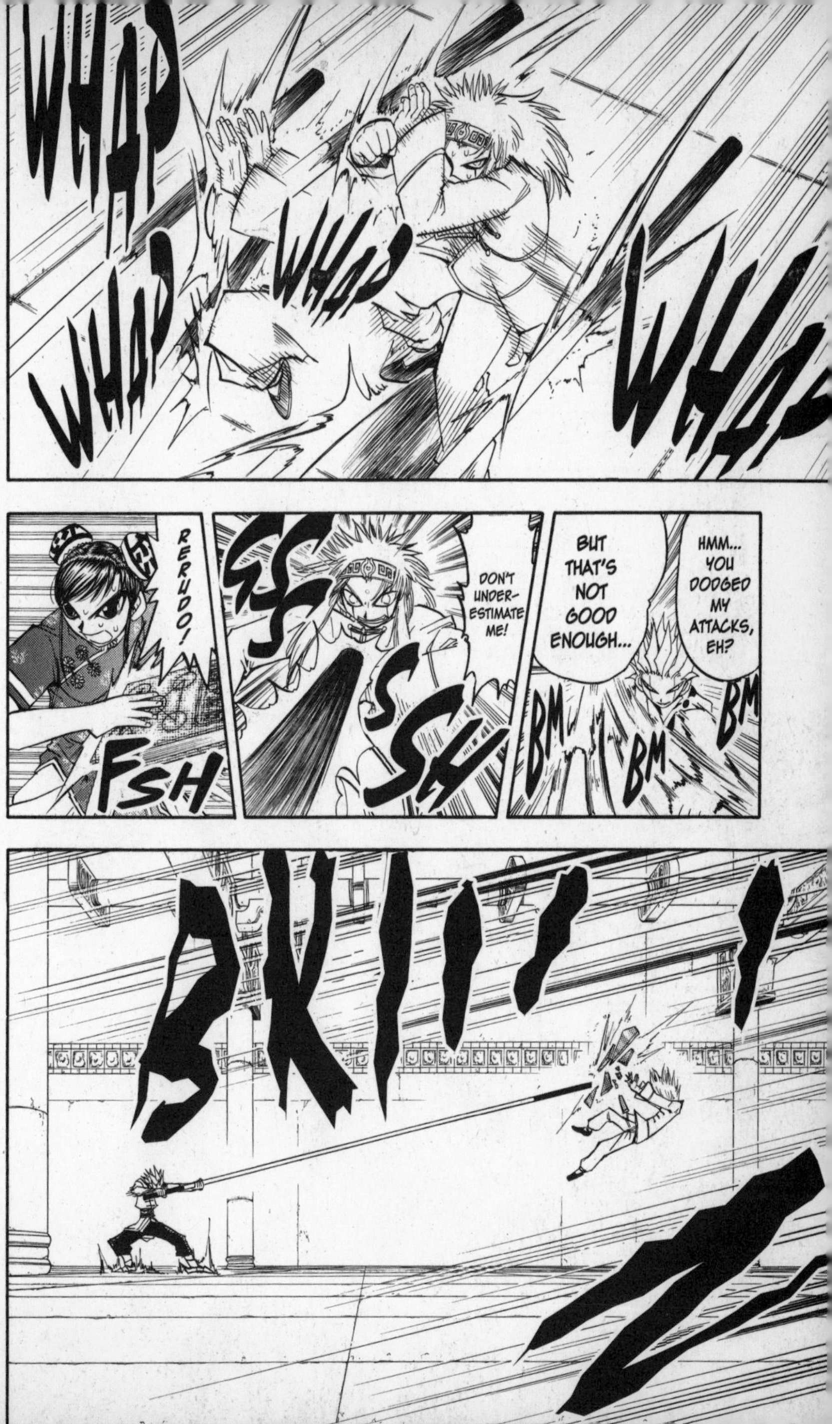

WHAP
WHAP
WHAP
WHAP
HMM... YOU DODGED MY ATTACKS, EH?
BUT THAT'S NOT GOOD ENOUGH...
BM
BM
BM
DON'T UNDER-ESTIMATE ME!
SSSH
RERUDO!
FSH
BKIII

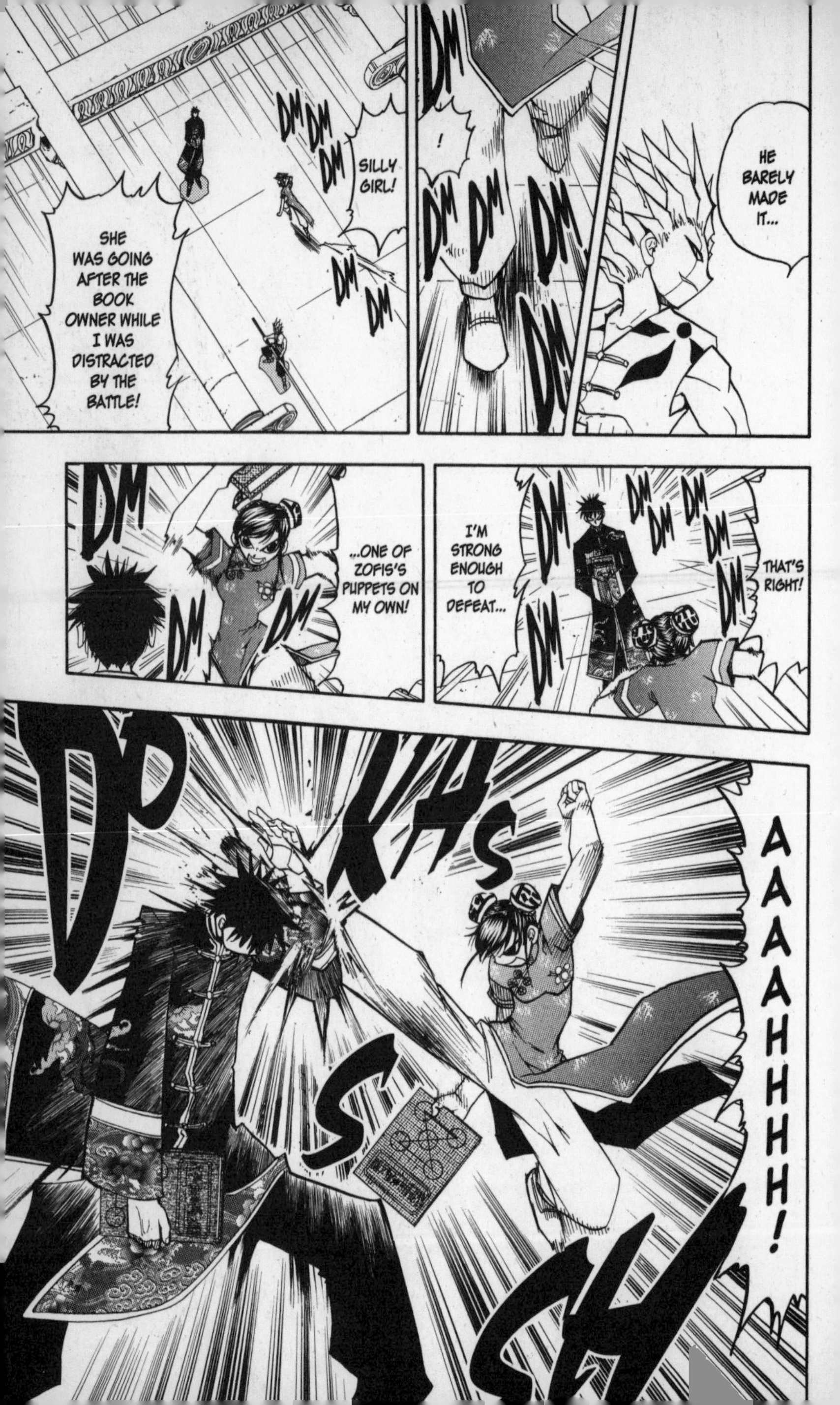
HE BARELY MADE IT...
DM
!
DM DM DM
DM
DM DM DM
SILLY GIRL!
SHE WAS GOING AFTER THE BOOK OWNER WHILE I WAS DISTRACTED BY THE BATTLE!
DM DM
DM DM DM DM DM
THAT'S RIGHT!
DM DM
I'M STRONG ENOUGH TO DEFEAT...
DM
...ONE OF ZOFIS'S PUPPETS ON MY OWN!
DM DM
AAAAHHHH!

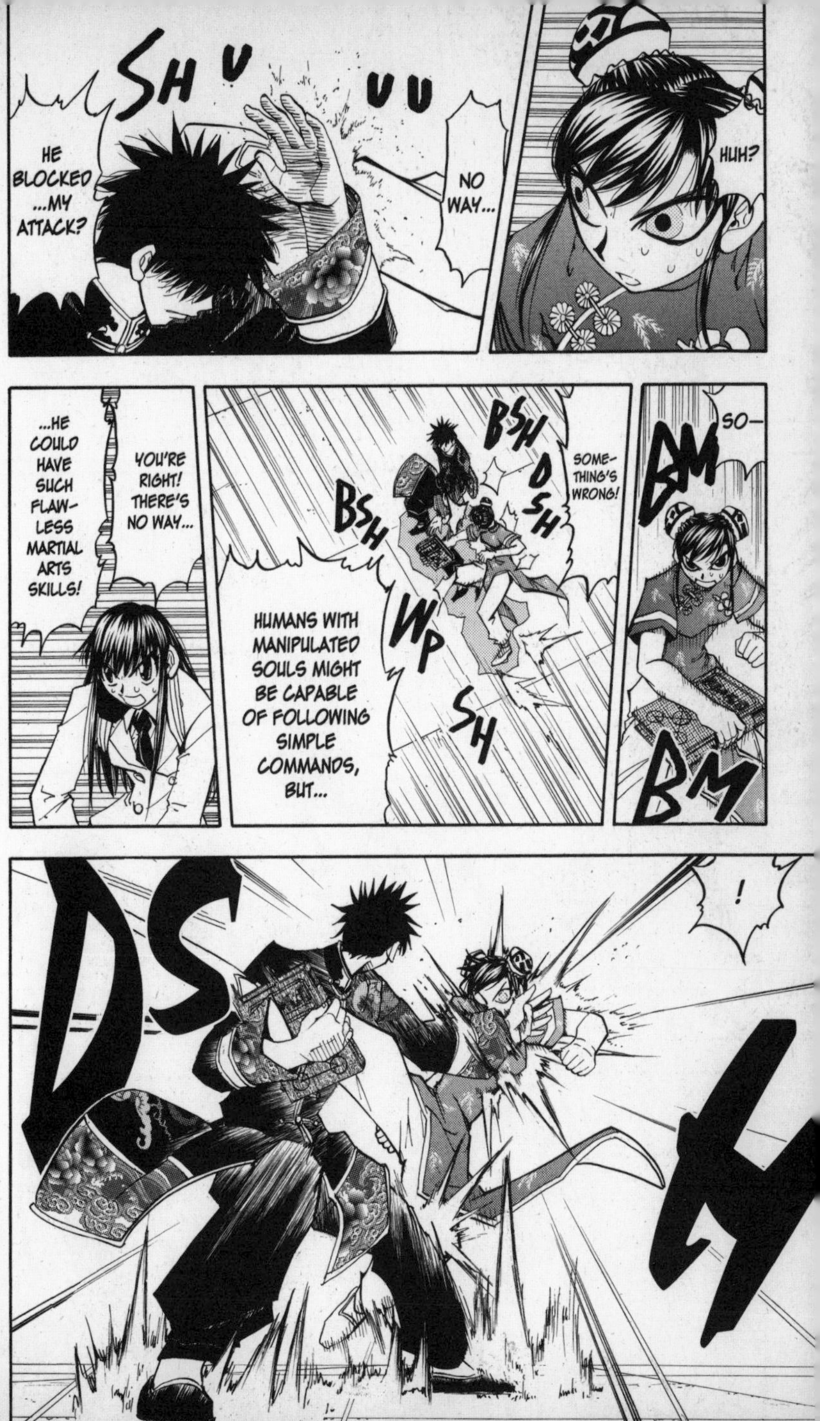
HUH?
SH U UU
NO WAY...
HE BLOCKED ...MY ATTACK?
SO—
BM
BM
SOME-THING'S WRONG!
BSH
DSH
BSH
WP
SH
HUMANS WITH MANIPULATED SOULS MIGHT BE CAPABLE OF FOLLOWING SIMPLE COMMANDS, BUT...
YOU'RE RIGHT! THERE'S NO WAY...
...HE COULD HAVE SUCH FLAW-LESS MARTIAL ARTS SKILLS!
!
DSCH

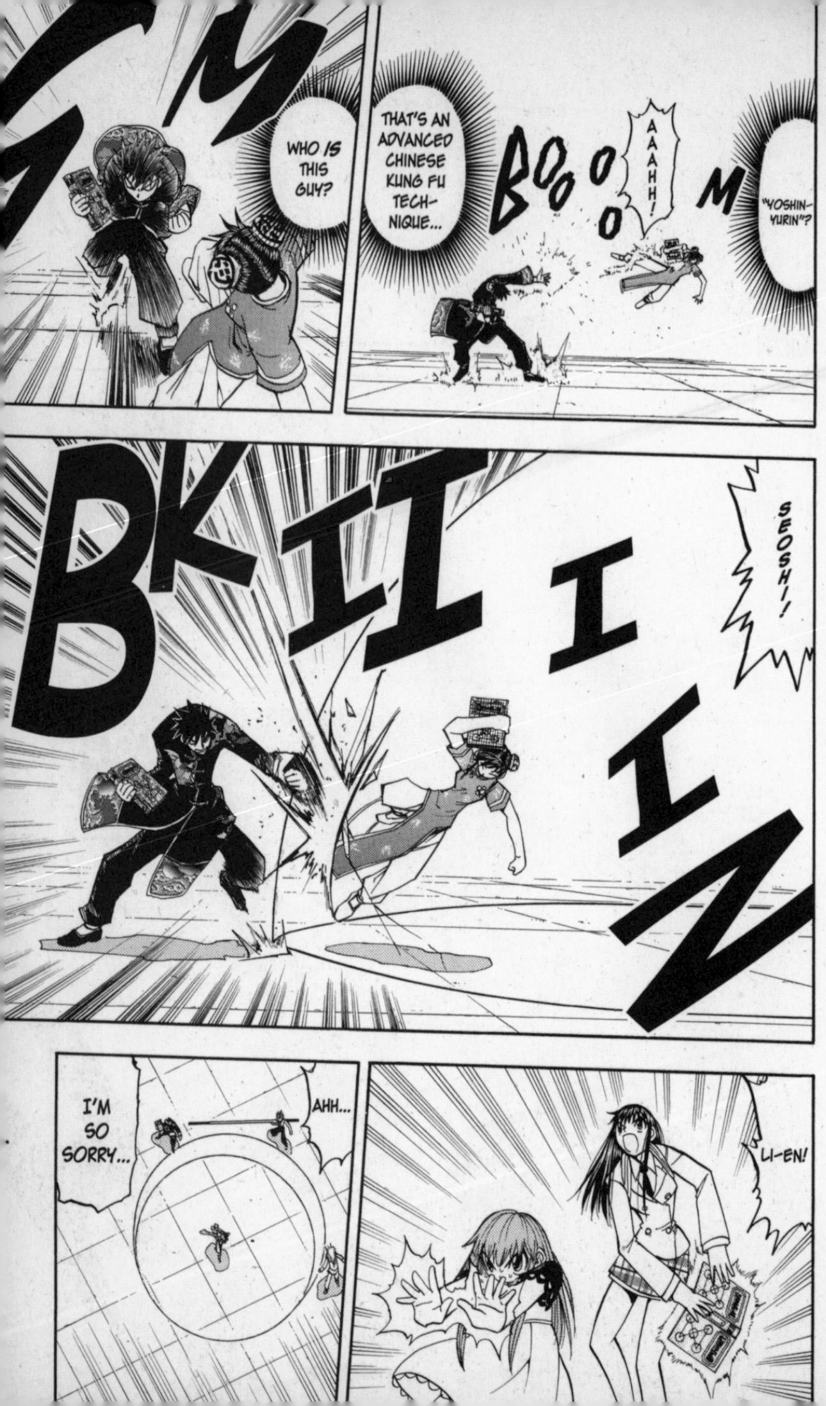
"YOSHIN-YURIN"?
AAAAHH!
BOOOOOM
THAT'S AN ADVANCED CHINESE KUNG FU TECH-NIQUE...
WHO *IS* THIS GUY?
SEOSHI!
BKIIIIN
LI-EN!
AHH...
I'M SO SORRY...

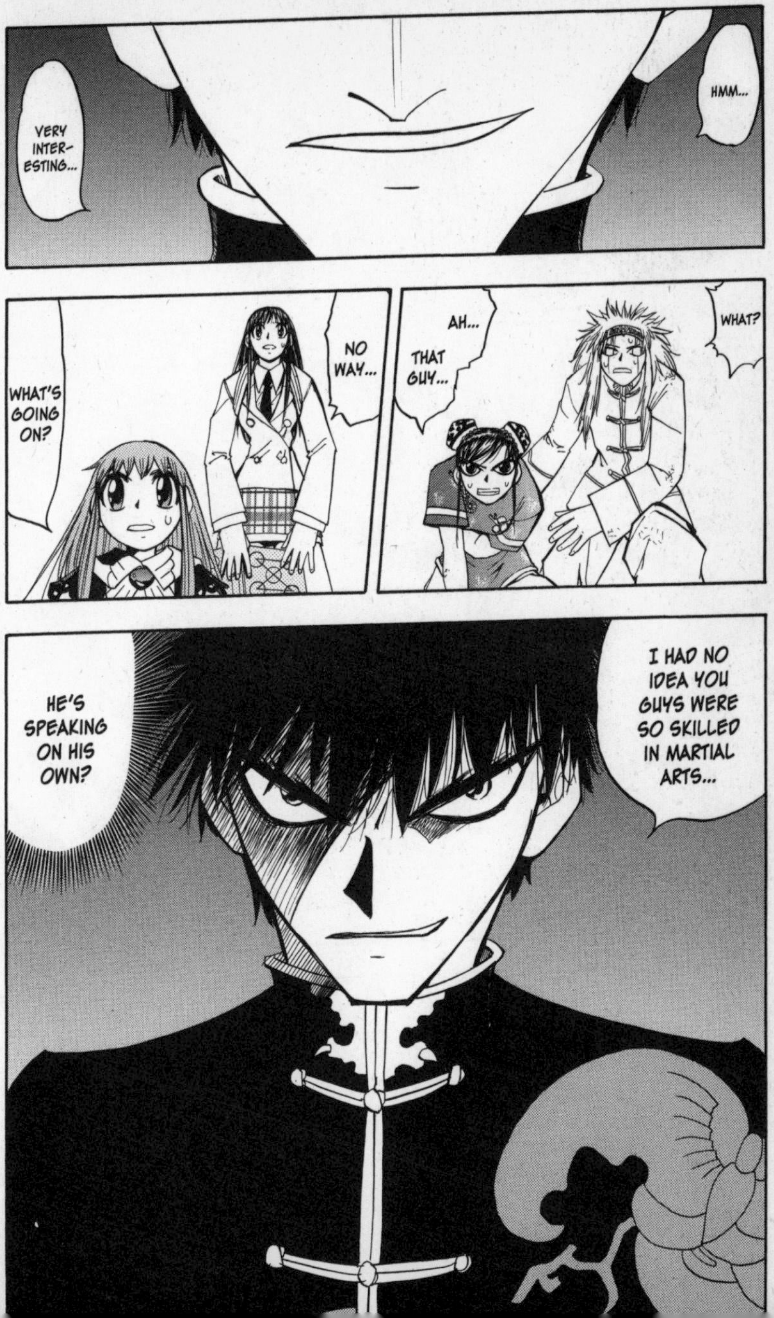
HMM...
VERY INTER-ESTING...
WHAT?
AH... THAT GUY...
NO WAY...
WHAT'S GOING ON?
I HAD NO IDEA YOU GUYS WERE SO SKILLED IN MARTIAL ARTS...
HE'S SPEAKING ON HIS OWN?

LEVEL 131: Seeking Strength

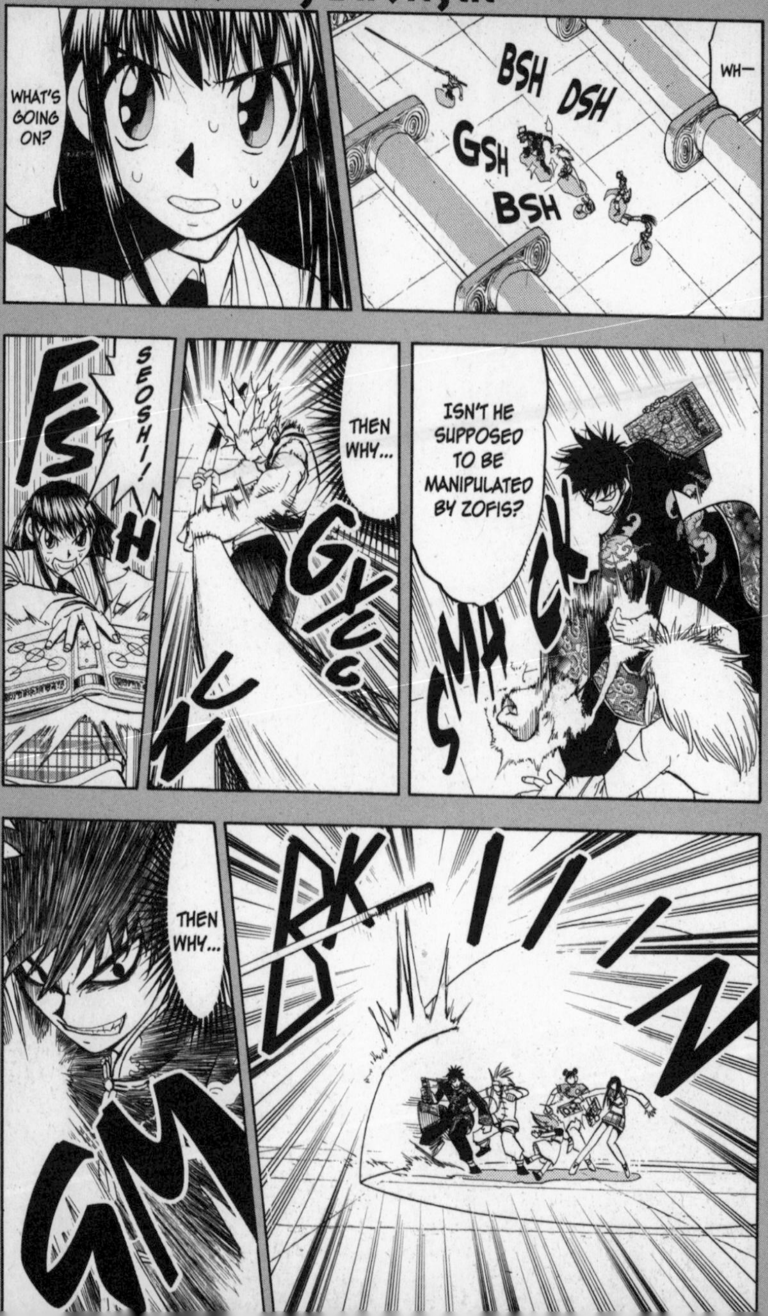
WH—
BSH
DSH
GSH
BSH
WHAT'S GOING ON?
ISN'T HE SUPPOSED TO BE MANIPULATED BY ZOFIS?
SMACK
THEN WHY...
SEOSHI!
THEN WHY...

LEVEL 131: Seeking Strength

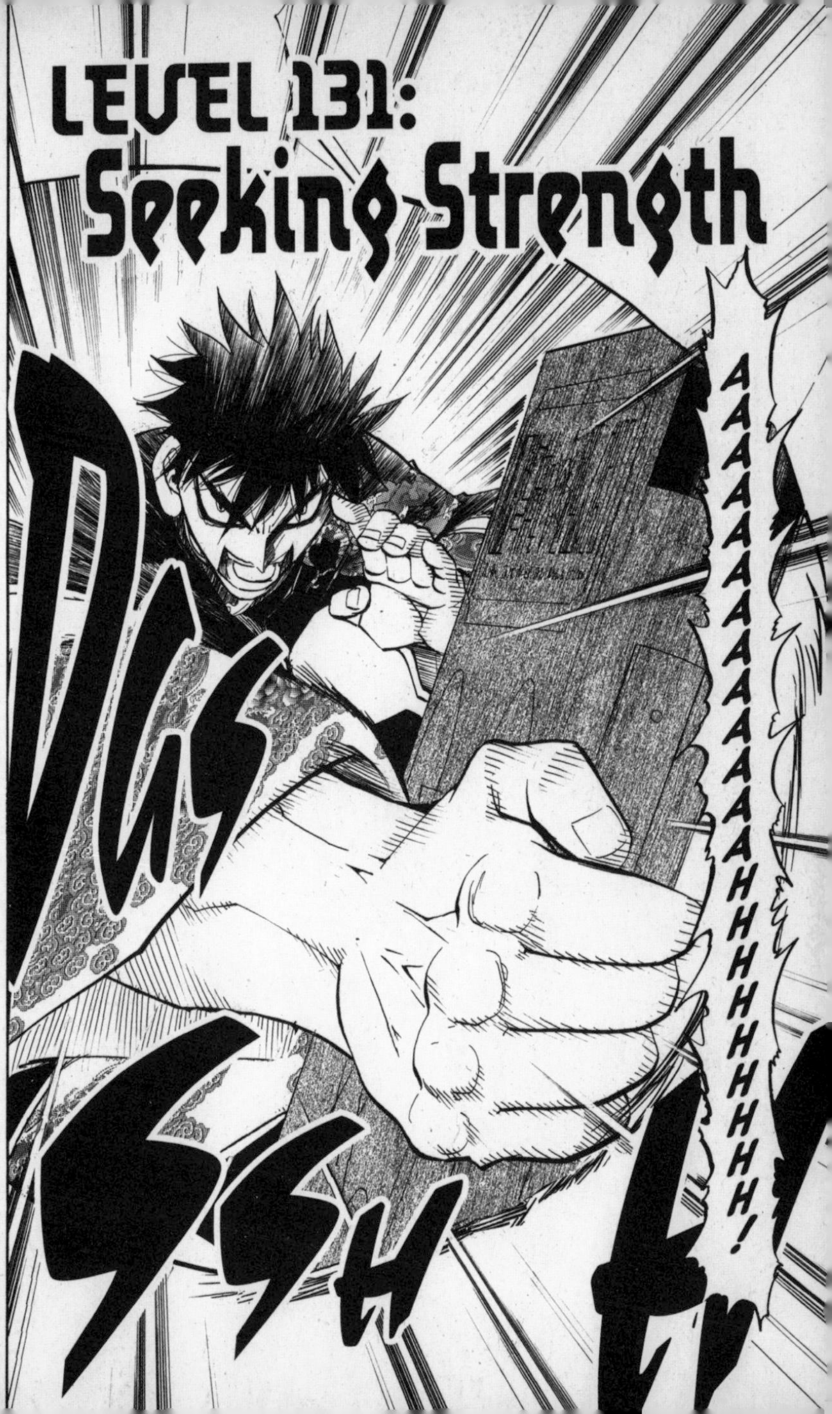
AAAAAAAAAAAAAAHHHHHHHH!

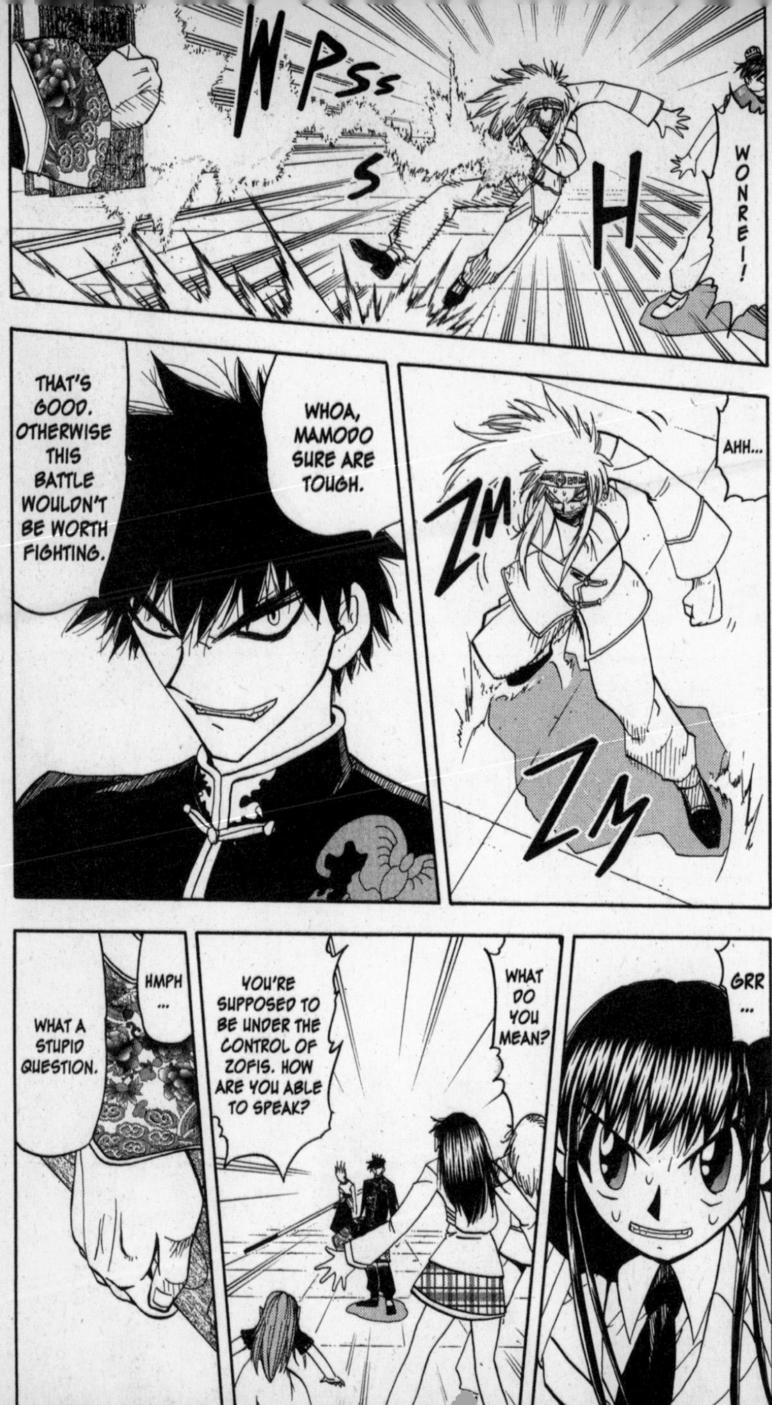
WONREI!
WPSss
S
H
AHH...
ZM
ZM
WHOA, MAMODO SURE ARE TOUGH.
THAT'S GOOD. OTHERWISE THIS BATTLE WOULDN'T BE WORTH FIGHTING.
GRR...
WHAT DO YOU MEAN?
YOU'RE SUPPOSED TO BE UNDER THE CONTROL OF ZOFIS. HOW ARE YOU ABLE TO SPEAK?
HMPH...
WHAT A STUPID QUESTION.

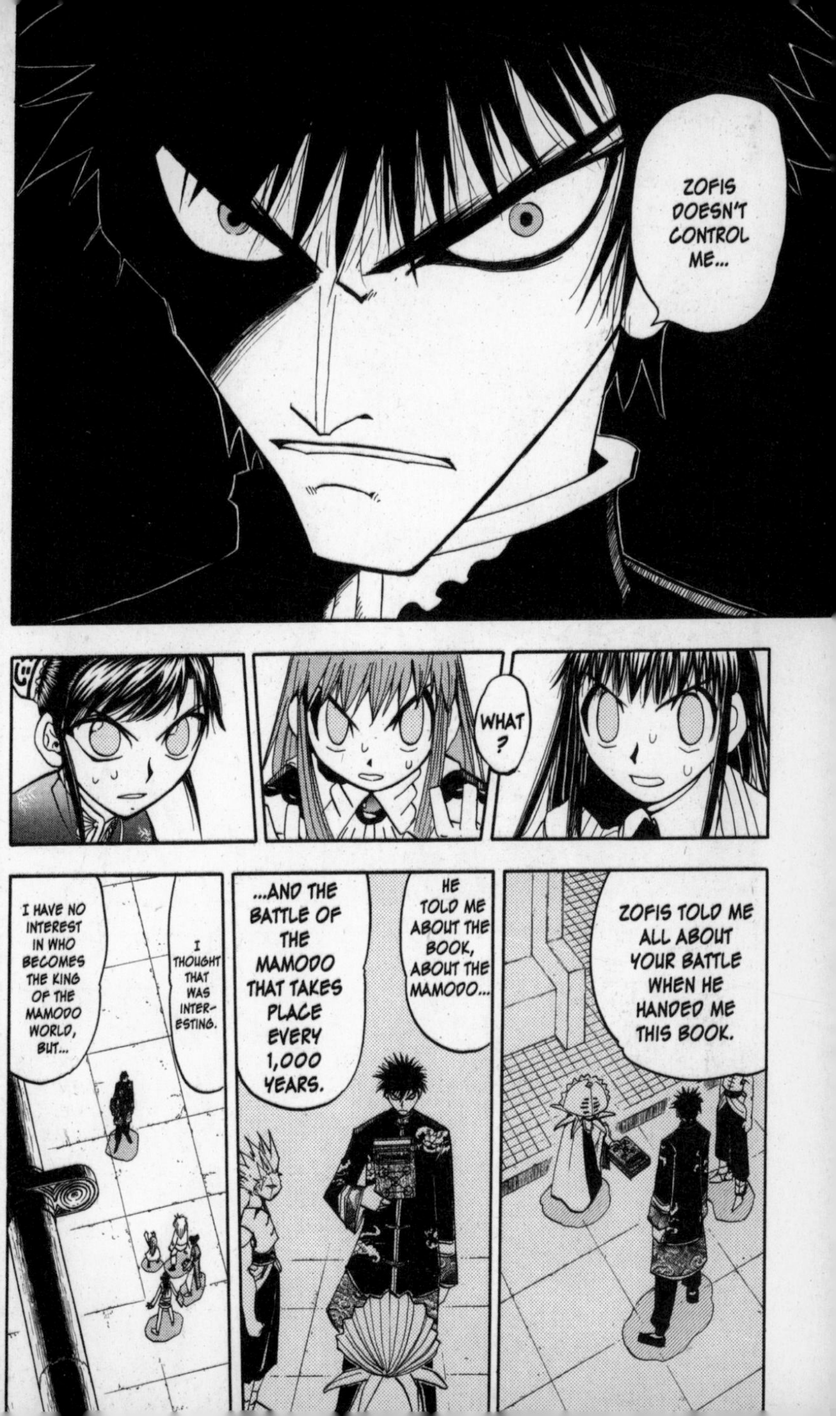
ZOFIS DOESN'T CONTROL ME...
WHAT?
ZOFIS TOLD ME ALL ABOUT YOUR BATTLE WHEN HE HANDED ME THIS BOOK.
HE TOLD ME ABOUT THE BOOK, ABOUT THE MAMODO...
...AND THE BATTLE OF THE MAMODO THAT TAKES PLACE EVERY 1,000 YEARS.
I THOUGHT THAT WAS INTER-ESTING.
I HAVE NO INTEREST IN WHO BECOMES THE KING OF THE MAMODO WORLD, BUT...

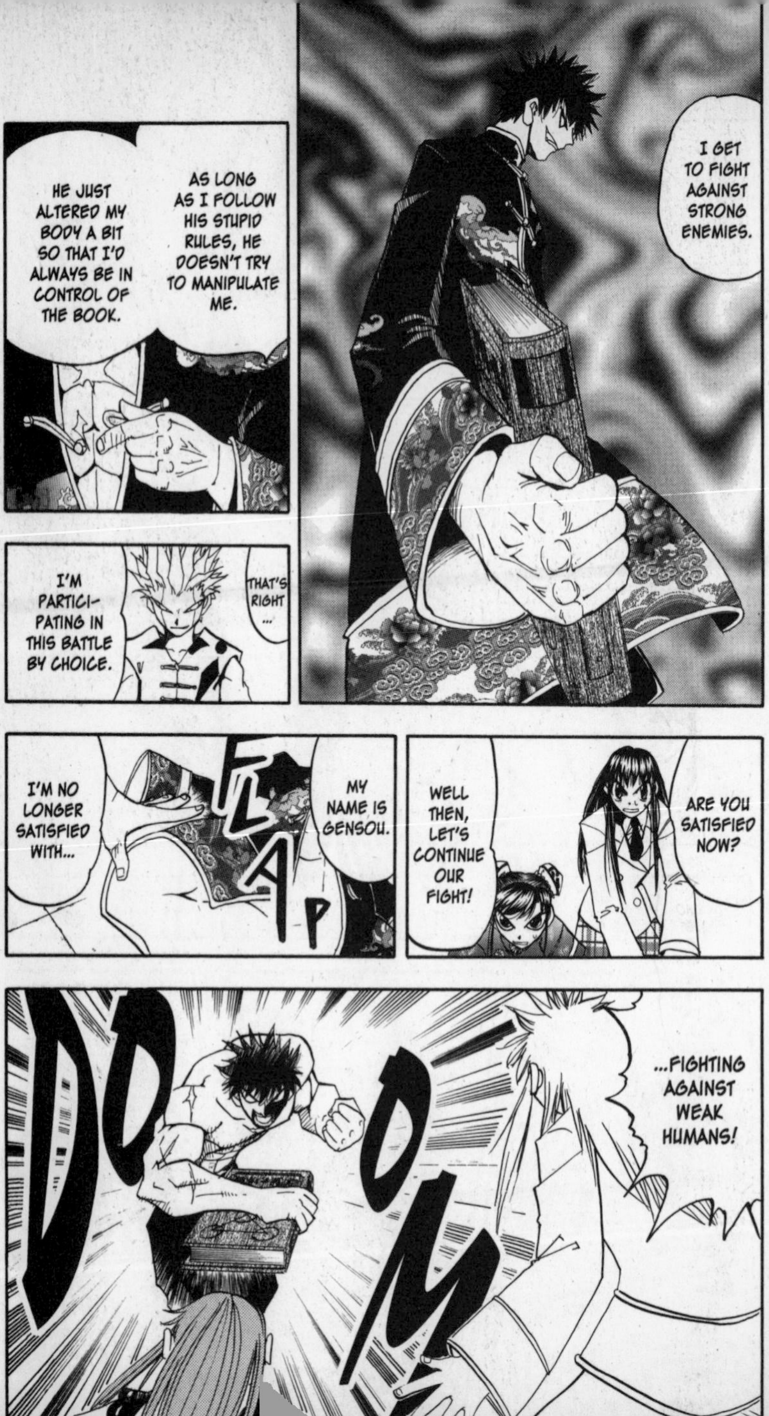
I GET TO FIGHT AGAINST STRONG ENEMIES.
AS LONG AS I FOLLOW HIS STUPID RULES, HE DOESN'T TRY TO MANIPULATE ME.
HE JUST ALTERED MY BODY A BIT SO THAT I'D ALWAYS BE IN CONTROL OF THE BOOK.
THAT'S RIGHT...
I'M PARTICI-PATING IN THIS BATTLE BY CHOICE.
ARE YOU SATISFIED NOW?
WELL THEN, LET'S CONTINUE OUR FIGHT!
MY NAME IS GENSOU.
FLAP
I'M NO LONGER SATISFIED WITH...
...FIGHTING AGAINST WEAK HUMANS!
DOOM

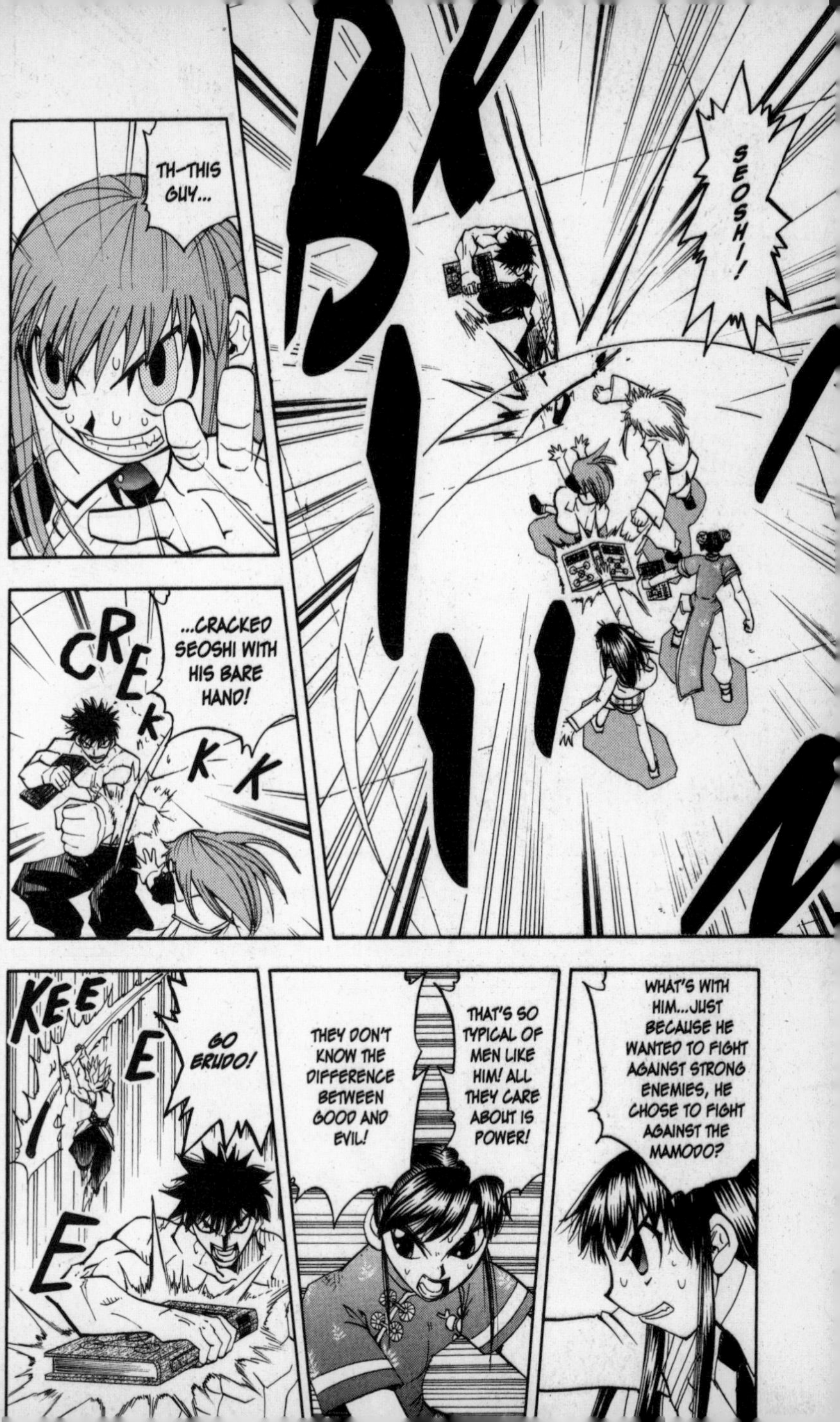
SEOSHI!!
TH-THIS GUY...
...CRACKED SEOSHI WITH HIS BARE HAND!
CREKKK
WHAT'S WITH HIM...JUST BECAUSE HE WANTED TO FIGHT AGAINST STRONG ENEMIES, HE CHOSE TO FIGHT AGAINST THE MAMODO?
THAT'S SO TYPICAL OF MEN LIKE HIM! ALL THEY CARE ABOUT IS POWER!
THEY DON'T KNOW THE DIFFERENCE BETWEEN GOOD AND EVIL!
GO ERUDO!

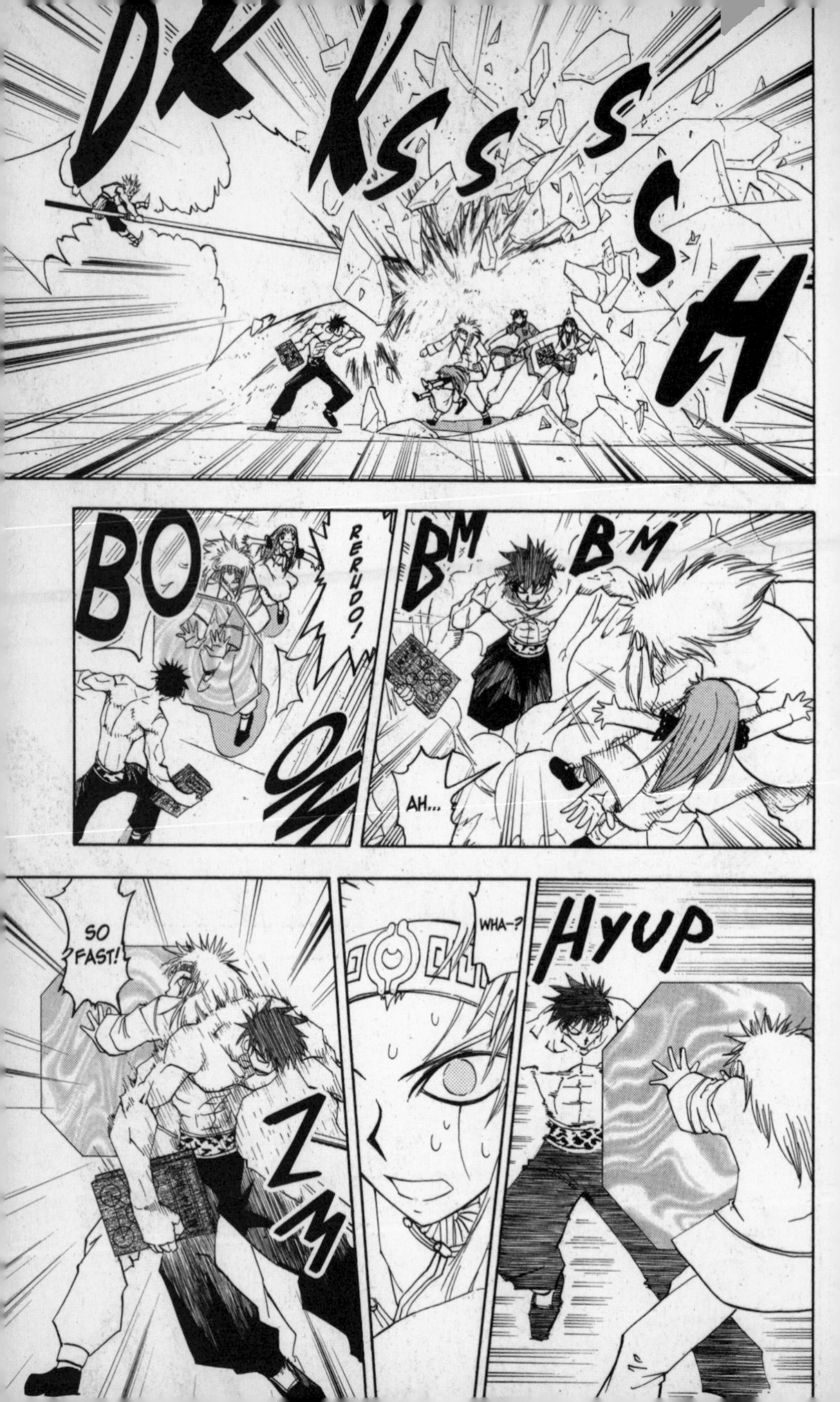
DKSSSSH
BM
BM
AH...
RERUDO!
BO
OM
HYUP
WHA-?
SO FAST!
ZM

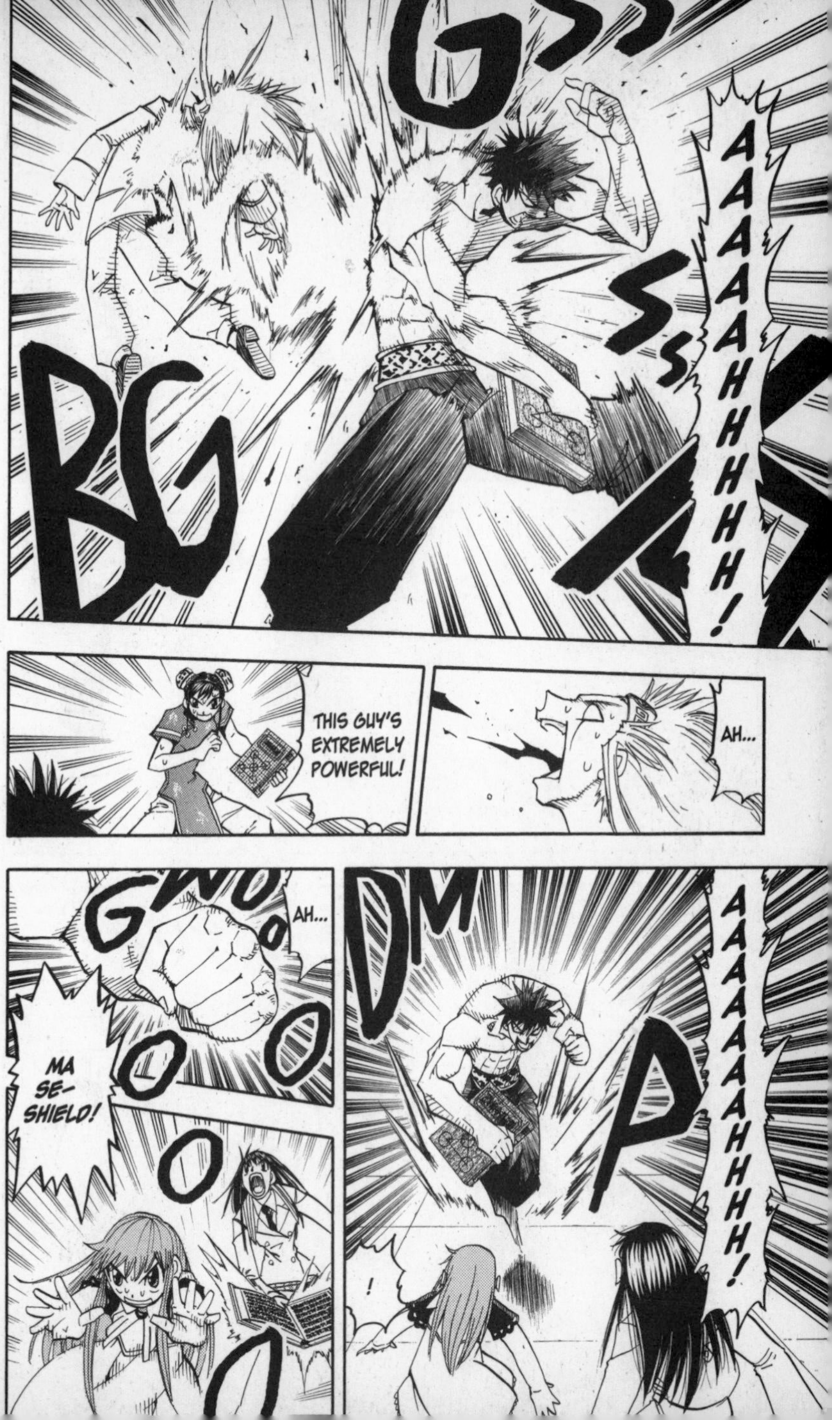

AAAAAHHHHHH!
G
SS
BG
AH...
THIS GUY'S EXTREMELY POWERFUL!
AAAAAAAHHHHH!
DMP
GWOOOOO
AH...
MA SE-SHIELD!
!

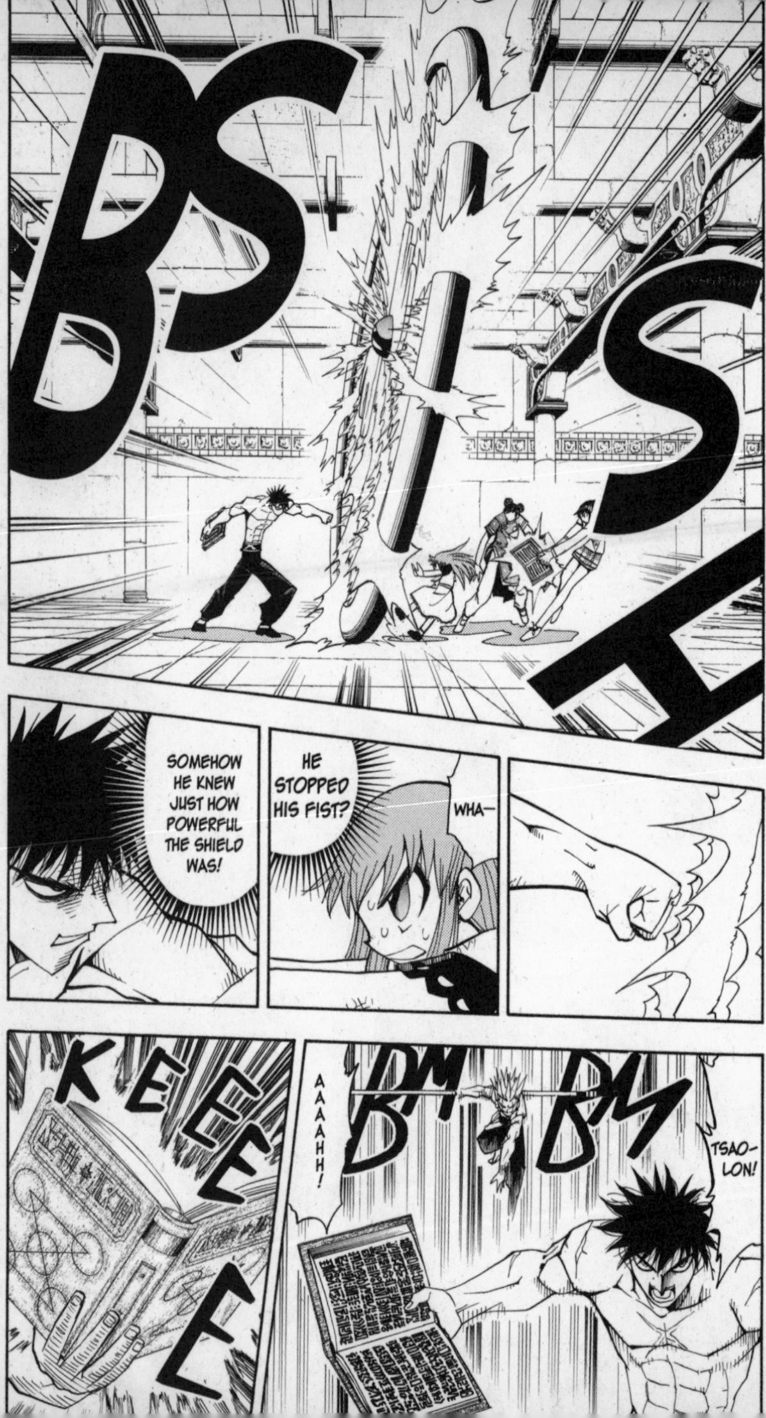
BSSH
WHA-
HE STOPPED HIS FIST?
SOMEHOW HE KNEW JUST HOW POWERFUL THE SHIELD WAS!
TSAO-LON!
BM BM
AAAAAHH!
KEEEE

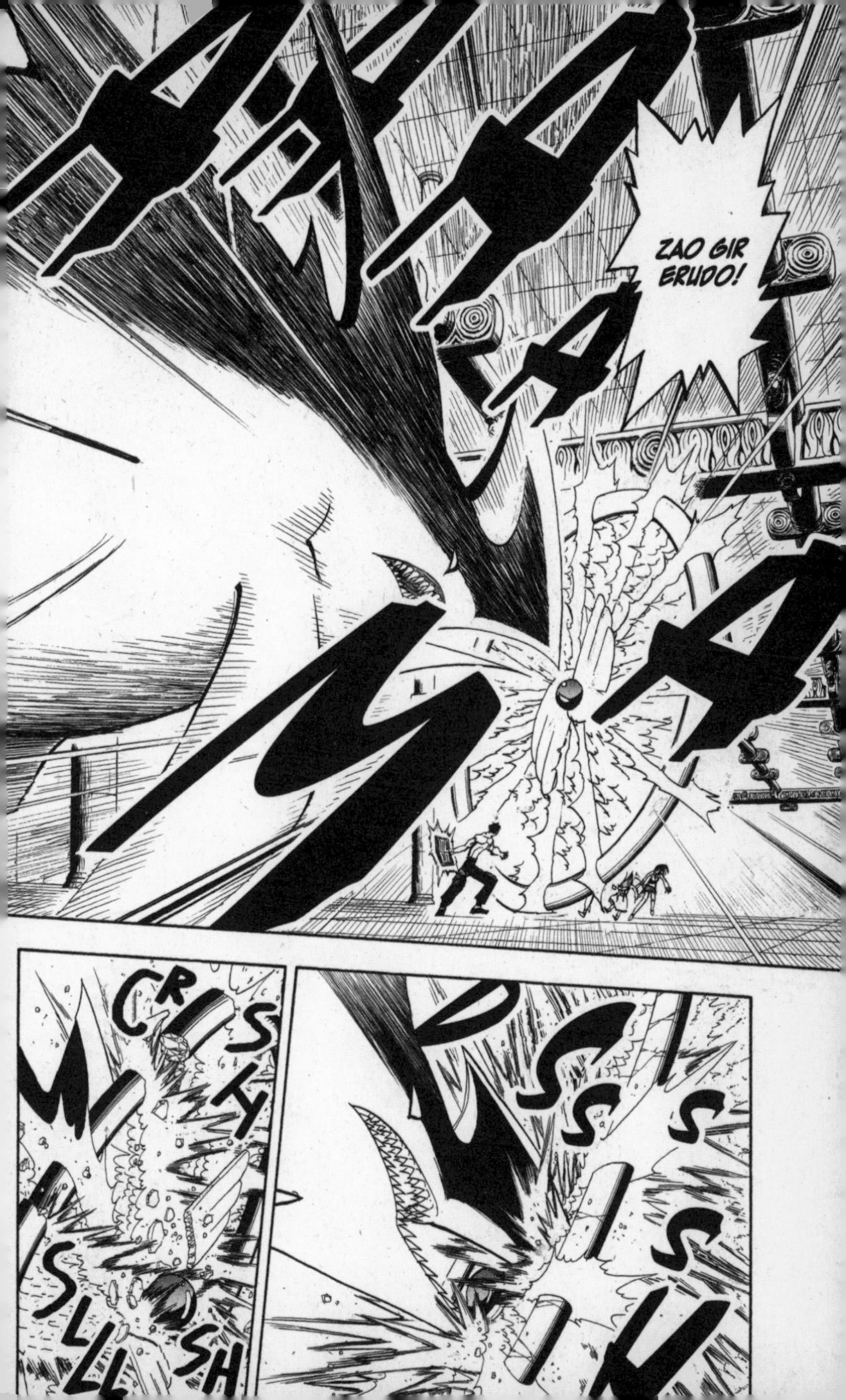
ZAO GIR ERUDO!

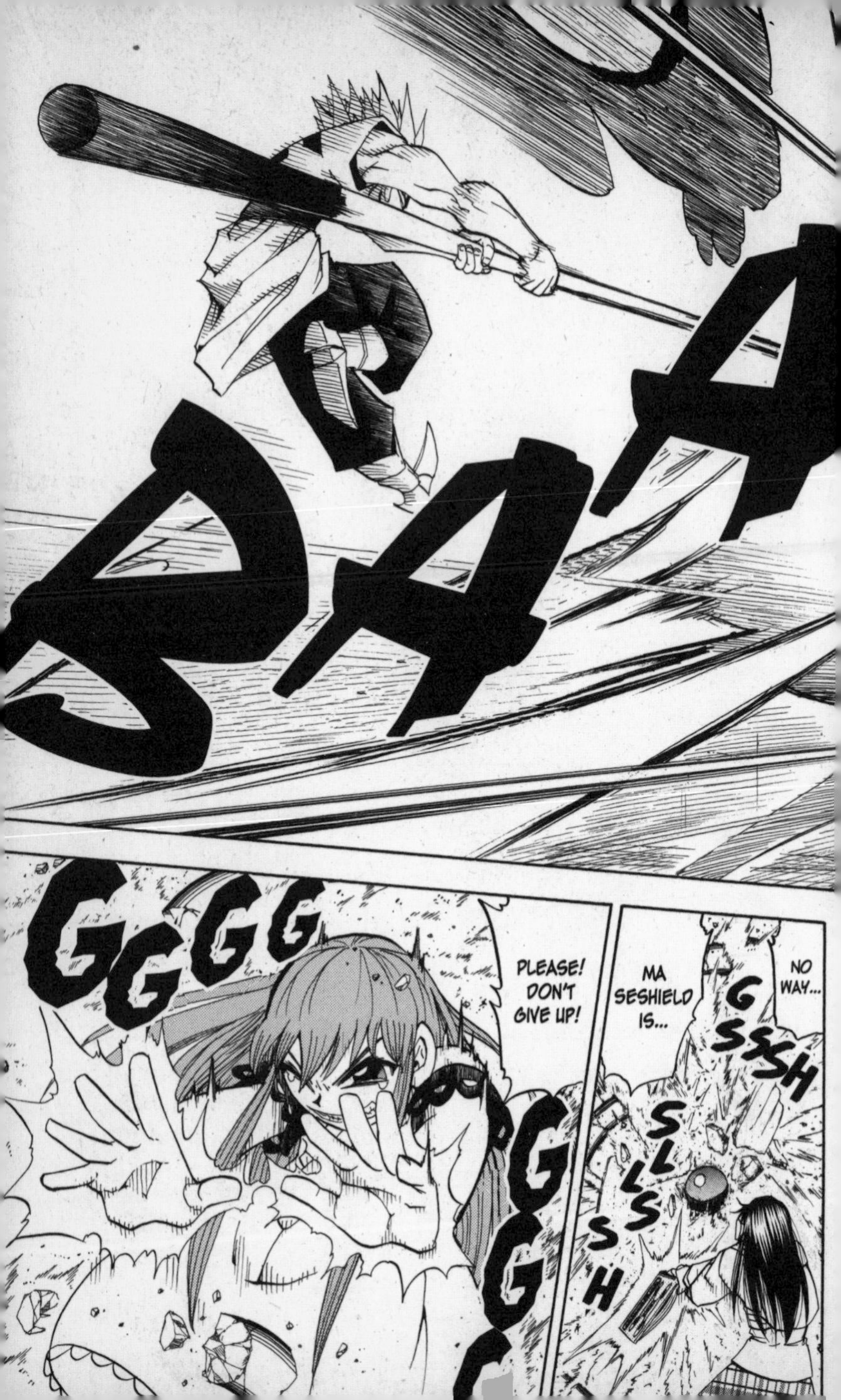
DAAA
NO WAY...
MA SESHIELD IS...
GSSSH
SLLSSH
PLEASE! DON'T GIVE UP!
GGGG
GG

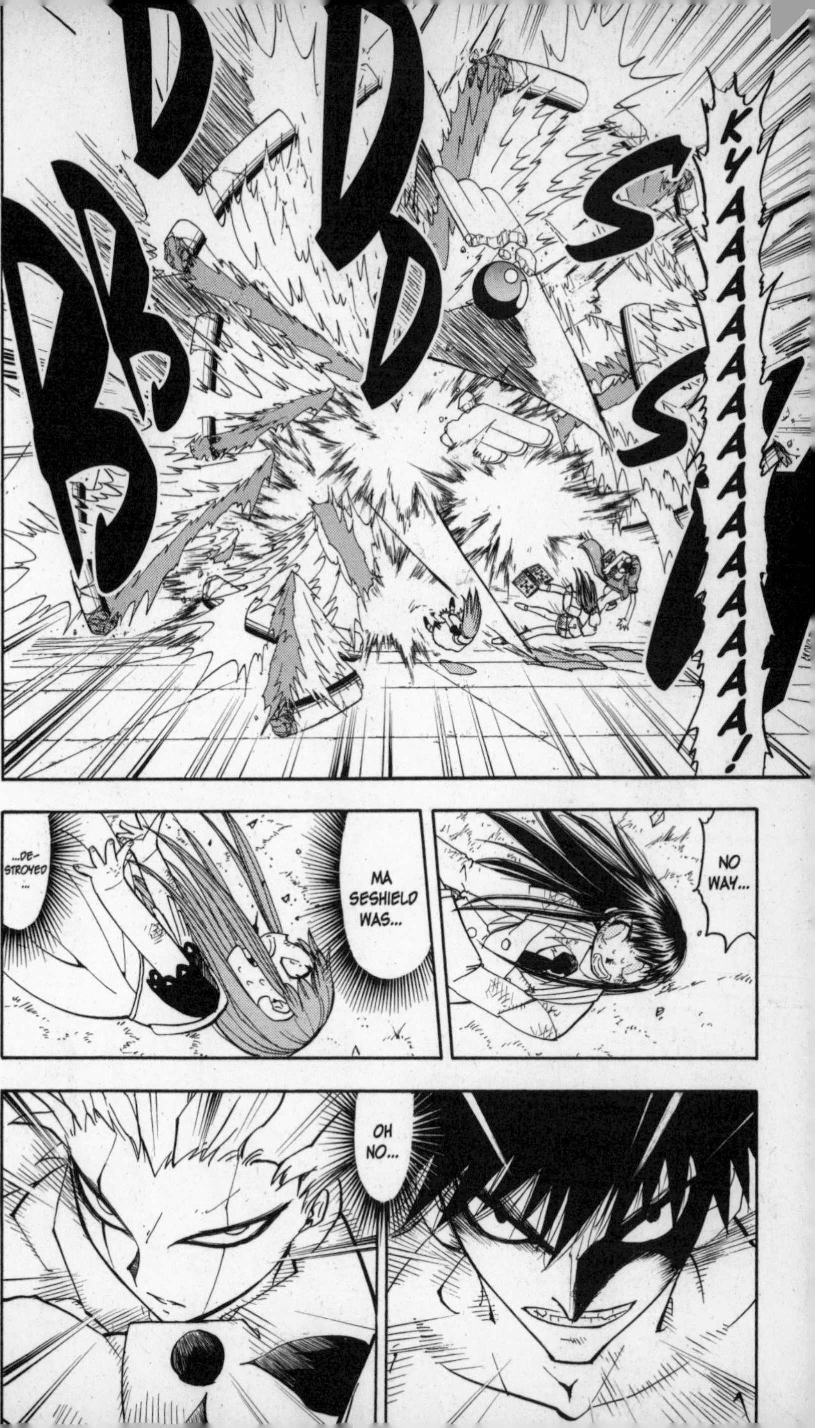
KYAAAAAAAAAAAAAA!
NO WAY...
MA SESHIELD WAS...
...DESTROYED...
OH NO...

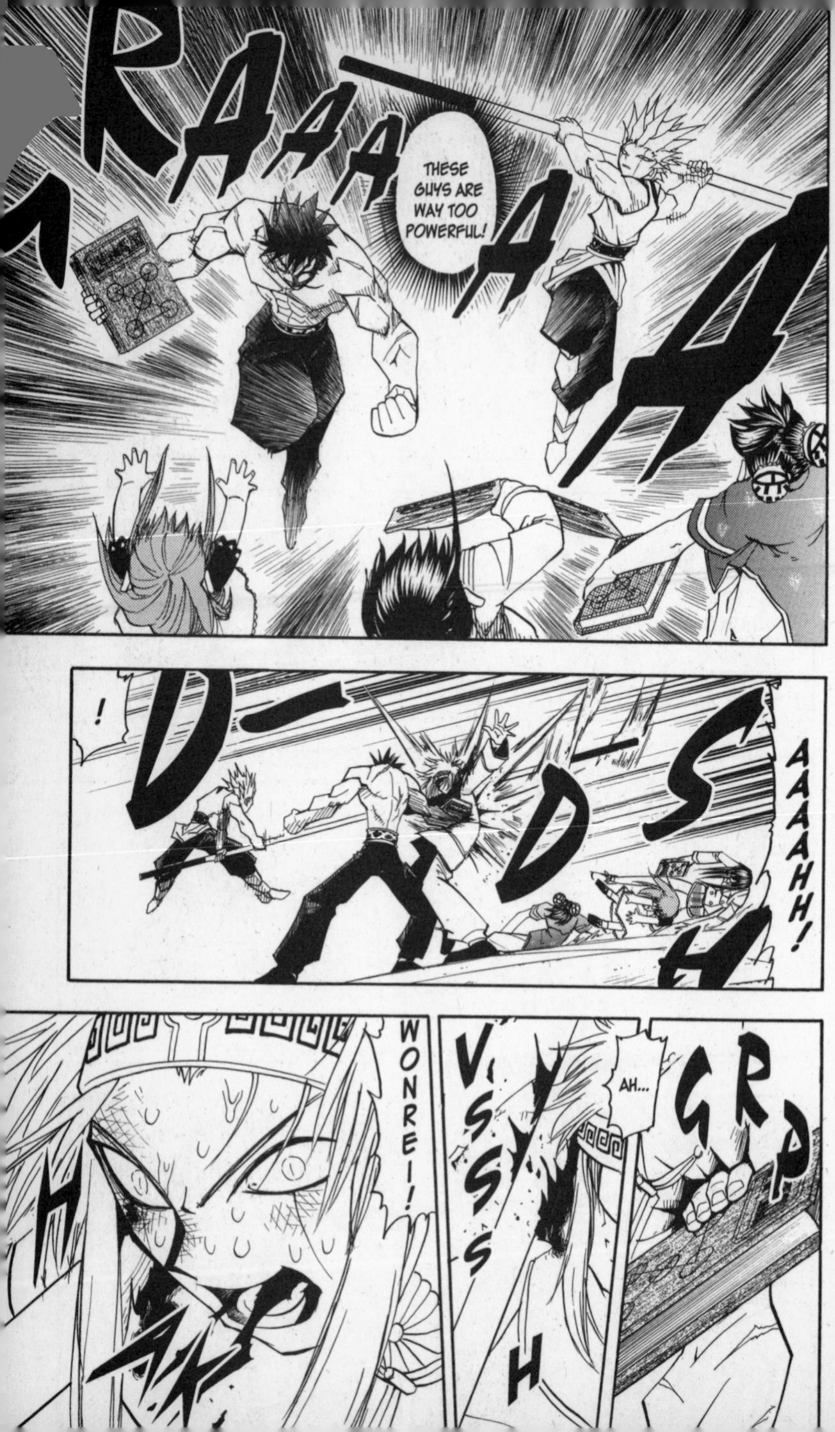
THESE GUYS ARE WAY TOO POWERFUL!
AAAAAHH!
!
AH...
WONREI!!

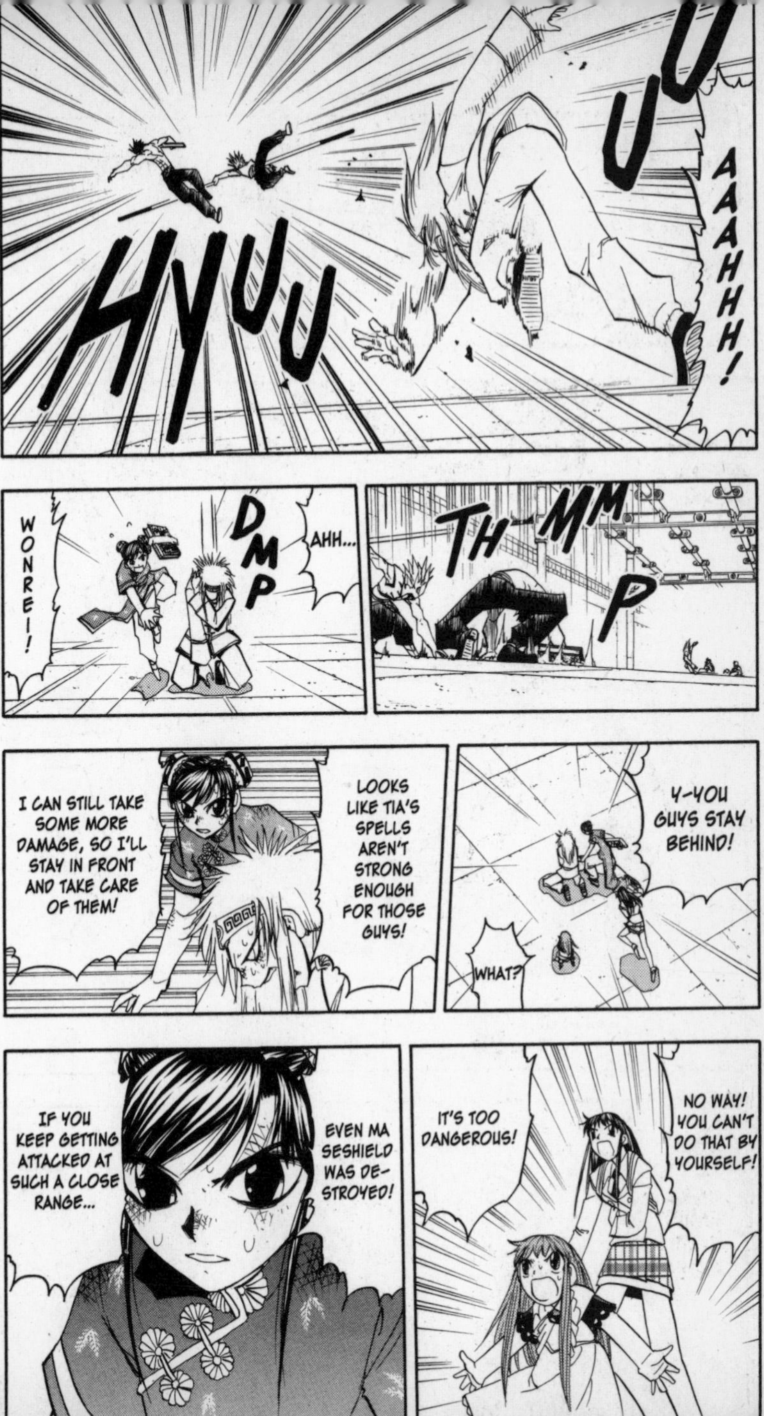
UUU
AAAHHH!
HYUUU
THMMMP
AHH...
DMP
WONREI!
Y-YOU GUYS STAY BEHIND!
WHAT?
LOOKS LIKE TIA'S SPELLS AREN'T STRONG ENOUGH FOR THOSE GUYS!
I CAN STILL TAKE SOME MORE DAMAGE, SO I'LL STAY IN FRONT AND TAKE CARE OF THEM!
NO WAY! YOU CAN'T DO THAT BY YOURSELF!
IT'S TOO DANGEROUS!
EVEN MA SESHIELD WAS DE-STROYED!
IF YOU KEEP GETTING ATTACKED AT SUCH A CLOSE RANGE...

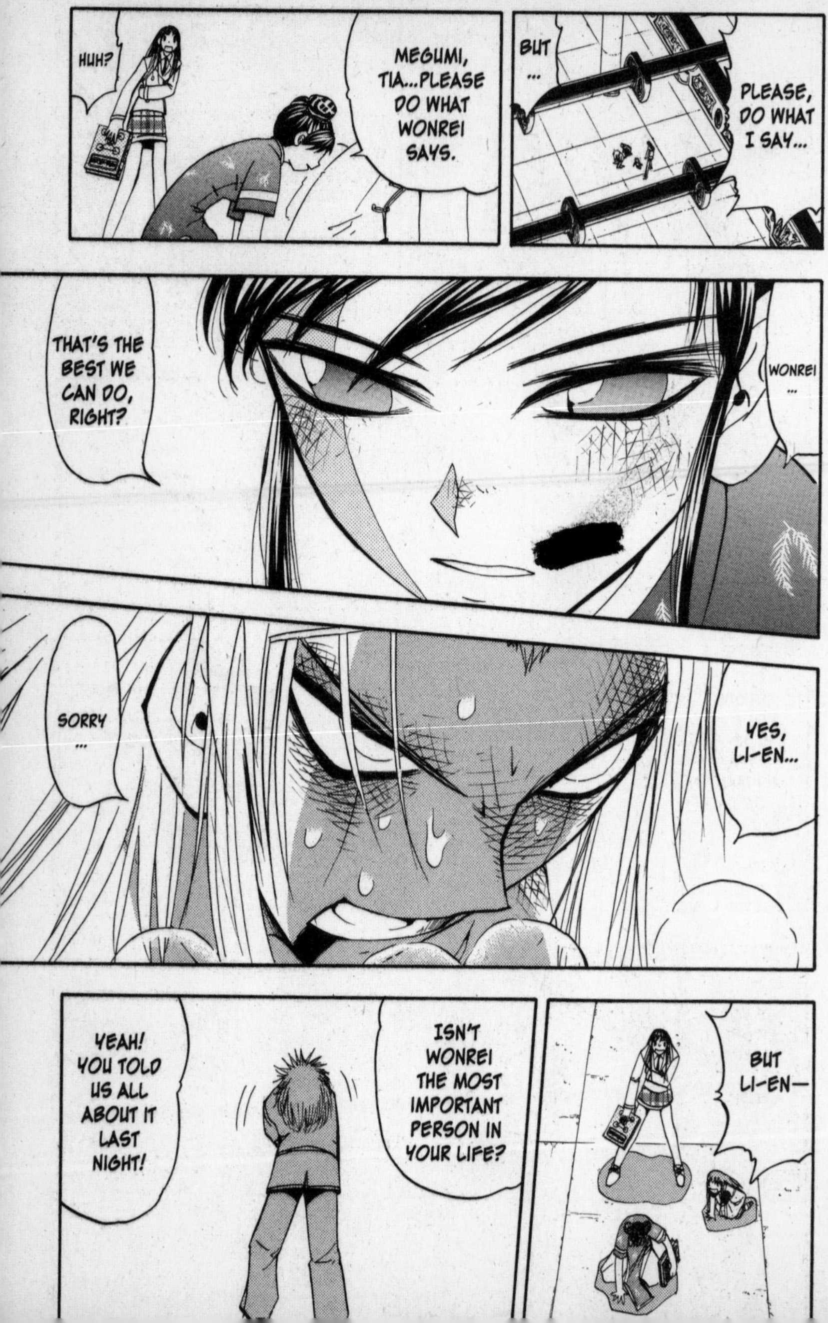

BUT ...
PLEASE, DO WHAT I SAY...
MEGUMI, TIA...PLEASE DO WHAT WONREI SAYS.
HUH?
WONREI ...
THAT'S THE BEST WE CAN DO, RIGHT?
YES, LI-EN...
SORRY ...
BUT LI-EN—
ISN'T WONREI THE MOST IMPORTANT PERSON IN YOUR LIFE?
YEAH! YOU TOLD US ALL ABOUT IT LAST NIGHT!

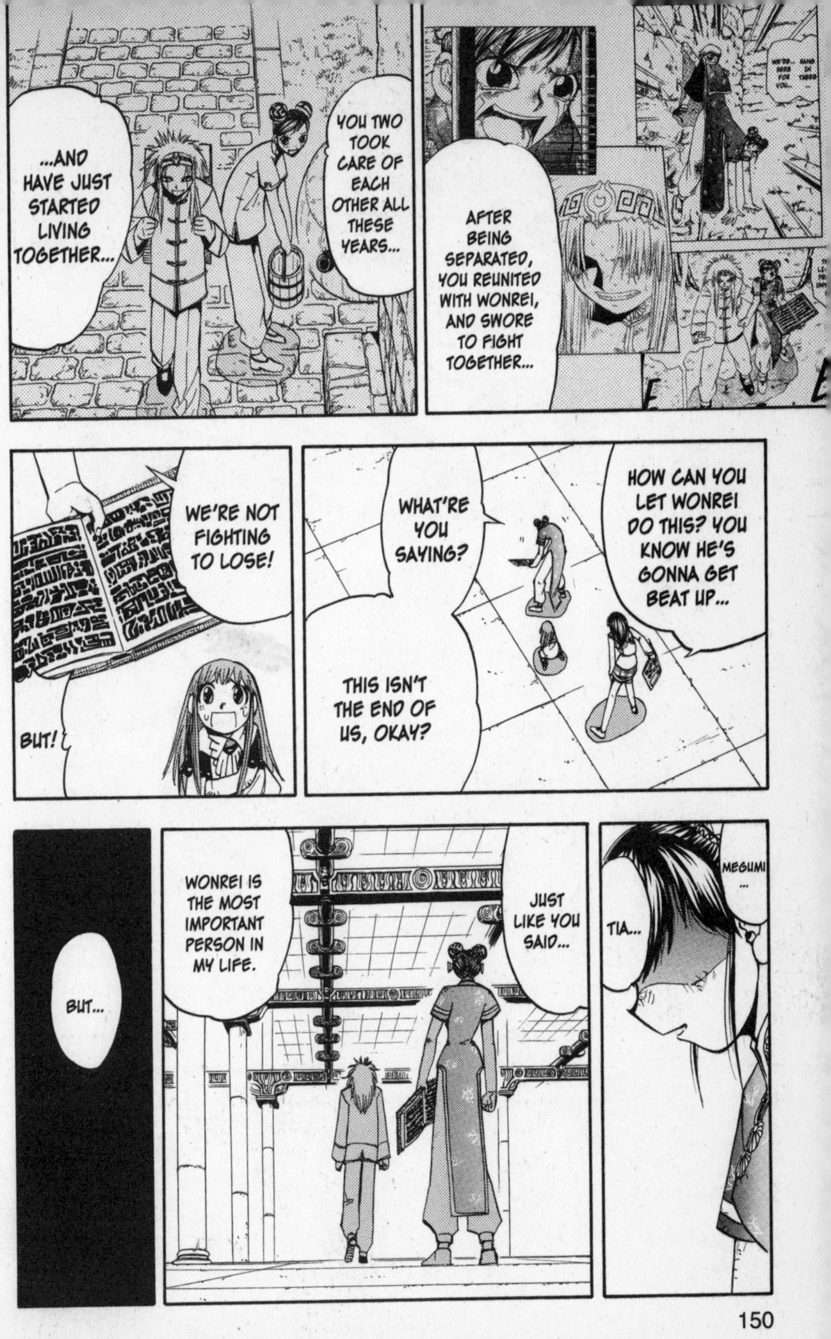
WE'RE... HERE FOR YOU...
HANG IN THERE...
AFTER BEING SEPARATED, YOU REUNITED WITH WONREI, AND SWORE TO FIGHT TOGETHER...
YOU TWO TOOK CARE OF EACH OTHER ALL THESE YEARS...
...AND HAVE JUST STARTED LIVING TOGETHER...
HOW CAN YOU LET WONREI DO THIS? YOU KNOW HE'S GONNA GET BEAT UP...
WHAT'RE YOU SAYING?
THIS ISN'T THE END OF US, OKAY?
WE'RE NOT FIGHTING TO LOSE!
BUT!
MEGUMI...
TIA...
JUST LIKE YOU SAID...
WONREI IS THE MOST IMPORTANT PERSON IN MY LIFE.
BUT...

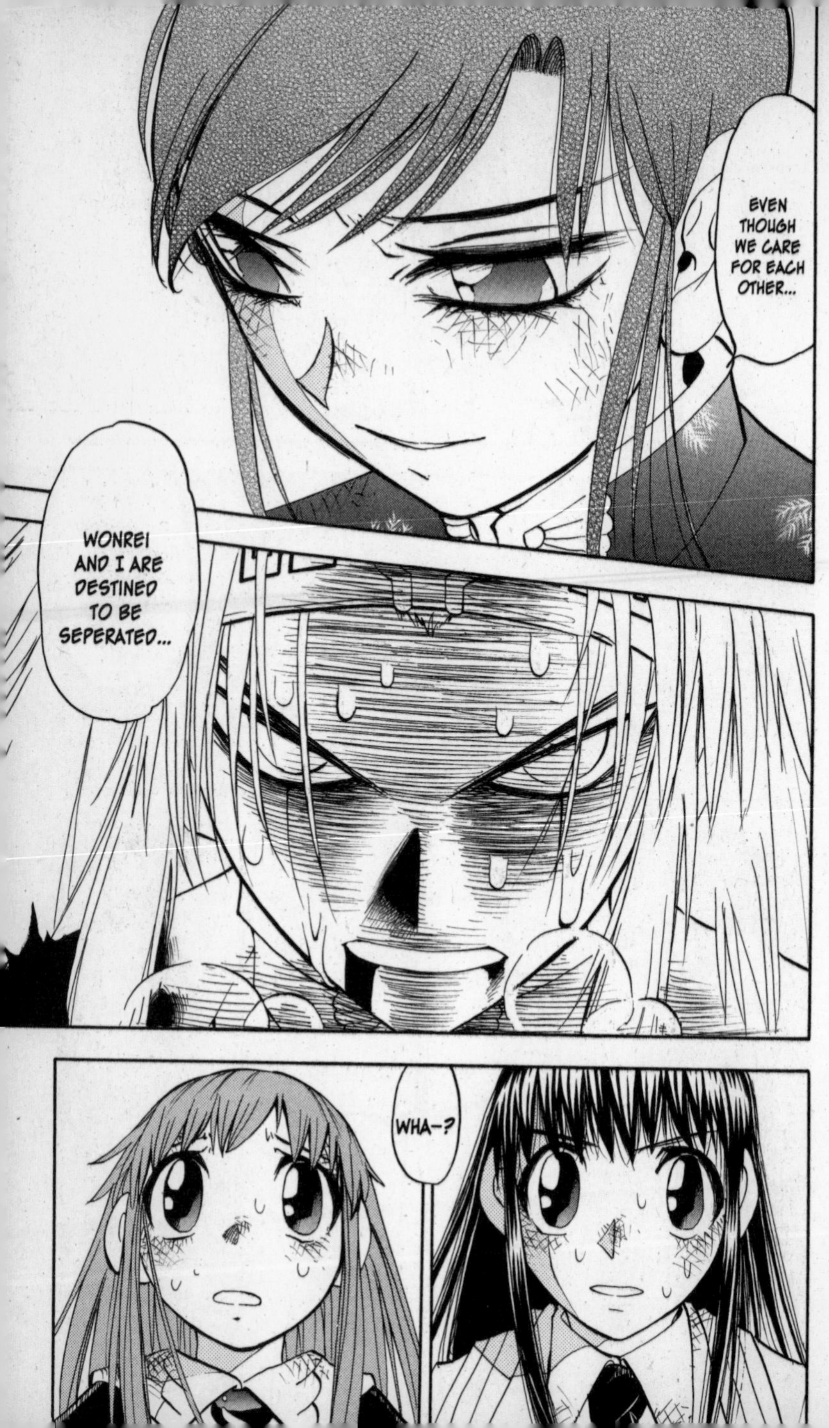
EVEN THOUGH WE CARE FOR EACH OTHER...
WONREI AND I ARE DESTINED TO BE SEPERATED...
WHA-?

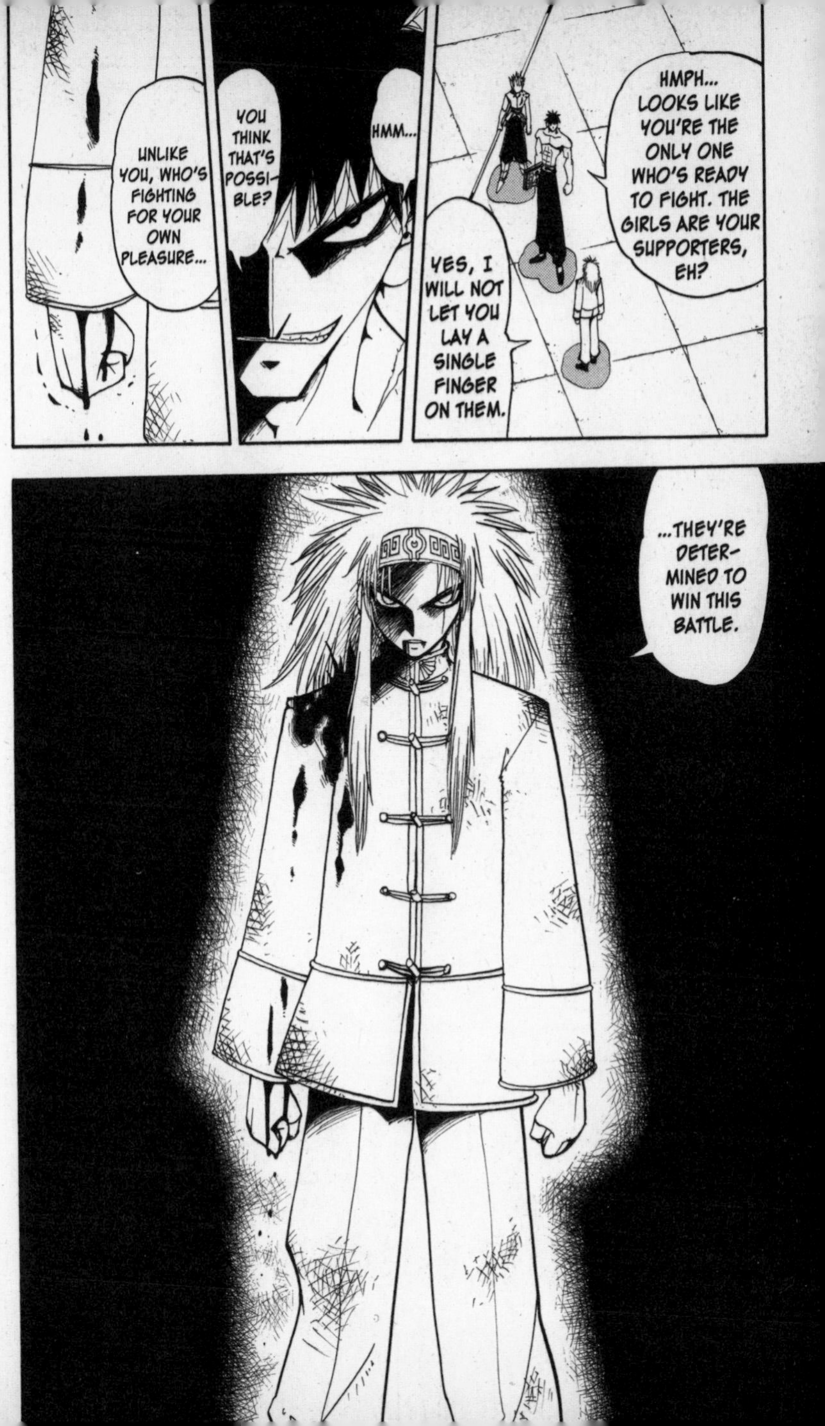
HMPH... LOOKS LIKE YOU'RE THE ONLY ONE WHO'S READY TO FIGHT. THE GIRLS ARE YOUR SUPPORTERS, EH?
YES, I WILL NOT LET YOU LAY A SINGLE FINGER ON THEM.
HMM...
YOU THINK THAT'S POSSI-BLE?
UNLIKE YOU, WHO'S FIGHTING FOR YOUR OWN PLEASURE...
...THEY'RE DETER-MINED TO WIN THIS BATTLE.

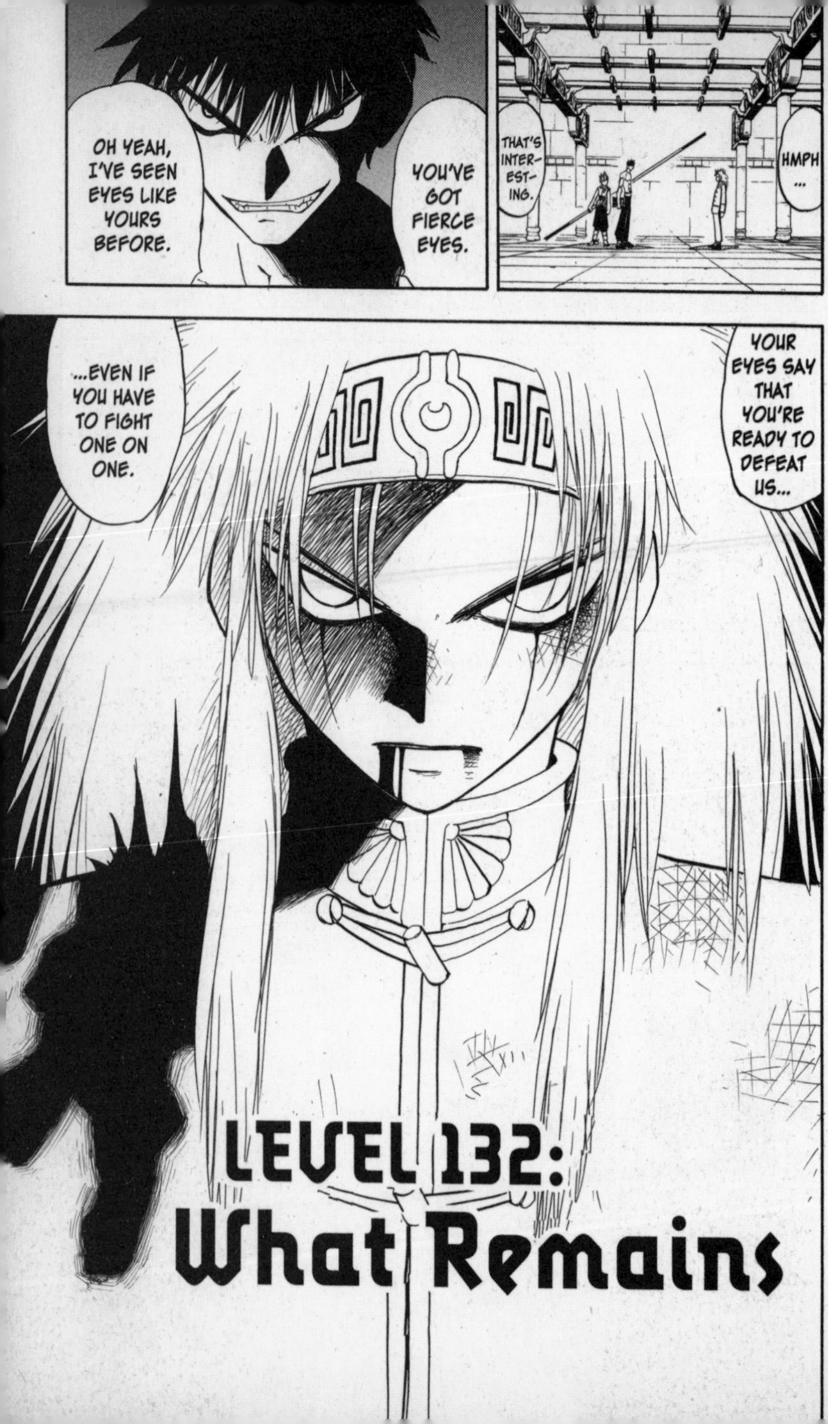
HMPH...
THAT'S INTER-EST-ING.
YOU'VE GOT FIERCE EYES.
OH YEAH, I'VE SEEN EYES LIKE YOURS BEFORE.
YOUR EYES SAY THAT YOU'RE READY TO DEFEAT US...
...EVEN IF YOU HAVE TO FIGHT ONE ON ONE.
LEVEL 132: What Remains

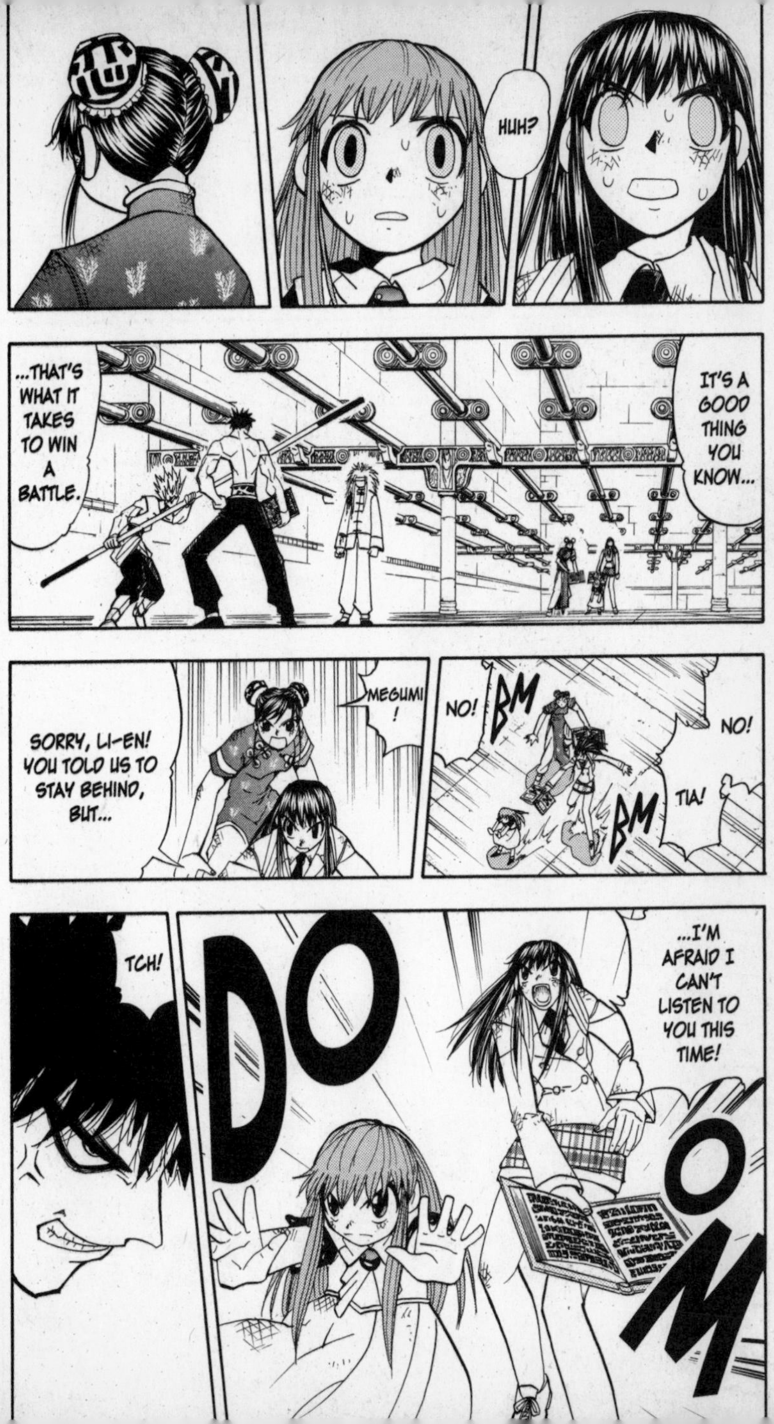
HUH?
IT'S A GOOD THING YOU KNOW...
...THAT'S WHAT IT TAKES TO WIN A BATTLE.
NO!
TIA!
NO!
BM
BM
MEGUMI!
SORRY, LI-EN! YOU TOLD US TO STAY BEHIND, BUT...
...I'M AFRAID I CAN'T LISTEN TO YOU THIS TIME!
DOOM
TCH!

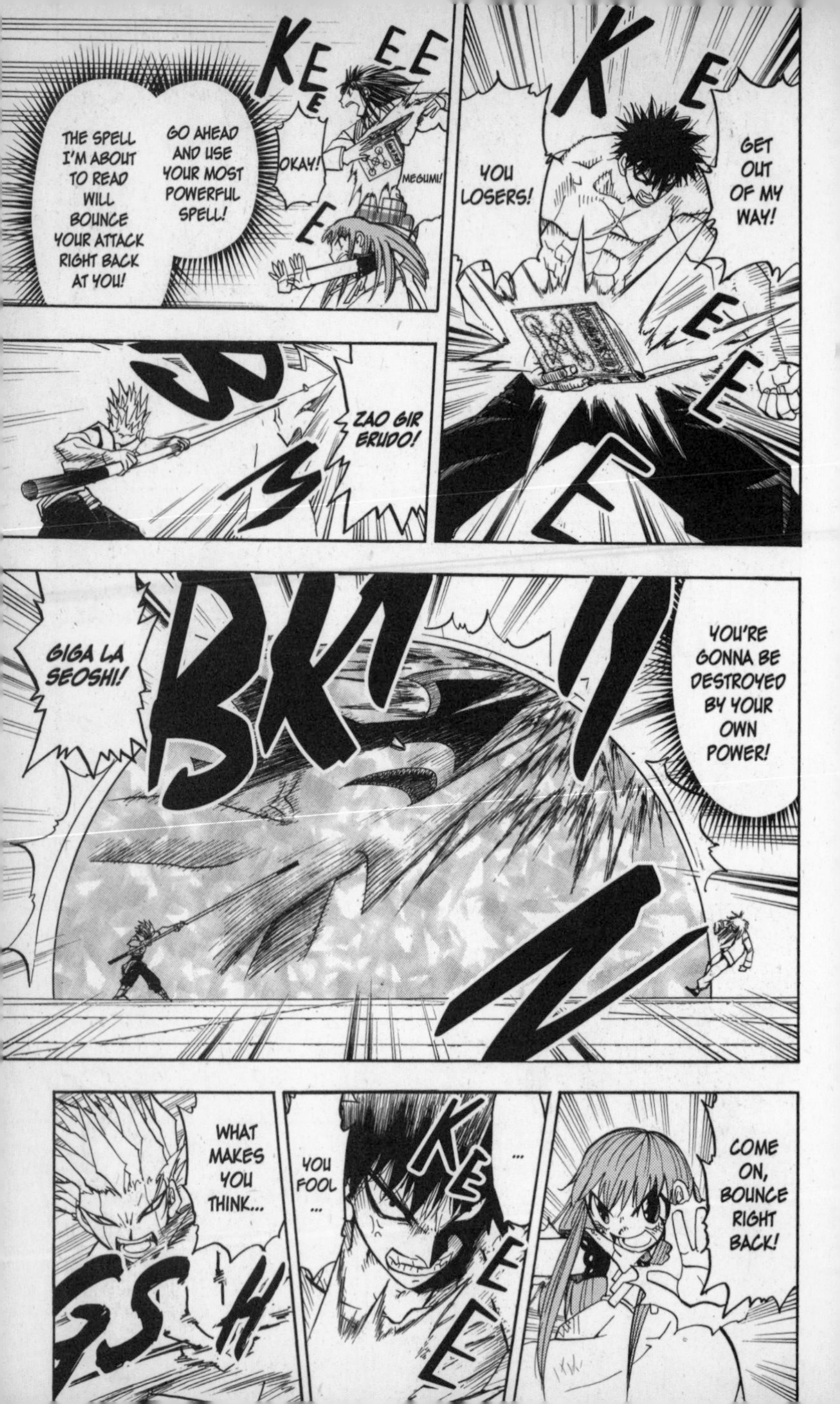
KEEEE
GET OUT OF MY WAY!
YOU LOSERS!
EEEE
MEGUMI!
OKAY!
GO AHEAD AND USE YOUR MOST POWERFUL SPELL!
THE SPELL I'M ABOUT TO READ WILL BOUNCE YOUR ATTACK RIGHT BACK AT YOU!
ZAO GIR ERUDO!
YOU'RE GONNA BE DESTROYED BY YOUR OWN POWER!
GIGA LA SEOSHI!
COME ON, BOUNCE RIGHT BACK!
...
KEEEE
YOU FOOL ...
WHAT MAKES YOU THINK...

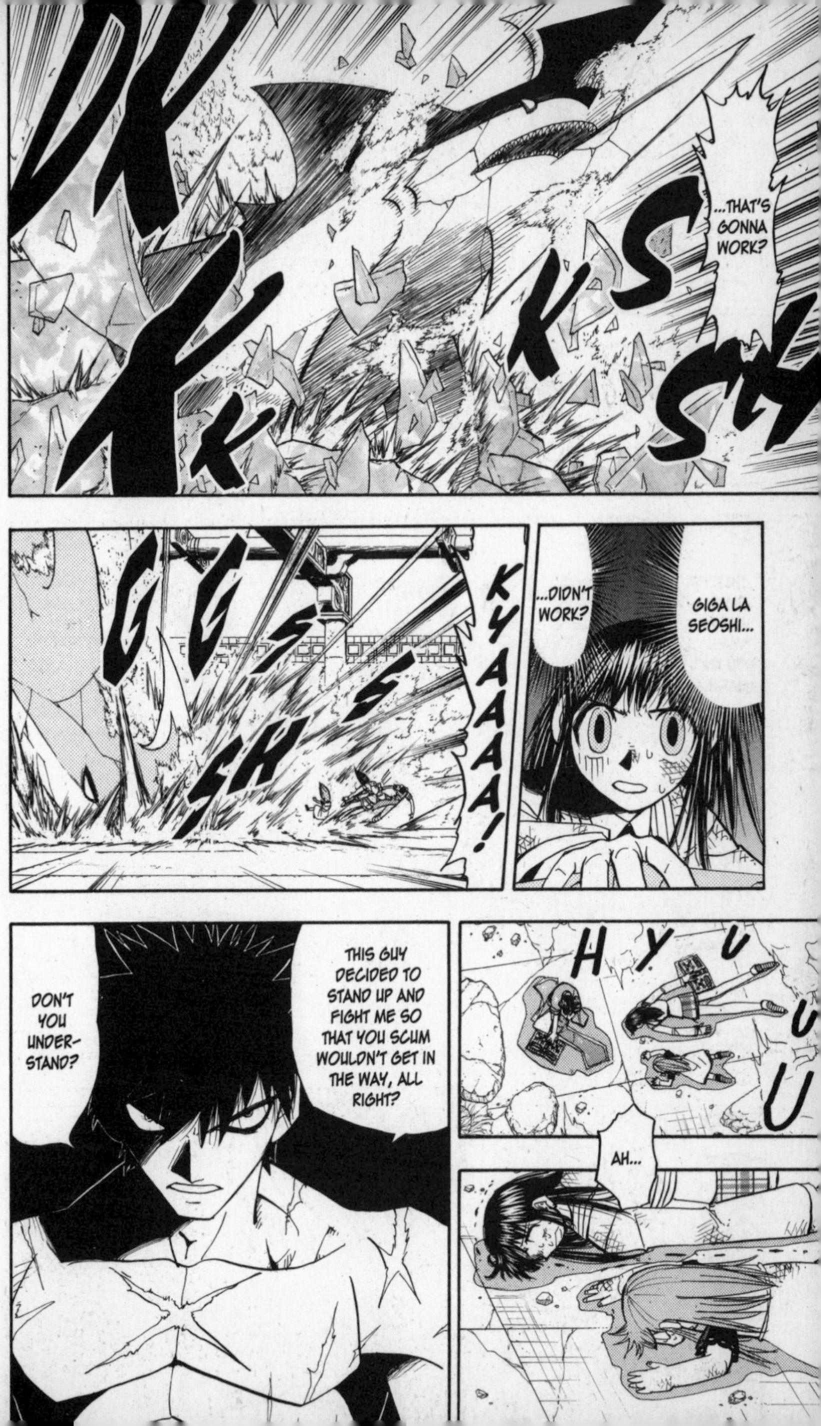
...THAT'S GONNA WORK?
GIGA LA SEOSHI...
...DIDN'T WORK?
KYAAAAA!
GUSSSH
HYUUUU
AH...
THIS GUY DECIDED TO STAND UP AND FIGHT ME SO THAT YOU SCUM WOULDN'T GET IN THE WAY, ALL RIGHT?
DON'T YOU UNDER-STAND?

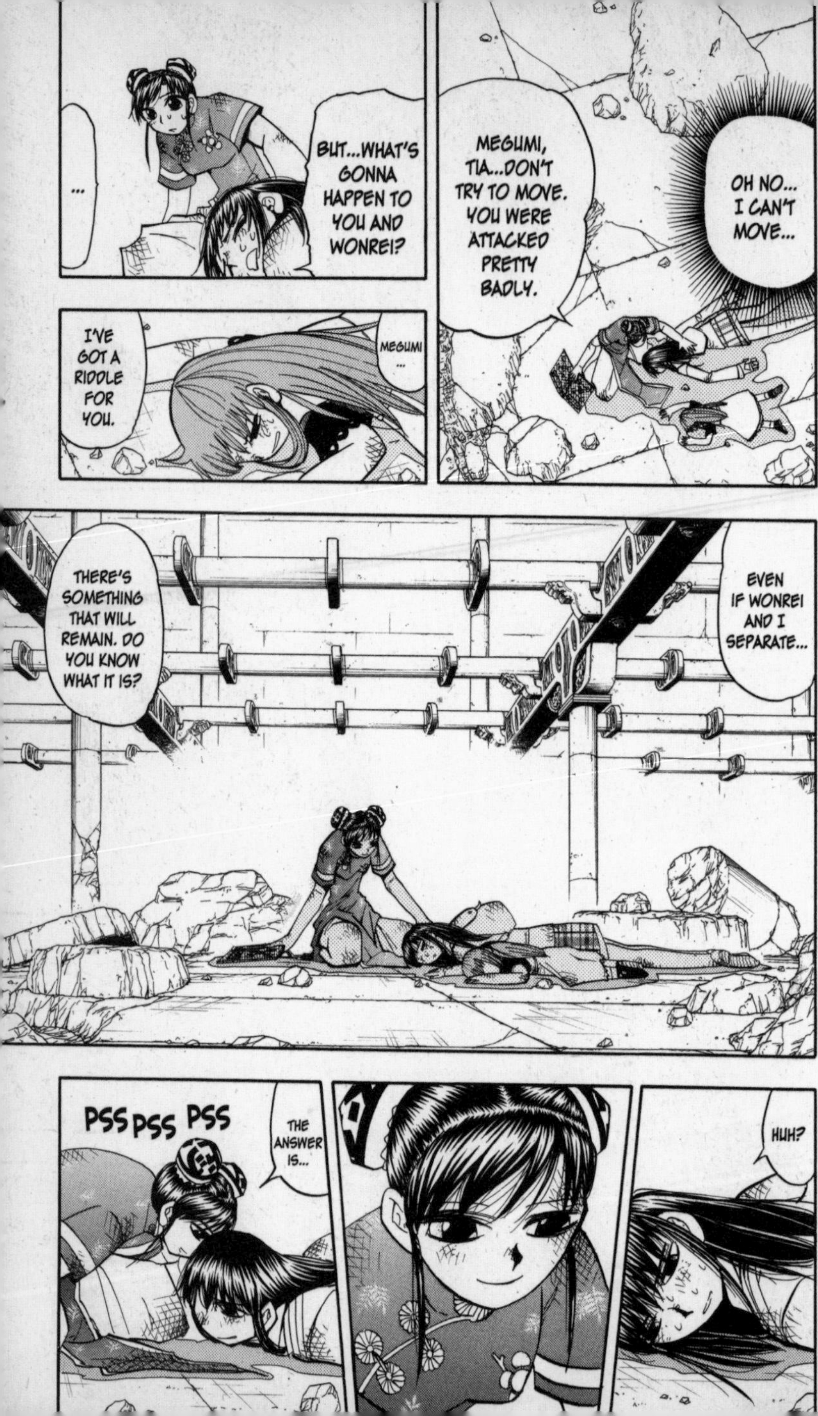
OH NO... I CAN'T MOVE...
MEGUMI, TIA...DON'T TRY TO MOVE. YOU WERE ATTACKED PRETTY BADLY.
BUT...WHAT'S GONNA HAPPEN TO YOU AND WONREI?
...
MEGUMI...
I'VE GOT A RIDDLE FOR YOU.
EVEN IF WONREI AND I SEPARATE...
THERE'S SOMETHING THAT WILL REMAIN. DO YOU KNOW WHAT IT IS?
HUH?
THE ANSWER IS...
PSS PSS PSS

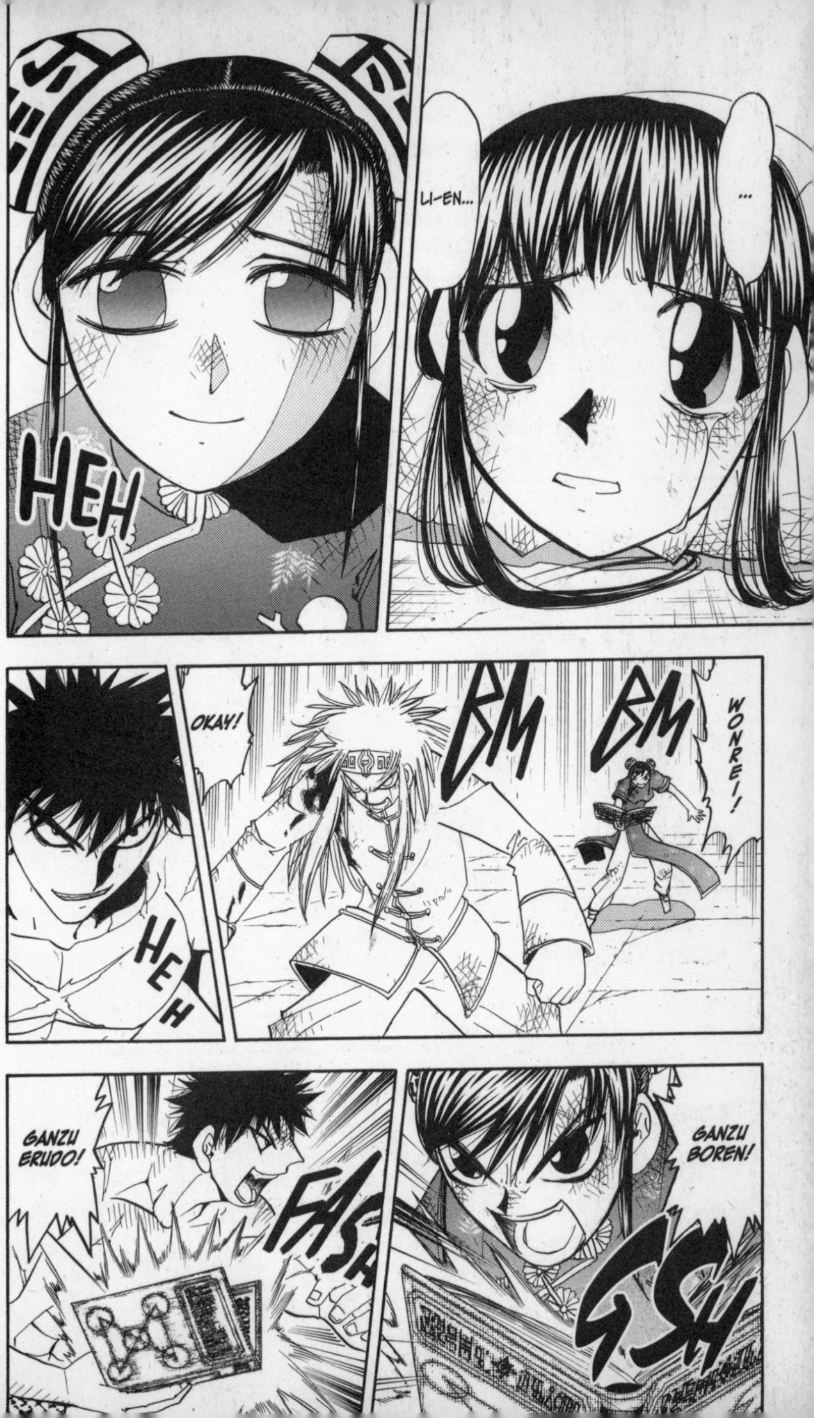
...
LI-EN...
HEH
WONREI!!
BM BM
OKAY!
HEH HEH
GANZU BOREN!
GSH
GANZU ERUDO!
FASH

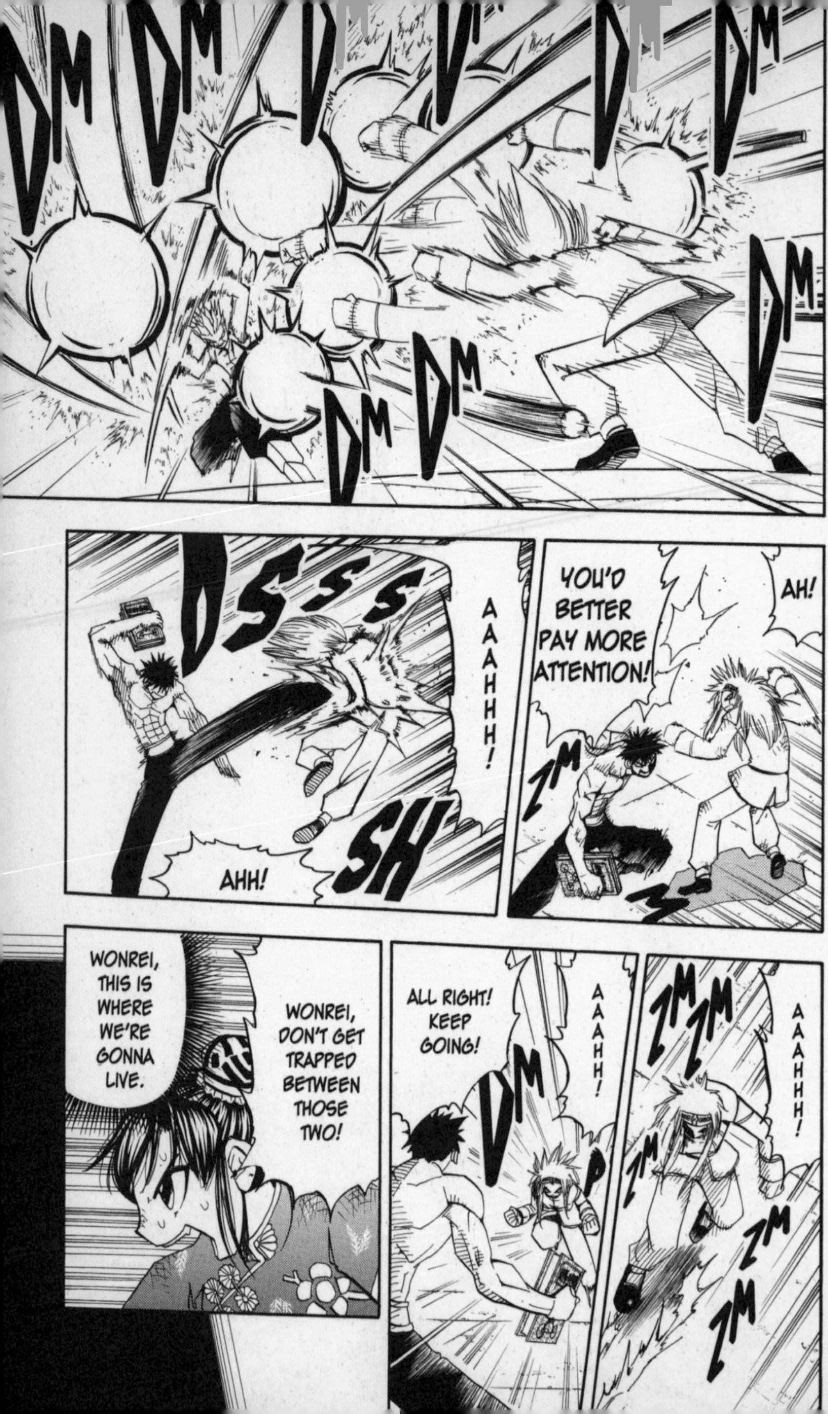
DM
DM
DM
DM
DM
DM
DM
AH!
YOU'D BETTER PAY MORE ATTENTION!
ZM
M
AAAAHHH!
DSSS
SH
AHH!
AAAAHHH!
ZM
ZM
ZM
ZM
AAAHH!
ALL RIGHT! KEEP GOING!
DM
P
WONREI, DON'T GET TRAPPED BETWEEN THOSE TWO!
WONREI, THIS IS WHERE WE'RE GONNA LIVE.

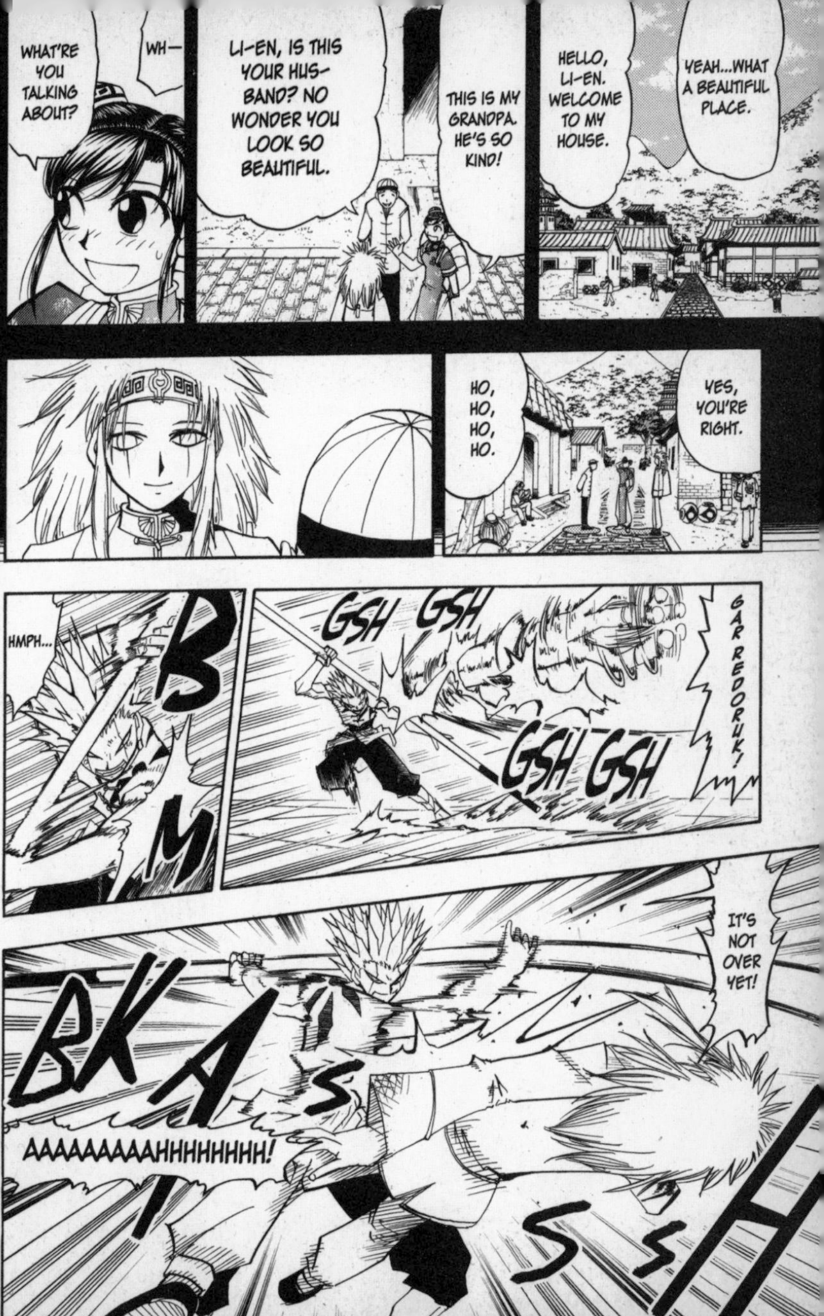

YEAH...WHAT A BEAUTIFUL PLACE.
HELLO, LI-EN. WELCOME TO MY HOUSE.
THIS IS MY GRANDPA. HE'S SO KIND!
LI-EN, IS THIS YOUR HUS-BAND? NO WONDER YOU LOOK SO BEAUTIFUL.
WH—
WHAT'RE YOU TALKING ABOUT?
YES, YOU'RE RIGHT.
HO, HO, HO, HO.
GAR REDORUK!
GSH GSH
GSH GSH
BM
HMPH...
IT'S NOT OVER YET!
BKASSH
AAAAAAAAAHHHHHHHH!

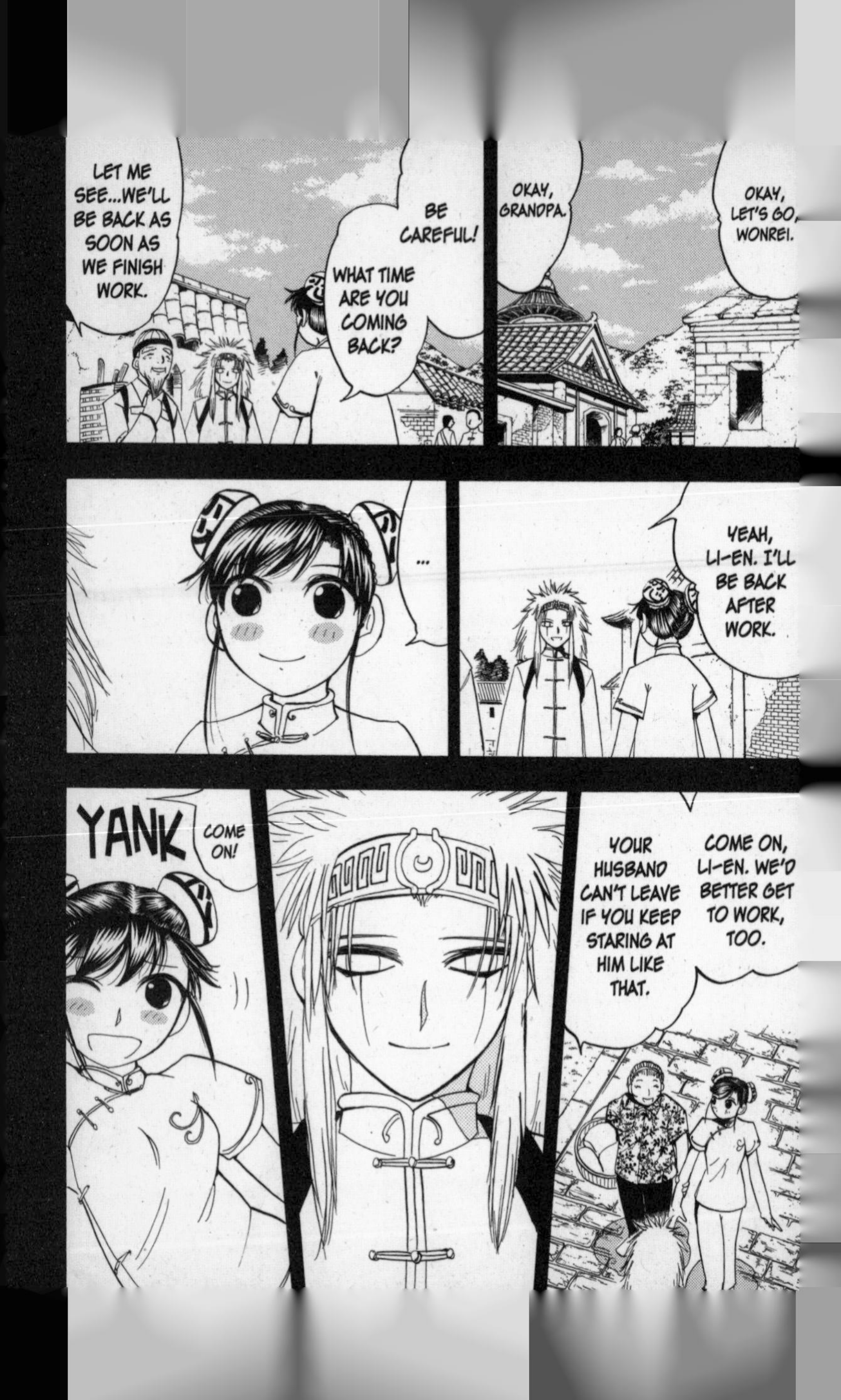
OKAY, LET'S GO, WONREI.
OKAY, GRANDPA.
BE CAREFUL!
WHAT TIME ARE YOU COMING BACK?
LET ME SEE...WE'LL BE BACK AS SOON AS WE FINISH WORK.
YEAH, LI-EN. I'LL BE BACK AFTER WORK.
...
COME ON, LI-EN. WE'D BETTER GET TO WORK, TOO.
YOUR HUSBAND CAN'T LEAVE IF YOU KEEP STARING AT HIM LIKE THAT.
COME ON!
YANK

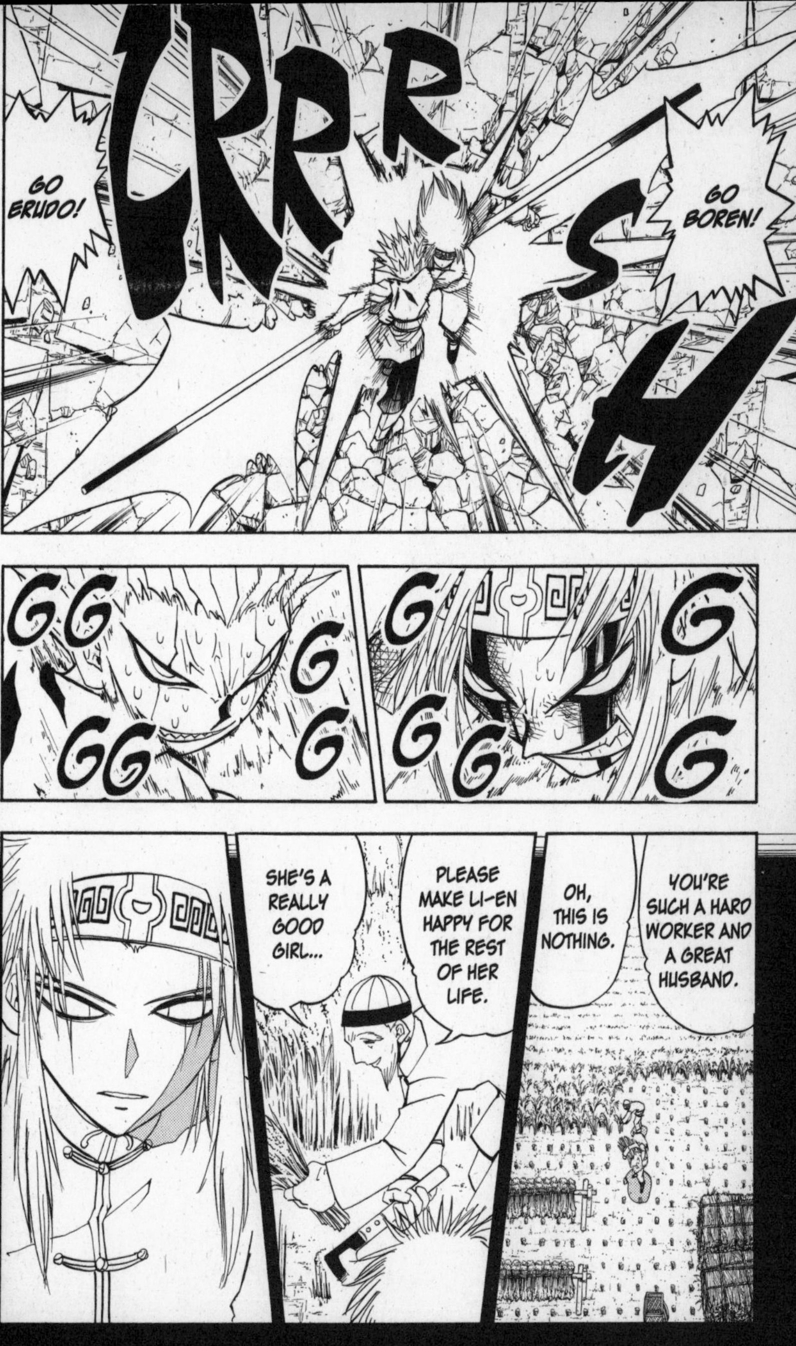
GO BOREN!
CRRRSH
GO ERUDO!
GGGGG
GGGGGG
YOU'RE SUCH A HARD WORKER AND A GREAT HUSBAND.
OH, THIS IS NOTHING.
PLEASE MAKE LI-EN HAPPY FOR THE REST OF HER LIFE.
SHE'S A REALLY GOOD GIRL...

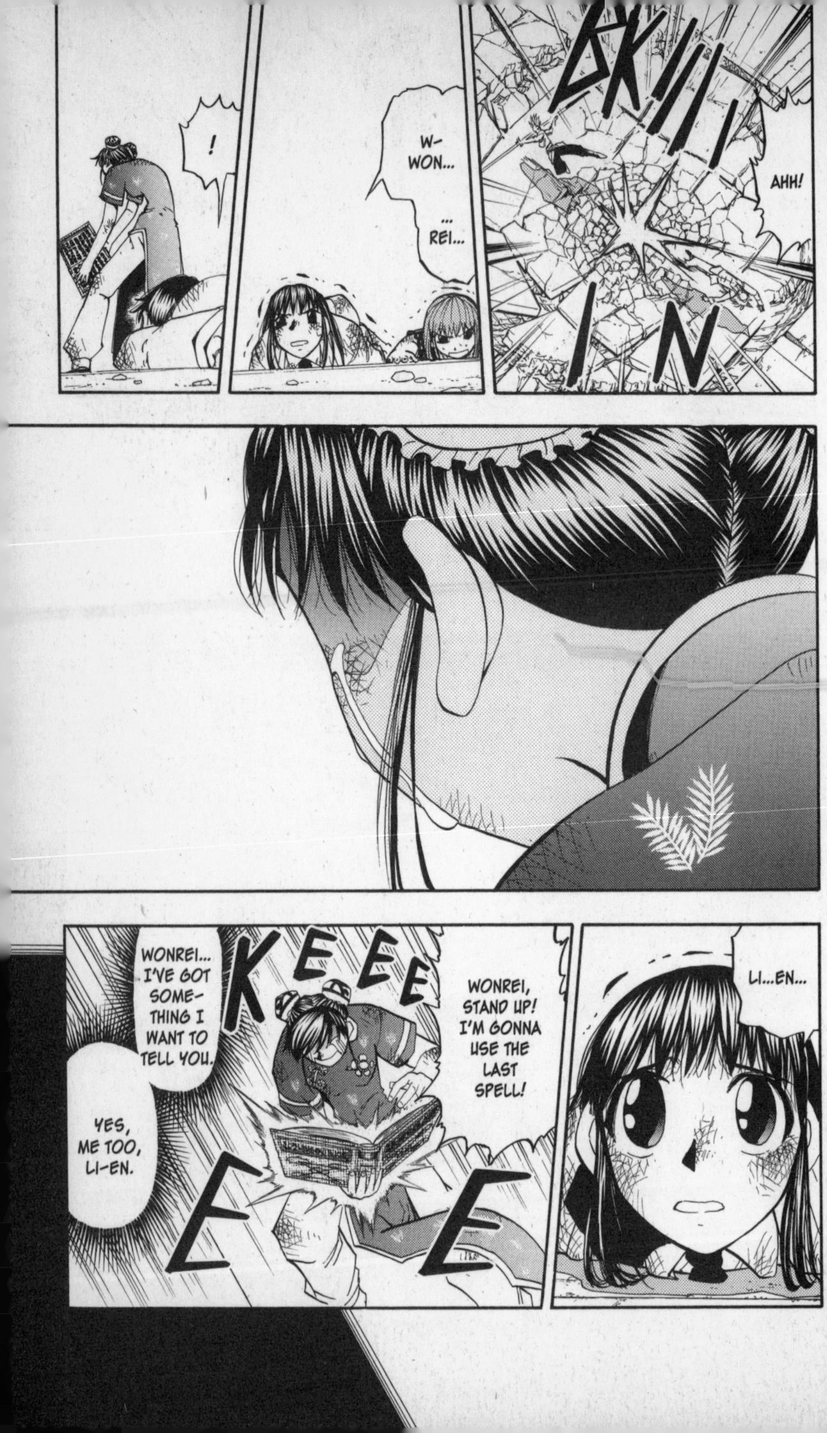
BKIIIIN
AHH!
W-WON...
... REI...
!
LI...EN...
WONREI, STAND UP! I'M GONNA USE THE LAST SPELL!
KEEEEE
WONREI... I'VE GOT SOME-THING I WANT TO TELL YOU.
YES, ME TOO, LI-EN.

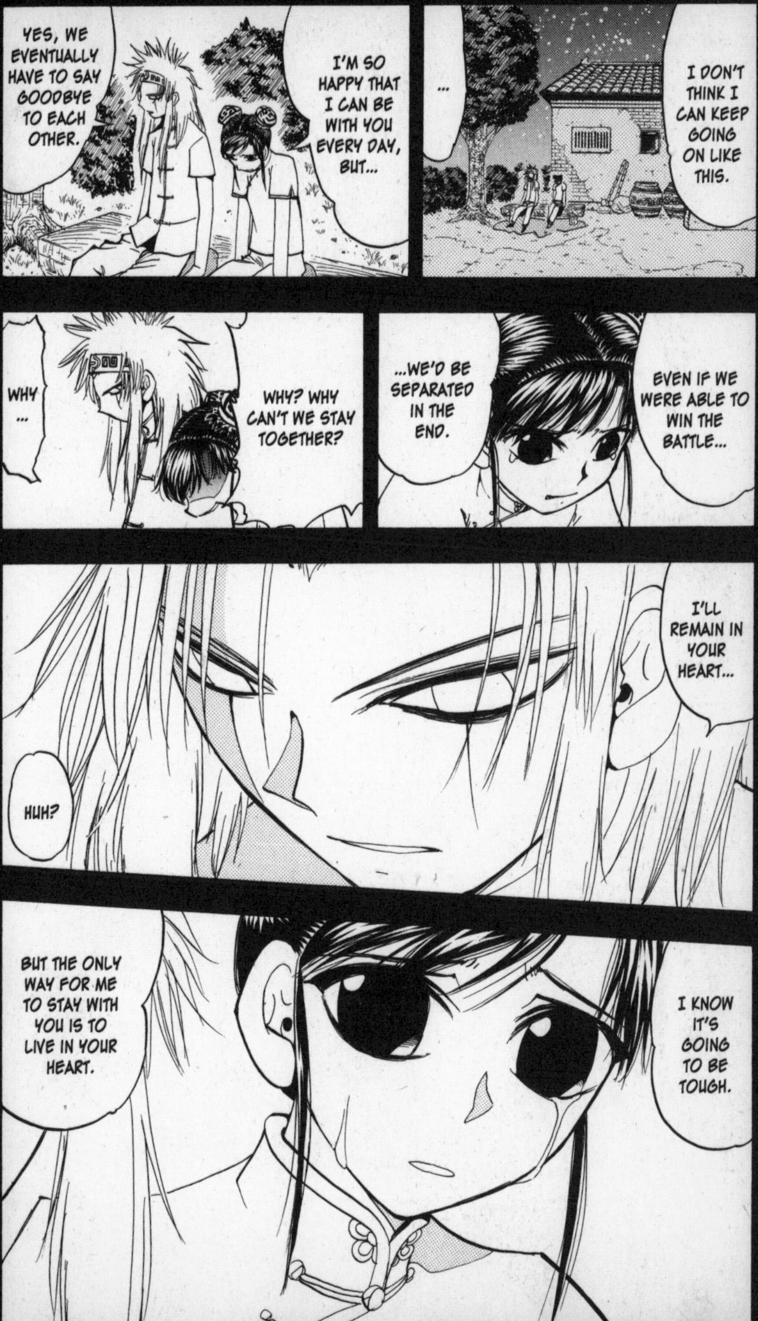
I DON'T THINK I CAN KEEP GOING ON LIKE THIS.
...
I'M SO HAPPY THAT I CAN BE WITH YOU EVERY DAY, BUT...
YES, WE EVENTUALLY HAVE TO SAY GOODBYE TO EACH OTHER.
EVEN IF WE WERE ABLE TO WIN THE BATTLE...
...WE'D BE SEPARATED IN THE END.
WHY? WHY CAN'T WE STAY TOGETHER?
WHY ...
I'LL REMAIN IN YOUR HEART...
HUH?
I KNOW IT'S GOING TO BE TOUGH.
BUT THE ONLY WAY FOR ME TO STAY WITH YOU IS TO LIVE IN YOUR HEART.

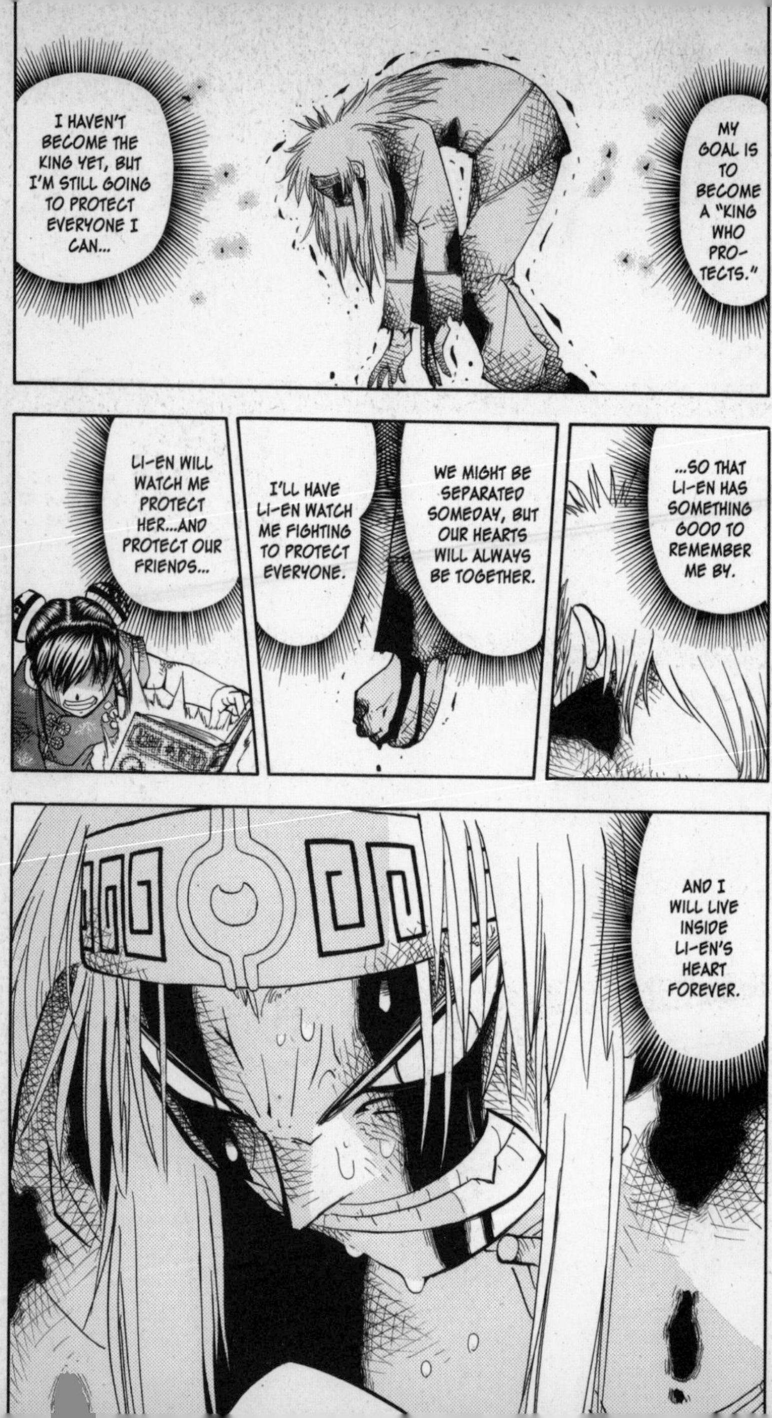
MY GOAL IS TO BECOME A "KING WHO PRO-TECTS."
I HAVEN'T BECOME THE KING YET, BUT I'M STILL GOING TO PROTECT EVERYONE I CAN...
...SO THAT LI-EN HAS SOMETHING GOOD TO REMEMBER ME BY.
WE MIGHT BE SEPARATED SOMEDAY, BUT OUR HEARTS WILL ALWAYS BE TOGETHER.
I'LL HAVE LI-EN WATCH ME FIGHTING TO PROTECT EVERYONE.
LI-EN WILL WATCH ME PROTECT HER...AND PROTECT OUR FRIENDS...
AND I WILL LIVE INSIDE LI-EN'S HEART FOREVER.

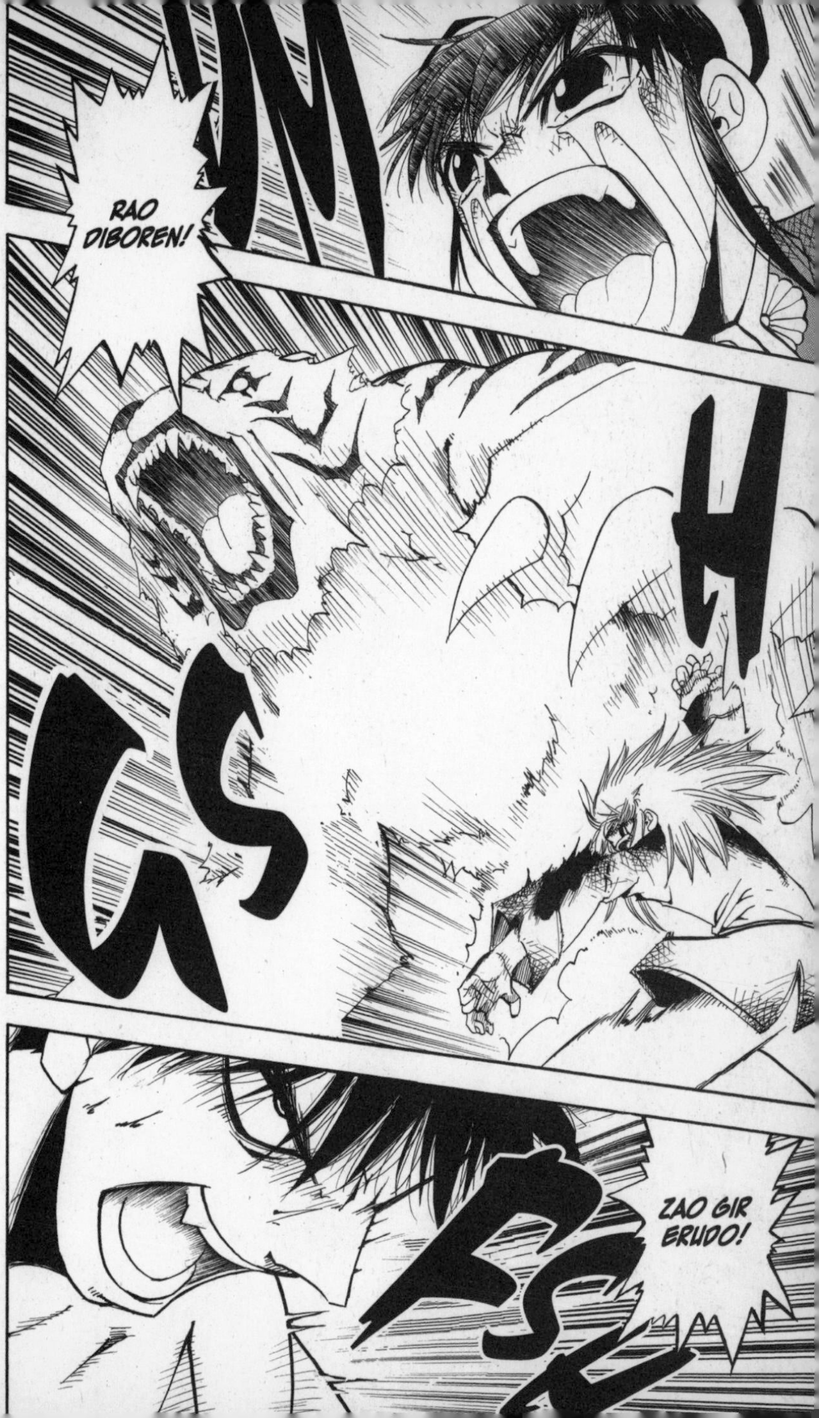
RAO DIBOREN!
ZAO GIR ERUDO!

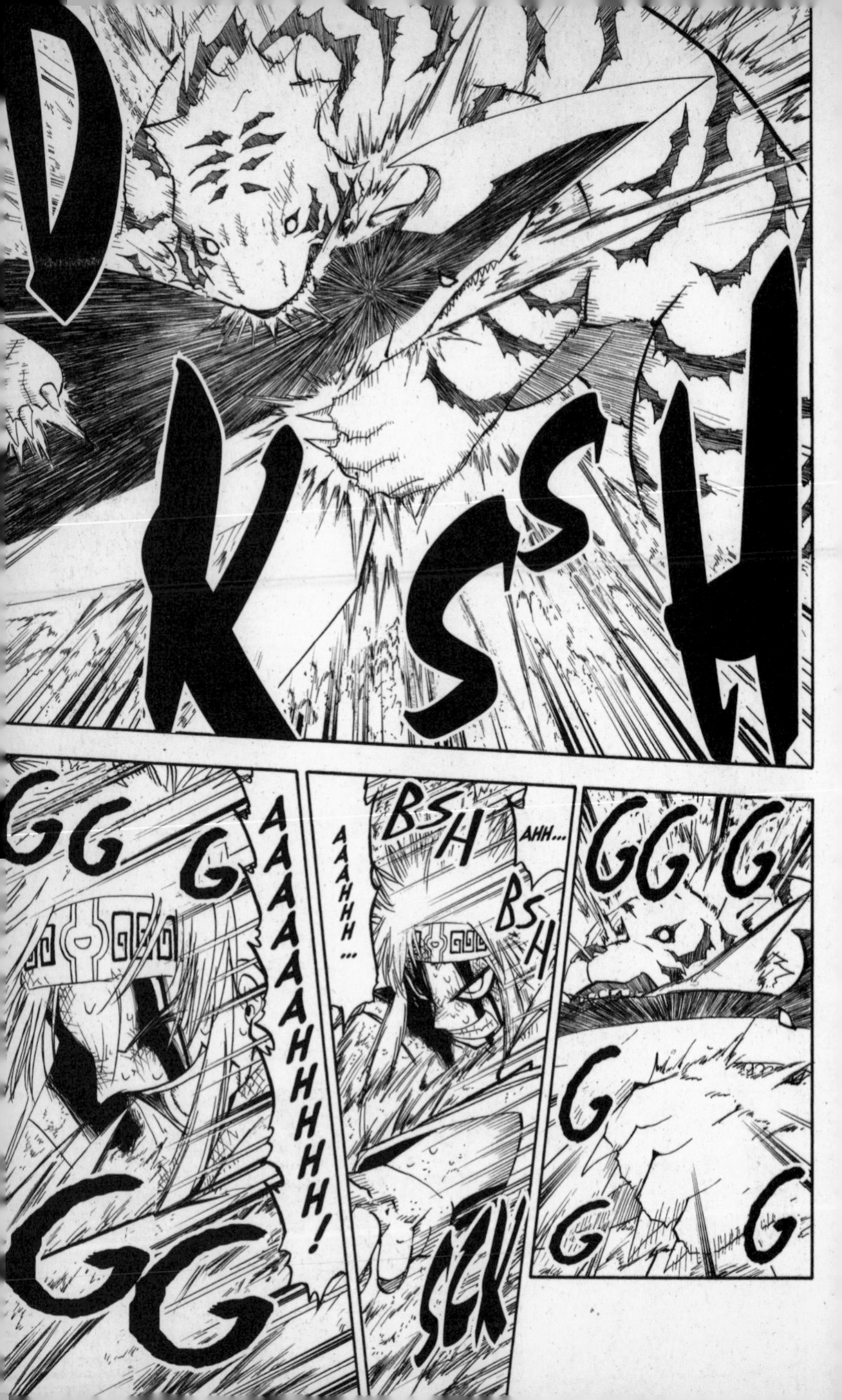
D
KSSH
GGGG
G
GG
AHH...
BSH
BSH
AAAHHHH...
AAAAAAAAHHHHHH!
GGG
GG

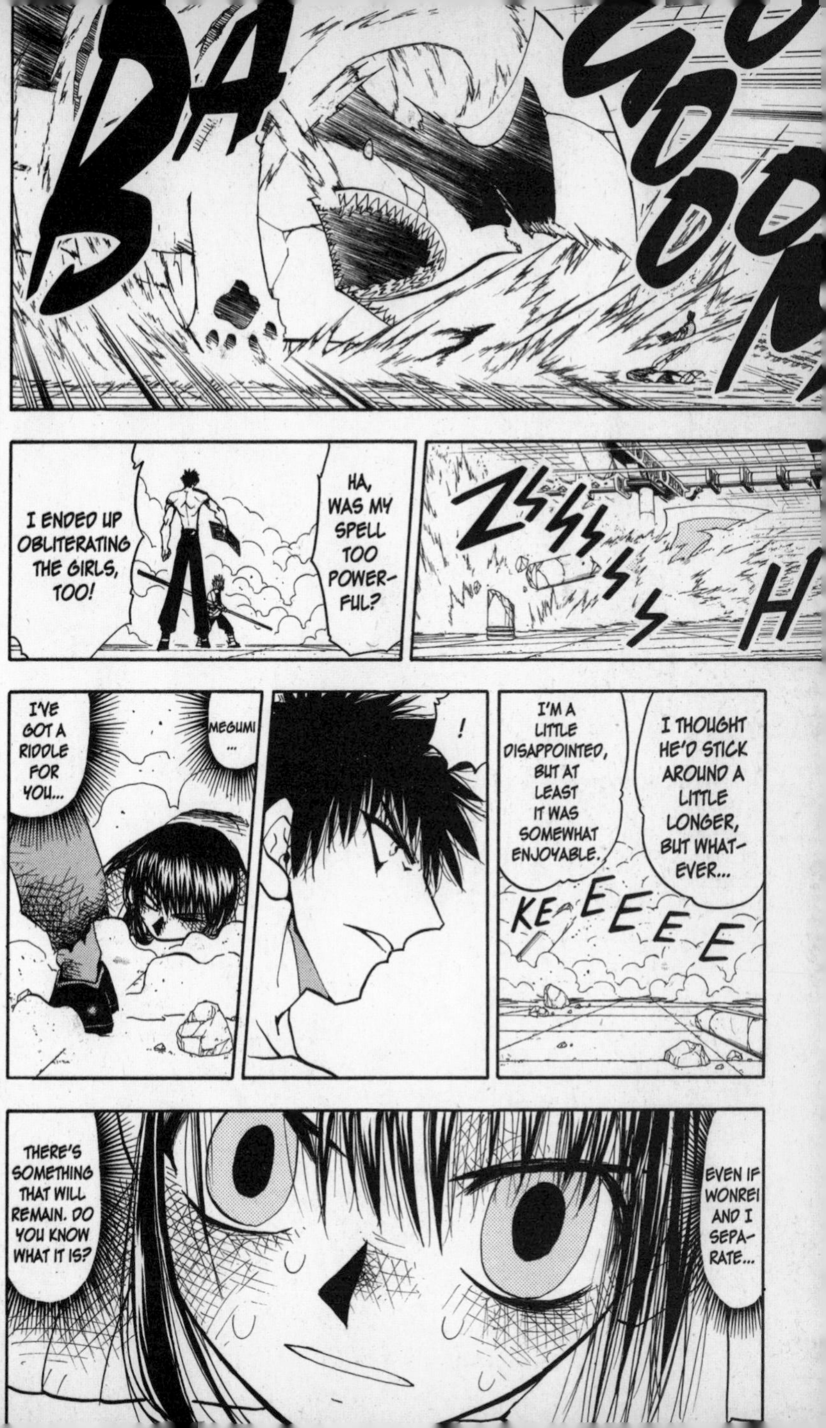
DA
B
ZSSSSSH
HA, WAS MY SPELL TOO POWERFUL?
I ENDED UP OBLITERATING THE GIRLS, TOO!
I THOUGHT HE'D STICK AROUND A LITTLE LONGER, BUT WHATEVER...
I'M A LITTLE DISAPPOINTED, BUT AT LEAST IT WAS SOMEWHAT ENJOYABLE.
KEEEEEE
!
MEGUMI ...
I'VE GOT A RIDDLE FOR YOU...
EVEN IF WONREI AND I SEPARATE...
THERE'S SOMETHING THAT WILL REMAIN. DO YOU KNOW WHAT IT IS?

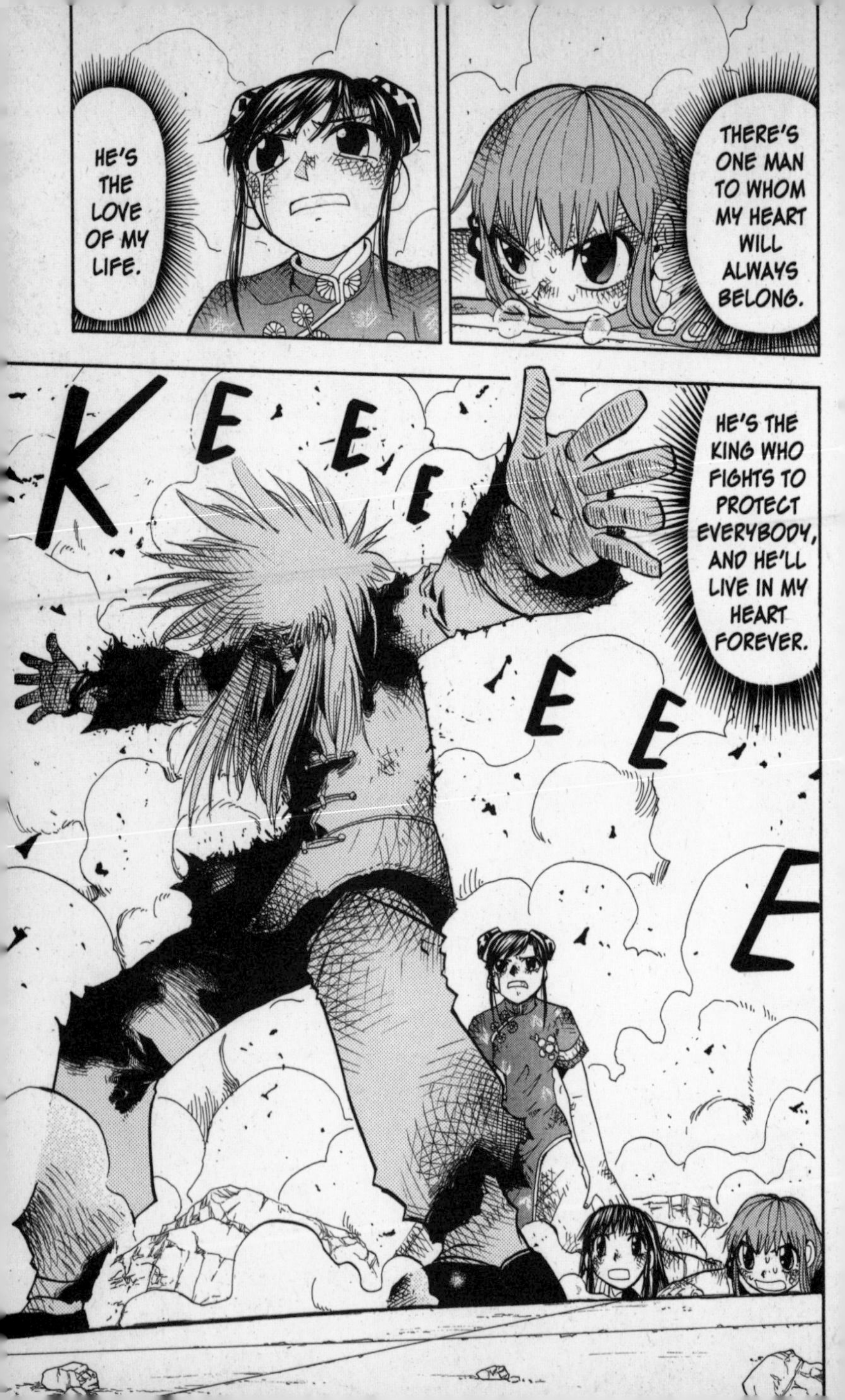
THERE'S ONE MAN TO WHOM MY HEART WILL ALWAYS BELONG.
HE'S THE LOVE OF MY LIFE.
HE'S THE KING WHO FIGHTS TO PROTECT EVERYBODY, AND HE'LL LIVE IN MY HEART FOREVER.
KEEEEEEE

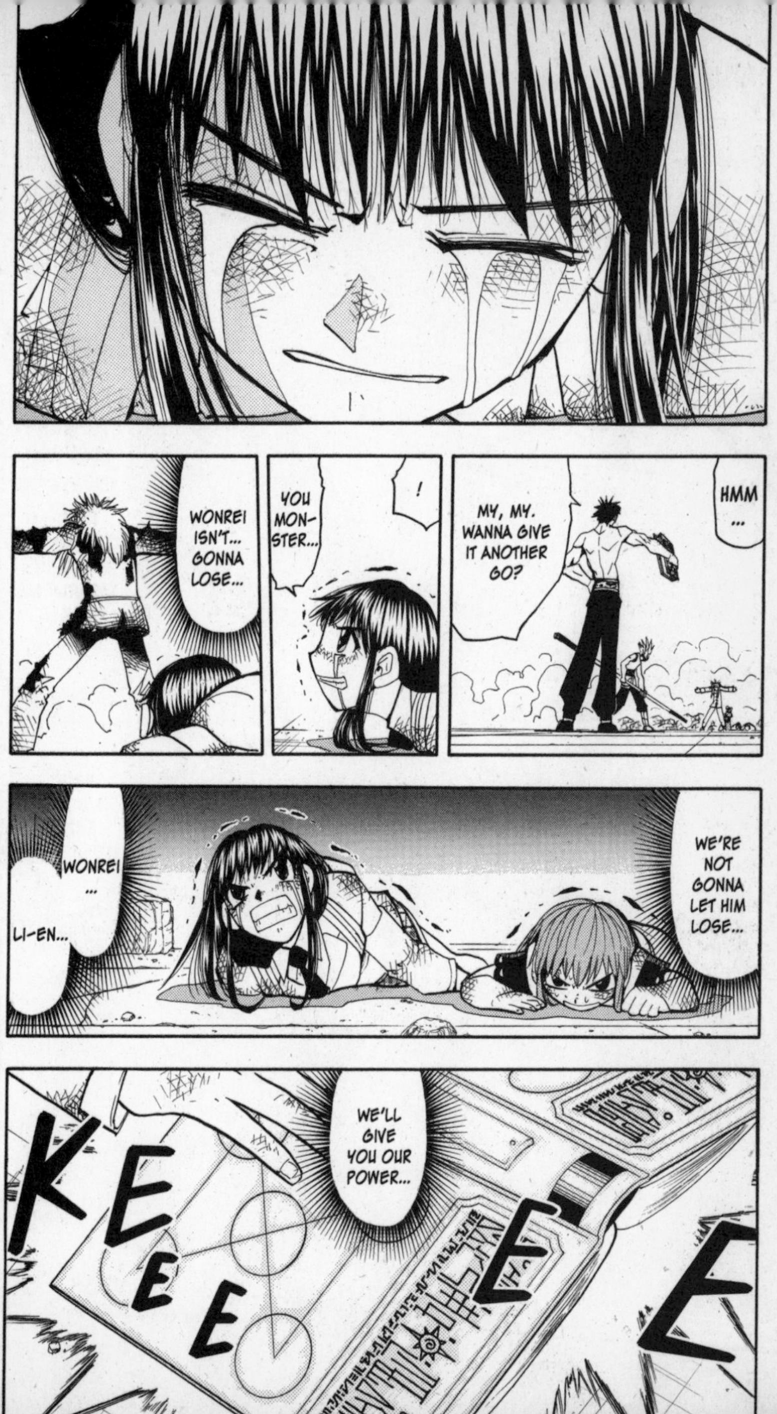
HMM ...
MY, MY. WANNA GIVE IT ANOTHER GO?
!
YOU MON-STER...
WONREI ISN'T... GONNA LOSE...
WE'RE NOT GONNA LET HIM LOSE...
WONREI ...
LI-EN...
WE'LL GIVE YOU OUR POWER...
KEEEEE

LEVEL 133: The King Who Protects

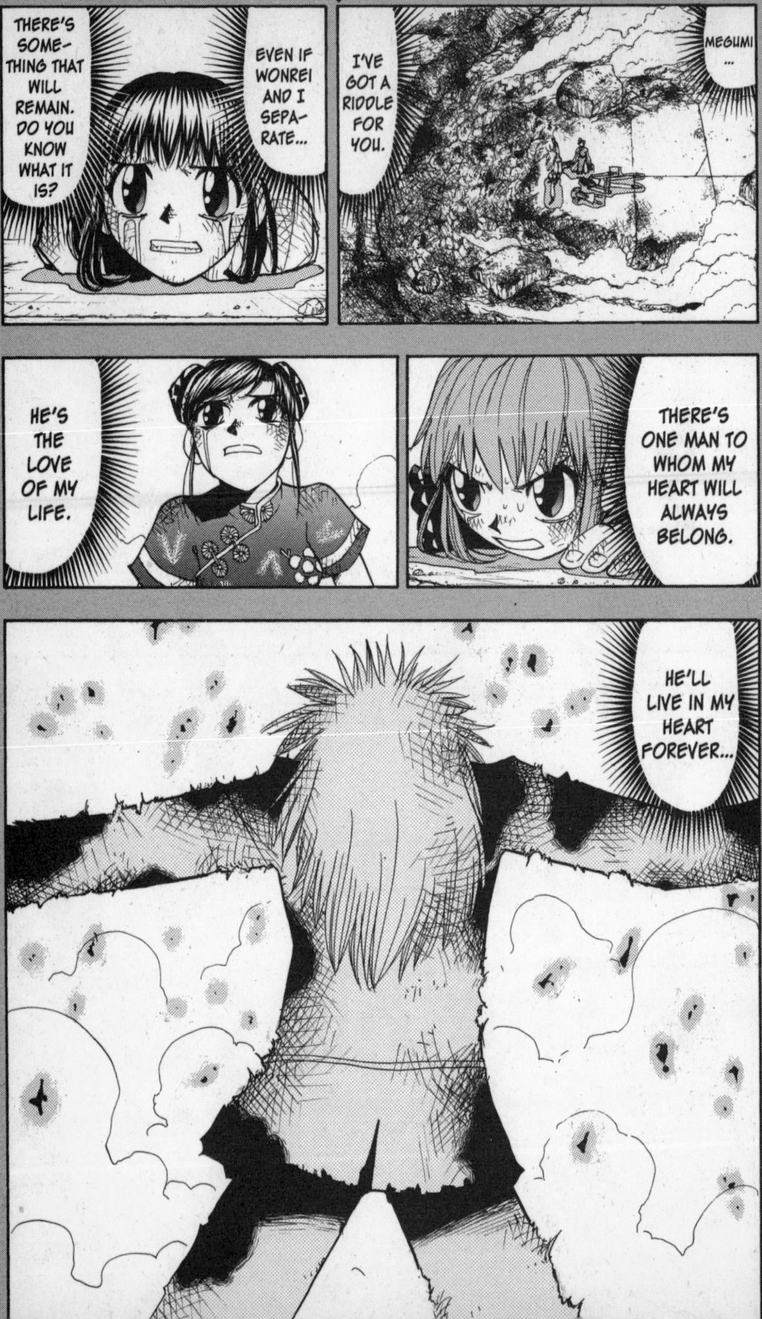
MEGUMI...
I'VE GOT A RIDDLE FOR YOU.
EVEN IF WONREI AND I SEPARATE...
THERE'S SOMETHING THAT WILL REMAIN. DO YOU KNOW WHAT IT IS?
THERE'S ONE MAN TO WHOM MY HEART WILL ALWAYS BELONG.
HE'S THE LOVE OF MY LIFE.
HE'LL LIVE IN MY HEART FOREVER...

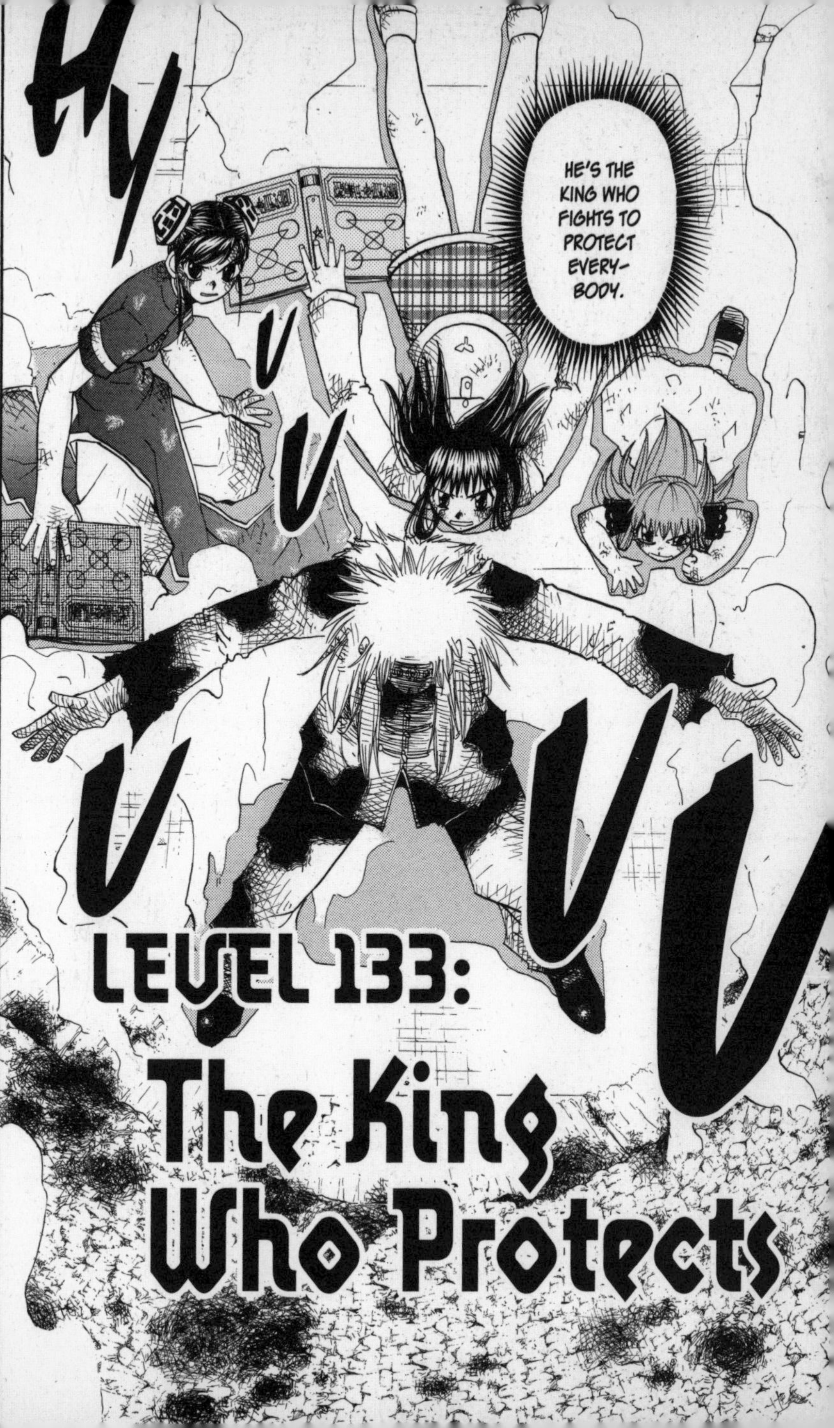
HE'S THE KING WHO FIGHTS TO PROTECT EVERY-BODY.
LEVEL 133:
The King Who Protects

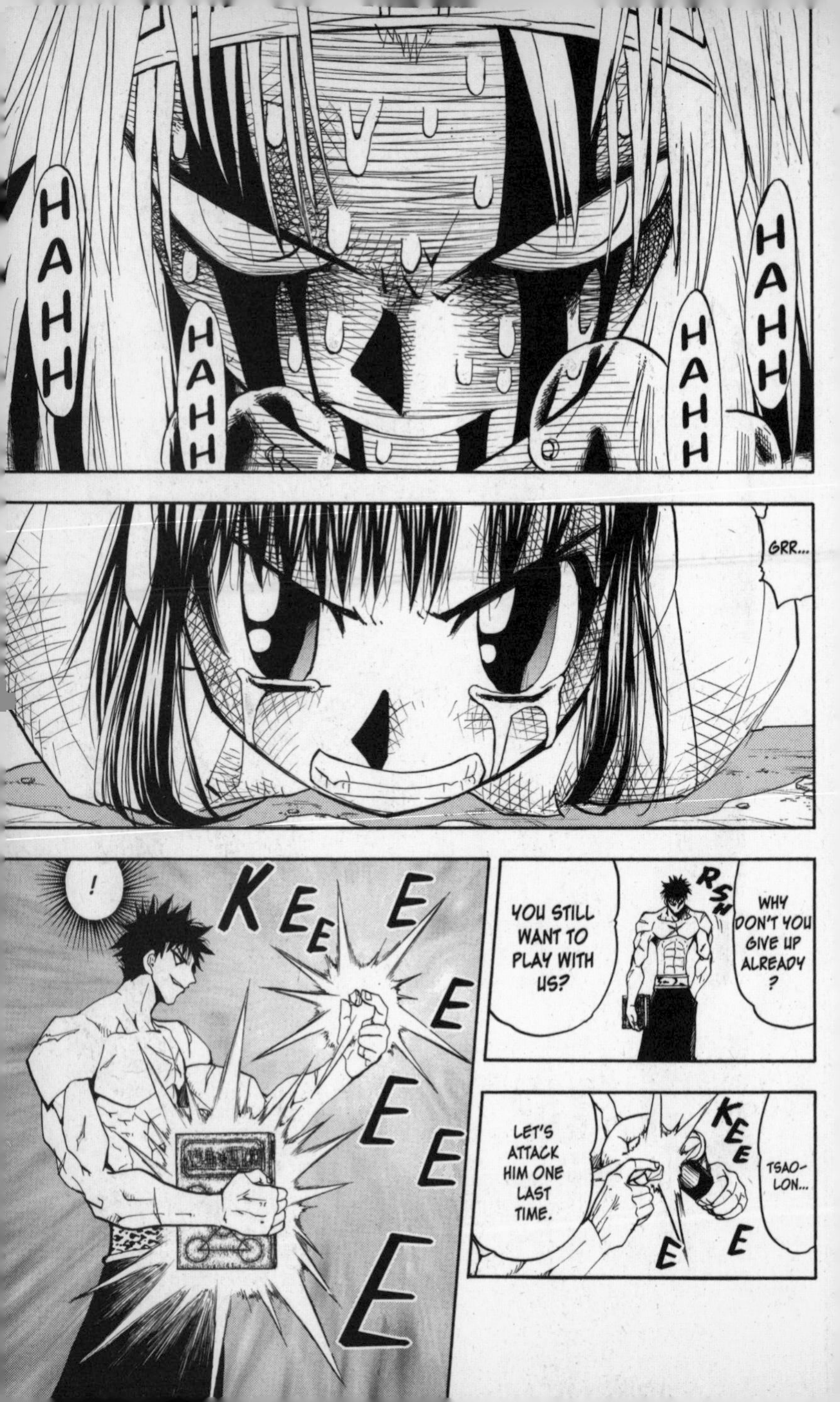
HAHH
HAHH
HAHH
HAHH
GRR...
WHY DON'T YOU GIVE UP ALREADY?
RSH
YOU STILL WANT TO PLAY WITH US?
TSAO-LON...
KEEEEE
LET'S ATTACK HIM ONE LAST TIME.
!
KEEEEEEE

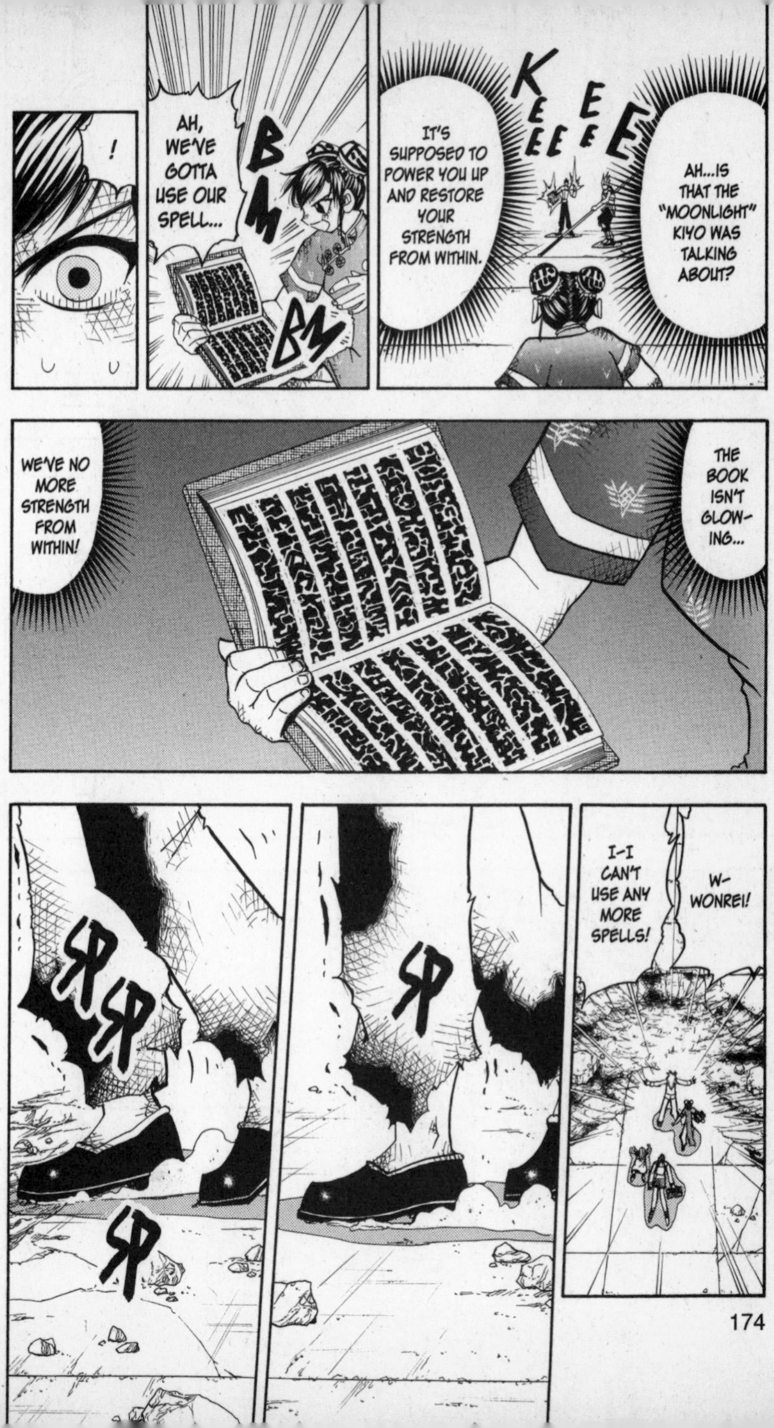
AH...IS THAT THE "MOONLIGHT" KIYO WAS TALKING ABOUT?
KEEEEE
IT'S SUPPOSED TO POWER YOU UP AND RESTORE YOUR STRENGTH FROM WITHIN.
AH, WE'VE GOTTA USE OUR SPELL...
BM
BM
!
THE BOOK ISN'T GLOW-ING...
WE'VE NO MORE STRENGTH FROM WITHIN!
W-WONREI!
I-I CAN'T USE ANY MORE SPELLS!
SP
SP SP
SP

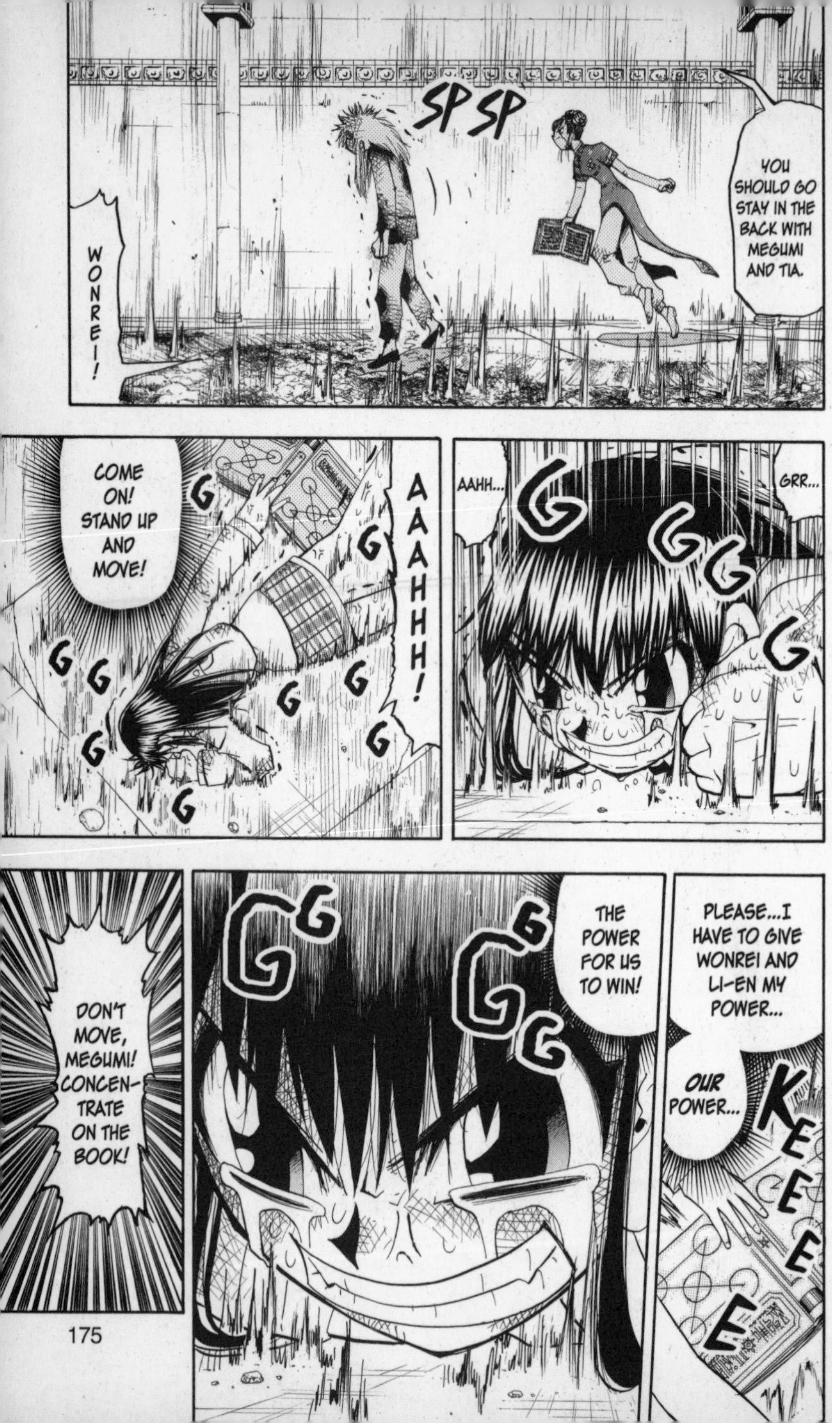
YOU SHOULD GO STAY IN THE BACK WITH MEGUMI AND TIA.
SP SP
WONREI!
GRR...
G G G G
AAHH...
AAAHHH!
COME ON! STAND UP AND MOVE!
G G G G G G G G
PLEASE...I HAVE TO GIVE WONREI AND LI-EN MY POWER...
OUR POWER...
KEEEEE
THE POWER FOR US TO WIN!
GG GGG
DON'T MOVE, MEGUMI! CONCENTRATE ON THE BOOK!

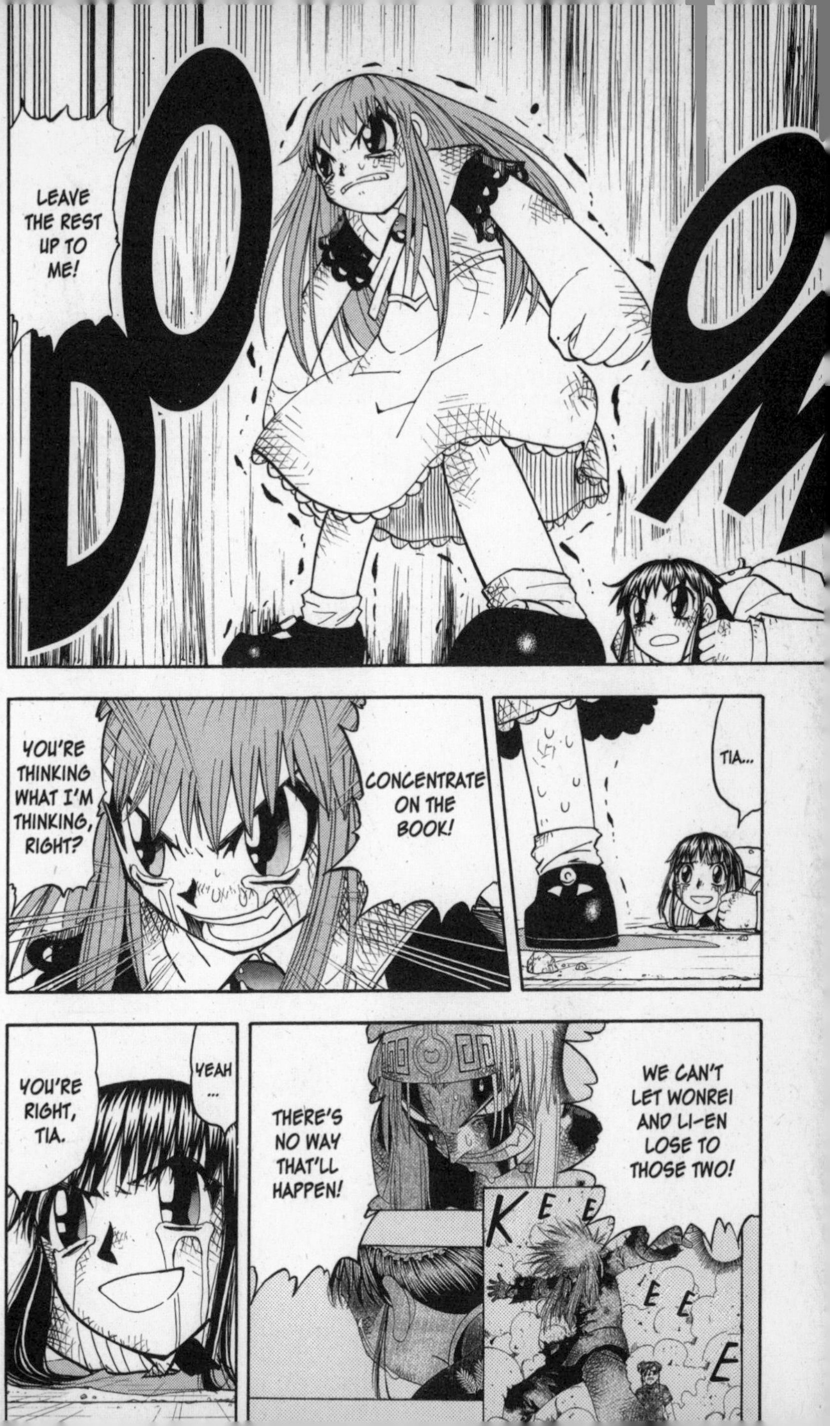
DOOM
LEAVE THE REST UP TO ME!
TIA...
CONCENTRATE ON THE BOOK!
YOU'RE THINKING WHAT I'M THINKING, RIGHT?
WE CAN'T LET WONREI AND LI-EN LOSE TO THOSE TWO!
THERE'S NO WAY THAT'LL HAPPEN!
KEEEEE
YEAH...
YOU'RE RIGHT, TIA.

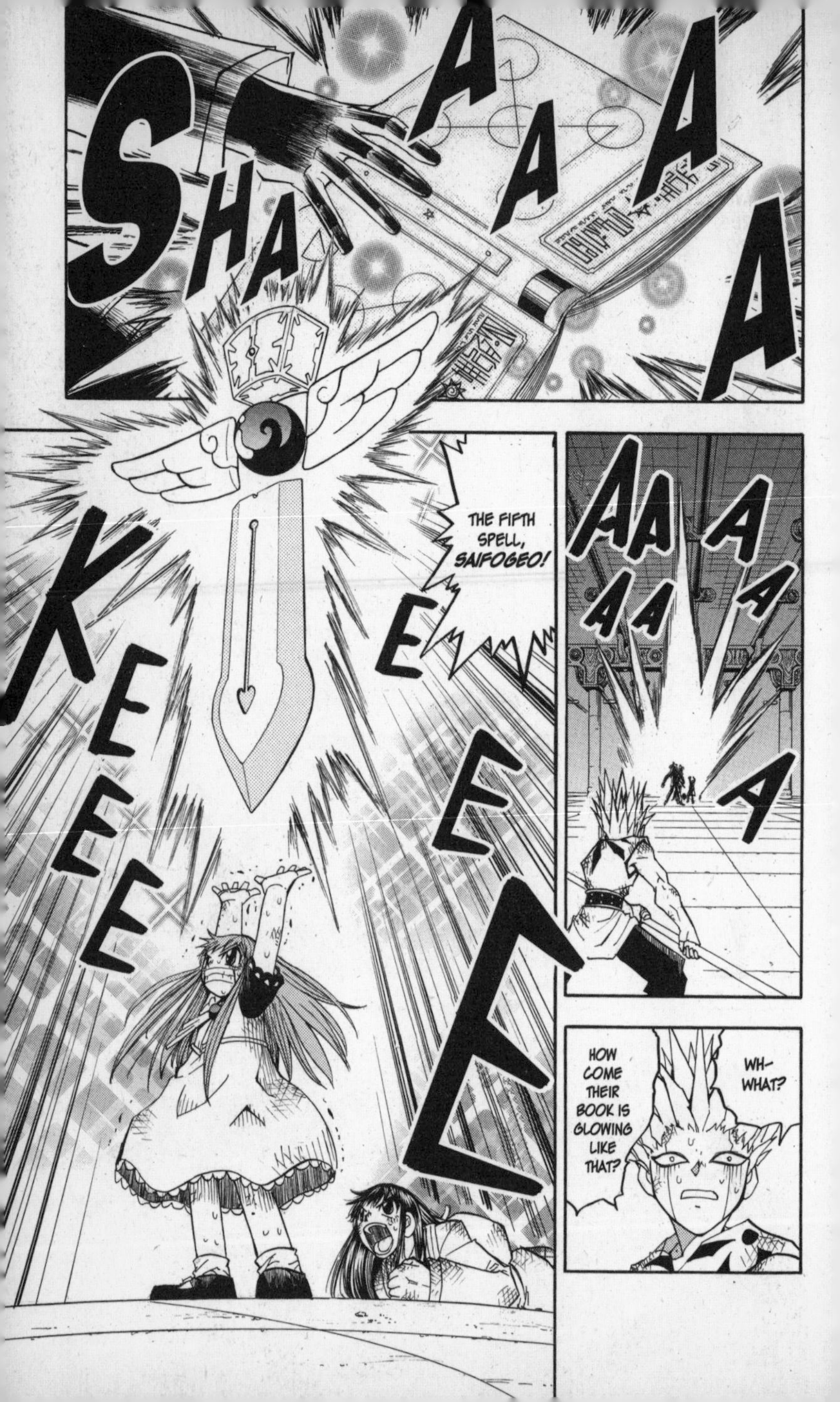
SHAAAAAA
AAAAAAAA
WH-WHAT?
HOW COME THEIR BOOK IS GLOWING LIKE THAT?
THE FIFTH SPELL, SAIFOGEO!
KEEEEEEEE

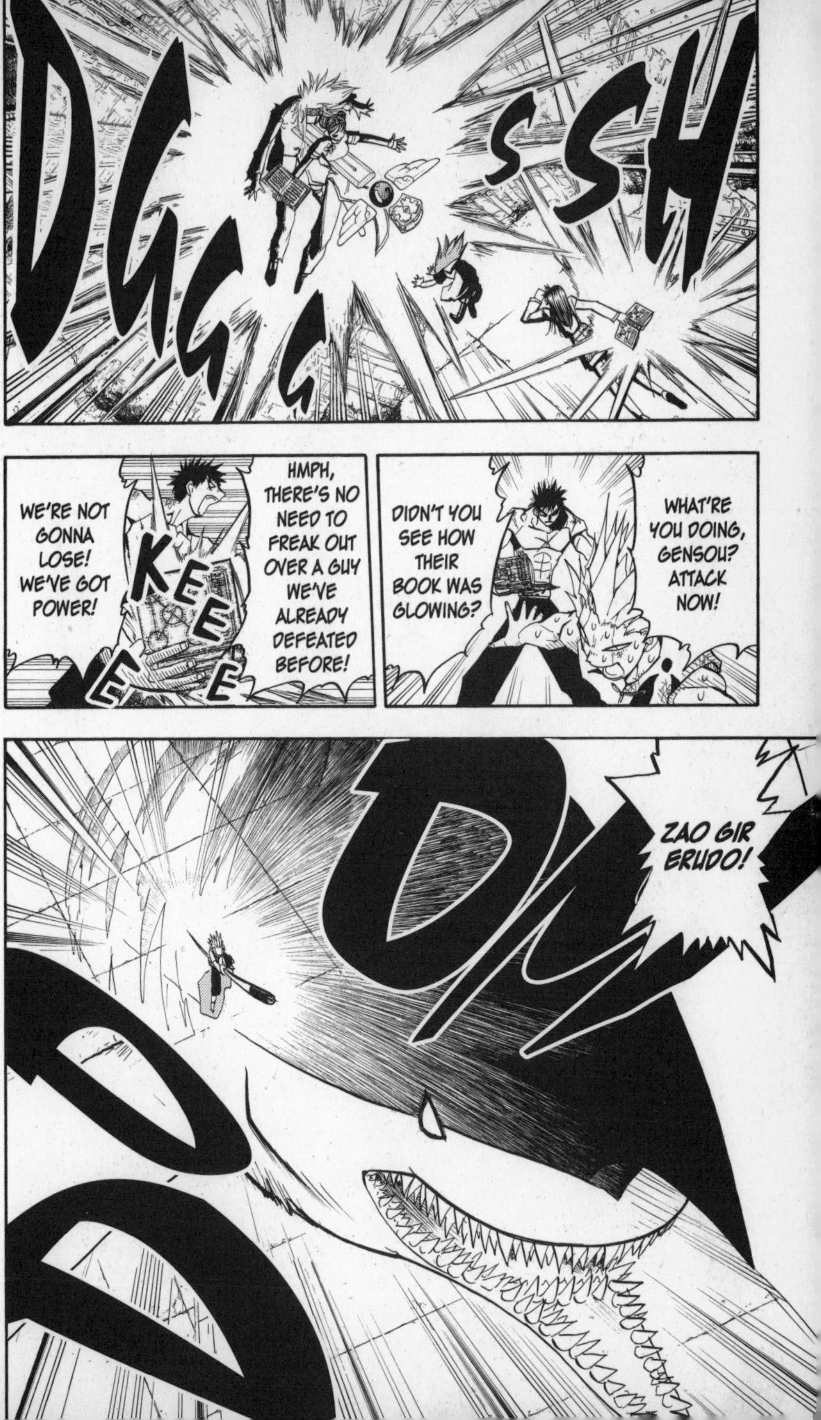
DUGG
SSH
WHAT'RE YOU DOING, GENSOU? ATTACK NOW!
DIDN'T YOU SEE HOW THEIR BOOK WAS GLOWING?
HMPH, THERE'S NO NEED TO FREAK OUT OVER A GUY WE'VE ALREADY DEFEATED BEFORE!
WE'RE NOT GONNA LOSE! WE'VE GOT POWER!
KEEEEE
ZAO GIR ERUDO!

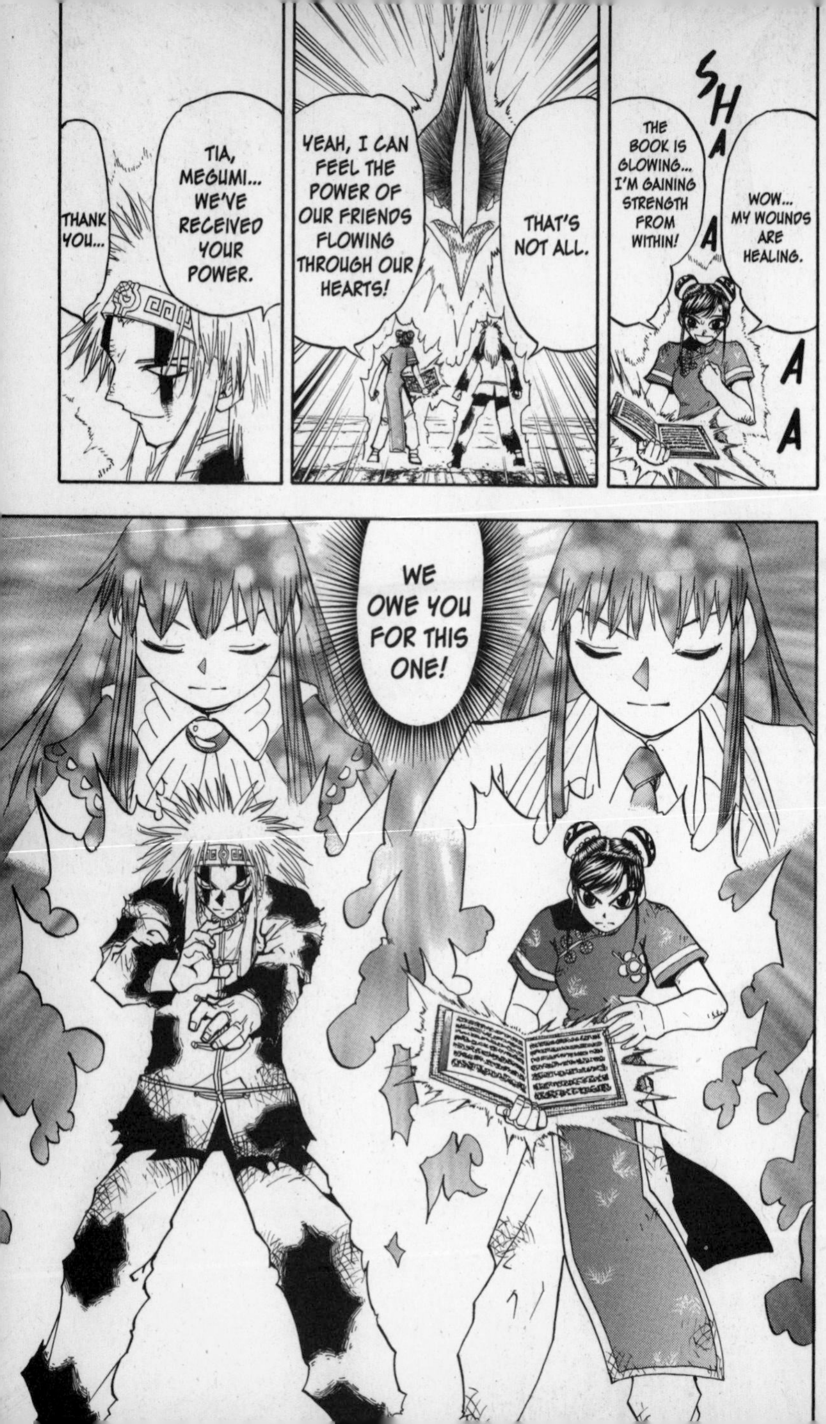
WOW... MY WOUNDS ARE HEALING.
THE BOOK IS GLOWING... I'M GAINING STRENGTH FROM WITHIN!
SHAAAAA
THAT'S NOT ALL.
YEAH, I CAN FEEL THE POWER OF OUR FRIENDS FLOWING THROUGH OUR HEARTS!
TIA, MEGUMI... WE'VE RECEIVED YOUR POWER.
THANK YOU...
WE OWE YOU FOR THIS ONE!

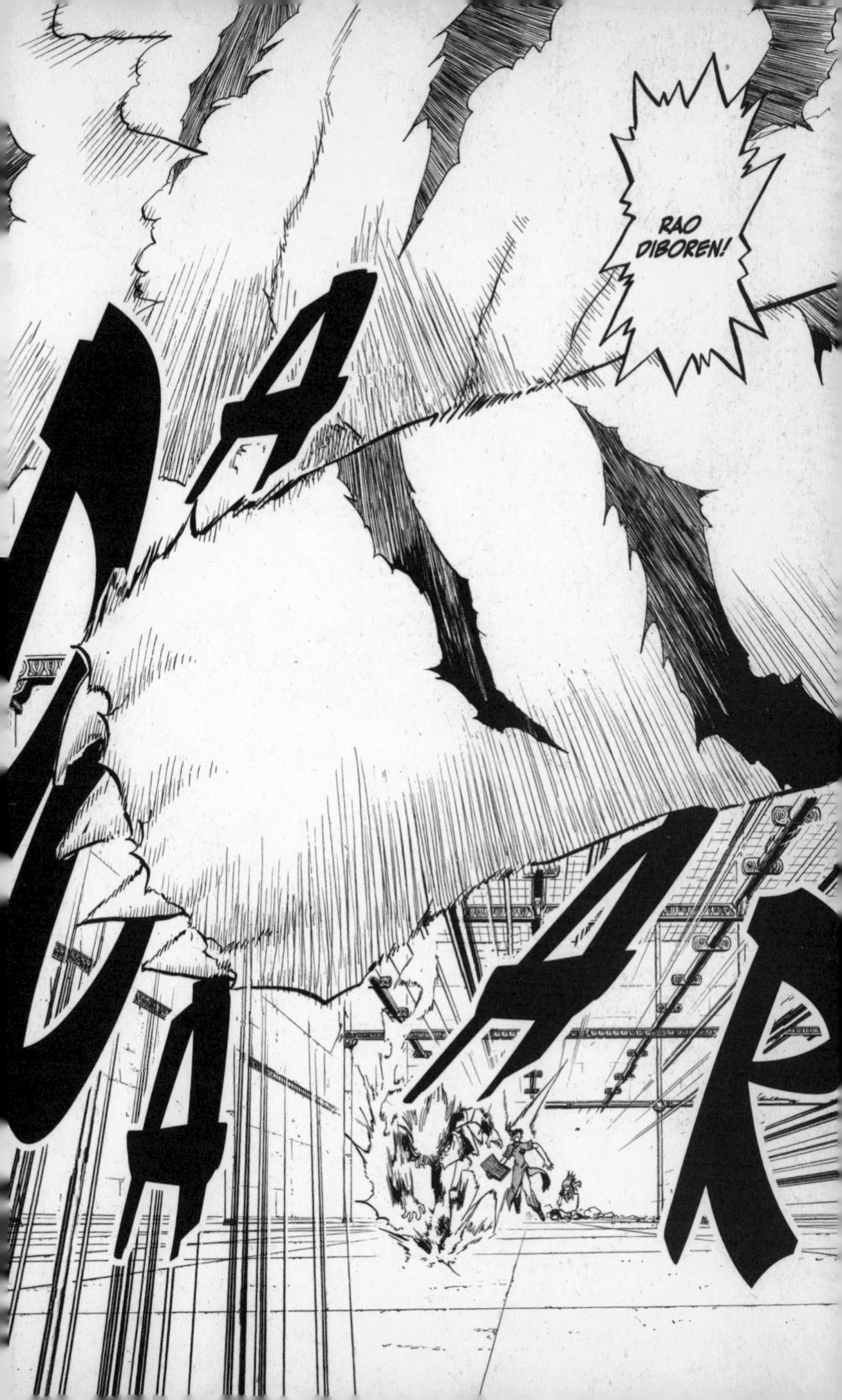
RAO DIBOREN!

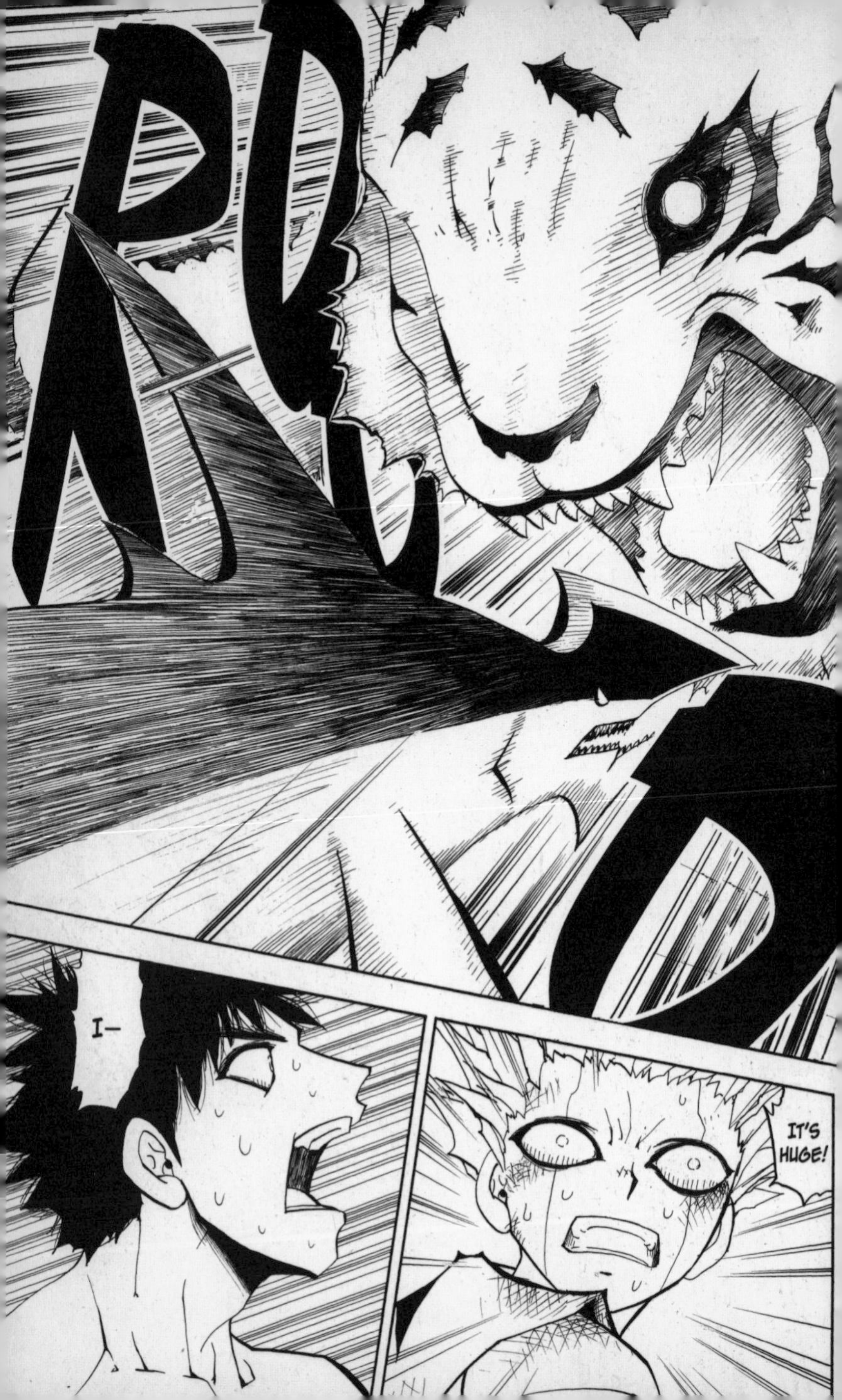
IT'S HUGE!
I—

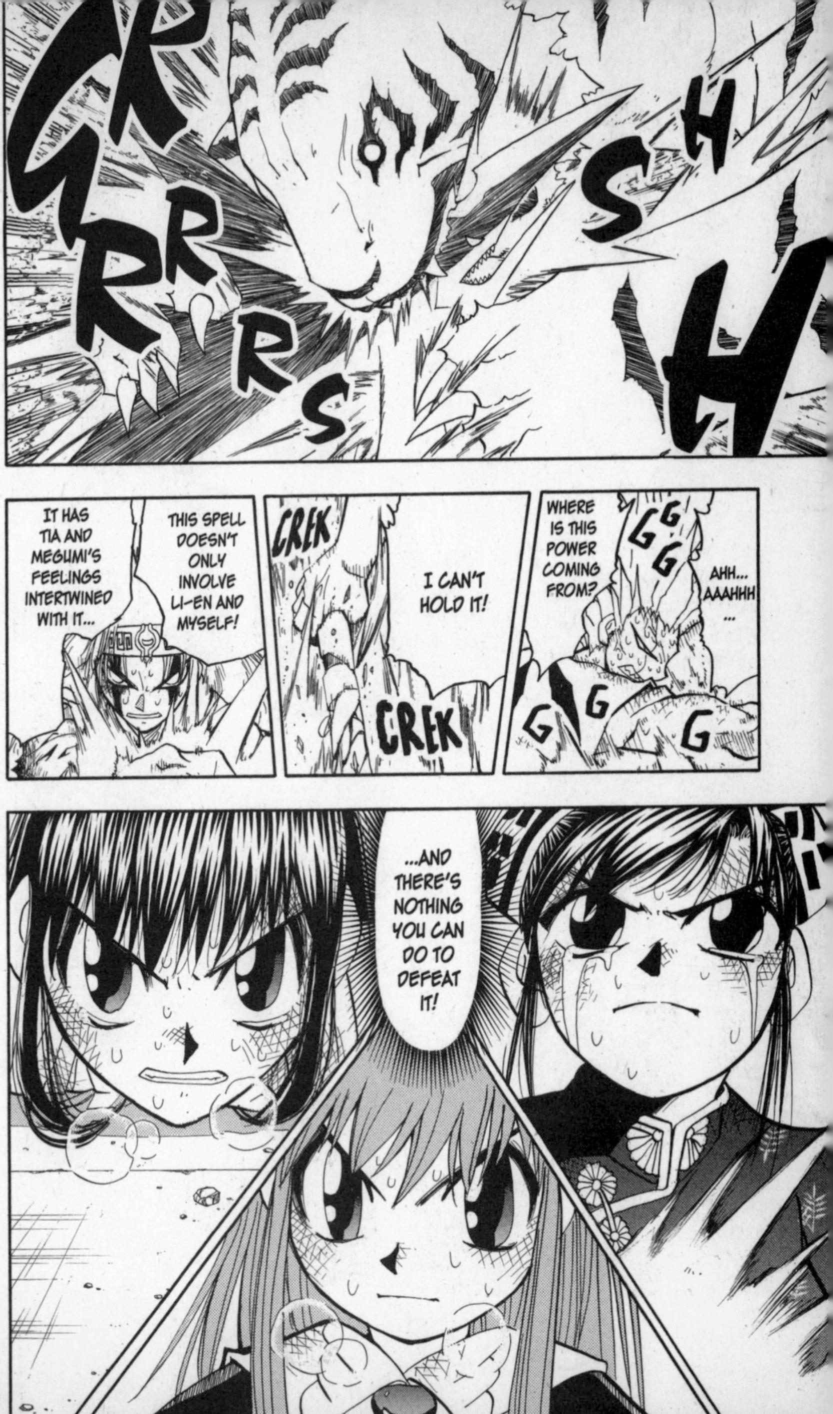
SHH
GRRRRS
GGG
WHERE IS THIS POWER COMING FROM?
AHH... AAAHHH...
GGG
CREK
I CAN'T HOLD IT!
CREK
THIS SPELL DOESN'T ONLY INVOLVE LI-EN AND MYSELF!
IT HAS TIA AND MEGUMI'S FEELINGS INTERTWINED WITH IT...
...AND THERE'S NOTHING YOU CAN DO TO DEFEAT IT!

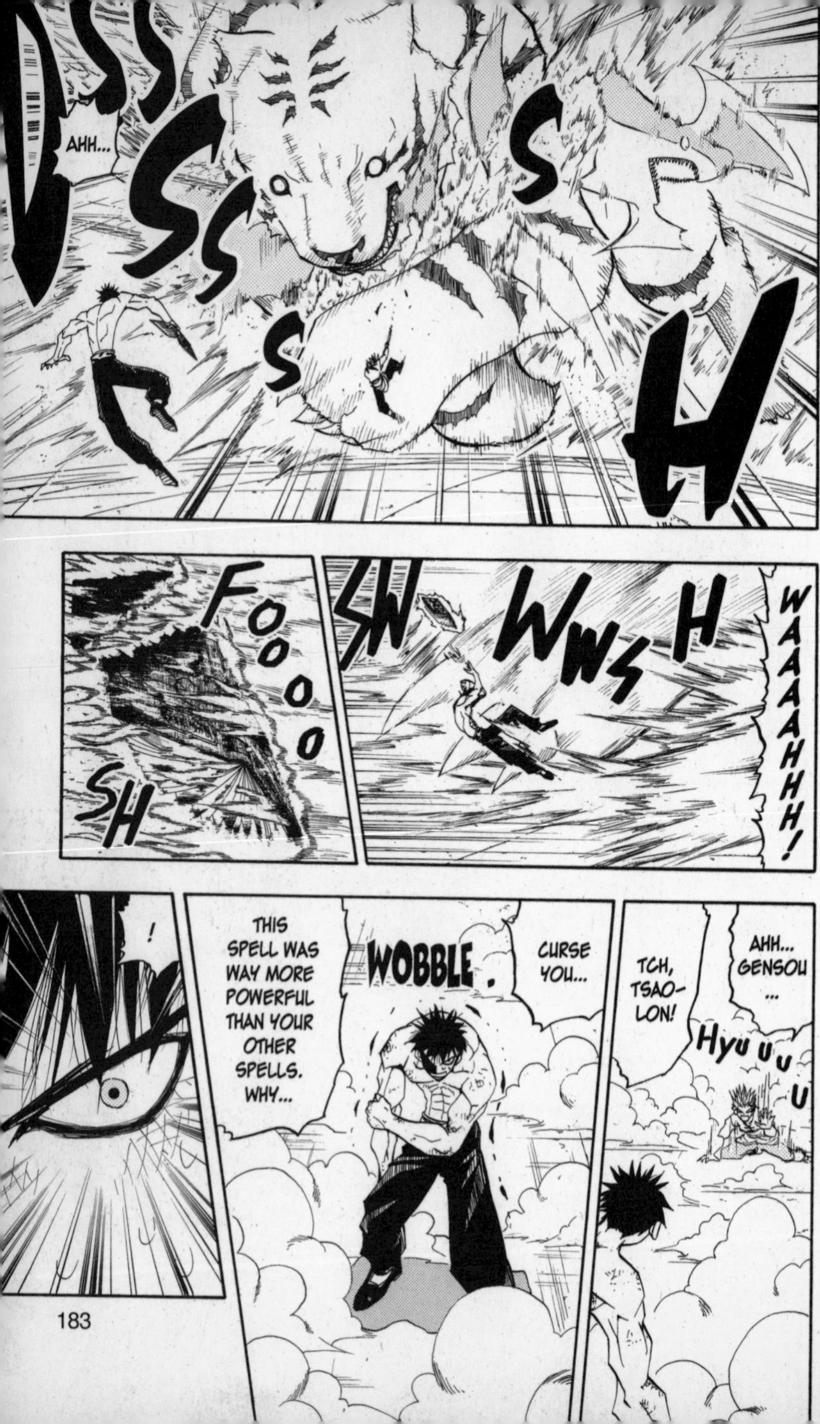

DSSSSSH
AHH...
WAAAAHHH!
SWWSH
FOOOOSH
AHH... GENSOU...
Hyuuuu
TCH, TSAO-LON!
CURSE YOU...
WOBBLE.
THIS SPELL WAS WAY MORE POWERFUL THAN YOUR OTHER SPELLS. WHY...
!

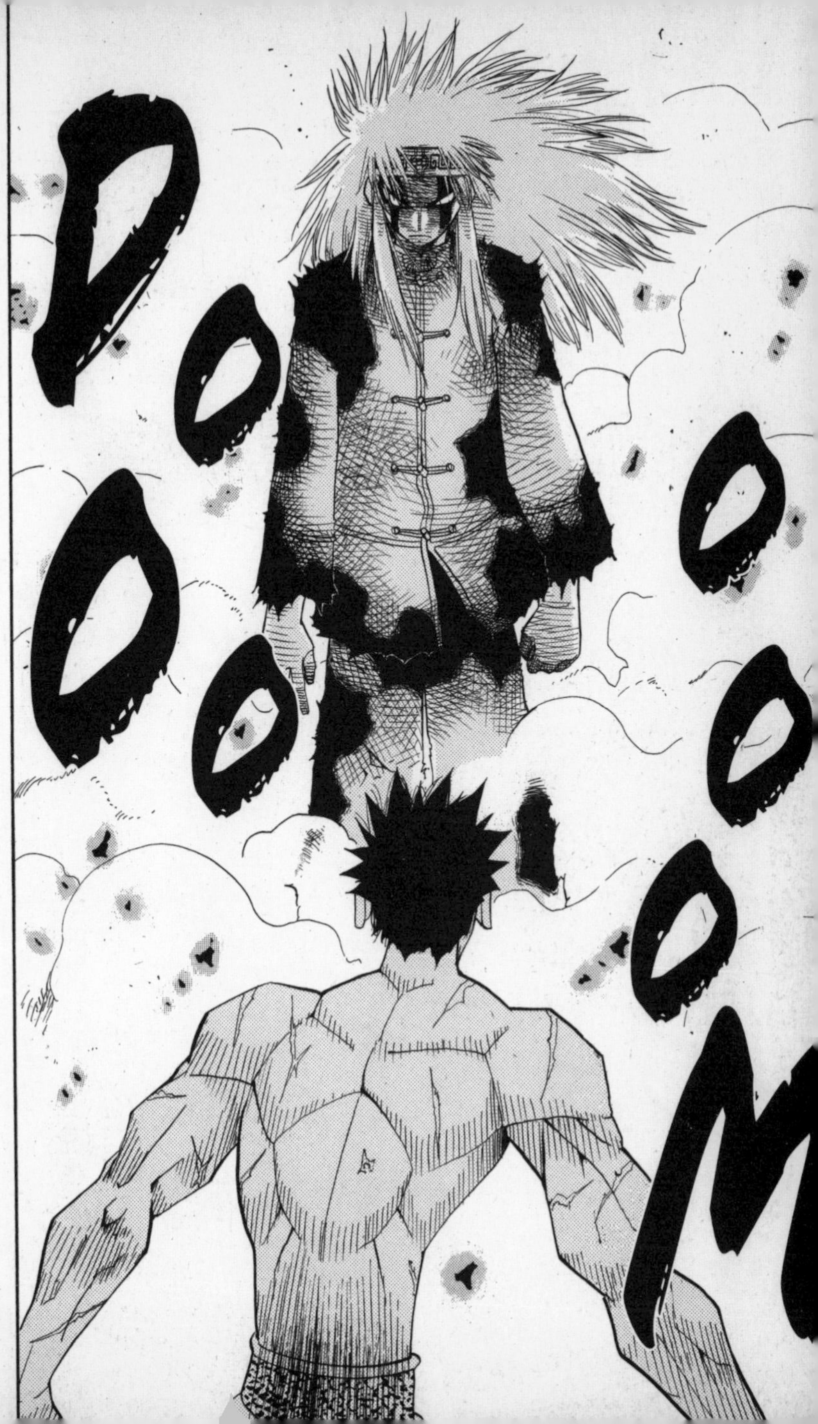
DOOOOOOM

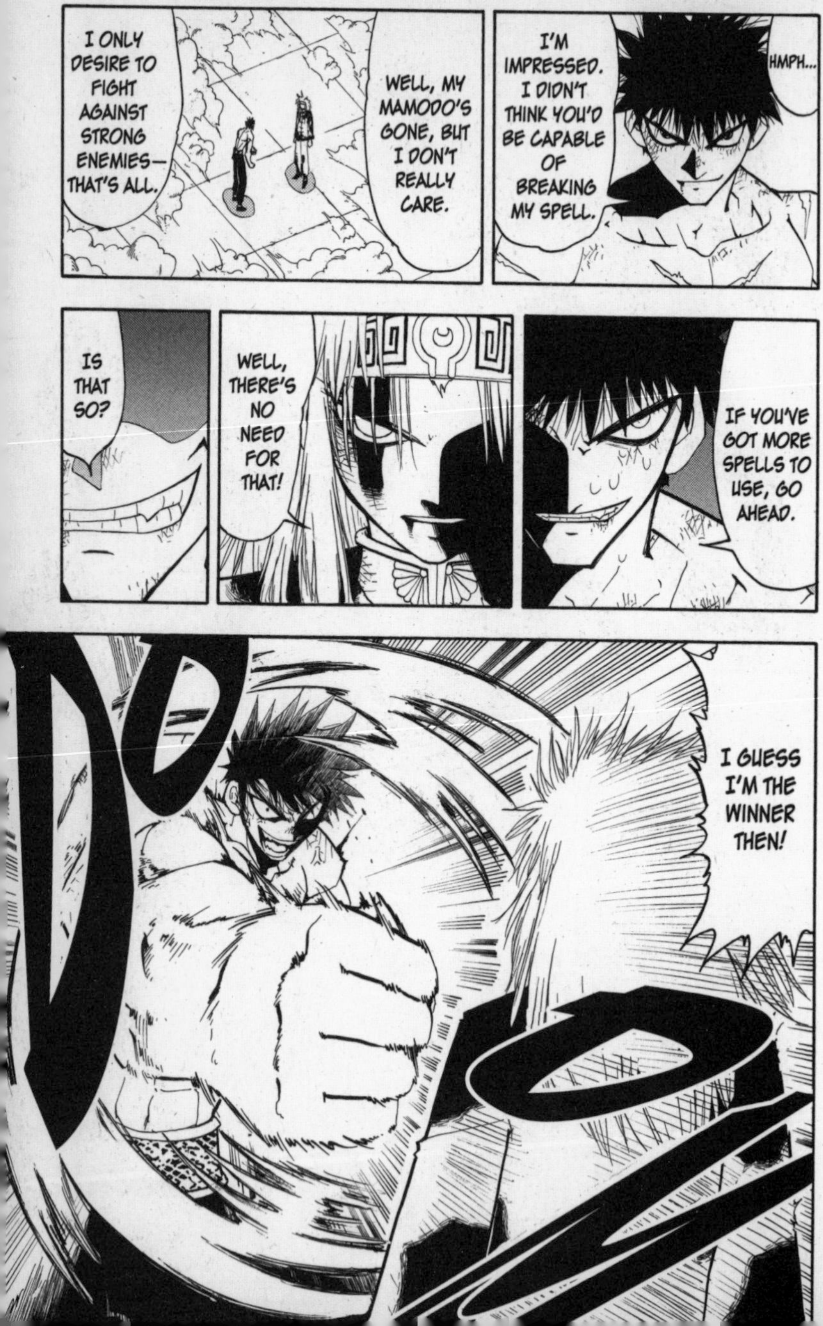
HMPH...
I'M IMPRESSED. I DIDN'T THINK YOU'D BE CAPABLE OF BREAKING MY SPELL.
WELL, MY MAMODO'S GONE, BUT I DON'T REALLY CARE.
I ONLY DESIRE TO FIGHT AGAINST STRONG ENEMIES—THAT'S ALL.
IF YOU'VE GOT MORE SPELLS TO USE, GO AHEAD.
WELL, THERE'S NO NEED FOR THAT!
IS THAT SO?
I GUESS I'M THE WINNER THEN!

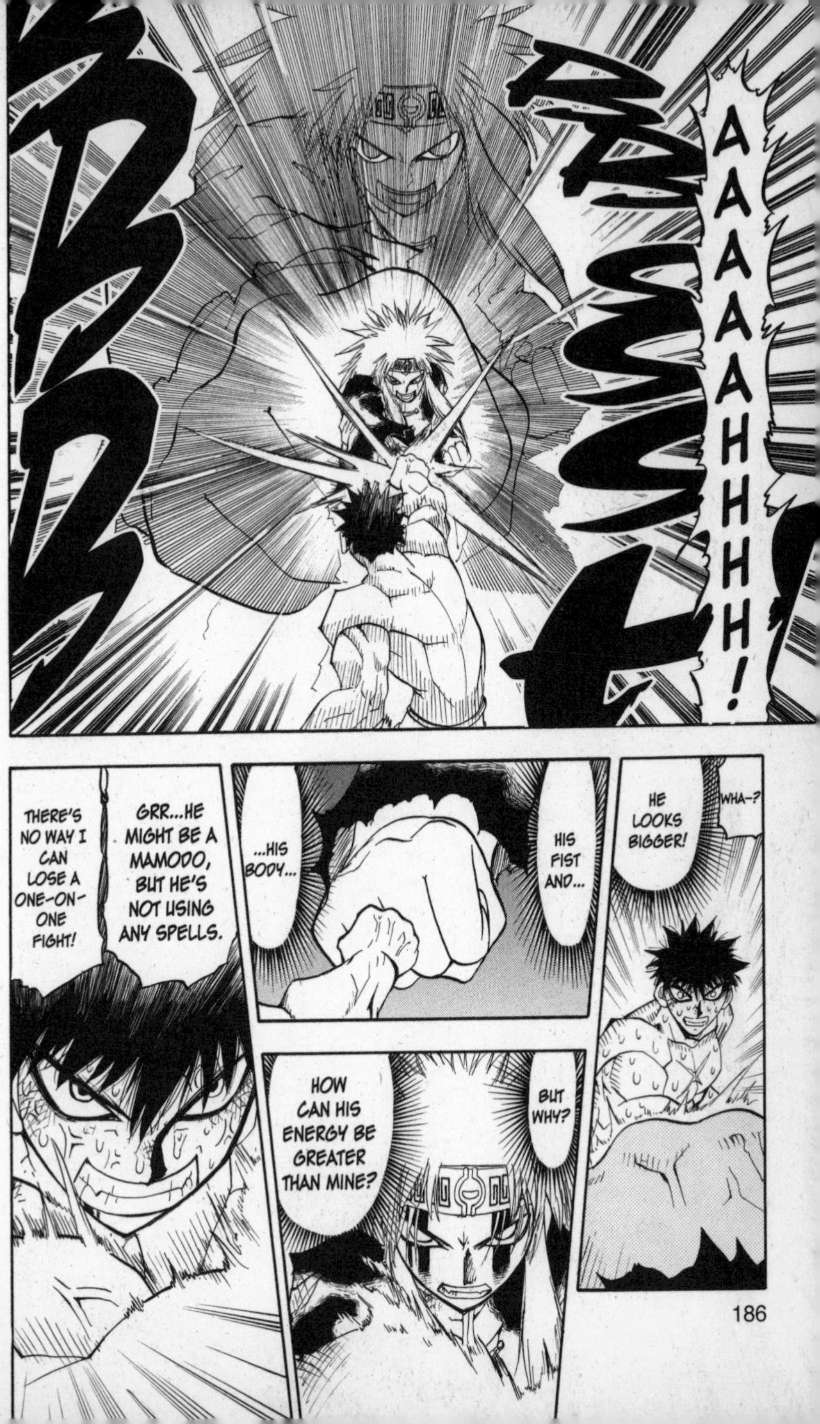
AAAAHHHH!
WHA-?
HE LOOKS BIGGER!
HIS FIST AND...
...HIS BODY...
BUT WHY?
HOW CAN HIS ENERGY BE GREATER THAN MINE?
GRR...HE MIGHT BE A MAMODO, BUT HE'S NOT USING ANY SPELLS.
THERE'S NO WAY I CAN LOSE A ONE-ON-ONE FIGHT!

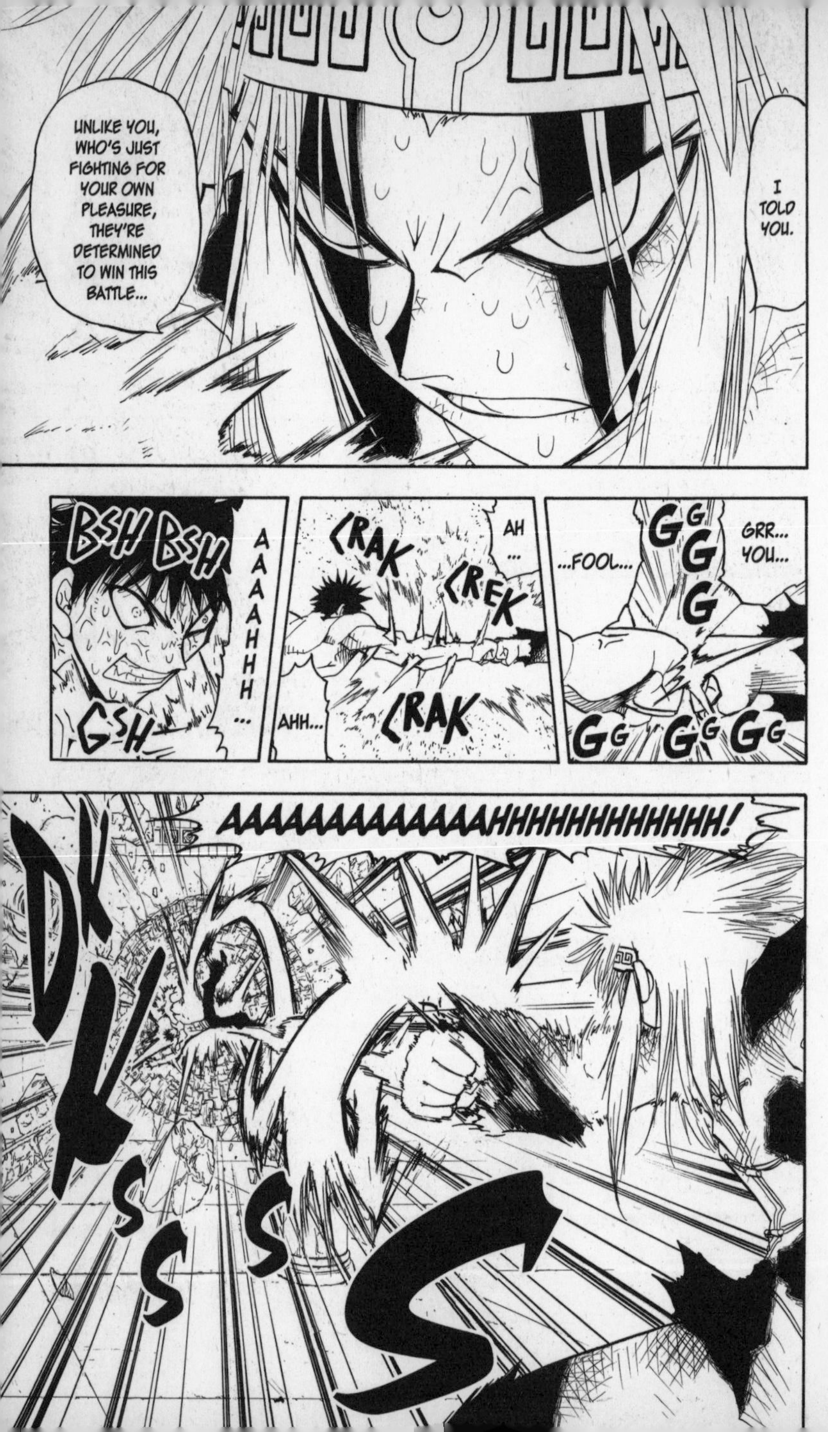
I TOLD YOU.
UNLIKE YOU, WHO'S JUST FIGHTING FOR YOUR OWN PLEASURE, THEY'RE DETERMINED TO WIN THIS BATTLE...
GRR... YOU...
GGG
...FOOL...
GG GG GG
AH...
CRAK
CREK
CRAK
AHH...
BSH BSH
AAAAAHHHH...
GSH
AAAAAAAAAAAAAHHHHHHHHHHHH!
DK
SSSS

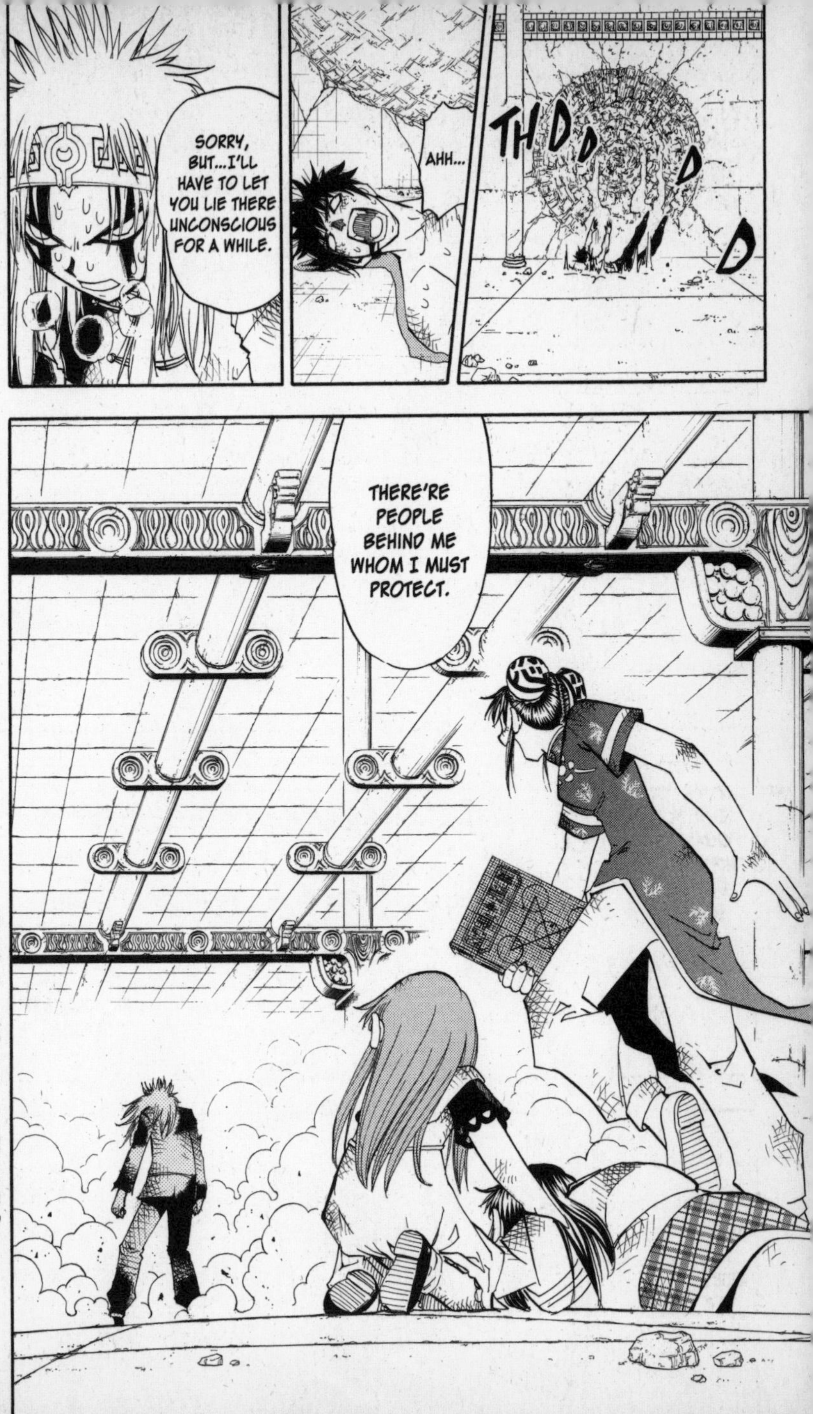
THDD D D D
AHH...
SORRY, BUT...I'LL HAVE TO LET YOU LIE THERE UNCONSCIOUS FOR A WHILE.
THERE'RE PEOPLE BEHIND ME WHOM I MUST PROTECT.

TO BE CONTINUED!!

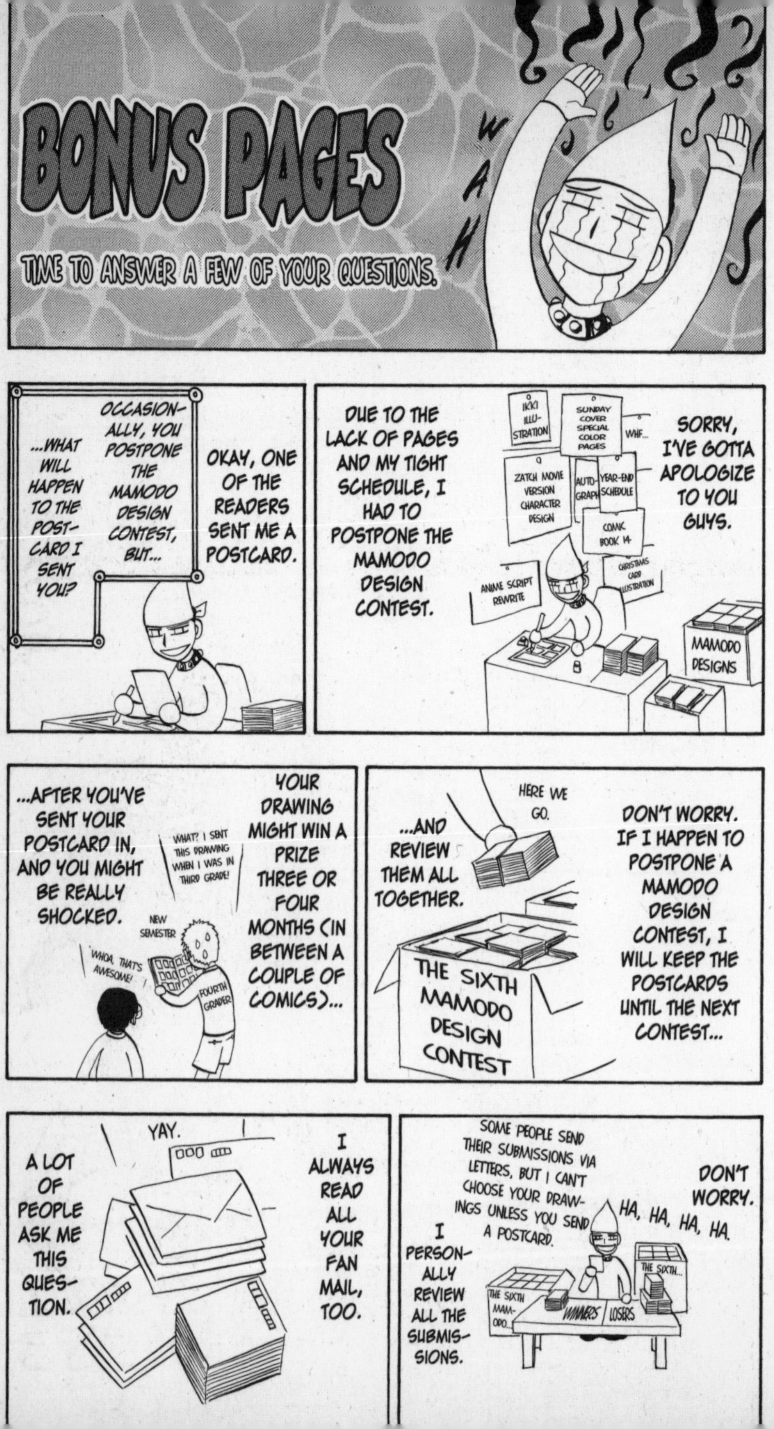
WAHH
BONUS PAGES
TIME TO ANSWER A FEW OF YOUR QUESTIONS.
SORRY, I'VE GOTTA APOLOGIZE TO YOU GUYS.
WHF...
SUNDAY COVER SPECIAL COLOR PAGES
IKKI ILLUSTRATION
YEAR-END SCHEDULE
AUTOGRAPH
ZATCH MOVIE VERSION CHARACTER DESIGN
COMIC BOOK 14
CHRISTMAS CARD ILLUSTRATION
ANIME SCRIPT REWRITE
DUE TO THE LACK OF PAGES AND MY TIGHT SCHEDULE, I HAD TO POSTPONE THE MAMODO DESIGN CONTEST.
MAMODO DESIGNS
OKAY, ONE OF THE READERS SENT ME A POSTCARD.
OCCASIONALLY, YOU POSTPONE THE MAMODO DESIGN CONTEST, BUT...
...WHAT WILL HAPPEN TO THE POSTCARD I SENT YOU?
DON'T WORRY. IF I HAPPEN TO POSTPONE A MAMODO DESIGN CONTEST, I WILL KEEP THE POSTCARDS UNTIL THE NEXT CONTEST...
HERE WE GO.
...AND REVIEW THEM ALL TOGETHER.
THE SIXTH MAMODO DESIGN CONTEST
YOUR DRAWING MIGHT WIN A PRIZE THREE OR FOUR MONTHS (IN BETWEEN A COUPLE OF COMICS)...
...AFTER YOU'VE SENT YOUR POSTCARD IN, AND YOU MIGHT BE REALLY SHOCKED.
WHAT? I SENT THIS DRAWING WHEN I WAS IN THIRD GRADE!
NEW SEMESTER
FOURTH GRADER
WHOA, THAT'S AWESOME!
DON'T WORRY.
HA, HA, HA, HA.
SOME PEOPLE SEND THEIR SUBMISSIONS VIA LETTERS, BUT I CAN'T CHOOSE YOUR DRAWINGS UNLESS YOU SEND A POSTCARD.
THE SIXTH...
I PERSONALLY REVIEW ALL THE SUBMISSIONS.
THE SIXTH MAMODO...
WINNERS
LOSERS
I ALWAYS READ ALL YOUR FAN MAIL, TOO.
YAY.
A LOT OF PEOPLE ASK ME THIS QUESTION.

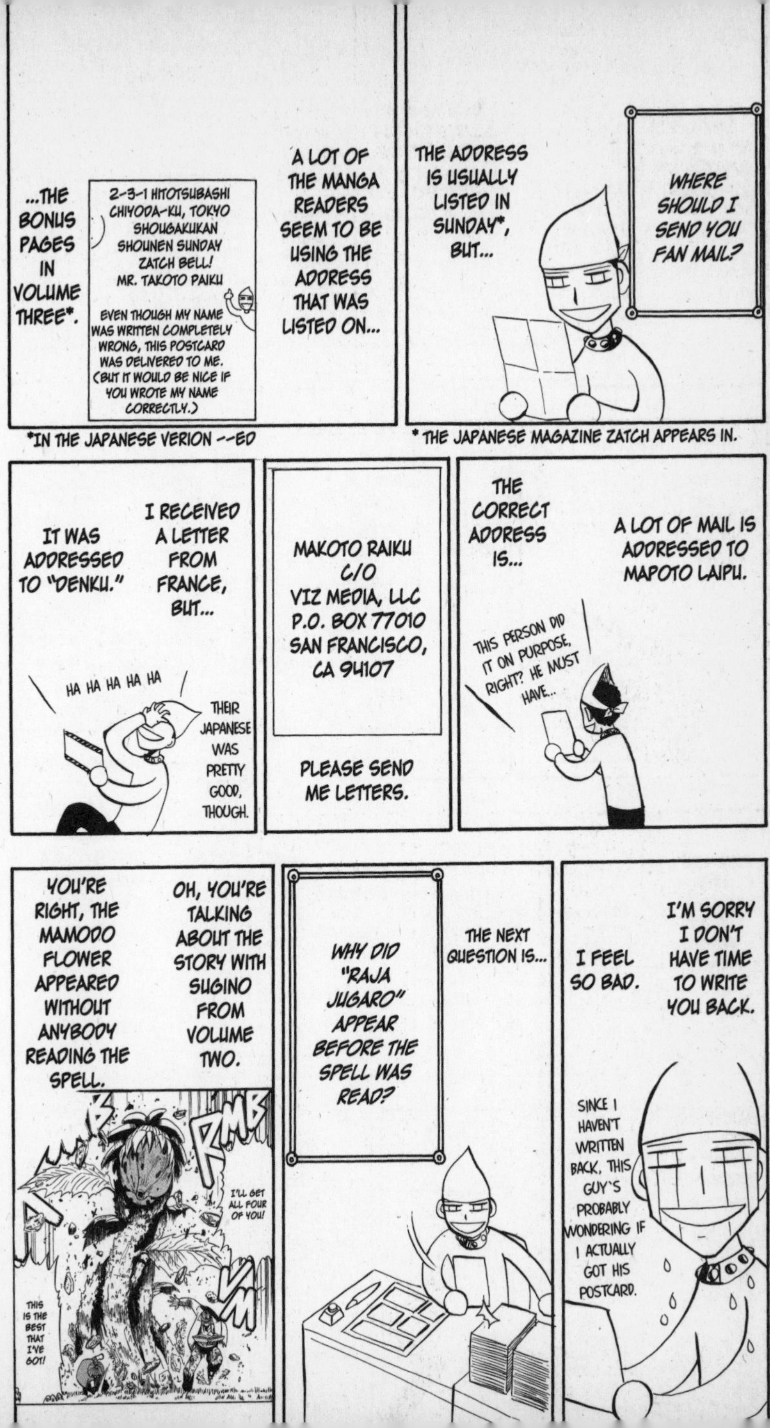
WHERE SHOULD I SEND YOU FAN MAIL?
THE ADDRESS IS USUALLY LISTED IN SUNDAY*, BUT...
* THE JAPANESE MAGAZINE ZATCH APPEARS IN.
A LOT OF THE MANGA READERS SEEM TO BE USING THE ADDRESS THAT WAS LISTED ON...
...THE BONUS PAGES IN VOLUME THREE*.
2-3-1 HITOTSUBASHI CHIYODA-KU, TOKYO SHOUGAKUKAN SHOUNEN SUNDAY ZATCH BELL! MR. TAKOTO PAIKU
EVEN THOUGH MY NAME WAS WRITTEN COMPLETELY WRONG, THIS POSTCARD WAS DELIVERED TO ME. (BUT IT WOULD BE NICE IF YOU WROTE MY NAME CORRECTLY.)
*IN THE JAPANESE VERION --ED
A LOT OF MAIL IS ADDRESSED TO MAPOTO LAIPU.
THE CORRECT ADDRESS IS...
THIS PERSON DID IT ON PURPOSE, RIGHT? HE MUST HAVE...
MAKOTO RAIKU C/O VIZ MEDIA, LLC P.O. BOX 77010 SAN FRANCISCO, CA 94107
PLEASE SEND ME LETTERS.
I RECEIVED A LETTER FROM FRANCE, BUT...
IT WAS ADDRESSED TO "DENKU."
HA HA HA HA HA
THEIR JAPANESE WAS PRETTY GOOD, THOUGH.
I'M SORRY I DON'T HAVE TIME TO WRITE YOU BACK.
I FEEL SO BAD.
SINCE I HAVEN'T WRITTEN BACK, THIS GUY'S PROBABLY WONDERING IF I ACTUALLY GOT HIS POSTCARD.
THE NEXT QUESTION IS...
WHY DID "RAJA JUGARO" APPEAR BEFORE THE SPELL WAS READ?
OH, YOU'RE TALKING ABOUT THE STORY WITH SUGINO FROM VOLUME TWO.
YOU'RE RIGHT, THE MAMODO FLOWER APPEARED WITHOUT ANYBODY READING THE SPELL.
RMB
I'LL GET ALL FOUR OF YOU!
VM
THIS IS THE BEST THAT I'VE GOT!

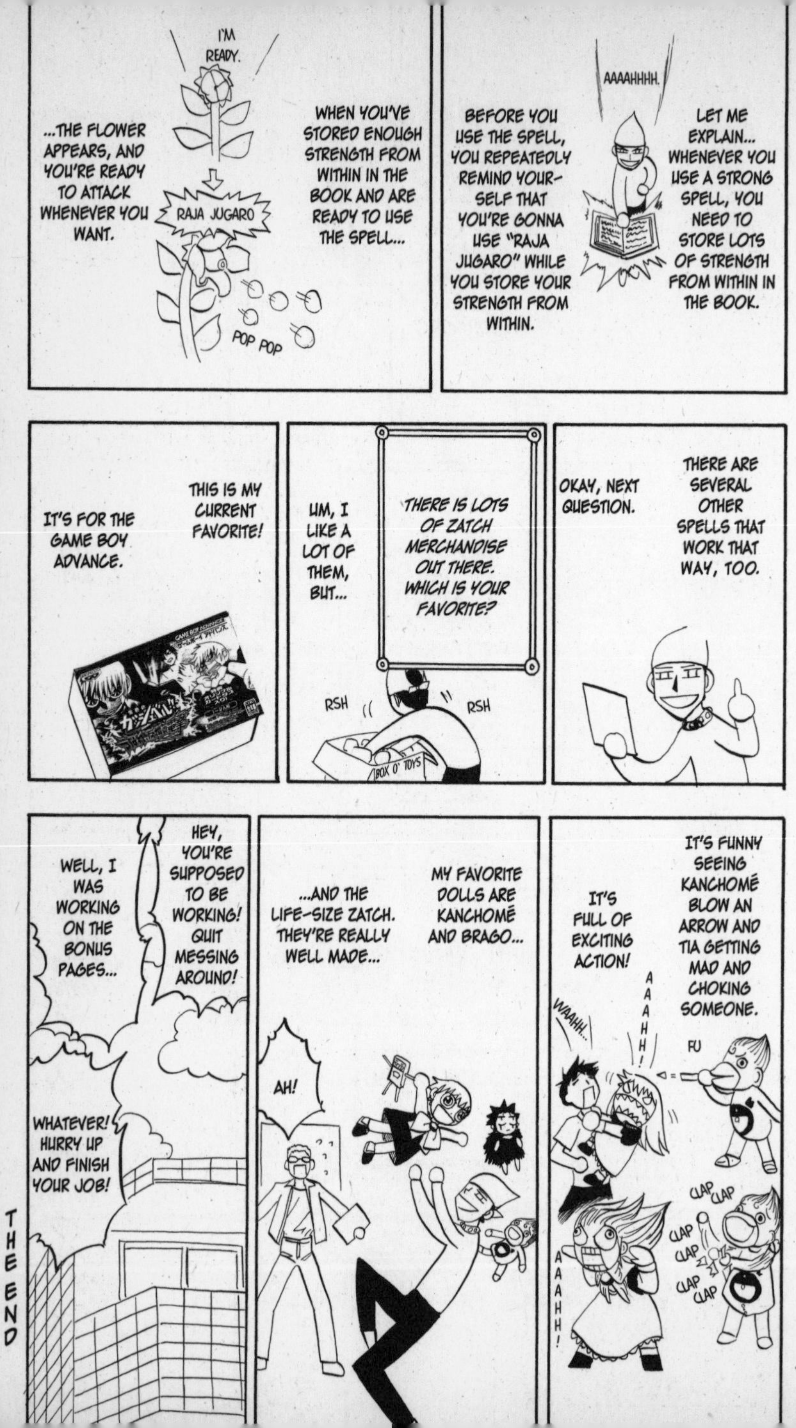
AAAAHHHH.
LET ME EXPLAIN... WHENEVER YOU USE A STRONG SPELL, YOU NEED TO STORE LOTS OF STRENGTH FROM WITHIN IN THE BOOK.
BEFORE YOU USE THE SPELL, YOU REPEATEDLY REMIND YOURSELF THAT YOU'RE GONNA USE "RAJA JUGARO" WHILE YOU STORE YOUR STRENGTH FROM WITHIN.
WHEN YOU'VE STORED ENOUGH STRENGTH FROM WITHIN IN THE BOOK AND ARE READY TO USE THE SPELL...
I'M READY.
...THE FLOWER APPEARS, AND YOU'RE READY TO ATTACK WHENEVER YOU WANT.
RAJA JUGARO
POP POP
THERE ARE SEVERAL OTHER SPELLS THAT WORK THAT WAY, TOO.
OKAY, NEXT QUESTION.
THERE IS LOTS OF ZATCH MERCHANDISE OUT THERE. WHICH IS YOUR FAVORITE?
UM, I LIKE A LOT OF THEM, BUT...
RSH
RSH
BOX O' TOYS
THIS IS MY CURRENT FAVORITE!
IT'S FOR THE GAME BOY ADVANCE.
GAME BOY ADVANCE
IT'S FUNNY SEEING KANCHOMÉ BLOW AN ARROW AND TIA GETTING MAD AND CHOKING SOMEONE.
IT'S FULL OF EXCITING ACTION!
FU
AAAAHH!
WAAHH...
CLAP CLAP
CLAP CLAP
CLAP CLAP
AAAAHH!
MY FAVORITE DOLLS ARE KANCHOMÉ AND BRAGO...
...AND THE LIFE-SIZE ZATCH. THEY'RE REALLY WELL MADE...
AH!
HEY, YOU'RE SUPPOSED TO BE WORKING! QUIT MESSING AROUND!
WELL, I WAS WORKING ON THE BONUS PAGES...
WHATEVER! HURRY UP AND FINISH YOUR JOB!
THE END

ZATCH & SUZY

BY MAKOTO RAIKU

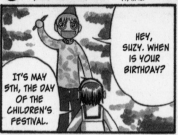

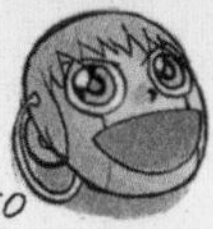

HEY, SUZY. WHEN IS YOUR BIRTHDAY?

IT'S MAY 5TH, THE DAY OF THE CHILDREN'S FESTIVAL.

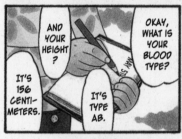

OKAY, WHAT IS YOUR BLOOD TYPE?

AND YOUR HEIGHT?

IT'S 156 CENTI-METERS.

IT'S TYPE AB.

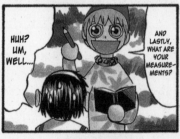

AND LASTLY, WHAT ARE YOUR MEASURE-MENTS?

HUH? UM, WELL....

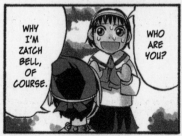

WHO ARE YOU?

WHY I'M ZATCH BELL, OF COURSE.

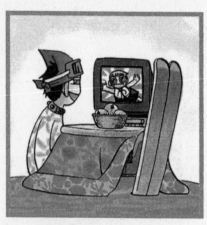

MAKOTO RAIKU

It's winter. It's snowing. I love skiing.
I couldn't go skiing before because I
was broke. Now I can't go because I
don't have any time... It's fun to sit
by the heater and eat tangerines
while watching TV.

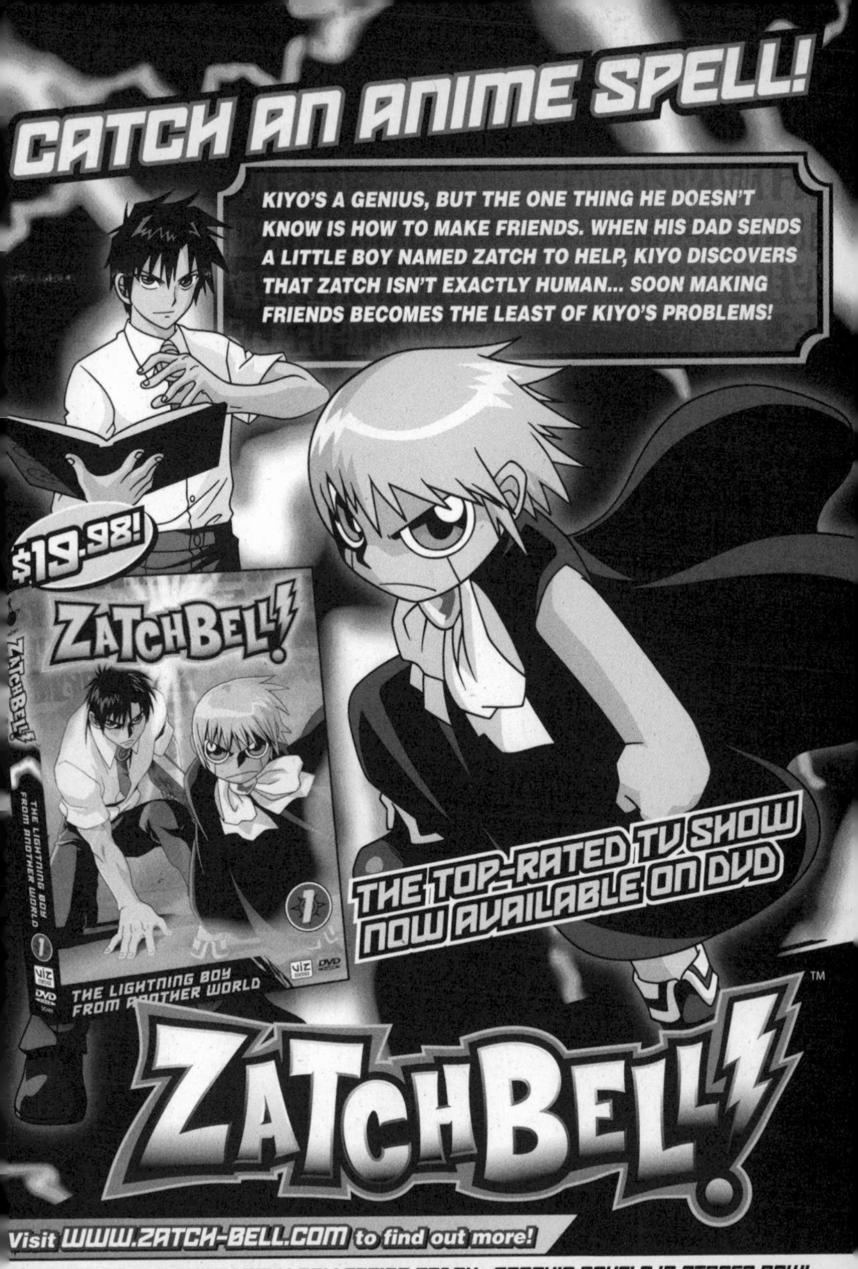

CATCH AN ANIME SPELL!
KIYO'S A GENIUS, BUT THE ONE THING HE DOESN'T KNOW IS HOW TO MAKE FRIENDS. WHEN HIS DAD SENDS A LITTLE BOY NAMED ZATCH TO HELP, KIYO DISCOVERS THAT ZATCH ISN'T EXACTLY HUMAN... SOON MAKING FRIENDS BECOMES THE LEAST OF KIYO'S PROBLEMS!
$19.98!
ZATCHBELL!
THE LIGHTNING BOY FROM ANOTHER WORLD
THE TOP-RATED TV SHOW NOW AVAILABLE ON DVD
ZATCHBELL!™
Visit WWW.ZATCH-BELL.COM to find out more!
COMPLETE YOUR ZATCH BELL! COLLECTION TODAY—GRAPHIC NOVELS IN STORES NOW!

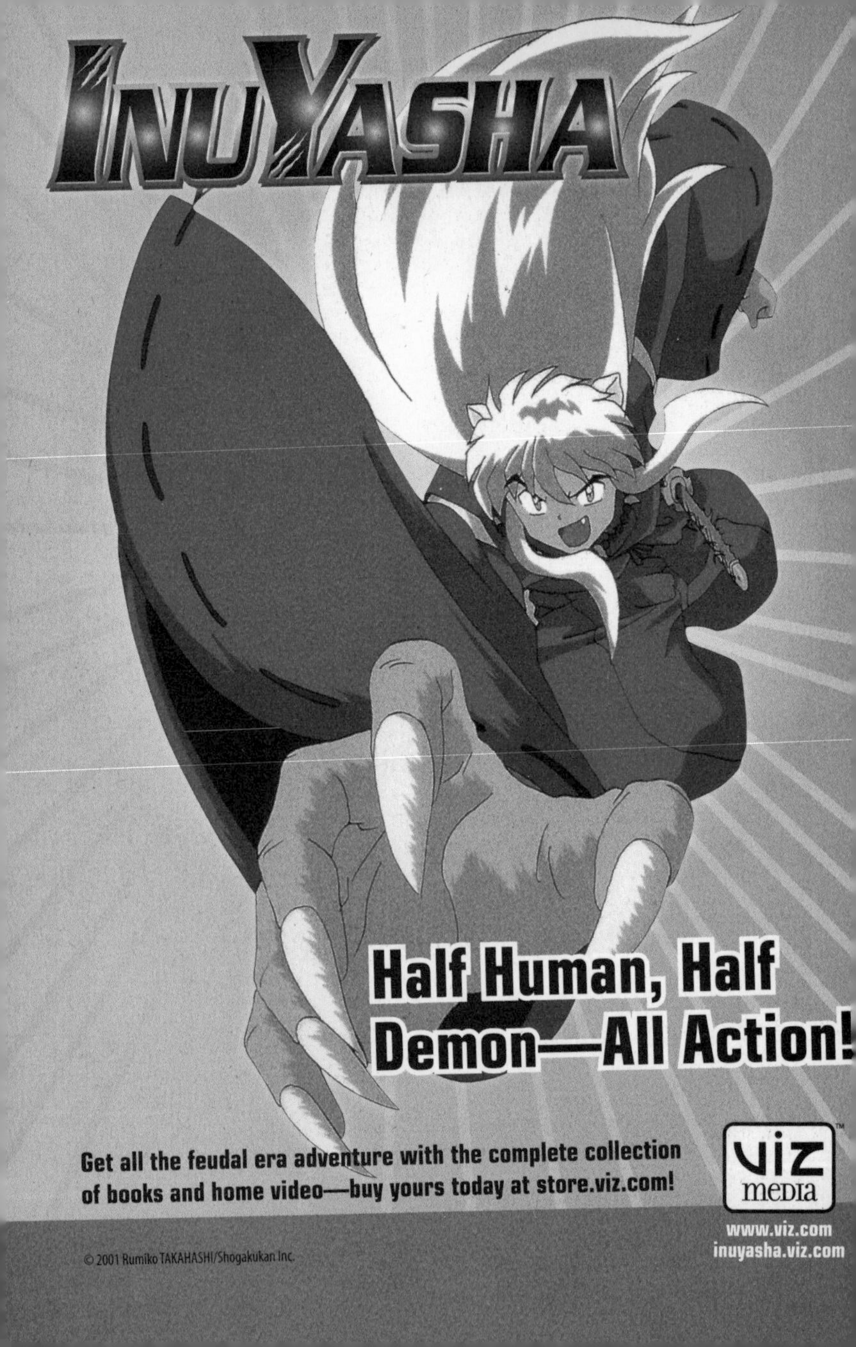
InuYasha
Half Human, Half Demon—All Action!
Get all the feudal era adventure with the complete collection of books and home video—buy yours today at store.viz.com!
viz media
www.viz.com
inuyasha.viz.com
© 2001 Rumiko TAKAHASHI/Shogakukan Inc.

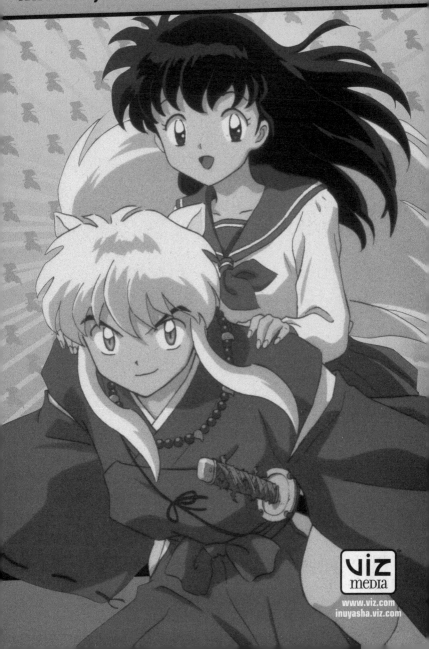

INUYASHA

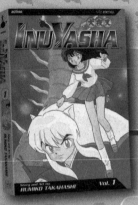

Read the action from the start with the original manga series

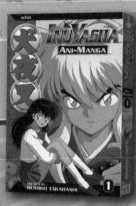

Full color adaptation of the popular TV series

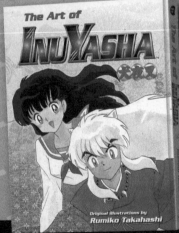

Art book with cel art, paintings, character profiles and more

TV SERIES & MOVIES ON DVD!

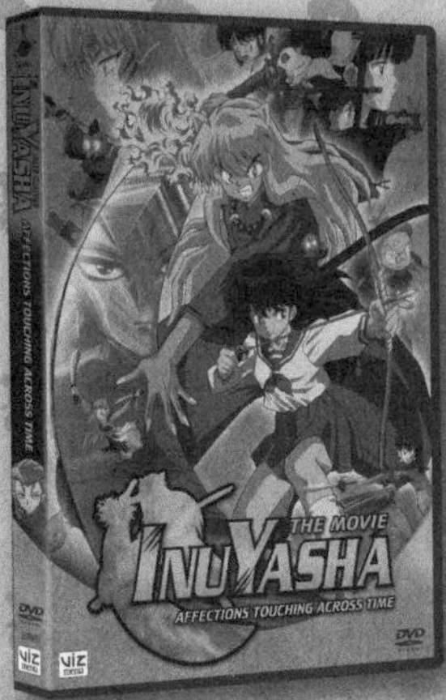
THE MOVIE
INUYASHA
AFFECTIONS TOUCHING ACROSS TIME
DVD
VIZ

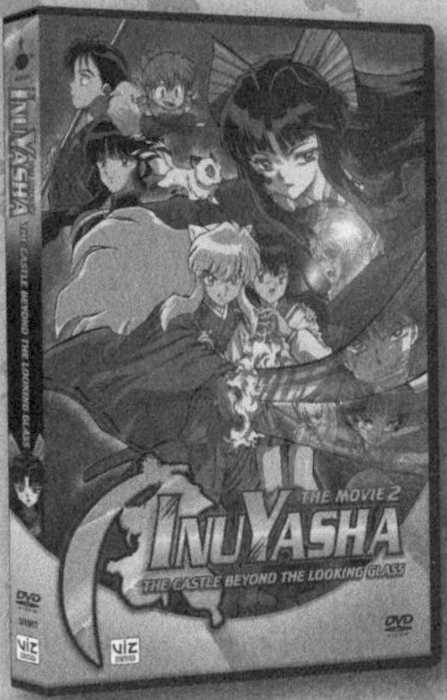
THE MOVIE 2
INUYASHA
THE CASTLE BEYOND THE LOOKING GLASS
DVD
VIZ

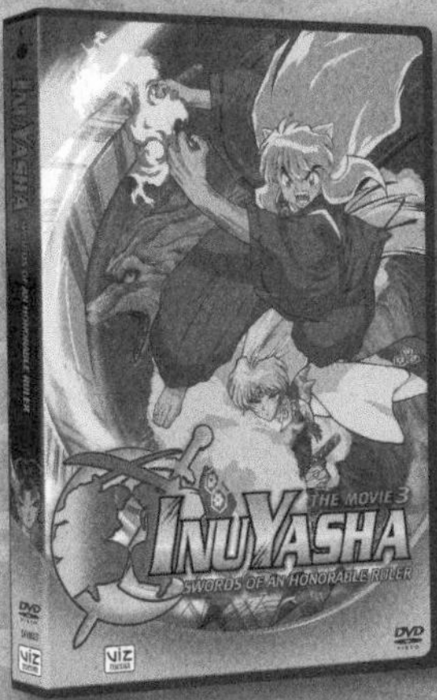
THE MOVIE 3
INUYASHA
SWORDS OF AN HONORABLE RULER
DVD
VIZ

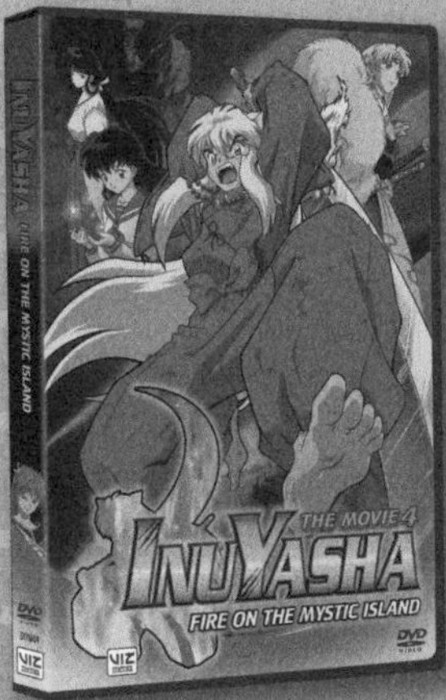
THE MOVIE 4
INUYASHA
FIRE ON THE MYSTIC ISLAND
DVD
VIZ

See more of the action in *Inuyasha* full-length movies

VIZ MEDIA

www.viz.com
inuyasha.viz.com

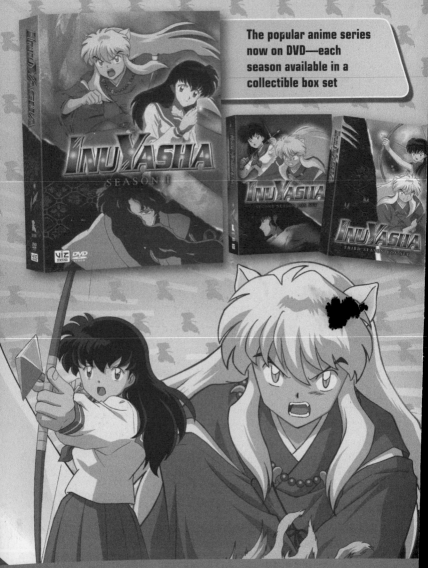

LOVE MA

LET US KNOW WHA

OUR MANGA SURVEY IS NOW AVAILABLE ONLINE. PLEASE VISIT: VIZ.COM/MANGASURVEY

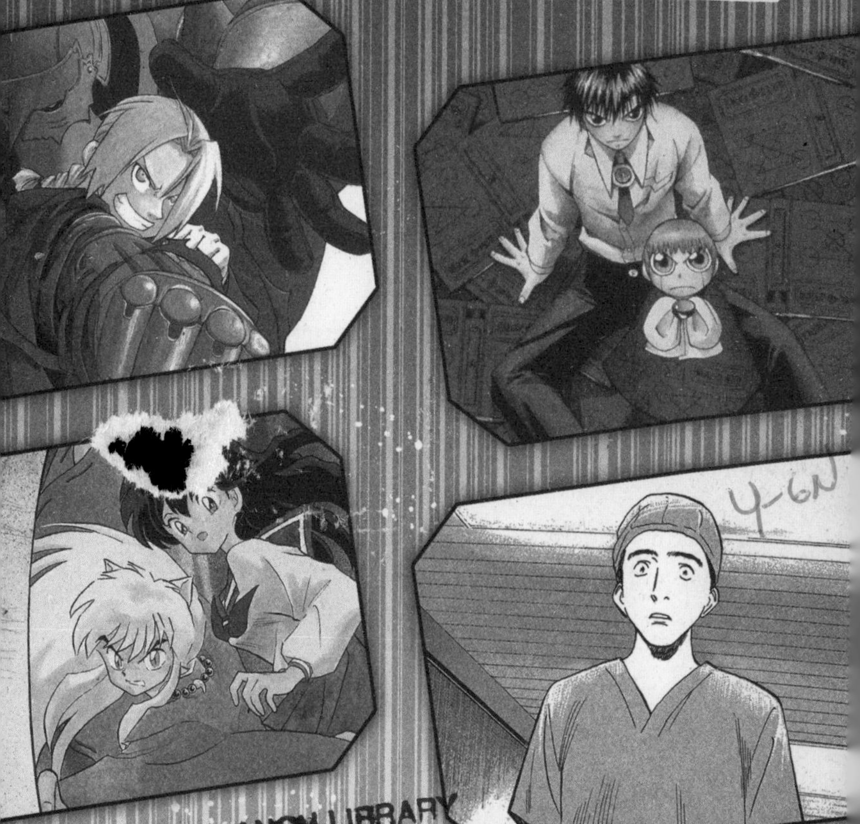

HELP US MAKE THE MANGA YOU LOVE BETTER!